Day by Day

IN
GALATIANS, EPHESIANS,
PHILIPPIANS & COLOSSIANS

Day by Day

IN

GALATIANS, EPHESIANS, PHILIPPIANS & COLOSSIANS

Chuck Gianotti

ECS

MINISTRIES

The Word to the World

Many ECS publications are also available in eBook formats.
For more information, visit our website www.ecsministries.org.

Day by Day in Galatians, Ephesians, Philippians & Colossians
Chuck Gianotti

Published by:
ECS Ministries
PO Box 1028
Dubuque, IA 52004-1028
phone: (563) 585-2070
email: ecsorders@ecsministries.org
website: www.ecsministries.org

First Edition 2014
Reprinted 2015

ISBN 978-1-59387-227-4

Code: B-DBDGEPC

Copyright © 2014 ECS Ministries

For additional information, contact:
Chuck Gianotti
27 Watchman Court
Rochester, NY 14624 USA
chuckgianotti@hotmail.com
www.bible-equip.org
www.BiblicalEldership.com

Other books by Chuck Gianotti:
Cosmic Drama: Men, Women & the Church
Day by Day in the Gospel of Matthew
The Formation of the New Testament
Biblical Foundations
Leadership Qualities
Leadership Principles
Practical Ministry

Printed in the United States of America

To Ross & Joan McIntee
who have demonstrated the character of Christ
and modeled true devotion to Him!

INTRODUCTION

These verse-by-verse expositional meditations follow the four epistles of Paul to the Galatians, Ephesians, Philippians and Colossians. The Bible text is accompanied by short textual commentaries and devotional thoughts for each day, spanning an entire year. The Bible version used is the New American Standard Version (NASB).

The reader will notice that the devotionals are divided up to suit a typical five-day work week. We have included suggested readings for the weekends from the four accounts of the Gospel of Christ: Matthew, Mark, Luke, and John.

Space has been left at the end of each week of readings for your own personal notes. A time-honored way to stimulate one's thinking about the Bible text itself is to answer the following questions:

> - What have I discovered here about God?
> - What have I discovered here about mankind (people in general)?
> - What have I discovered here about the relationship between God and man?

We suggest you spend a few minutes in conversation with the Lord, using the prayer at the end of each day's meditation and adding your own thoughts. Also for your reference, a general outline of the four books is provided on page XI.

May God use these brief daily thoughts to spur you on to greater discipleship of our Lord and King, Jesus Christ, and to enjoy ever-deepening contemplations about His person and work.

Acknowledgments

A ny publication is a team effort. The author provides the content in raw form, but, at least in this case, the raw content needs the refinement of competent editing. For this I thank Ruth Rodger who has provided expertise in correcting misspellings, typos of various sorts, awkward wording and other sundry things that needed fixing. To the many who have received these devotionals in blog form and responded with comments, corrections and general feedback—thanks to all. Greatly appreciated is Rob Tyler, Executive Director of ECS Ministries, for believing in this project and Mark Wainwright who has been faithful in shepherding the manuscript all the way through publication. Of course, any errors that remain go back to the one who originally made them, which would be the author. I take full responsibility.

Thank you to my life partner, Mary, for all her love and support. She has read every one of these devotionals, and offered great interactions and feedback.

Finally, and most importantly, to the Lord Jesus Christ be all the glory,

–Chuck Gianotti, 2014

GENERAL OUTLINE

Galatians

Authoritative Introduction

Galatians 1:1

¹ Paul, an apostle (not sent from men nor through the agency of man, but through Jesus Christ and God the Father, who raised Him from the dead) ...

So begins Paul's defense of the doctrine of justification, the centerpiece of his theology. The Galatian churches were being tempted to draw away from the living grace of the Lord Jesus Christ and to return to a legalistic religion requiring compliance with the Law of Moses. The issue is so foundational to Christian faith, so crucial to all the Lord had revealed to Paul through direct revelation that he begins with no uncertain terms about his authority to address the issue.

As in all his letters, Paul identifies himself up front. But, unlike some of his other letters, he has no collaborators in writing to the Galatians. In light of the seriousness of his subject, he asserts his prerogative as an apostle for speaking authoritatively. As such, he carries great authority. He did not assume such a position for himself, but he affirms that this commissioning had come, not by human ecclesiastical ordination, but directly from God through the agency of none other than Jesus Christ. This is the One whom God raised from the dead and who is, therefore, still alive.

Paul's authority was frequently challenged, especially through his early ministry when this letter was written. The bulk of his ministry was comprised of three missionary journeys throughout the eastern Mediterranean areas. Jewish pseudo believers dogged his steps, often entering into areas after Paul evangelized and attempting to bring the new believers in Christ back under the law. It was mixing law and grace, which as Paul demonstrates in this letter, completely undermines grace. This letter is a polemic, or a defense, against such efforts. At its core, such false teaching negates the very gospel message that God had sent Paul to propagate. In other words, this is no small issue.

His ministry was all about the Lord Jesus Christ; it was authorized by God the Father, and it carried out the implications of the resurrection. The centrality of justification by grace is the keynote message of the book and of his ministry. It is the proverbial hill on which Paul took his stand and planted his flag. This is his ultimate "go to the wall" issue. Take this away, and you gut the message of the gospel. So, he begins the letter with no ambiguity concerning his authority as an apostle of the Lord and his independence from any human ecclesiastical sources. He speaks as a mouth piece of God.

Lord, help me to understand the foundational truth of the gospel of Jesus Christ—justification by grace. If it was so important for You to give the letter defending this truth, help me to see its importance for my life and ministry.

Gracious Greetings

Galatians 1:2-3

² ... and all the brethren who are with me, to the churches of Galatia: ³ Grace to you and peace from God our Father and the Lord Jesus Christ ...

Paul's letters were personal, written in the context of his ministry with people. No ivory tower academic, his doctrine was not separated from people where they lived. So, while he speaks with the authority of an apostle, he reminds his readers that his teaching is not unique to him, but the sentiments of the letter are shared by "all the brethren who are with me." This is similar to when he appealed to the Corinthians on a gender issue based on the general practice of the churches—a sort of positive peer pressure to conform to the truth (1 Cor. 11:16).

Who were these "brethren?" Possibly he was referring to the apostles, elders and others present at the Jerusalem Council in Acts 15. Paul and Barnabas had just returned from their first missionary journey, arriving in Jerusalem from the area of Galatia where a number of Gentile churches had been established (Acts 13-14). A council in Jerusalem had been called to work out the ramifications of the new teaching of grace and the issue of Gentiles being required to become Jewish proselytes before being added to the church. His letter to the Galatians could possibly have been written and delivered at the same time as the letter from the council to the churches of Galatia (see Acts 15:22ff). At any rate, the contents of both letters are related to the issue of whether the Mosaic law is required (in particular the Jewish rite of circumcision) for Gentile believers.

The hallmark of Paul's writing comes next, "Grace to you and peace . . .", which he includes in every one of his letters. At the core of his teaching is the desire that all to whom he ministers would understand and experience both grace and peace. Grace is the means by which we are brought into right relationship with God (justification) and the means by which we continue and grow in that relationship (i.e. sanctification). Peace is the result both personally in ourselves and relationally with God and with others. Both grace and peace are essential to life. Grace, because we cannot win God's favor with our efforts at keeping His commandments, and peace because we separated ourselves from God by our wrong doings. This grace is sourced in God and comes through the Lord Jesus Christ (Paul uses His full title). Paul's writing was intended to convey that grace and peace, and we would do well to make it our goal to understand and to live in that grace and peace.

Dear Lord Jesus Christ, thank You for the grace and peace which You have so freely given to me. I deserved none of it.

A Concise Glory

Galatians 1:4-5

⁴ ... who gave Himself for our sins so that He might rescue us from this present evil age, according to the will of our God and Father, ⁵ to whom be the glory forevermore. Amen.

The apostle never strayed from this core truth; it was absolutely central to everything he taught (at this point, he had been a follower of Christ for at least 17 years (see 1:18 & 2:1). In the opening words, Paul can't help but expound on "the Lord Jesus Christ." In one concise sentence, he captures the plan and the purpose of His coming into our world.

First, the Lord Jesus Christ gave Himself. He had said of Himself, "The Son of man did not come to be served, but to serve" (Matt. 20:28a). Self-giving is the essence of love. His gift to us was Himself. Second, He gave Himself for our sins. This was the nature of His gift. He gave "His life as a ransom for many" (Matt. 20:28b)—His payment for our debt. Third, the immediate purpose of His gift was to rescue us. We were in trouble, in danger of spiritually dying. Indeed, we were already "dead in our trespasses and sins" (Eph. 2:1).

Fourth, the context of our spiritual death was "this present evil age." This is often taught as referring to the world "system" which is contrary to God's ways, the fallen world of Satanic influence. It's the predominate influence on the unregenerate person. But now the Lord Jesus Christ has liberated us from that persuasive dominance in our lives. This does not transfer blame, but simply recognizes one perspective, but a very significant one, on the non-Christian state—slavery, bondage, an inability to do what God requires of us.

Fifth, the blue-print behind this self-giving sacrifice to rescue us was nothing other than strategy of the Father, that is, "the will of God." The apostle Peter put it this way at Pentecost, "this Man, delivered over by the predetermined plan and foreknowledge of God, you nailed to a cross by the hands of godless men and put Him to death" (Acts 2:23). He later wrote, "For He was foreknown before the foundation of the world, but has appeared in these last times for the sake of you" (1 Peter 1:20). Paul personalizes it further, "He chose us in Him before the foundation of the world . . ." (Eph. 1:4). Salvation, the event of the cross and also our own individual salvation, was planned out well ahead of time!

Finally, the ultimate goal in God's plan of salvation is the Father's eternal glory! God's purpose in the world is doxological—to show His Glory! Everything else flows from this God-centric purpose.

Father, thank You for saving me. While I benefit from it, You far more—for my salvation will show how great a God You are, throughout all eternity.

The Go-To-The-Wall Issue

Galatians 1:6-7

⁶ I am amazed that you are so quickly deserting Him who called you by the grace of Christ, for a different gospel; ⁷ which is really not another; only there are some who are disturbing you and want to distort the gospel of Christ.

Few things amazed the apostle Paul, and this is one of them—that new believers so easily and summarily abandon their new faith. He was extremely tolerant in many areas (see Philippians 1:15; 1 Corinthians 8:7-8), but one thing he would not tolerate was any message that compromised the message of grace through faith in the Lord Jesus Christ. It boggled his mind that the first converts of his worldwide mission would become like withering plants (Matt. 13:5).

They were now holding to a façade of the gospel, but denying the very foundation on which it was established. What they were believing now was masquerading as the "gospel," or good news. It appealed to them as "better news" than what Paul preached, an improvement, but they were rejecting the true gospel, Paul says, for "a different gospel; which is really not another."

The message of the grace of the Lord Jesus Christ is not just one of many angles on what could be construed as a better way of life. It is "the truth," and it admits to no variations. It was Paul's "go to the wall issue," and he wouldn't tolerate any modifications, adjustments, rewordings or other manipulations which cut the core out of the message—the grace of God. This has nothing to do with a minor theological variation within the accepted stream of the Christian faith. It is not simply an intramural debate among Christians, a variant part of legitimate "Christendom." Rather, to use the terms of theologians, it is not orthodoxy, but heterodoxy—"a different word of glory." Genuine Christianity as was revealed to Paul and as he taught opposes everything else that is essentially law-based. This would include not just other religious systems, but also much of present day "Christendom" that is a facade for law-based religion.

This aberration among the Galatians found its source in false teachers who were intentionally "distorting the gospel of Christ." Historically, certain Jewish "so-called" believers moved in after Paul would leave an area to subvert his teachings. With great duplicity, they ostensibly affirmed faith in Jesus Christ, but also pressed the new Gentile believers to follow the law of Moses, in particular, to be circumcised. The issue of whether Gentiles needed to become Jewish proselytes was the central concern of the early church. In this letter, Paul answers the question in unambiguous terms—"NO!" We today should be as clear in our thinking about this as he was.

Father, thank You for the simplicity of the gospel message of grace. I commit to defending it and teaching it as You revealed it to Your apostles.

Don't Tamper With the Gospel

Galatians 1:8-9

⁸ But even if we, or an angel from heaven, should preach to you a gospel contrary to what we have preached to you, he is to be accursed! ⁹ As we have said before, so I say again now, if any man is preaching to you a gospel contrary to what you received, he is to be accursed!

Purity of the gospel message was inviolable in Paul's teaching. He was unbending, uncompromising—he would take no quarter. Here he uses the strongest possible words to denounce purveyors of such false teaching. Tampering with the gospel incurred his greatest censure.

Notice his invective would even fall on himself if he so much as altered his original message. That is how certain he was of the absolute centrality of the gospel message to everything he taught and propagated. The focus is the original gospel message he preached to the Galatians. There was no room for "development" that some modern interpreters would suggest is appropriate for the gospel message that ostensibly, in their minds, needs to be "adapted" to the culture and sensibilities of our day. The truth is that the gospel in its purest form is still as needed today as when Paul first preached it.

Paul uses the strongest possible condemnation, "he is to be accursed," which in the Greek is "anathema." This word refers to one who is condemned. Strong words! He even pronounces this anathema on angels should any of them distort the message. And then, not to be misunderstood, Paul repeats himself almost verbatim.

The gospel message, as Paul goes on to show in this letter to the Galatians, was the message of grace, a salvation freely given through faith akin to Abraham's before the law came. Therefore, it was faith available to Gentiles and Jews alike, without any necessity for keeping the law or circumcision. It is a salvation that originates in God with the meritorious work of Christ on the cross. We humans are simply recipients through faith of this wonderful gift of forgiveness, reconciliation, regeneration and new life. Anything different is a false gospel and undermines any possibility of living a life pleasing to God in conformity to His purpose for creating us. There can be no genuine Christ-like love, human grace or true benevolence apart from the genuine message that God has saved us apart from anything we have done—other than simple, Abrahamic-like faith, the faith of a child. This is the message Paul preached; this is the message he guarded; this is the message the distortion of which he condemned in no uncertain terms!

Lord, thank You for reminding me of the need to hold to the purity of the gospel of grace—for it is the foundation on which I live my life to please You.

Weekend Reading

Saturday – Matthew 1
Sunday – Matthew 2

PERSONAL REFLECTIONS

_____
_____
_____
_____
_____
_____
_____
_____
_____
_____
_____
_____
_____
_____
_____
_____
_____
_____
_____
_____
_____
_____
_____
_____
_____
_____
_____
_____
_____
_____
_____
_____

Being a God-Pleaser

Galatians 1:10

¹⁰ For am I now seeking the favor of men, or of God? Or am I striving to please men? If I were still trying to please men, I would not be a bond-servant of Christ.

Man-pleasing was not what the apostle Paul was about. He had received his orders directly from God. From his commissioning in Acts 9:15-19, he was a bond-servant of the Lord Jesus Christ (Rom. 1:1). He was charged with "the promise in Christ Jesus through the gospel, of which I was made a minister, according to the gift of God's grace which was given to me according to the working of His power" (Eph. 3:6-7). He recognized, "To me, the very least of all saints, this grace was given, to preach to the Gentiles the unfathomable riches of Christ, and to bring to light what is the administration of the mystery which for ages has been hidden in God who created all things" (Eph. 3:8-9). So, Paul's defense of the purity of the gospel came by divine authority, and he steadfastly stayed on message, regardless of what anyone said—even if it meant standing up to the other apostles, as we will see in chapters 2 and 3!

Paul recognized that you cannot serve both God and humans. Being a man-pleaser automatically removes a person from the realm of being a God-pleaser. But, ". . . it is God who is at work in you, both to will and to work for His good pleasure" (Eph. 2:13). Therefore, our goal as Christians, following Paul's example, is to be God-pleasers, which is God's purpose in us. A wise, godly woman told me as I embarked into fulltime ministry for the Lord, "Just remember, you are not going out to serve people . . . You are going out to serve the Lord." Wiser words are seldom spoken. It is so easy to fall into the pattern of serving the Lord in ways that are more intended to please people. Maybe it is the need for accolades. Maybe it is the desire to win the approval of those whom you admire, your parents, a mentor, church leaders, etc.

These words of Paul echo Jesus' teachings, "He who loves father or mother more than Me is not worthy of Me; and he who loves son or daughter more than Me is not worthy of Me" (Matt. 10:37). The disciples, when commanded by the high priest to cease preaching Christ, responded, "We must obey God rather than men" (Acts 5:29). Joshua said it most exquisitely, "If it is disagreeable in your sight to serve the LORD, choose for yourselves today whom you will serve: whether the gods which your fathers served which were beyond the River, or the gods of the Amorites in whose land you are living; but as for me and my house, we will serve the LORD" (Josh. 24:15).

Lord, You have created me to serve You. Help me to recognize when I am living to please others so that I might repent and return to pleasing You.

Authority Through Revelation

Galatians 1:11-12

[11] For I would have you know, brethren, that the gospel which was preached by me is not according to man. [12] For I neither received it from man, nor was I taught it, but I received it through a revelation of Jesus Christ.

Paul was clear about the source of his message. The message itself was not unique to Paul, nor was the origin of it different than that of the other apostles. But he was not dependent upon the other apostles for the core message of the gospels. To be sure, there were many things he received from them. For example, "Now I praise you because you remember me in everything and hold firmly to the traditions, just as I delivered them to you" (1 Cor. 11:2). The word "traditions" literally means "that which is passed down." He was probably referring to things which the official twelve witnesses (Acts 1:8) had passed on to him through the perfect recall given them by the Holy Spirit (John 14:26), and which he passed on to others. Even his writings refer to things of which he was not personal witness (1 Cor. 11:23; 1 Tim. 5:18; Matt. 10:10; 1 Cor. 9:14, etc.).

However, one of the most strenuous points Paul makes to the Galatians is that he specifically did not receive the message of the gospel from the other apostles, even though he himself was not one of the twelve. It came by direct revelation from Jesus Christ. Why was it so important for him to make this point so strenuously?

Clearly his authority as an apostle was under attack. The so-called "Judaizers," those who dogged his ministry with charges that he was undermining the Mosaic Law, kept trying to pervert the message to a law-based system, to essentially make the new converts to Paul's message into Jewish proselytes. In arguing against this false message, the purveyors of which are to be cursed (Gal. 1:8-9), his first argument has to do with his authority. He teaches the gospel as one who has received it directly from God personally. It has not been mediated by any human being, not even the 12 apostles. In modern vernacular, we might say he is pulling rank by appealing to a higher authority. His standing as an authority will be established in the following chapter and a half as he outlines his dealings with the twelve, especially with Peter.

Then, in chapters three and four, he presents the doctrinal basis for the purity of the gospel, that salvation comes by grace apart from the works of the law. He will show that circumcision is not only unnecessary for salvation but also detrimental to salvation. This is not just something manmade or the result of theological deliberation—this truth comes directly from Jesus Christ!

Lord, thank You that the gospel message was not an invention of human origin. Because it comes by Your divine authority, we can trust it to be true.

A Case For Credibility

Galatians 1:13-14

¹³ For you have heard of my former manner of life in Judaism, how I used to persecute the church of God beyond measure and tried to destroy it; ¹⁴ and I was advancing in Judaism beyond many of my contemporaries among my countrymen, being more extremely zealous for my ancestral traditions.

H is reputation preceded him, so the Galatians needed only to be reminded of Paul's life before Christ. He was a convert away from those who were now persecuting him and the message of grace in Jesus Christ. In fact, there had been no greater antagonist against this new movement of Christ-followers, commonly referred to as "The Way" (see Acts 9:2; 19:9, 23; 24:14, 22). He had persecuted the church prior to being a proponent of the church. In fact, his reputation had been widely known among the Jews (Acts 26:4-5). The historical record shows that he "ravaged the church" (Acts 8:3). On the one hand, he looked back on this time with shame, "For I am the least of the apostles, and not fit to be called an apostle, because I persecuted the church of God" (Acts 15:9). But his argument against the Judaizers is made more effective because he was once one of them! Converts always lend credibility to the legitimacy of a new way—they know whereof they speak.

Paul, however, had not been your run-of-the-mill religious person, a Jew in name only. He was crazy insane with attacking the new movement, also called "the church of God," the "ekklesia," or the "people gathered out by God." He was obsessed with obliterating it out of existence. Neither was he simply a fringe fanatic during his years of antagonism. He was upwardly mobile, making a name for himself among the religious elite. He was mainstream; in fact, he was the up and coming bright young star of Judaism. He was not a radical innovator of cutting edge theology; rather, his standing was that of a firmly rooted traditionalist in the historic, accepted Jewish customs. His pedigree was solid (Phil. 2:4-6). In other words, he was unparalleled in his qualification to speak on the subject of the Mosaic Law, the very thing the Judaizers were promoting.

Thus, Paul begins his tense theological debate with the establishment of his credentials. He speaks as one who is a leader in the new movement of God (that is, an apostle authorized by God), and as one who had previously been a leader of the old movement of God, traditional Judaism. So, Paul was not just a brainwashed lackey of the movement. His conversion was powerful testimony. Never was there a time to be more adamant and faithful to the message of Jesus Christ. Paul was both!

Lord, the credibility of the gospel message was enhanced when You saved me from my old way and brought me into the new way of Jesus Christ.

Christ Revealed In Me

Galatians 1:15-16a

* But when God, who had set me apart even from my mother's womb and called me through His grace, was pleased to reveal His Son in me so that I might preach Him among the Gentiles ...*

Paul's authority rested in a greater background than his religious credentials; his was a sovereign commissioning by God. Some might object, "Where are the witnesses of this commissioning?" However, the Holy Spirit validated Paul's authority using supernatural events, "The signs of a true apostle were performed among you with all perseverance, by signs and wonders and miracles" (2 Cor. 12:12). As he did with the Roman believers (see Romans 1:1), Paul here asserted his authority without reserve and did not rely on any human ordination or endorsement. The supernatural evidence speaks for itself!

His "set apartness" for the gospel took place at birth, which presupposes a prior contemplation by God in His "predetermined plan" (see Acts 2:23; Ephesians 1:4). This selecting at or before birth also marked the prophet Jeremiah (Jer. 1:5). Further, it marked the Messiah (Isa. 49:1). So this is a big deal! Likewise, it is a big deal for all of us as well, who are redeemed by grace.

A few applications can be made, using God's work in Paul's life as our model (for following Paul's example, see 1 Corinthians 4:16; 11:1; Philippians 3:17; 4:9). First, God's plan for our lives began long before we were converted, for God "chose us in Him before the foundation of the world" (Eph. 1:4). Second, His plan for us is bathed in grace, it is a gift of life and service. Serving Him is a privilege.

Third, it all has to do with revealing Jesus Christ in us. God's great purpose is to show off His Son! Fourth, this plan excites God, He is thrilled ("pleased") with this magnificent scenario, for it restores what God originally intended, that we exist "in His image" (Gen. 1:27). Sin has obscured that picture. Now Christ, as the "second Adam" (1 Cor. 15:45; Rom. 5:14), perfectly reveals God: "He is the image of the invisible God, the firstborn of all creation . . ." (Col. 1:15a, see also 2 Cor. 4:4); "He is the radiance of His glory and the exact representation of His nature . . ." (Heb. 1:3). As with God's working in Paul's life, the Lord's purpose is to reveal the image of His Son in each of us, for that is the picture God has in mind. Paul later addressed his readers, "My children, with whom I am again in labor until Christ is formed in you . . ." (Gal. 4:19). That is the goal of the ministry to which he was called.

Finally, we, for our part, need to "be all the more diligent to make certain about His calling and choosing you . . ." (2 Peter 1:10)

Lord, thank You for choosing me as a showpiece for revealing Your Son. Let me be the mantel piece on which the trophy of Christ might stand.

Not A Man-Made Message

Galatians 1:16b-18

16 ... I did not immediately consult with flesh and blood, 17 nor did I go up to Jerusalem to those who were apostles before me; but I went away to Arabia, and returned once more to Damascus. 18 Then three years later I went up to Jerusalem to become acquainted with Cephas, and stayed with him fifteen days.

Paul was converted on the road to Damascus, somewhere between 30-35 AD, at most within a few years of the crucifixion and resurrection of Christ. (Dating of these events is determined by detailed comparison of the biblical record with secular sources of history). Paul zeroes in on the aspects of his personal history that support the independence of his message from human influence. He stressed that significant time had passed after his conversion before he even met the other apostles (three years). He simply did not "consult with flesh and blood" about the content of the gospel message, nor did he receive a commissioning from anyone. His authority came from God.

The salient details are as follows. According to the book of Acts, while in Damascus, after his conversion, ". . . immediately he began to proclaim Jesus in the synagogues, saying, 'He is the Son of God.'" (Acts 9:20). Severe persecution forced him out and, although the book of Acts doesn't record what happened next, Paul writes here that he went to Arabia for some time before returning again to Damascus. It was only then that he went to Jerusalem where he met the apostles (see Acts 9:27), specifically meeting with Peter for a little over two weeks (Paul tended to refer to Peter by his Hebrew name, Cephas).

The total elapsed time from conversion to this first Jerusalem visit was at least three years. During that time, Paul had preached the message of Christ he had received from God, without seeking or receiving any confirmation or authorization from the other apostles.

A few observations are in order. First, Paul's authority was independent of Peter and the others. Therefore, even from the beginning, Peter did not hold a position of primacy (later in the letter, Paul relates how he rebuked Peter for hypocrisy). Second, Paul was not disrespectful of the other apostles, for he did acknowledge them as apostles. Third, his insistence on the divine origin of his message was not born out of jealousy or insecurity, for he had been preaching the gospel long before ever meeting them. Fourth, it is a matter of fascinating conjecture to consider what Paul and Peter discussed for 15 days. Was Paul eager to learn the details of Christ's earthly life from an eyewitness and frequent companion of the Lord? That shall remain a mystery until we arrive in glory!

Lord, just as Paul looked to You for his authority, help me look only to Your Word for my authority, for it is the message of divine origin.

Weekend Reading

Saturday – Matthew 3
Sunday – Matthew 4

Not On Human Authority

Galatians 1:19-20

¹⁹ But I did not see any other of the apostles except James, the Lord's brother. ²⁰ (Now in what I am writing to you, I assure you before God that I am not lying).

James was the only other significant Christian leader with whom Paul met in Jerusalem (besides Peter) on his first visit; not for lack of his efforts though, ". . . he [Paul] was trying to associate with the disciples; but they were all afraid of him, not believing that he was a disciple" (Acts 9:26). His reputation as a persecutor of the church did not dissipate easily even after three years.

This James was not the apostle and brother of John, but the half-brother of Jesus. They had the same mother, Mary, but since Jesus was virgin born, they did not have the same father (see Matthew 13:55). That Paul was not using the term "brother" in the generic sense of "brother in Christ" or as an affectionate reference to James the apostle is virtually certain because of the following reasons: The apostle James was martyred early on (see Acts 12:2) and never showed prominence in the early church. In Acts 15, another James came to the fore as the rumored source of agitation which Paul describes in later in this letter (see Galatians 2:12). That James became the chief spokesperson in resolving the issue of how the Gentiles were to be accepted based on faith and not on adherence to the law. Further, this James is the one specifically mentioned in Galatians 1:19 in what definitely appears to be a reference to the same James of Acts 15, and therefore, not the apostle James. Thus, our reference here must refer to Jesus' half-brother, as stated. (The direct implication of all this is that Jesus was virgin born, but Mary did not remain a virgin after that).

The Scripture never tells us when James came to faith, but prior to Jesus going to Jerusalem, James and the other biological half-brothers did not believe in Him as the Messiah (John 7:5). How ironic that those who grew up with him were so slow to become His disciples! Yet, after the crucifixion, we find at least that this half-brother, James, became not only an ardent follower of Christ but also a prominent leader among the early Christians.

Paul's emphasis was on the originality and independence of his message; he did not receive the gospel from such prominent leaders as Peter or James. In fact, he adds oath, "I assure you before the Lord." The importance of this will become evident shortly when he writes about confronting Peter in his hypocritical behavior toward the Gentile believers. Here Paul was establishing his full authority for confronting the highly respected Peter.

Lord, help me to fully understand that my faith in the gospel of Jesus Christ does not rest in highly esteemed preachers, but in the revealed Word of God.

Glorify God Because of Me

Galatians 1:21-24

²¹ Then I went into the regions of Syria and Cilicia. ²² I was still unknown by sight to the churches of Judea which were in Christ; ²³ but only, they kept hearing, "He who once persecuted us is now preaching the faith which he once tried to destroy." ²⁴ And they were glorifying God because of me.

During Paul's first visit to Jerusalem, Barnabas paved the way by vouching for him to the believers. Paul quickly began preaching the gospel there (Acts 9:27-28). His work was mainly among the Greek-speaking Jews, those who were ethnically and religiously Jews, but culturally more Greek than Hebrew. Paul, having been a child of Roman citizens (and, thus, himself a Roman citizen) and having been raised in the Roman city of Tarsus with all its Greek culture, related easily to the Greek Jews. After only two weeks, threats on his life by the unbelieving Greek Jews he was trying to reach prompted the believers (converted Hebrew Jews) to wisely spirit Paul out of Jerusalem for his own safety. From there, Paul travelled to "Syria and Cilicia" as our text today reads and spent time in his home city of Tarsus (Acts 9:29-30).

Paul now, as he writes to the Galatians, brings the assessment of his "credentials" to a close with a brief analysis of his exposure in Jerusalem. He had not personally met the churches in Judea (obviously referring to those outside of Jerusalem— His gospel preaching was confined to that city). His reputation, though, had changed (in large part due to Barnabas' influence as well as Paul's own actions of preaching the gospel) and news of the change spread throughout Judea: He was a different man! They had known him quite well as the chief antagonist against the church (see Acts 8:1-3). But now, astonishingly, his reputation was growing as the one who was "now preaching the faith he once tried to destroy." In the end, the churches of Judea embraced Paul sight unseen and saw his conversion as an amazing act of God. What an affect this one man had on the early church!

Paul indeed saw his conversion as God's wonderful example to the believers. He later wrote, "I thank Christ Jesus our Lord . . . though I was formerly a blasphemer and a persecutor and a violent aggressor. Yet I was shown mercy . . . and the grace of our Lord was more than abundant . . . Christ Jesus came into the world to save sinners, among whom I am foremost of all. Yet for this reason I found mercy, so that in me as the foremost, Jesus Christ might demonstrate His perfect patience as an example for those who would believe in Him . . ." (1 Tim. 1:12-16).

Lord, let my life be an example of Your grace so others might glorify You because of me.

Not In Vain

Galatians 2:1-2

¹ Then after an interval of fourteen years I went up again to Jerusalem with Barnabas, taking Titus along also. ² It was because of a revelation that I went up; and I submitted to them the gospel which I preach among the Gentiles, but I did so in private to those who were of reputation, for fear that I might be running, or had run, in vain.

Considerable time passed before Paul re-visited Jerusalem. He was not summoned by the church leaders, but was prompted by a revelation directly from God. His traveling companions were Barnabas and Titus. Barnabas was Paul's early mentor, from shortly after his conversion through his first missionary tour. During preparation for the second tour, the two had a falling out and went their separate ways (Acts 15:39-40). So, Paul refers here in our text to a time between the 1st and 2nd tours, which places this event at the time of Acts 15, the Jerusalem council, when the two were still together. Although we know little of Titus' background or how he came to associate with Paul, we do know he was a faithful and frequent companion of Paul and the latter wrote him a letter which is included in the New Testament writings

After fourteen years of Paul preaching the gospel and after some conflict had ensued over Gentile converts to the faith, it was important to establish solidarity in the gospel, that what he was preaching and teaching, though authorized independently of the other apostles, was consistent and cohesive with their teachings. The unity of the church was at stake; there was not to be two separate movements, a true Jewish church and a lesser Gentile church. Paul's letter to the Ephesians focused on that very issue. "For He Himself is our peace, who made both groups [Jews and Gentiles] into one and broke down the barrier of the dividing wall, by abolishing in His flesh the enmity, which is the Law of commandments contained in ordinances, so that in Himself He might make the two into one new man, thus establishing peace . . ." (Eph. 2:14-15).

Paul approached the other apostles "privately" lest the work of the gospel in establishing a unified, new community of believers would be thwarted at such an early stage. Further, he did not want any "skirmish" with the apostles to go public until he had opportunity to talk with the Jerusalem leaders first. His referring to them as being "those who were of reputation" emphasizes that he was concerned about avoiding public conflict that could diminish their stature. Solidarity and the purity of the gospel were the main issues. Paul was a man of truth and grace. What an example for us to follow.

Lord, I pray for the unity of the church. Despite all the different doctrinal persuasions, help us to rally around the pure gospel of grace.

Guarding the Freedom

Galatians 2:3-4

³ But not even Titus, who was with me, though he was a Greek, was compelled to be circumcised. ⁴ But it was because of the false brethren secretly brought in, who had sneaked in to spy out our liberty which we have in Christ Jesus, in order to bring us into bondage.

The gospel brought liberty, real freedom, not simply a theological platitude. Freedom from the external requirements of the Mosaic law. Paul enjoyed it completely and his converts likewise. Titus, himself a Gentile (referred to here as "Greek"), was fully employed in ministry without being circumcised.

Circumcision was the watershed separating Jews from Gentiles. Before Christ, any non-Jew who wanted to be right with God had to embrace the Law of Moses, which was the moral and religious constitution of the Jewish people. They had to become what are called "proselytes" or converts to Judaism. Circumcision was the hallmark, the sign that indicated a person's commitment to the Law of Moses (now, this had immediate implications for the males physically, but also for the females in principle). However, Paul did not require circumcision of the Gentiles, and thus, did not require them to convert to Judaism to be followers of Christ.

This alarmed the Jewish believers in Jerusalem, and resulted in some of them traveling 300 miles north to Antioch in Syria where Paul was ministering among a large number of Gentile believers—to spy out their behavior. The very way Paul writes about this reveals his great irritation at the efforts to bring these new believers into "bondage." They had been set free from the very oppressive mandates that plague all religious efforts of the world, namely, that humans must labor under systems of laws to appease their guilt before God. Such thinking enslaves people in fear. Later in his letter, Paul says, "It was for freedom that Christ set us free . . ." (Gal. 5:1). The freedom Christians have comes through the Lord Jesus Christ, and Paul goes to wall for this very issue.

Perversions of the gospel are on the rise today, just as in Paul's day. Many teach that baptism is necessary for salvation. Others assert that good works maintain their salvation. Some minimize the message of grace as being just a character of behavior, and that behavior is what saves a person. But the message of forgiveness of sins freely given by a righteous, gracious, forgiving God through Jesus Christ is the pure gospel. ". . . for [gospel] is the power of God for salvation to everyone who believes, to the Jew first and also to the Greek" (Rom. 1:16). This the hill on which Paul plants his flag!

Lord, thank You for the freedom I have in Christ. He saved me freely and keeps me securely. Help me enjoy that freedom and not be again enslaved by the law.

No Respecter of Reputation

Galatians 2:5-6

⁵ But we did not yield in subjection to them for even an hour, so that the truth of the gospel would remain with you. ⁶ But from those who were of high reputation (what they were makes no difference to me; God shows no partiality)—well, those who were of reputation contributed nothing to me.

Unequivocating and unyielding was Paul's terse response to the threats of legalism to the gospel message. He would not bend to human pressure, regardless of the source. There could be no modification of the gospel of grace that brings freedom from the law, not in the slightest.

We simply point out the obvious in his statements. First, he was motivated to preserve the "truth of the gospel." Doctrine, contrary to cultural Christians of today, does matter, particularly at the core issue of God's work in Christ. The gospel was completely new and was of a completely different nature than the law of Moses. There can be no mixture of the two. This was not merely an intramural debate among differing persuasions in the broader context of the Christian religion—it struck at the core, the very nature of the Christian faith.

Second, Paul was unconcerned with the reputation of any individual who might be seen as modifying the core message of the gospel. Earlier, he said even if he himself were to change the message, then let himself be accursed (Gal. 1:8-9). Reputation meant nothing to Paul, neither his nor anyone else's.

Third, his attitude modeled that of God, who shows no partiality. The Lord uses people, but He is not beholden to them. It is only by His grace that He uses any of us, and we dare not abuse that role by tampering with the truth.

Finally, Paul asserts dogmatically that the so-called "pillars" of the early church, Peter, James and the rest of the Jerusalem leaders "contributed nothing to me." He bows to no man when it comes to preserving the truth of the gospel.

The early church was struggling with overcoming old prejudices against the Gentiles. It took time for them to transition their behavior to coincide with their belief in the gospel of grace, and to fully understand the commissioning of Acts 1:8 that the message was to the "uttermost parts of the world." Acts 10 chronicles the apostle Peter's early struggle with preaching the gospel to the Gentiles. It didn't come easily for him and required a revelation from God in the form of a sheet lowered from heaven with unclean animals. After the ensuing conversion of Cornelius in Caesarea, in Acts 11, he reported in detail the whole event to the church in Jerusalem. Paul cemented the issue—the gospel did not require the law!

Lord, help us not to treat the doctrine of the gospel of grace as simply one of many theological interpretations. It is the core of Your message to us today.

WEEKEND READING

Saturday – Matthew 5
Sunday – Matthew 6

PERSONAL REFLECTIONS

_____
_____
_____
_____
_____
_____
_____
_____
_____
_____
_____
_____
_____
_____
_____
_____
_____
_____
_____
_____
_____
_____
_____
_____
_____
_____

Solidarity in the Gospel

Galatians 2:7-9

⁷ But on the contrary, seeing that I had been entrusted with the gospel to the uncircumcised, just as Peter had been to the circumcised ⁸ (for He who effectually worked for Peter in his apostleship to the circumcised effectually worked for me also to the Gentiles), ⁹ and recognizing the grace that had been given to me, James and Cephas and John, who were reputed to be pillars, gave to me and Barnabas the right hand of fellowship, so that we might go to the Gentiles and they to the circumcised.

Solidarity achieved! Paul had not run in vain (Gal. 2:2). The most prominent leaders in the Jerusalem church, namely James, Peter (also called "Cephas") and John, recognized four things in Paul's ministry. First, they saw that Paul had indeed been entrusted with the gospel message by God in the same way as Peter. Second, the only difference between Peter's and Paul's ministry was in the target audience: Paul was sent to reach the Gentiles; whereas, Peter was to focus on the Jews (referred to here as "the circumcised"). Yet, Paul continued to have a burden for his people the Jews, "For I could wish that I myself were accursed, separated from Christ for the sake of my brethren, my kinsmen according to the flesh . . ." (Rom. 10:3) and the Jewish synagogue was often his first stop when visiting a city for the first time. He understood that the Gospel was for "the Jew first and also for the Gentile" (Rom. 1:16).

Third, the Jerusalem leaders recognized that Paul's ministry to the Gentiles was validated by the results, which were called "effective." He was no self-proclaimed evangelist that accomplished nothing. Though the Jewish people rejected the message coming from him, many Gentiles did respond. Peter, on the other hand, was used mightily by God to more effectively reach the Jews (notice the results of his Day of Pentecost message where 3000 were saved in one day—Acts 2:41). From a human perspective, we might have thought a better plan would be for Paul, the learned Jewish scholar, to appeal to the Jews, but God's ways are not our ways.

Fourth, they recognized the grace Paul had been given. This was the grace of the gospel, first in his conversion, but also replicated through him in the preaching of the gospel to those in need of the Savior. Paul had the unmistakable finger print of God on his ministry. In the end, James, Cephas and John, the ones considered as pillars of the church in Jerusalem (as Paul understood it from rumor), symbolically extended to Paul the sign of solidarity, "the right hand of fellowship." The unity of the gospel was preserved, by those who were faithfully committed to obeying the Lord and shepherding His church.

Lord, help me to recognize the God-ordained work You are doing in others, even though some aspects of their ministries challenge my prejudices.

Of Poverty and Benevolence

Galatians 2:10

[10] They only asked us to remember the poor—the very thing I also was eager to do.

Social concern was high on the priority list in the early church. Paul had been infected with this concern through his association with Barnabas, if not earlier. Early on, the latter had been sent from Jerusalem to Antioch to investigate reports of a huge number of Gentiles coming to faith. He recruited Paul from Tarsus to help in the teaching work there. It was during this time that a famine broke out, which was especially severe in Judea. The mostly-Gentile believers in Antioch sacrificially gave of their resources for the famine relief, sending the funds to the church in Jerusalem by the hand of Barnabas and Paul (Acts 11:22-30). That was Paul's second visit to Jerusalem, the third one being the one referenced presently in our text.

We see this emphasis on benevolence continue into Paul's later ministry. On his third mission tour, he actively solicited financial support for the struggling believers in Jerusalem (see Romans 15:25-28; 1 Corinthians 16:1-3; Acts 24:17). Though he was adamant about his independence from the Jerusalem leaders and about the Gentiles not needing to convert to Judaism in order to be saved, he none-the-less felt compelled to honor the Jerusalem church and their leaders, "For if the Gentiles have shared in their [believers in Jerusalem] spiritual things, they [i.e. Gentile believers] are indebted to minister to them also in material things" (Rom. 15:27b).

Paul was clear that benevolence did not provide a basis for salvation, yet was still compelled to be generous to the poor. He taught the Ephesian elders, "You yourselves know that these hands ministered to my own needs and to the men who were with me. In everything I showed you that by working hard in this manner you must help the weak and remember the words of the Lord Jesus, that He Himself said, 'It is more blessed to give than to receive.'" (Acts 20:34-35).

Today the poor are all around us. Certainly, there are beggars on the streets and those who make their rounds looking to churches for financial aid, but there are also people in our churches who struggle with making ends meet, astronomical medical bills, single mothers, struggling students. Not to mention those in third world countries, especially children, who live in dire poverty. Let this mind be in us that was also in the apostle Paul and the Jerusalem leaders; let us remember the poor in tangible, real ways. Let us open our wallets and checkbooks—and our lives. Let us give sacrificially to help others.

Lord, help me to remember the poor, for You said, "You will always have the poor with you." (Matt. 26:11)

Not on Human Foundation

Galatians 2:11

11 But when Cephas came to Antioch, I opposed him to his face, because he stood condemned.

Controversy was brewing in Antioch, and Paul attacked it at the highest level. The gospel was being watered down, as we shall see in the next verses. However, here Paul takes on one of the reputed "pillars" of the church, none-other than Peter himself. As mentioned before, Paul often used Peter's Hebrew name Cephas, rather than the name Jesus gave him, Peter. Was this done as a slight? That certainly is a possibility, but it could have been rather Paul's way of emphasizing that Peter had not been acting faithfully in the gospel message. Paul's adamant stand for the truth showed no respect for persons, because he had a clear understanding of his mission. The purity of the gospel message trumps all else, there can be no wavering, even if it came from an angel or himself or any man (1:8-10) . . . Peter is no exception.

In the history of Christendom, there has been much hype over Peter being the chief apostle, the "vicar of Christ" and having the keys to the kingdom. This has evolved into an elaborate pontificate with magisterial authority and pomp, complete with detailed canon law and sophistry. The ultimate ascension of the clergy/laity divide is supposedly traced to an "apostolic succession" of bishops, the foremost of which is the bishop of Rome, more well-known as the pope of the Roman Catholic Church. However, biblical support for this is quite lacking. In this case, Peter is called out for his hypocrisy in communicating the gospel. Further, nowhere in the New Testament record do we read of anyone giving Peter the primacy over the other apostles. True, Peter was given the keys to the kingdom (Matt. 16:19a), but as was often the case, Peter was standing in for the other disciples. In fact, the "loosing and binding" authority given him (Matt. 16:19b), was also given to all the apostles (Matt. 18:18). Keys open doors, and historically, we see that Peter (in some cases with John) opened the door of the gospel to Jews (Acts 2), the Samaritans (Acts 8) and the Gentiles (Acts 10). The Lord used a play on words in Matthew 16:18 telling Peter that his name was "stone" (Greek petros) and that Jesus would build His church on the "rock" (Greek petra). The church is built on rock-like faith, which Peter expressed so simply and clearly.

Therefore, when, by his actions, Peter denied the simple and clear gospel, Paul took him to task. No man dare tamper with the gospel message. Paul was unequivocal: Peter stood condemned!

Lord, thank You that the church is not built on fallible human beings or ecclesiastical courts, but on the rock solid truth of the gospel of Jesus Christ!

Targeting Integrity

12 For before certain men came from James, he was eating with the Gentiles; but when they came he drew back and separated himself, fearing the circumcision party. 13 And the rest of the Jews acted hypocritically along with him, so that even Barnabas was led astray by their hypocrisy.

Here is the crux of Peter's failing: he acted hypocritically. Of all sin, this ranks near the top in severity of judgment. Did not Jesus save his harshest condemnations for the Pharisees on this very point? What led Paul to level this accusation against Peter?

The number of Gentile believers in Antioch had grown exponentially, and word had gotten down to Jerusalem. The Jewish believers knew that Gentiles would benefit from the gospel message of Jesus Christ, but they had expected the Gentiles would be enfolded into the Jewishness of the faith. This was not happening in Antioch. Peter himself was not initially deterred by this, as he enjoyed delightful fellowship with them ("eating with Gentiles" would normally have been taboo for a Jew.). He did not come by this freedom easily, for in Acts 10 when he was confronted with Cornelius, the Gentile centurion, God needed to convince Peter through a vision that Gentiles were indeed acceptable to God. Peter concluded, "If then God gave the same gift to them as he gave to us when we believed in the Lord Jesus Christ, who was I that I could stand in God's way?" (Acts 11:17).

Some others went from Jerusalem to Antioch "to spy out our liberty which we have in Christ Jesus" (2:4). Ostensibly, these "came from James." Some scholars suggest that James tended more toward legalism, in contrast to Paul's message of grace. In this line of thinking, they pit the teaching of James with his emphasis on "faith without works is dead" thinking against Paul and his central teaching of "justification apart from works of the law." This tension is superficial, however, as a correct understanding of the book of James shows. A more probable interpretation of our passage here is that as the early church was working through the transition from law to grace, those men overstepped their commissioning "from James."

Their arrival had a pronounced effect on Peter—he began to avoid the Gentiles, just like unbelieving Jews did. He fell to the pressure of what the men from Jerusalem thought. Even Barnabas, Paul's companion in ministry of the gospel of grace was caught up in the obvious duplicity. Oh, that Christians would make a priority of walking in integrity of our beliefs and our actions.

Lord, help me to root out hypocrisy in my life, even when no one else sees or knows. "Search me and know my heart . . ." (Ps. 139:23).

Justification through Faith

Galatians 2:14-16

[14] But when I saw that they were not straightforward about the truth of the gospel, I said to Cephas in the presence of all, "If you, being a Jew, live like the Gentiles and not like the Jews, how is it that you compel the Gentiles to live like Jews? [15] We are Jews by nature and not sinners from among the Gentiles; [16] nevertheless knowing that a man is not justified by the works of the Law but through faith in Christ Jesus, even we have believed in Christ Jesus, so that we may be justified by faith in Christ and not by the works of the Law; since by the works of the Law no flesh will be justified."

Paul delivered to Peter a pointed lecture in theology—the grace of our Lord Jesus Christ supersedes the Law of Moses. Chapters three and four flesh this out more, but his comment here was wry. He pulled no punches. Peter was living two different lives, depending on who was present. Hypocritical!

On the one hand, Peter was living like a Gentile, as one apart from the law. This was the natural extension of the gospel of grace, freeing believers up from the yoke of the law. Yet, when the legalists from Jerusalem arrived, he pulled away from the Gentiles, and in effect, sent them a message by his behavior. It had the effect of pressuring the Gentiles to follow the law.

When Paul referred to Jews as not being "sinners from among the Gentiles," he was speaking in the sense of Gentiles not keeping the Law of Moses, and therefore, being sinners. The Jews kept the law, at least ostensibly. He went on to say that despite that, justification is not about keeping the Law. That is impossible to do, as he shows later. Justification comes through faith in Christ. This is one of the clearest statements in the NT distinguishing faith from works, and it highlights the core issue of justification. Indeed, the book of Galatians has sometimes been referred to as the Magna Carta of the Christian faith. We are freed by the grace of Christ from the bondage of the law. Jews are justified apart from works of the law—this is also true for the Gentiles. So, there is no basis for Jewish believers to pull back from non-Jewish believers or to pressure them into keeping the law.

Many "so-called" Christian denominations teach just the opposite, that a person must keep the law in order to be saved. For some, it is the requirement of baptism, as a kind of surrogate for circumcision. For others, is it giving to charity, doing good or obeying church laws. On an individual basis, many call themselves Christians because they are trying with all their effort to live rightly. But Paul was unequivocal. Justification comes through faith, apart from works. Anything else is "another gospel" and is anathema to God (Gal. 1:8-9).

Lord, help me to rest fully in Your grace, knowing that I am accepted, not based on my works which can never be enough. Your grace is sufficient, Amen!

WEEKEND READING

Saturday – Matthew 7
Sunday – Matthew 8

PERSONAL REFLECTIONS

Free From the Law

Galatians 2:17-19

17 "But if, while seeking to be justified in Christ, we ourselves have also been found sinners, is Christ then a minister of sin? May it never be! 18 For if I rebuild what I have once destroyed, I prove myself to be a transgressor. 19 For through the Law I died to the Law, so that I might live to God.

All have sinned and come short of the glory of God, as Paul writes in Romans 3:23. However, that is not his point here. In context "sinners" refers to the Gentiles who do not keep the Law of Moses. What he is saying here is that, according to the legalist's thinking, if in the process of being justified in Christ through faith, people are led to freedom from the law—which the Jews would consider sinful—then believing in and following Christ would in fact be encouraging sinfulness.

First, the legalists' way of reasoning would mean Christ Himself encourages sin, for His Gentile followers have not embraced circumcision and the Mosaic Law. Paul responds to this with a tight, concise retort—*me gnoita* ("may it never be"). He frequently used this explosive phrase in the book of Romans when addressing objections to justification by grace (Rom. 3:4; 6:2 etc.).

Second, if Paul began to require circumcision and the law, he would be essentially admitting guilt to transgressing the law by not having required it before then. He would be rebuilding the message of the gospel to require the law, something he had tried hard to not do (i.e. to destroy).

However, Paul had already gone on the line by saying that anyone who preached a different gospel (and that would include those who preached a gospel which required circumcision) is to be cursed (anathema) (Gal. 1:8-9). Furthermore, in his own life, he "died to the Law", and this came about "through the Law," so that he might "live to God." In other words, by living the way of the Law, he discovered his inability to live fully the way the law circumscribed, and therefore, became spiritually dead; the law did not have the intended effect in his life; thus, he "died to the Law." However, the happy result was his living for God; something the law could not accomplish. Of course, this came about through faith in Christ. As Paul said on his first missionary tour, ". . . everyone who believes is freed from all things, from which you could not be freed through the Law of Moses" (Acts 13:39).

Someone has said a majority of people attending Christian churches today are unsaved, still trying to merit their salvation by keeping the commandments. Let each of us examine our heart to see if we really do believe.

Lord, thank You for setting me free from the law of sin and judgment. Your grace is wonderfully sufficient, and I praise and worship You for this, Lord!

Christ Living in Me

Galatians 2:20-21 (part 1)

20 "I have been crucified with Christ; and it is no longer I who live, but Christ lives in me; and the life which I now live in the flesh I live by faith in the Son of God, who loved me and gave Himself up for me. 21 I do not nullify the grace of God, for if righteousness comes through the Law, then Christ died needlessly."

This was Paul's personal vision statement for his life. And if Philippians 3:17 is taken seriously, we then ought to imitate Paul, and set that as our own personal vision statement for life. As Christians, we have identified with His crucifixion, so much so that we see ourselves as being there on the cross with Christ, dying with Him. Just as Peter walked on the water with Christ, we choose to relate to Him in the dying process. But, as Paul continues to speak figuratively, we likewise identify with His life. The old way of living is no longer in control, or as Paul writes elsewhere, the old self is crucified (Rom. 6:6), with its passions and lusts (Gal. 5:24).

Christ lives in Paul—and so should we see this as true for ourselves. Christ lives in me. The life I now live is characterized by the life of faith in Christ. It was Christ who loved me and gave Himself up for me—not vice versa. That is precisely where the legalists were fouling up the message. Legalism really has at its core the need for the initiative for salvation to lie within the human heart. But, not so. The initiative lies with God. As John says, "We love because He first loved us" (1 John 4:19).

His great truth is mutually exclusive with a righteousness that comes through the law. If law was still in effect, two things would then follow: 1) The grace of God would be nullified—in other words, God is either gracious or He is not, He is all about law, or He is all about grace—the two concepts are mutually exclusive and cannot be mixed, or 2) Christ died needlessly—the sacrificial system of Moses must continue on—Christ's death, although a good model of self-sacrifice, was just another death, inspiring as it was. If law is required for salvation, Christ's death was worthless.

Some have said salvation is by faith and works, and if it is later discovered that works were not required, faith would be enough. However, by its very nature, believing that works of the law are required for salvation, necessarily exposes the faith being claimed as insufficient. For the faith required for salvation is a faith in the ultimate sufficiency of Christ, undiluted by faith in the law. So then, a person who believes in Christ and also the law of Moses, does not really have a saving faith after all!

Lord, help me to live a Christ-centered life—alone, for He alone saves, and He alone keeps me in the faith.

Christ Living in Me

Galatians 2:20-21 (part 2)

---

[20] *"I have been crucified with Christ; and it is no longer I who live, but Christ lives in me; and the life which I now live in the flesh I live by faith in the Son of God, who loved me and gave Himself up for me.* [21] *"I do not nullify the grace of God, for if righteousness comes through the Law, then Christ died needlessly."*

Studying and expounding this passage is one thing. Living it is another. Early in my Christian life, I committed verse 20 to memory, so that I could not just remember it, but also meditate on it. It was in this meditation that the heart of the Christian life became more clear. Some passages in Scripture lend themselves to our consideration more poignantly than others—and this is one of them.

To live, yet not live; to consider oneself to have died with someone else living life through him has the ingredients of psychological imbalance in a world that teaches us to "find ourselves," "love yourself," "look out for number one." This is no new concept, for Jesus said, "He who has found his life will lose it, and he who has lost his life for My sake will find it" (Matt. 10:39). In our passage, germane to the core of Christian living is a dying and a living, but a kind that is radically Other-centered, with the "Other" being God. This is described by Paul as believing ultimately that "Christ lives in me." My life at that point became indistinguishable from Christ's life. It is as though He were living in me, animating my every move.

So when confronted with a particular life difficulty, I remind myself of this verse: I am dead with Christ, it is not I that is living in this body anymore; Christ lives in me; I live by faith in Christ; He loved me first. Simple words to say, and to be sure ascetic or mystical sounding. But the Christian who forgets those things that lie behind and reaches forward to the mark of the prize of the upward call in Christ Jesus (Phil. 3:13-14) reorients his thinking and imagination to where he acts on the truth and reality of our passage. It is not spiritual mumbo jumbo, but the very words of revolutionary life-change.

In Romans 7, Paul records his struggle with sin and the weak human will, the duplicity of life forces within his body. The solution for finding freedom from the guilt problem is found in Romans 8:1 "Therefore there is now no condemnation for those who are in Christ Jesus." The solution to living in freedom from sin is found in this verse, Galatians 2:20. This is the grace of God. Not that we live a good life that merits anything, but that Christ lives His life in us. We are His hands, His feet, His eyes, and His mouth. He lives His life through us. All for His glory!

Lord, thank You for giving me a new life to live, the life of Christ.
I want to reflect Him in my every thought and action.

Not By Works of Law

Galatians 3:1-2

¹ You foolish Galatians, who has bewitched you, before whose eyes Jesus Christ was publicly portrayed as crucified? ² This is the only thing I want to find out from you: did you receive the Spirit by the works of the Law, or by hearing with faith?

They should have known better, the Galatian believers! They had left the truth for an error. Paul is flabbergasted by the report of how they had so quickly devolved from a life of faith into life under the law. It is the propensity of fallen human nature, as evidenced in the multitude of human religions, to move in the direction of spirituality through human efforts, that is, through law. The Galatians, even though redeemed people, were proving this to be so.

It was not for lack of knowledge that they fell into error, for Paul had himself "portrayed" to them the Lord as crucified. It was "before whose eyes," that is, they had personally seen and heard Paul's testimony about Christ and the crucifixion of Christ. There was simply no excuse.

His use of "foolish" to describe the Galatians is reminiscent of Jesus' words to the two disciples on the road to Emmaus after the resurrection, "O foolish men and slow of heart to believe in all that the prophets have spoken! Was it not necessary for the Christ to suffer these things and to enter into His glory?" (Luke 24:25-26). Foolishness is to clearly know the truth and to turn away from it—there is no rationale or justification for it. It can only be described as foolish.

The Galatians were deceived, as though under a spell, into embracing something infinitely inferior. They were rejecting the central significance of the crucifixion of Jesus Christ. The source of this deception, according to the Greek syntax, is singular. This could refer to a single, unnamed false teacher, but it more like refers to the father of lies, Satan himself, in contrast to the Spirit in verse 2. The devil is the master of deception, subtly perverting the truth ever so slightly, yet with eternal ramifications. Does it not appeal to the fallen human nature to think that laws are required in order to receive blessings from God? This plays into the prideful thought that possibly a person can become good enough in himself if he could only follow the right behavior. Yet Paul undercuts this by simply noting, with rhetorical question, that they received the Spirit of God, the ultimate blessing, simply through faith, and not by keeping any law. The truth continues today. No works of the law are required: neither baptism, nor church membership, nor the ten commandments; nothing is required to become right with God. We only need believe in Christ, crucified for our sins!

Lord, I do believe that Christ died for my sins because I could not be good enough in keeping the works of the law. Your grace is my hope!

Perfected Not By Flesh

Galatians 3:3-4

³ Are you so foolish? Having begun by the Spirit, are you now being perfected by the flesh? ⁴ Did you suffer so many things in vain—if indeed it was in vain?

Paul chastises the Galatians again, using a different word for "foolish." One lexicon defines the underlying word here as "pertaining to an unwillingness to use one's mental faculties in order to understand." There is a fundamental inconsistency in their behavior as compared to their salvation. God does not save a person by the working of His Spirit, and then expect that person to finish the work of sanctification through his own efforts.

The great anomaly of this is that there is an inner compulsion in the "old man," the flesh, to perform and to work. Paul is not talking about spiritual passivity, for he says in other places "work out your salvation with fear and trembling" (Phil. 2:12). We are to "walk by the Spirit" (Gal. 6:25), or as the NIV puts it, "keep in step with the Spirit." We must learn what God is accomplishing in us and cooperate with Him, for He will complete what He began in us (Phil. 1:6).

The perfecting of the Christian is accomplished by the work of the Spirit in us by faith. It is not something we merit or earn through our righteous deeds, whether it be circumcision, keeping the law of Moses, or our own rules and regulations. Many today have overlooked the teachings of grace and Spirit in the New Testament and have created "Christian laws," thereby forfeiting the freedom they have in Christ (see Colossians 2:20-23). This is not of the Spirit.

To be sure, the Spirit does not lead us into lawlessness. Outward fleshly desires lead us to sin that imprisons us in guilt and spiritual uselessness. Inward fleshly desires attempt to overcome the outward fleshly desires with rules and conformity. So both the inward and the outward fleshly desires work together to hinder the Spirit's work in our life. That's why it is so foolish to attempt perfection by the flesh—it simply won't work. The Spirit has a better way.

A further appeal is made to their experience of suffering, which was due to Jewish persecution for embracing faith as opposed to the Law of Moses. This harassment went back to Paul's first visits when the Jews stoned him and left him for dead (Acts 14:19). The Galatians were willing to suffer for their new-found faith. However, if it turns out that the Law of Moses was required, all that suffering would have been for nothing. We must resist all efforts at legalism; living by a set of Christian laws. Yes, we discipline ourselves for maximum spiritual effectiveness, but we dare not confuse this with sanctification, which is a work of the Spirit.

Lord, help me to continuously rest in Your finished work on the cross and not rely on my religious or moral efforts.

WEEKEND READING

Saturday – Matthew 9
Sunday – Matthew 10

_____
_____
_____
_____
_____
_____
_____
_____
_____
_____
_____
_____
_____
_____
_____
_____
_____
_____
_____
_____
_____
_____
_____
_____
_____

The Greatest Miracle

Galatians 3:5-6

---

⁵ So then, does He who provides you with the Spirit and works miracles among you, do it by the works of the Law, or by hearing with faith? ⁶ Even so Abraham BELIEVED GOD, AND IT WAS RECKONED TO HIM AS RIGHTEOUSNESS.

The Christian life is begun "by the Spirit" (vs. 4) because God has provided us "with the Spirit" (vs. 5). This is a miracle of the first rank, that the Spirit of the very God of the universe should become ours. The greatest miracle we can experience is spiritual regeneration, for that moves a soul from spiritual death to eternal life in the Spirit. This is nothing less than spectacular from God's perspective. He is not the least bit influenced by any person's ability to perform "works of the Law." In fact, all of us fall far short (Rom. 3:23). The only hope is in God doing the work that we couldn't do. That is miraculous!

Knowing that we are prone to believe what we can physically see, the Lord also provided outwardly tangible miracles to confirm the inner workings of the Spirit: "God [was] also testifying with them, both by signs and wonders and by various miracles and by gifts of the Holy Spirit according to His own will" (Heb. 2:4). Paul's gospel ministry, likewise, was confirmed in the same way, "The signs of a true apostle were performed among you with all perseverance, by signs and wonders and miracles" (2 Cor. 12:12). These "proofs" during the foundational time of the church and the early spread of the gospel gave assurance to the divine origin of the gospel message.

Whether or not God is still doing miracles today to the same extent and character as in the beginning, we can clearly see that the miraculous does not happen as a result of good moral or religious behavior. Even faith does not cause miracles, so that one person's faith in miracles is somehow better than another's lack of faith in miracles. Abraham had virtually no miraculous events to aid his faith. He simply, at the Lord's behest, observed the starry sky and believed His promise that the number of his descendants would rival the number of stars in the sky (Gen. 15:6; Rom. 4:3; James 2:23). God may or may not give miraculous signs to affirm His message—faith is not to be in miracles, but in God whose Spirit sovereignly and graciously works in supernatural ways. Abraham's faith came through hearing of the Word of God (Rom. 11:17).

The result was the patriarch being declared righteous in God's eyes. The same is true also for the Galatian believers and for us today. Righteousness does not come by human efforts, but through faith in God, particularly in what He has done in "Jesus Christ who [was] publically portrayed as crucified" (vs. 1).

Lord, thank You for miraculously saving me, moving me from death into life. Help me to live now by faith, not by works of the Law.

Related to Abe

Galatians 3:7-9

⁷ Therefore, be sure that it is those who are of faith who are sons of Abraham. ⁸ The Scripture, foreseeing that God would justify the Gentiles by faith, preached the gospel beforehand to Abraham, saying, "ALL THE NATIONS WILL BE BLESSED IN YOU." ⁹ So then those who are of faith are blessed with Abraham, the believer.

S alvation through faith is tied inextricably to God's dealings with Abraham, who lived 800 years before the time of Christ (3800 years before our time). God had made a promise to the patriarch in Genesis 12, which Paul here quotes in verse 8. God's dealing with Abraham precedes the giving of the law by hundreds of years and, therefore, takes priority.

Abraham is considered the Father of the Jewish people. He was the one called out by God from pagan worship, from Ur of the Chaldeans (Gen. 15:7) to the land of Canaan. God promised him three things: a land, a seed, and a blessing. He would possess a land; his descendants would become a great nation, and he would be both blessed and a blessing to all the nations of the world. The Jewish people have held on to these promises through the centuries. But in Christ, the blessing part of the promise is given its proper and intended fulfillment—and that is Paul's point here. John affirms this. God has blessed both the Jewish people and the Gentiles (non-Jews) by the coming of the Messiah, a descendant of Abraham. This blessing was extended to all the world, to "as many as received Him . . . to those who believed in His name" (John 1:12).

Gentile believers in Jesus Christ are described here in two ways: 1) sons of Abraham and 2) blessed with Abraham. In other words, God sees them as being related to Abraham in the most essential way, without any mention of the Law of Moses. It is all about faith, and so Paul explains the Abrahamic promise as, "God would justify the Gentiles by faith" (vs. 8). That is the core message of the gospel as it pertains to the non-Jews. It is no different than for the Jews: ". . . the righteous will live by his faith" (Hab. 2:4). Gentiles are made right in God's eyes, not by becoming Jews and keeping the law, but by believing like Abraham believed. The result is a relationship with Abraham that the Jews had claimed exclusively for themselves.

So this truth of a faith-based justification, that is, to be made right with God, was not a new invention of Paul's. We are believers together with Abraham, the archetype of faith. This continues to be Paul's "go-to-the-wall" issue, and we should stand with him in embracing and defending this truth at all costs.

Lord, thank You for making me right in Your eyes and putting me into good company, in the Abrahamic household of faith!

Escaping the Curse

Galatians 3:10

¹⁰ For as many as are of the works of the Law are under a curse; for it is written, "Cursed is everyone who does not abide by all things written in the book of the law, to perform them."

Acerbic would be an apt description of Paul's terse comment here, as he comes to the crux of his argument; he pulls no punches. There is a fundamental problem with human efforts at keeping the Law of Moses. The stakes are extreme (cursing if you fail), and the bar is set impossibly high (you must keep "all" of the law (Deut. 27:26)! James put it this way, "For whoever keeps the whole law and yet stumbles in one point, he has become guilty of all" (James 2:10). This is a problem for people who assert that a person must keep certain moral or legal standards in addition to faith in order to be saved and go to heaven. Paul wrote to the Romans, "All have sinned and come short of the glory of God" (Rom. 3:23).

Now the problem is not that the law is unreasonable, but that humans are sinners who cannot meet God's standards. The law reflects God's perfect holiness, and it demonstrates human sinfulness. It is like a tape measure, sizing us up to see if we meet up to God's standard. Since His standard is perfection, the law measures us as coming up short. How ironic to attempt to justify themselves by the very measuring tape that God uses to show them they fail. Their attempts are self-incriminating. One can imagine a soul standing before God insisting that the Eternal Judge and Law giver use the law to judge him. For all those who reject Christ, that is essentially what they are doing. One can imagine God saying, "If you insist . . . therefore you have failed and are cursed."

Today, various Christian denominations assert things necessary to be in right standing before God, including baptism, keeping the "ordinances," attending church, giving indulgences, avoiding "mortal" sins and various other "do's and don'ts." They think these things earn them good standing with God and entrance to heaven. I grieve to think what it will be like when they realize that the curse of God is what they have earned!

To say such things is not callous fear-mongering. Some resist teaching the "harsh" things of Scripture. However, this forms the basis for teaching the grace of God. Salvation is a free gift, given through the work of the Holy Spirit, based on the Lord Jesus Christ who was "publically portrayed as crucified" (Gal. 3:1). To warn someone of the danger of a works-based justification is to show them grace in preventing disaster in their lives.

Lord, I owed a debt I could not pay; I needed You to take my sins away (adapted from "He paid a debt"). Thank You.

Justified by Faith!

Galatians 3:11-12

[11] Now that no one is justified by the Law before God is evident; for, "THE RIGHTEOUS MAN SHALL LIVE BY FAITH." [12] However, the Law is not of faith; on the contrary, "HE WHO PRACTICES THEM SHALL LIVE BY THEM."

Nothing could be more clear in the writings of the apostle Paul than his teaching on how to become righteous before God. In this case, his point is that one cannot become righteous by practicing the Law of Moses. He grounds this in Old Testament teaching, in particular Habakkuk 2:4 (which is also quoted in Romans 1:17 and Hebrews 10:38). Equating "live" with "is justified," he reasons that, if a righteous man is to live by faith, justification cannot possibly come about by the works of the law. This is because keeping the law is not, on the surface of it, a matter of faith. Rather, the law is a matter of simply keeping it, all of it. The contrast is clearly being made; a person either lives by faith, or he lives by law. He is either justified by faith, or he is justified by law. Paul doesn't allow for a mixture of the two.

Paul will shortly show the relationship of faith to law; but suffice it to say at this juncture, the two options for justification are all there is, and they are diametrically opposite of each other. The term "no one" does not admit any exceptions. "There is no one who does good. The LORD has looked down from heaven upon the sons of men to see if there are any who understand, who seek after God. They have all turned aside, together they have become corrupt; There is no one who does good, not even one" (Ps. 14:1-3).

Some people feel that salvation comes through faith plus law. But the minute one adds law as a requirement for justification, then he must keep all of the law, he must live by it completely—or else be cursed (vs. 10). That is not something Paul invented that is contrary to God's standards of the Old Testament. Rather he is giving insight to the patent truth of the matter. The Law of Moses was an exacting task-master, and as a result, all have fallen short (Rom. 3:23)—there has to be a different way. That is Paul's point. We need to live by faith, because that is how salvation began, namely, by faith.

Living by law is like having a checklist, disassociated from a relationship with God. Living by faith is believing not in the Law, but in the One who gave the Law, trusting in His word. So we live, not to achieve greatness through adherence to strict ordinances, but we live to grow in our relationship with our Maker. We live life trusting Him, rather than our own fallen reason and the inclinations of our hearts.

Lord, help me move more and more away from a works-based lifestyle to a walk of faith in You and Your word. In them there is life!

A Curse For the Cursed

Galatians 3:13-14

---

13 Christ redeemed us from the curse of the Law, having become a curse for us—for it is written, "CURSED IS EVERYONE WHO HANGS ON A TREE"— 14 in order that in Christ Jesus the blessing of Abraham might come to the Gentiles, so that we would receive the promise of the Spirit through faith.

Redeeming from a curse with a curse—that is God's plan. In verse 10, we saw that being under the law and not keeping the law perfectly results in a person being under the curse of the law. A standard definition of a curse is "a directly expressed utterance which brings harm by its very expression to the one against whom it is directed." In this case, the curse is brought by God, and pity the person to whom this applies! The magnitude of this is great; that's why Paul, in chapter 1, doubly stresses that anyone who preaches that the law needs to be added to faith in order to be justified is "anathema" (which is sometimes translated "accursed"). That message leaves a person to remain under the curse of the law—so the good news is really just the same old news, with no hope for being justified before God.

The surprise of eternity, which even the angels had previously longed to see (1 Peter 1:12), was how God would be able to justify sinners, those under the curse. Now Paul makes it absolutely clear; God did it by having the Lord Jesus Christ stand in our place, on our behalf, becoming a curse for us. How that happened came through His death on the cross. Paul here refers to Deuteronomy 21:23 where the word "tree" is used for the cross. In Old Testament culture, when a person sinned and was executed, and his body fastened to a tree for public display, he was cursed by God. But, Christ released us from that curse by becoming a curse for us. Elsewhere we read, "He made Him who knew no sin to be sin on our behalf, so that we might become the righteousness of God in Him" (2 Cor. 5:21).

The purpose of all this was so that non-Jews could share in the blessing promised to Abraham long ago, which came by faith. The law stood in the way of that blessing. Not the law per se, but man's failure to live by the law, the perfect standard of God's holiness. And Gentiles and Jews are put on common ground in terms of the righteousness of God. It comes through faith—that is the promise of the Holy Spirit.

What better news can there be, but that through Christ's death on the cross, we have been set free from the curse of the law! We cannot keep to God's righteous standards, but through faith the Spirit has fulfilled the promise of justification and blessing to Abraham in us. What a magnificent plan for our salvation!

Lord, thank You for releasing me from the curse and giving me the blessing of righteousness before You and forgiveness for my sin.

WEEKEND READING

Saturday – Matthew 11
Sunday – Matthew 12

PERSONAL REFLECTIONS

_____

_____

_____

_____

_____

_____

_____

_____

_____

_____

_____

_____

_____

_____

_____

_____

_____

_____

_____

_____

_____

_____

_____

_____

_____

_____

_____

_____

A "Singular" Promise

Galatians 3:15-16

15 Brethren, I speak in terms of human relations: even though it is only a man's covenant, yet when it has been ratified, no one sets it aside or adds conditions to it. 16 Now the promises were spoken to Abraham and to his seed. He does not say, "And to seeds," as referring to many, but rather to one, "And to your seed," that is, Christ.

Paul has just finished writing that the blessing of Abraham would come to all, including Gentiles, who receive the promised Spirit by faith (vs. 14). That blessing refers to having a right standing before God—in other words, justification; and that justification comes to us apart from the Law of Moses.

Paul now continues to build his epic defense of the gospel of grace. God had made a binding agreement with Abraham that the whole world would be blessed through him (Gen. 12:1-3; 22:18). That agreement still stands. Using a human analogy, he points out that a legal contract is binding once it is signed (ratified); it cannot be changed. In the same way, the agreement between God and Abraham is no less binding.

Paul uses the word "promises" to refer to the covenant with Abraham, for it was in reality a unilateral agreement. There were three aspects to the covenant: the promise of a land, descendants (i.e. seed) and a blessing. Blessing to the world would come through God's blessing of Abraham's descendants in the land God would and did give them. The Lord made this commitment prior to Abraham's believing, not as a result of his belief (Gen. 12). What Abraham's faith produced was not the promise of blessing, but his own personal righteousness. That was how he himself entered into the blessing, "Then he believed in the LORD; and He reckoned it to him as righteousness" (Gen. 15:6). The blessing comes to all who believe with the same kind of faith as Abraham.

The promise, therefore, was not to Abraham only, but to his "seed." In the original Hebrew, the word *sera* translated seed is used in reference to Abraham's descendants, in the sense that Abraham impregnated his wife, who bore the fruit of children—and all their descendants are called "seed." The word when used in the sense of descendants never occurs in the plural, but always in the singular (like in English, the singular seed can be used in a collective sense). So the word can refer to a single seed (or descendant) or to multiple seeds (or descendants). Although we ourselves would never have caught this in the OT reading, Paul, under the inspiration of the Holy Spirit, points out this profoundly significant nuance to emphasize that God had one particular seed in mind, namely Christ.

Lord, thank You that though humans may break their contracts and covenants, You do not. Your Son proved to be the ultimate "Promise Keeper."

A Promise Is a Promise

Galatians 3:17-18

[17] What I am saying is this: the Law, which came four hundred and thirty years later, does not invalidate a covenant previously ratified by God, so as to nullify the promise. [18] For if the inheritance is based on law, it is no longer based on a promise; but God has granted it to Abraham by means of a promise.

The relationship between the Law and faith has vexed Christianity from the earliest times, as evidenced by this crucial letter of Paul's to the Galatians. Down through history to our present day, this problem continues. Many so-called Christian denominations have added all sorts of requirements to attaining salvation beyond simple faith in Christ. Baptism, church laws, even the 10 commandments (or at least avoiding the more egregarious violations of such) are all necessary for gaining a favorable judgment in the afterlife. Against all these, Paul speaks out pointedly by addressing the core issue. In our passage today, he lays out clearly the relationship between the promise of God (on which faith is built) and Law (the central structure of Jewish life and practice).

Paul's reasoning is based on chronology and then on the nature of a promise. The covenant with Abraham preceded the Law by 430 years. The Judaizers (who asserted that Gentiles must keep the Law in order to be accepted by God) would have no doubt recognized this, but would have taught that the Law superseded or refined what happened with Abraham, so that the Law took precedent. So, in their thinking, although Gentiles may have initially been saved by faith, now they must keep the Law.

While the actual number of years (430) presents some challenge in matching up with the Genesis-Exodus record, the point is served. And, the promise to Abraham was certainly not fulfilled in his own life time, nor in the lifetime of Isaac, Jacob or his 12 sons. In fact, by the time of the giving of the Law (Exodus 20ff), the people were still not in the land (one of the three parts to the Abrahamic covenant). Further, the promise to Abraham was to him and his seed (singular), which refers to Messiah, Who came after the law (in the person of Jesus). Therefore, the Law couldn't possibly invalidate the promise which came prior and continues on after. To say otherwise, that the inheritance of the Abrahamic promise comes by keeping the Law, would be to invalidate the promise of God. It would, therefore, be inferred that God would be a promise-breaker, a liar—which is impossible. So the Judaizers requiring keeping the law is patently contrary to the promise to Abraham. This, of course, leaves the question, "Why then was the Law given?" That is what Paul draws us to next.

Lord, You promised salvation to all who believe, so I trust that You will keep Your word to Abraham and to me.

The Unilateral Priority

Galatians 3:19-20

19 Why the Law then? It was added because of transgressions, having been ordained through angels by the agency of a mediator, until the seed would come to whom the promise had been made. 20 Now a mediator is not for one party only; whereas God is only one.

Up until this point, Paul has made the point that the Law "did not annul or add conditions to the promise God made to Abraham" (see William MacDonald's, "Believer's Bible Commentary"). So, using one of his favorite techniques for advancing his argument, Paul asks a question his readers will most naturally have in mind at this juncture: "Why then did God give the Law?"

The answer is "because of transgressions." Notice, it doesn't say, "because of sin." Sin existed before the law was given, but, "through the Law comes the knowledge of sin." (Rom. 3:20b). Consciousness of sin was heightened by the Law. In fact, Paul says, ". . . where there is no law, there also is no violation" (Rom. 4:15). Put simply, the Law turns sin into transgression and accentuates it (Rom. 5:20).

So, the Law did not annul the blessing. But, it is also true that the blessing did not annul sin. God knew that, in setting Abraham and his descendants apart as His special people, there was a danger of their minimizing the significance of rebelling against God. Since the days of the Garden of Eden, humans have rebelled against their Creator, and God's plan of eternity has been to bring His image-bearers back to Himself. The promise to Abraham gave the great hope that has kept them from spiraling into nihilism and despair. The Law of Moses kept them from the myth that "I'm OK, You're OK." The promise leads us to look upward, and then to look inward. The first shows us our salvation, the second our need.

The law, therefore, cannot be added to the promise to effect salvation or even to enhance or preserve it. It was, in fact, a temporary measure, useful until Christ (the "seed") came. Whereas the promise was made directly to Abraham, the Law was given to Moses through angels (see Hebrews 2:2). The Law was a bi-lateral agreement, involving responsibilities by two parties (God and the Israelites). The promise was unilateral, involving only one party with responsibility, namely God. Abraham and his descendants are beneficiaries of this agreement, but they had no responsibilities. There was no mediator in the promise to Abraham, since God is the single party involved (see Hebrews 6:13-18). What a magnificent plan for showing our need and giving us hope!

Lord, thank You for the promise You made to Abraham, of which I am a beneficiary today. Help me not fall into the inferior life of living by the law.

Shut Up For a Promise

Galatians 3:21-22

²¹ Is the Law then contrary to the promises of God? May it never be! For if a law had been given which was able to impart life, then righteousness would indeed have been based on law. ²² But the Scripture has shut up everyone under sin, so that the promise by faith in Jesus Christ might be given to those who believe.

We have seen now that the Law of Moses had a different purpose than the promise to Abraham. The Law's purpose was to expose sin, the rebelliousness of the human heart. The promise to Abraham, the unilateral covenant, was designed to give hope of the ultimate solution to the sin problem— namely, God would finally bring His blessing to the world, and that through the promised "seed."

So, the question naturally arises whether the Law and the promise were opposing principles, contrary to each other. Paul answers his own setup question in typical fashion, "May it never be!" (Gal. 2:17; Rom. 6:1, 15; 7:7, 13). Or as another translation puts it, "Absolutely no!" Though the question may logically follow, the answer is unequivocal. Both the promise and the Law came from God, and they serve complementary purposes. The Law was never intended to give life. If it could do that, then, Paul reasons, righteousness would be based upon the law. The problem, then, would be absolute hopelessness, for the Law proves (that is, demonstrates beyond all shadow of doubt) that everyone is a sinner and, therefore, unrighteous. As Paul says in another place, "All have sinned and fall short of the glory of God" (Rom. 3:23). One cannot use that which by design exposes sin to make one righteous. That is patently absurd. The law is like a pair of glasses which, when one puts them on, shows him how much dirt is on his hands. The glasses cannot be used to clean his hands, that is not their purpose. Likewise, the law was given to show us how unrighteous we are; it cannot be used to make us righteous!

What then is the hope for people who are hopelessly unrighteous? This is where the promise comes in. The promise of blessing to Abraham and to "his seed" is obtained, not by keeping the law, but by faith in Jesus Christ. It is obtained by faith, and it is found in the fulfillment of the Abrahamic promise in the Lord Himself.

How misled people are who strenuously strive for righteousness by their good deeds and religious acts. At best, those efforts are useless. How blessed are those who have discovered a righteousness found only in Jesus Christ.

Lord, help me not become entrapped by the law again, the vanity of thinking I can add to my righteousness with good deeds and religious works.

The Law Did Well

Galatians 3:23-24

²³ But before faith came, we were kept in custody under the law, being shut up to the faith which was later to be revealed. ²⁴ Therefore the Law has become our tutor to lead us to Christ, so that we may be justified by faith.

Our passage today explains that the Law served a very useful purpose, namely to provide a guideline for right living between the time when the promise was made to Abraham and when it was fulfilled in Jesus Christ. An analogy pictures life for the people of God before Jesus Christ came as like a child (Greek *paidos*) in custody of a tutor (Greek *paidagogos*). In Greek culture, a 'paidagogos' functioned as a personal life-trainer for a child and had authority over the child until it became an adult.

So, how was the Law a 'paidagogos' for the people of God? It taught them the holiness of God, a reflection of the standard that would make a person acceptable to God. It demonstrated to the Jews (and to all people) that we all fall hopelessly short of being like God. Ever since the Garden of Eden, humankind has endeavored to be like God (Gen. 3:5). The irony is that since we are created in God's image, we are already like Him by virtue of our creation. So, the effort to become like Him is futile and can only be seen as a rejection of God's pattern already in us, and therefore, a rebellion against our Creator. Adam and Eve's taking of the fruit was tantamount to settling for a godlikeness of human making, rather than of divine origin.

The Law inherently teaches that godliness must come from some other means than by keeping the Law. Because that proves disastrous, it is a constant reminder of our failure. The godliness God desires is a righteousness that is given to us—His righteousness. And that is available to all who believe, not just to those under the Law. The advantage of the Jews is that they had the tutor (that is, the Law) while the Gentiles did not. Now that faith has come through Jesus Christ, like a child reaching adulthood, why would one go back to the Law, like an adult going back to a 'paidagogos'? Furthermore, why demand other adults take on the 'paidagogos.' Why then should Gentile Christians who have already come to faith in Christ take on the tutor of the Law? That would be absurd.

Praise God, the Law did what it was supposed to do—it led people to the need for a new kind of righteousness, one that comes through faith in Christ. This is true in particular for the Jewish people, but also for all people who have had a sense of religious and moral law.

*Lord, thank You for teaching me through the Law that I needed a Savior.
There is no doubt that I needed a righteousness that is not my own.*

WEEKEND READING

Saturday – Matthew 13:1-35
Sunday – Matthew 13:36-58

_____
_____
_____
_____
_____
_____
_____
_____
_____
_____
_____
_____
_____
_____
_____
_____
_____
_____
_____
_____
_____
_____
_____
_____
_____
_____
_____
_____
_____
_____

We Are Sons of God

Galatians 3:25-27

25 But now that faith has come, we are no longer under a tutor. 26 For you are all sons of God through faith in Christ Jesus. 27 For all of you who were baptized into Christ have clothed yourselves with Christ.

Continuing the analogy, like a child coming to adulthood no longer needs to submit to the authority of his tutor, so also when a person comes to faith in Christ, he no longer needs to submit to the Law of Moses. It has completed its task and is no longer needed; it has no more authority over a person of faith.

Paul is speaking now specifically to the Galatian believers and affirms their new identity in Christ. Being Gentiles, the question of their relationship to God is settled: it doesn't require becoming Jewish, and it does not require keeping the Law. They are sons of God, part of the family of His people. In other places, he writes of being adopted, "For you have not received a spirit of slavery leading to fear again, but you have received a spirit of adoption as sons by which we cry out, 'Abba! Father!'" (Rom. 8:15). Sons in Greek and Roman culture had full rights and status as family members, they were no longer treated as children.

The sonship of believers is a big topic in the Christian life. "For both He who sanctifies and those who are sanctified are all from one Father; for which reason He [Jesus] is not ashamed to call them brethren." (Heb. 2:11). Because we are sons, we can refer to God the Father as Jesus did. "And He [Jesus] was saying, 'Abba! Father! All things are possible for You' . . ." (Mark 14:36). "For you have not received a spirit of slavery leading to fear again, but you have received a spirit of adoption as sons by which we cry out, 'Abba! Father!'" (Rom. 8:15). We have the same familial prerogative of approaching the Father as did our brother, Jesus. What a privilege!

Our baptism signifies the new relationship we have. Of course Paul is not writing about water baptism, but just as he wrote to the Romans, this is a spiritual baptism, a placing ourselves into Christ (see Romans 6:3-4). Here baptism is likened to having "clothed yourselves with Christ." Because we are in Him, we have the same access to God. We are now sons because He is the Son. The question is, do we really believe it and act like it is true? Going back to the law and requiring it for being right with God is not acting like sons.

So many Christians today act like children who still need the law; they live by their lists of regulations and requirements. But Christ has set us free by making us sons of God. Let us walk as sons. Christian, remember who you are!

Lord, thank You for giving me a new identity. Your one and only begotten Son is not ashamed of me! So I know I am fully accepted by You, because I am in Him.

Equal Standing

Galatians 3:28

²⁸ There is neither Jew nor Greek, there is neither slave nor free man, there is neither male nor female; for you are all one in Christ Jesus.

Hard to believe as it may be, our passage today is controversial among Christians. The issue has to do with whether the Gospel of Jesus Christ has removed all distinctions between men and women. Evangelical Christianity today is split on this very issue, particularly on whether leadership in the church should be restricted to men only or extended to women as well. In addition, the roles in marriage are disputed, whether the man is "the head" of his wife, or whether husband-wife roles are equal and interchangeable.

We believe that this verse does not eliminate all distinctions, for there are clearly anatomical differences that remain. While this observation is obvious, it forces us to admit that this verse is not absolute. Once doing that, we must look for a principle that will control what applications might be made or not made. For this, we turn to one of the most basic rules of interpretation, namely, to consider the context of a verse.

In this case, the context has to do with an equal standing before God, and there is no mention of role relationships in the church or marriage. All along Paul has been addressing the question of whether Gentiles need to become Jewish in order to have a right and acceptable standing before God. His answer has been a resounding, "No!" (see Galatians 3:21). The lead off doublet in this verse indicates that he is still addressing the same issue.

In the second and third doublets, Paul expands the truth to include two other spiritual prejudices that were widely held in the ancient world. We have seen that a Gentile doesn't need to become Jewish to be saved. So also, a slave doesn't need to become free in order to be saved. And a women has an equal standing before God as does a man. All are considered "sons." Now, through faith in Jesus Christ, all have equal access to God, being part of His family, regardless of gender. This was revolutionary thinking in ancient times.

There are social implications to this verse, to be sure. Believing slave owners are to treat their slaves as brothers (see book of Philemon). Husbands are to treat their wives as "fellow heirs of the grace of life" (1 Peter 3:8) and to "love your wives, just as Christ also loved the church . . ." (Eph. 5:25). In the transformation, God still preserved certain role distinctions, for example, "The husband is the head of the wife . . ." (Eph. 5:23). The burden of church leadership rests on male elders, rooted in the created order (1 Tim. 2:13-15; 3:2; Titus 1:6).

Lord, thank You for making us equal in salvation and righteousness; You accept all based on faith in Christ, regardless of ethnic, economic or gender issues.

Our Legacy

²⁹ And if you belong to Christ, then you are Abraham's descendants, heirs according to promise.

One of the greatest truths in Scripture is that, as a believer, you belong to Christ. You are more than an object that He owns; you belong to Him as a "son" (Gal. 3:26). Ethnicity doesn't matter, nor does gender or economic situation. When people come to God by faith in Jesus Christ, they are placed on an equal footing. As God said elsewhere, "Let every valley be lifted up, And every mountain and hill be made low; And let the rough ground become a plain, And the rugged terrain a broad valley" (Isa. 40:4). He is the great Leveler.

What is our response to this? "The brother of humble circumstances is to glory in his high position; and the rich man is to glory in his humiliation, because like flowering grass he will pass away" (James 1:9-10). We all join the ranks of Abraham's descendants, humbling in the eyes of the world but exalting in view of God's promise.

Consider for a moment the import of this thought. Nearly 3,800 years ago, God called Abraham out of a pagan culture and revealed Himself as the one true God, re-establishing monotheism in a world that had strayed from the truth. He made the epic promise to Abraham to, among other things, bless him and also to bless the world through him. Everything following that has been and continues to be a working out of that promise. Salvation through Jesus Christ is a direct result of God's commitment to Abraham.

Abraham's descendants through Isaac and Jacob are the Jewish people, and they occupy a privileged standing before God. Though they have been oppressed through the years, God sees them as special. They are His chosen people; they belong to Him. Others, in order to know and to be rightly related to God, needed to either covert to Judaism (that is, become a proselyte) or at least be favorable to the God of Israel (sometimes called a "God-fearer").

But now through faith in Christ, we have equal standing before Him. And in the context of the book of Galatians, Gentile believers now "belong" to God, in the same way that Jews belong to God; believing Gentiles do not need to become Jews.

One tangible result, and a big one, is that Gentiles (in fact, all Christians), share in the inheritance that once belonged only to the Jews. But now, since the promise applies to Gentiles as well as Jews, the inheritance is shared by all who believe in the Lord Jesus Christ.

Lord, though once I was an outsider to the blessings that belonged only to Your people, now I have great things to look forward to, because I am now Yours.

No Longer Slaves

Galatians 4:1-3

[1] Now I say, as long as the heir is a child, he does not differ at all from a slave although he is owner of everything, [2] but he is under guardians and managers until the date set by the father. [3] So also we, while we were children, were held in bondage under the elemental things of the world.

Continuing the analogy from chapter 2, Paul makes clear application. People who live by the Law are like infants (literally) and not like mature adults. What is pictured here is a child who is the heir of his father's wealth. In Roman times, a child under a certain age (which varies from culture to culture) may own an inheritance, but he has no control of it, or over himself for that matter. He is under the management of a legal guardian or teacher. This was an individual set in place by the father to look after the child's life and growth into adulthood. In many regards, the child was treated like a slave in that he had no rights of his own. Once he reached the age of "majority" and was no longer a minor, he was free to possess and manage his inheritance without the need for a personal manager. He was no longer a child to be treated like a slave.

So, Paul likens this to a person's pre-Christ days. Before faith, he was like a child who was still under guardianship. He had in himself the potential for being all the Lord designed him to be, as he was made in the image of God. But, attempts to live by the Law (for the Jews) or the "basic elemental things of the world," kept him under that guardianship. The potential was there for a right relationship with God but was not experienced before faith in Christ.

We must not overlook the subtle point that the transition point from childhood to adulthood was set by the father. In the family situation, that came at a specific age. By analogy, God the Father set the transition point from spiritual childhood to maturity; that point is when the person comes to faith in Christ. He leaves behind his guardian and manager, the Law. Furthermore, he leaves behind all attempts based on human effort. He is now free to live the life He was created to live, without fear of judgment by the law.

In another place, Paul chastises believers for living like they are still children under law, "If you have died with Christ to the elementary principles of the world, why, as if you were living in the world, do you submit yourself to decrees, such as, 'Do not handle, do not taste, do not touch!' (which all refer to things destined to perish with use)—in accordance with the commandments and teachings of men?" (Col. 2:20-22). Praise God we have been set free from such things.

Lord, I praise You that I am no longer under the guardianship of the Law. The inheritance of blessing is now mine, and I can truly walk in freedom.

Pregnant Times

⁴ But when the fullness of the time came, God sent forth His Son, born of a woman, born under the Law, ⁵ so that He might redeem those who were under the Law, that we might receive the adoption as sons.

The pivotal in the space-time continuum of creation was encapsulated in the life and death of Jesus Christ. All history had been building to the entry of the Son of God into His world. It was truly the fullness of time. The world was unified under Roman imperialism; there was a common language (Greek), an extensive road system (Roman), a heightened sense of the supernatural, a yearning for a Messianic deliverer in Israel—all made the times pregnant for the delivery of the Lord's entry as the God-man redeemer. It was a Creator-creation warp, where divinity and humanity intersected, the supernatural collided with the natural. Eternity and time merged. Grace delivered the final blow to law. Death gave way to life; rebellion turned into restoration, judgment to forgiveness. The fullness of times had indeed come, a time to bring fullness in the most spiritually full sense, as it were, from fullness to fullness!

God sent His Son, from His place at the Father's side, setting aside the glory about which He prayed before the cross, "Now, Father, glorify Me together with Yourself, with the glory which I had with You before the world was" (John 17:5). He left glory for the life of a peasant in Israel and to live under the Law He had given His people to order their lives by. That was the same Law that resulted in the condemnation of all, because "all have sinned and come short of the glory of God" (Rom. 3:23). He, the holy One, came to live under the Law that showed all humans to be sinners. Yet, as Hebrews points out, "[He] has been tempted in all things as we are, yet without sin" (Heb. 4:15). He lived fully under the Law, yet He never sinned. The time was ripe for a God-man to live like that, because history showed no mere man was able to.

As a result, praise God, there is redemption for people under law, and that would come by adoption as sons. Continuing to live under the Law would be like remaining as infants, with the Law as our manager. But as adopted sons, we no longer need the law-manager but have a vital relationship with the Law-giver, God Himself. We are now redeemed, and no longer in need of redemption—it is the blessing of Abraham that is already ours through faith. We no longer need to strive for a righteousness good enough to be saved; we already have a new kind of righteousness—not by law, but one that comes from the righteousness of Christ.

Lord, in the fullness of my times, You sent Your son, the Lord Jesus Christ into my world, into my life and redeemed me. Hallelujah, what a Savior!

WEEKEND READING

Saturday – Matthew 14
Sunday – Matthew 15

_____
_____
_____
_____
_____
_____
_____
_____
_____
_____
_____
_____
_____
_____
_____
_____
_____
_____
_____
_____
_____
_____
_____
_____
_____
_____
_____
_____
_____

Son and Heir!

Galatians 4:6-7

⁶ Because you are sons, God has sent forth the Spirit of His Son into our hearts, crying, "Abba! Father!" ⁷ Therefore you are no longer a slave, but a son; and if a son, then an heir through God.

To be sons of God, what a thrill! We Christians, though, are so used to this terminology that we often take it for granted. The implications are enormous, to have such an intimate relationship with the Creator and Sovereign of the universe. The One who spoke the cosmos into existence with a mere word. The One of whom Isaiah asked, "Who has measured the waters in the hollow of His hand, and marked off the heavens by the span, and calculated the dust of the earth by the measure, and weighed the mountains in a balance and the hills in a pair of scales?" (Isa. 40:12). The "King of kings and Lord of lords" (1 Tim. 6:15; Rev. 19:16). We are HIS sons!

Ancient monarchs often had scores of children by multiple wives; most of whom had little relationship their father. If at all, it was usually a business or legal arrangement, rather than a father-child relationship. But, our relationship with our Heavenly Father is instinctively personal. The new relationship with God through faith results in the Spirit motivating our inner spirits to react to God in familial terms, "Abba! Father!" The term, "Abba," is well known to be the affectionate call of a child to his tender father. It was reserved for those with a special relationship. This is the same manner of speaking to God as Jesus used of His Heavenly Father (see Mark 14:36; Romans 8:15). Today's equivalent might be "Papa."

Paul's logical sequence then goes like this: Because of faith in Christ, 1) we are not slaves, 2) we are "sons" and, therefore, 3) since we are sons, we are heirs. What this means is that everything that belongs to God is rightfully ours, by virtue of our family relationship to God. Elsewhere, Paul writes, "and if children, heirs also, heirs of God and fellow heirs with Christ . . ." (Rom. 8:17). This Christ is the Son of God, "whom He appointed heir of all things, through whom also He made the world." (Heb. 1:2). This is just another way of saying that the blessing promised to Abraham is now ours through faith!

Finally, when Paul says we are heirs, this is not because of any effort or good works on our part. It comes "through God." It is not through being a physical descendant of Abraham or from attempts to keep the Law. Nor is it from practicing circumcision, or for just males or free men (see Galatians 3:28). All who believe are heirs of the great promise of blessing made to Abraham.

*Lord, thank You for giving me the great hope of my inheritance.
I am so blessed by what You have done in redeeming me.*

Why Go Back?

Galatians 4:8-10

⁸ However at that time, when you did not know God, you were slaves to those which by nature are no gods. ⁹ But now that you have come to know God, or rather to be known by God, how is it that you turn back again to the weak and worthless elemental things, to which you desire to be enslaved all over again? ¹⁰ You observe days and months and seasons and years.

W hy would a believer who has an intimate relationship with the one true God revert to a system of belief that enslaves him to religious rules? Laws don't bring the knowledge of God, but rather fear of judgment. For the unregenerate person, that is a strong motivator toward behavior modification. But, it cannot bring about justification before God, because no one can keep the law perfectly. We all fail (see Romans 3:23).

True enough, some of the Galatians thought they were serving God by holding to religious laws. The multiplicity of all law-based religions believe they are serving deities, but in reality, they are serving that which, "by nature are no gods." Even some forms of so-called Christendom fall prey to teachings that mix Christ and the Law! Many denominations and churches preach a form of legalistic requirement to be acceptable to God. This is why Paul so adamantly condemns anyone as being "accursed" who preaches a different gospel (1:8-9). Such religions are completely false. Though such mixing of Christ and law is historically part of church heritage through the centuries, such teaching is antithetical to true faith in Christ as Paul taught.

Yes, the Law of Moses was good, and it was the true religion—that is, before Jesus Christ. Now that He has come, the purpose of the Law has been fulfilled; it is no longer needed. It pointed to God's mercy and grace in Christ. To use the Law as a way to merit God's blessing now becomes a curse! Even using is as a way to enhance our acceptability to God is false. The specifics for the Galatians had to do with keeping to holy days and times. These things are not wrong in themselves, but when treated as mandatory for maintaining a right relationship with God, it amounts to serving a false god.

The difference is that through faith in Christ, a believer has come into a relationship with God; here described as knowing Him and being known by Him. In previous verses, we are proclaimed to be "sons of God" and can now call Him, "Abba." The Law could never bring about that kind of relationship. Why go back from living as sons and knowing God to enslaving ourselves to "worthless elemental things" and forfeiting an intimate relationship with God?

Lord, help me always keep the grace of my Lord Jesus Christ in the forefront of my thoughts, so that I don't fall prey to legalistic living.

Don't Let It Be Vain

Galatians 4:11-12a

¹¹ I fear for you, that perhaps I have labored over you in vain. ¹²ᵃ I beg of you, brethren, become as I am, for I also have become as you are ...

What would Paul have written to Christians today, if he was so terse with the Galatians? Would he not, as William MacDonald suggests, "condemn the traditions brought into Christianity from Judaism—a humanly ordained priesthood, distinctive vestments for the priest, Sabbath-keeping, holy places, candles, holy water, and so forth?"

Yet, Paul turns personal in his burden for the Galatians. His was not a fondness for sterile, academic truth, but for the Galatians (and us) to live truly in God's way and in His truth. His penchant for defending right doctrine emanates from a genuine concern for their souls. His labor was for people; truth was the means, the good news that rescues people from the hopelessness of religious efforts. Paul worked hard and sacrificed greatly to bring the message and to persuade people of the truth of Jesus Christ. However, he had no control over whether they would believe. Precisely at this point, he was anxious.

Earlier in this letter, he had expressed similar reservations, that his efforts at maintaining the unity of the gospel might have been in vain (2:2). He realized he simply could not control other people's reaction to his ministry. This anxiety, or worry, prompted him to write to the believers in Galatia. But, it also prompted him to pray, for he later wrote to another group of believers that the best antidote to anxiety is prayer (Eph. 4:6-7).

Paul, when he first preached the gospel to the Corinthians, feared his message would be rejected, "I was with you in weakness and in fear and in much trembling" (1 Cor. 2:3). While this could refer to fear of the physical beatings, his greater fear was that people might reject the message—he understood the enormity of such a response. In a similar vein, he wrote to the Thessalonians, "For this reason, when I could endure it no longer, I also sent to find out about your faith, for fear that the tempter might have tempted you, and our labor would be in vain" (1 Thess. 3:5).

He appeals to them to "become as I am," that is, to live free from the law as sons of God. He himself was a Jew who became like them; he lived like a Gentile apart from the law. They as Gentiles should not, therefore, become like Jews and live under the law, but become like Jews who are now free to live like Gentiles, apart from the law! The Gospel makes a difference in how we live our daily lives. We should let no one rob us of our freedom under the guise of "obedience."

Lord, help me live in freedom as Your child and not by religious regulations.

Despite Weakness

Galatians 4:12b-14

[12b] You have done me no wrong; [13] but you know that it was because of a bodily illness that I preached the gospel to you the first time; [14] and that which was a trial to you in my bodily condition you did not despise or loathe, but you received me as an angel of God, as Christ Jesus Himself.

P hysical illness in the ancient world was often associated with a person falling out of favor with a deity, or seen as a personal weakness resulting in a social judgment of sorts. So, it is noteworthy, as Paul points out, that the Galatians had not dismissed him because of his physical difficulties. They accepted him based solely on his message. They received him as an angel. In fact, they received him as the Lord Himself!

Paul's ministry among the Galatians was not one of personal strength as might be expected of someone who was seemingly starting a new religious movement. His effectiveness was due solely to the work of God in his ministry. As he later wrote to the Corinthians, "But we have this treasure in earthen vessels, so that the surpassing greatness of the power will be of God and not from ourselves . . ." (2 Cor. 4:7).

Apostleship was not easy, but it was part of the assignment he received from the Lord at his conversion: "But the Lord said to [Ananias], 'Go, for he is a chosen instrument of Mine, to bear My name before the Gentiles and kings and the sons of Israel; for I will show him how much he must suffer for My name's sake.'" (Acts 9:15-16). He affirmed another group of Christians: ". . . so that no one would be disturbed by these afflictions; for you yourselves know that we have been destined for this" (1 Thess. 3:3).

And when he was first evangelizing among the Galatians, he suffered greatly: "But Jews . . . having won over the crowds, they stoned Paul and dragged him out of the city, supposing him to be dead. But while the disciples stood around him, he got up and entered the city" (Acts 14:19-20, see also 2 Tim. 3:11). So, when Paul refers to illness this could have been brought on by his physical beatings while among the Galatians. The word translated "illness" can also be translated "weakness." (For other descriptions of Paul's sufferings, see 2 Corinthians 6:4-5; 11:23-27).

What's Paul's point here? He is calling the Galatians back to the circumstances of their salvation and their initial response to him—and to the original message (Gal. 3:1-5). They overlooked the superficialities, believing the word Paul spoke to them. So, also, they must listen to him now!

Lord, help me not to stray from the simple message of the gospel that was so clear when I first believed.

The Unchanging Message

Galatians 4:15-16

15 Where then is that sense of blessing you had? For I bear you witness that, if possible, you would have plucked out your eyes and given them to me. 16 So have I become your enemy by telling you the truth?

Poignant questions, the two in our passage for today. Paul had a proclivity to penetrating, challenging interrogations. He recalls to them the "sense of blessing" they had experienced when he was with them for the first time—the joy of salvation, their first love (see Rev. 2:4). Their overwhelmingly positive experience at Paul's ministry among them was such that they would gladly have sacrificed their own eyesight for his.

What's that all about? One suggestion is that Paul may have had noticeably weak eyesight. We do know that he had some sort of limitation, a thorn in the flesh (2 Cor. 12:7). Although he never reveals what exactly that was, it may very well have been damaged eyes from his many beatings. After all, he had been whipped five times, beaten too often to count, and stoned frequently (2 Cor. 11:23-24). One time, he was beaten so severely they left him for dead. (Acts 14:19). Surely, he must have had lingering physical effects.

Whether or not poor eyesight was the cause for their sacrificial attitude toward him, Paul was calling them back to their first joy in the message of salvation and their love for him. He was the source of their blessing, that is, he was the beloved messenger that brought the good news of the fulfillment of God's promise to bless the whole world through Abraham's descendant. The promise came before and apart from the Law of Moses. There was salvation for the Gentiles with the supreme Creator God of the universe. And, they didn't have to become Jews in order to receive the blessing of salvation!

Despite their initial experience, the Galatians had come to think of him as their enemy. How could this have happened? Evidently, someone had "bewitched you" (Gal. 3:1). Who were these people? On the face of it, Peter (whom Paul calls Cephas) influenced them by his example. Paul had charged him, "If you, being a Jew, live like the Gentiles and not like the Jews, how is it that you compel the Gentiles to live like Jews?" (Gal. 2:14). Actions speak as loud as words! Yet, Peter himself was influenced (bewitched?) by "certain men from James . . . the party of the circumcision" (Gal. 2:12). Paul had not changed, the message had not changed. But, the circumcision party was trying to change the gospel, and the Galatians believed that lie. Their enemy was not Paul, but those who taught a different gospel.

Lord, I am still holding on to the message of salvation that brought me forgiveness, restoration and eternal life—by grace alone, through faith alone.

WEEKEND READING

Saturday – Matthew 16
Sunday – Matthew 17

_____

_____

_____

_____

_____

_____

_____

_____

_____

_____

_____

_____

_____

_____

_____

_____

_____

_____

_____

_____

_____

_____

_____

_____

_____

_____

_____

_____

Standing Firm, Alone

Galatians 4:17-18

[17] They eagerly seek you, not commendably, but they wish to shut you out so that you will seek them. [18] But it is good always to be eagerly sought in a commendable manner, and not only when I am present with you.

Shady, smooth-talking politicians today promise sweeping changes for the good of the people, but often are interested only in gaining power for their own sakes. Not all are like that, but for many, the people really mean nothing to them. The same might be said of some religious leaders. In the Galatians' situations, certain men were seeking to gain a following among the new believers, but with insincere motives. Yes, they eagerly sought the Galatians, as did Paul. However, the Judaizers really cared nothing for the Galatians.

This reminds us of Jesus' blistering condemnation, "Woe to you, scribes and Pharisees, hypocrites, because you travel around on sea and land to make one proselyte; and when he becomes one, you make him twice as much a son of hell as yourselves" (Matt. 23:15). No wonder Paul twice pronounced a curse on those who preach a different gospel (Gal. 1:8-9). They disturb and distort (1:7), bring Christians into bondage (2:4), bring fear (2:12), foster hypocrisy and duplicity (2:13-14), destroy what Paul had built (2:18), nullify grace (2:21), bring people back under the curse of the law (3:10), turn people back to the weak and worthless things (4:9), and render Paul's work vain (4:11).

Paul, in contrast, genuinely had the Galatians' wellbeing in mind. "For I am jealous for you with a godly jealousy; for I betrothed you to one husband, so that to Christ I might present you as a pure virgin" (2 Cor. 11:2).

The false teachers "wish to shut you out." But, Paul's message of grace freed people from being "shut up" by the law (Galatians 3:23 same word). Now that grace is here through the message of Jesus Christ; the law is no longer needed, its work is done. To continue teaching the law is a complete negation of grace. Adding moral or religious behavior to the message of grace is not simply a modification of Paul's message of grace, nor is it an improvement on or clarification of Paul's message. It is a complete nullification of the message! Grace plus anything is not grace at all. Grace plus works of the law equals works of the law—and is, therefore, under God's severest condemnation.

On an interesting personal note, it is not wrong to want to feel wanted ("eagerly sought"). However, the desire to feel accepted should be kept in check so as not to end up following whatever false teachers happen to be present. Believers need to stand firm, and if necessary, stand alone, in grace.

Lord, You accept me in Your grace. Help me stay focused, so I don't fall back into the worthless things of legalistic religion that leaves me feeling insecure.

Are You Listening?

Galatians 4:19-21

¹⁹ My children, with whom I am again in labor until Christ is formed in you— ²⁰ but I could wish to be present with you now and to change my tone, for I am perplexed about you. ²¹ Tell me, you who want to be under law, do you not listen to the law?

Compassion and tenderness defined Paul's heart, though his writings could be terse. It seemed to him, though, that the pains of child-birth were taking place all over again. In preaching the gospel to them the first time, he expended much effort to convince them of its truth. For example, the chronicle of his time with them records this instance, "But the Jews who disbelieved stirred up the minds of the Gentiles and embittered them against the brethren. Therefore they spent a long time there speaking boldly with reliance upon the Lord . . ." (Acts 14:2-3). It was hard work evangelizing the Galatians; there was opposition.

Yet, now Paul was forced to argue with the Galatians again the same message of grace. He likened it to a mother going into labor all over again. The goal of the Christian walk is the same as the goal of salvation, namely, the formation of Christlikeness. The law does not bring that about, it cannot—only grace can. This is not just a trivial doctrinal issue that has no bearing on the real world. The consequences are huge—the very transformation of a person's life.

Paul was perplexed; what the Galatians (at least some of them) were doing made no sense. The issue was so simple, yet they were failing so greatly. The law cannot bring about life change. Grace can! God's grace working through simple belief is the key to sanctification, and that is the goal of Christ coming into the world—to not only save sinners, but to restore us to God's original purpose for us, who were created in His image, to reflect His glory. Grace is the key to saving us and to perfecting us—God wants to work that directly into our lives. Our role is simply to cooperate with Him in faith.

Paul's passion for them was so great; his desire compelled him to visit them again. If we are correct in assuming this letter was written shortly after his first missionary journey where the Galatian believers were saved, Paul did return to Galatia during his second missionary trip (Acts 15:41–16:2). (On a side note, it was on that second visit that Paul discovered Timothy and, thus, began the well-known association of the mature apostle with his young protégé).

Bottom line, if a person desires to still live under the law, they should take a good hard look at the Law of Moses—it should become obvious that there is no hope there, but only condemnation—for all have sinned (Ps. 14:1-3; 53:1-3).

Lord, thank You that by Your grace Christlikeness is being formed in me. I stand amazed by Your goodness to me.

Controlled Interpretation

Galatians 4:22-24

²² For it is written that Abraham had two sons, one by the bondwoman and one by the free woman. ²³ But the son by the bondwoman was born according to the flesh, and the son by the free woman through the promise. ²⁴ This is allegorically speaking, for these women are two covenants: one proceeding from Mount Sinai bearing children who are to be slaves; she is Hagar.

Perplexing is the description some have for this passage; Paul's method of interpreting the Old Testament is curious. The question is posed whether he legitimized an uncontrolled and fanciful use of the allegorical method of interpretation. In other words, can we Christians today, based on Paul's example, give symbolic meanings to biblical events without any evidence from Scripture that such interpretation is reasonable? For example, can we proclaim that the Tabernacle tent pegs refer to the Christian's security in Christ, when Scriptures does not even hint at such an interpretation? Why would it not refer to the need for Christians to be anchored in the Word? Did Paul make an arbitrary connection in our passage? Are there no constraints to fanciful interpretations?

In our passage today, the Old Testament narrative of Hagar and Sarah gives no sense of the meaning that Paul gave it. Some use this to justify their wild interpretations of Scripture, claiming authority as a prophet or having a special word of knowledge. Conservative interpreters, though, have traditionally used what is called a "Grammatical-Historical" method of interpretation. This means a passage must be understood in its normal grammatical sense that would have been understood in the time it was written. Further, a passage should be understood in the context of the cultural and geographical setting. What did it mean to the original author and to his original audience? Paul's interpreting of the story of Hagar and Sarah seems to disregard all this.

However, Paul was using the story for illustration purposes. He was not giving a definitive interpretation of the event and reading that meaning back into it. Rather, he was using the story to bring his readers to a conclusion he had already written about. But in using this story, Paul brings in an emotive element as well as a certain irony. Emotive because the story leads to Hagar's children being cast out, and, therefore, the Judaizers being cast out by the Galatians. Irony because Paul is using "The Law" (which term the Jews used to refer to the five books of Moses, namely, Genesis through Deuteronomy) to argue against living by the Law. In other words, he turned the legalizers' arguments back on them, using their own methods against them. As it was, he is fighting them on their turf.

Lord, help me to rightly understand Your Word and to not be influenced by wild and uncontrolled teachings that are not based on clear, proper interpretations.

Not Slave But Free

Galatians 4:24-26

²⁴ This is allegorically speaking, for these women are two covenants: one proceeding from Mount Sinai bearing children who are to be slaves; she is Hagar. ²⁵ Now this Hagar is Mount Sinai in Arabia and corresponds to the present Jerusalem, for she is in slavery with her children. ²⁶ But the Jerusalem above is free; she is our mother.

An allegory is a "representation of an abstract or spiritual meaning through concrete or material forms; figurative treatment of one subject under the guise of another" (Dictionary.com). Paul used the story of Hagar and Sarah to illustrate a crucial difference between law and grace. The meaning he gave does not arise from an unbiased analysis of the story itself. But, he was inspired by the Holy Spirit; therefore, his illustration carries the authority of God.

Paul applied the story to Law and grace. Hagar represents the Law, that which Moses received on Mt. Sinai. Hagar was a servant (slave) of Abraham, not a wife. Her children, then, were also slaves. The analogy is that those who live under the Law are slaves to the Law like Hagar's children who were slaves. That is the covenant of Law. Paul extended the analogy to Jerusalem, at that time representing Sinai and the Law. This is an indictment on Israel of his day, who saw Jerusalem as the center of their religious life. They were slaves of the Law and were not truly free.

On the other hand, grace found in the Lord Jesus Christ is likened to Sarah, Abraham's wife, and her offspring. She represents the line of promise, and ultimately, those who come to faith in Christ. Paul likens that to a new and different Jerusalem, that which is above. Or to put it another way, the true spiritual Jerusalem, not the earthly one run by legalist religious rulers.

Jeremiah spoke of this new covenant that would come, "'But this is the covenant which I will make with the house of Israel after those days,' declares the LORD, 'I will put My law within them and on their heart I will write it; and I will be their God, and they shall be My people'" (Jer. 31:33). This is the new covenant that Jesus spoke of in the last supper, "He took the cup after they had eaten, saying, 'This cup which is poured out for you is the new covenant in My blood'" (Luke 22:20). This covenant sets people free from slavery to the Law! So, believers now trace their roots back, not to the Law, but to grace—the spiritualized Jerusalem! For the Jews, this was also significant, because in Christ their connection to Abraham is not one primarily of physical lineage, but of spiritual heritage by grace through faith. It is in this sense that there is no difference between Jew or Greek (Gal. 3:28).

Lord, thank You for the covenant of grace written in my heart! What a heritage!

Children of the Promise

Galatians 4:27-28

27 For it is written, "Rejoice, barren woman who does not bear; Break forth and shout, you who are not in labor; For more numerous are the children of the desolate Than of the one who has a husband." 28 And you brethren, like Isaac, are children of promise.

Some portions of Scripture are more oblique than others—this section on Hagar and Sarah is one of them. As already mentioned, Paul employs allegory to illustrate his point; he used the story of Abraham's offspring from two different women (one a servant girl, the other his wife).

The question naturally arises that, if the new covenant of grace is in fact traced back to Abraham, how then does one explain the delay in its manifestation among God's people? Why had the Law been in force all that time, from Moses to Jesus? Although Paul doesn't give an answer to that question directly, he does find an analogy in Isaiah. Israel struggled with the same issue during the prophets' time. Paul quotes the verse that immediately follows Isaiah 53, the so-called Suffering Servant song, depicting Christ's death. The Jews tend to see that chapter as depicting the sufferings of the people of Israel; they are the "suffering servant." The point is that long suffering is intrinsic to Israel's existence, waiting on God's promises. Paul likens the wait for grace to Isaiah's depiction of a barren woman who waits long for a child. The coming of the message of grace through Jesus Christ is like such a woman who finally gives birth.

Gentile believers (since that is who Paul is writing to) have now, through faith, come into the standing of sons of the promise. Isaac was the son of Sarah; he was the one through whom the promise of blessing was to pass. Though the promise passed down the genealogical line through Isaac, Jacob and the descendants of the twelve sons of Jacob, now the line of inheritance is passed on to and through those who have faith in the Lord Jesus Christ. The choice, then, is whether to forever associate with the Law of Moses or to embrace the coming of the blessing promised beforehand to Abraham.

The quotation from Isaiah also points out that the children in question, those of the new, heavenly Jerusalem, will be more numerous than those of the old, earthly Jerusalem. In fact, they will include both believing Jews and believing Gentiles. All those who believe are raised up in status, not to the position of being fellow children under the Law which brings slavery to the Law, but to the higher position, fellow children of promise, citizens of the new, heavenly Jerusalem, which brings freedom in Christ. Praise God.

Lord, what a tremendous standing You have given me, to be a child of Abraham's promise and a citizen of the new Jerusalem.

WEEKEND READING

Saturday – Matthew 18
Sunday – Matthew 19

PERSONAL REFLECTIONS

_____
_____
_____
_____
_____
_____
_____
_____
_____
_____
_____
_____
_____
_____
_____
_____
_____
_____
_____
_____
_____
_____
_____
_____
_____
_____
_____
_____
_____
_____
_____
_____
_____
_____

Whose Son Are You?

Galatians 4:29-31

²⁹ But as at that time he who was born according to the flesh persecuted him who was born according to the Spirit, so it is now also. ³⁰ But what does the Scripture say? "CAST OUT THE BONDWOMAN AND HER SON, FOR THE SON OF THE BONDWOMAN SHALL NOT BE AN HEIR WITH THE SON OF THE FREE WOMAN." ³¹ So then, brethren, we are not children of a bondwoman, but of the free woman.

Before Paul moves on to the practical application of his teaching, he wraps up the defense of his gospel message of grace. Continuing the analogy of Hagar and Sarah, he uses their respective sons to further illustrate the contrast between living under the Law versus freedom through Christ. From the time Ishmael, Hagar's son "born according to the flesh," mocked Sarah at the birth of Isaac (Gen. 21:9), there was animosity between the two sons and their descendants. Sarah had Ishmael expelled from the clan (Gen. 21:10).

This story pictures Paul's teaching on the Galatian situation. First, Ishmael corresponds to the false teaching infiltrating the church and those who espouse it. Combining the Law with faith is "according to the flesh." It appeals to man-centered efforts performed by human ability—which never bring justification. In contrast, the teaching about salvation by grace and those who promote it, are like Isaac, who was born "according to the Spirit." Paul equates that with his being the son of the promise. God's covenant with Abraham was passed down through Sarah's physical descendants, not through Hagar, thus, through Isaac, not Ishmael.

Second, even though both sons were Abraham's, only Isaac inherited the promise and was, therefore, "born according to the Spirit." So also, both Law and grace are from God, but only grace is "according to the Spirit."

Third, Paul inherently applies the words of Sarah to his recommended dealings with the false teachers of Galatia, "Cast them out!" There is to be no co-inheritance. Neither with Isaac and Ishmael, nor with Law and grace.

Fourth, the genuine brotherhood of believers is not among those who espouse Law and grace, but only those who espouse grace alone. We who believe through the grace of our Lord are like children of Sarah, not like children of Hagar. There is no admixture! Law and grace do not, they cannot mix. The 16th century reformers were right: faith alone through grace alone!

Paul, therefore, concludes his defense of the doctrine of grace alone for both salvation and for Christian living. Grace has a significant impact on how we live—and that is the subject Paul turns to next.

Lord, thank You so much for liberating us from a system of life that only leads to failure. Your grace wonderfully motivates us to live robustly in Your grace.

Keep Standing Firm

Galatians 5:1-2

¹ It was for freedom that Christ set us free; therefore keep standing firm and do not be subject again to a yoke of slavery. ² Behold I, Paul, say to you that if you receive circumcision, Christ will be of no benefit to you.

Paul has been called "The Apostle of the Heart Set Free" (see title of the classic book by F.F. Bruce), and rightly so. The book of Galatians drips with freedom. For Paul, this was a heart issue. Prior to his conversion, his heart was set on the Law and defending it. He later wrote to the Philippian believers, "If anyone else has a mind to put confidence in the flesh, I far more: circumcised the eighth day, of the nation of Israel, of the tribe of Benjamin, a Hebrew of Hebrews; as to the Law, a Pharisee; as to zeal, a persecutor of the church; as to the righteousness which is in the Law, found blameless" (Phil. 3:4b-6). When it came to living under the Law, Paul knew whereof he wrote. Looking back on it, he clearly saw that he had been a slave to it.

Today, religions abound that enslave people. In Islam, for example, adherents see themselves primarily as servants or slaves of God. Christians, in contrast, see ourselves as children of God. "For you have not received a spirit of slavery leading to fear again, but you have received a spirit of adoption as sons by which we cry out, 'Abba! Father!'" (Rom. 8:15). We have an affectionate relationship with Him. Further, we believers in Christ also view ourselves as God's friends, "No longer do I call you slaves, for the slave does not know what his master is doing; but I have called you friends . . ." (John 15:15).

The practical application of the difference between Law and grace, therefore, is relational. We are children of God, friends with God, no longer slaves of the Law. And, it is all through the grace of our Lord. We are set free!

If then we are set free, why in the world would we go back to slavery? No one in their right mind would do such a thing! Therefore, the Galatians, indeed we Christians, need to stand firm for this truth. Too much is at stake to consider it simply an intramural debate in Christendom.

Circumcision was symbolic of the entire Law of Moses. Today many see Christian baptism as symbolic of the new covenant through Christ and require it for salvation. But that is wrong—it just shifts the symbol; Paul still denounces the principle. Such requirements render the word "freedom" to be completely empty. Requiring baptism for salvation becomes, then, symbolic of a "Christian law, which is in essence the Mosaic Law in "Christian" garb. Paul's message still resonates, the purveyor of such teaching "is to be accursed" (Gal. 1:8-9).

Oh Father, help me live in the freedom of Christ, avoiding any so-called "Christian" teaching that requires me to earn Your love by keeping laws.

What You Believe Matters

Galatians 5:3-4

³ And I testify again to every man who receives circumcision, that he is under obligation to keep the whole Law. ⁴ You have been severed from Christ, you who are seeking to be justified by law; you have fallen from grace.

A person's doctrinal belief has tremendous implications. Paul signals this with his intensely personal wording, first in verse 2, "I, Paul, say to you . . ." and now "And I testify again . . ." If a person receives circumcision, there is then no benefit in being a follower of Christ (vs. 2); he is still obligated to keep the entire Law of Moses. He places himself back under a system of legalistic righteousness and removes himself from life under grace.

The message here is this: Do you wish to live a holy life? Then get your doctrine straight. Avoid legalism. Get hold of grace! The Law mandates, but does not enable. Grace provides what the Law commands (Wm. MacDonald).

The consequences of getting this wrong is weighty. The person who lives by the Law is: 1) obligated to keep the whole Law, 2) severed from Christ, and 3) fallen from grace. Being obligated to keep the whole Law means we can't be content with keeping just the more easily attained laws—every law becomes a cruel master. Further, we cannot just simply add the Law to faith in Christ; it is either Christ alone, or Christ not at all, severed. In other words, "God would put a minus sign before Christ in the lives of the Galatians if they put a plus sign before anything else" (J.M. Boice, Expositor's Bible Commentary).

Fallen from grace is not just a modification of grace to ensure there is motivation for doing what is right. It is a departure from the high, glorious truth, that it is God alone who justifies us through His grace. And it is this same grace alone that enables us to live out what the Law demands, not human effort.

Does this mean, as some teach, that a Christian can fall from grace and, therefore, lose his justification? No! Paul had already addressed the foolishness of the believing Galatians, "Are you so foolish? Having begun by the Spirit, are you now being perfected by the flesh?" There he was speaking to believers, "you" who have already begun the life of the Spirit by grace. But here in Galatians 4:3-4, he speaks to "every man who receives circumcision" to be justified; "you" whose attempts at justification are based not on faith in Christ alone, but on the works of Law—which is futile. They are still lost souls, not justified believers. Though they have heard the message of grace through Christ, they have separated themselves from Christ, and fallen away from the message of grace.

Lord, convict those who appear to be Christians but who hold on to man-made efforts to justify themselves before You. Show them the magnitude of their error.

Spirit-Enabled Hope

Galatians 5:5-6

⁵ For we through the Spirit, by faith, are waiting for the hope of righteousness. ⁶ For in Christ Jesus neither circumcision nor uncircumcision means anything, but faith working through love.

Hope breeds patience, so hope, therefore, is immensely practical—this is not dry doctrine. While the impatient heart wants results now, propelling him to achieve what he desires, true hope brings a Spirit-enabled patience.

Notice our passage does not speak of hoping for righteousness, but a hope of righteousness. Being right before God is something a believer has already attained through faith (Gal. 2:16). Rather, Paul speaks of a hope that results from the knowledge that righteousness is already ours; it is the "hope of righteousness."

Biblical hope encompasses expectancy with desire. Because of the knowledge of righteousness that comes through faith, energized by the Holy Spirit, we actually look forward with eagerness to the return of Christ. For those who live under Law, having spurned the truth of Christ, there is an inherent fear of judgment (Heb. 10:26-27).

This hope is well grounded in the believer's knowledge of the truth. We eagerly await our citizenship in heaven (Phil. 3:20), our adoption and full redemption as sons (Rom. 8:23-25), the return of Christ (Rev. 9:28) and "the revelation of our Lord Jesus Christ, who will also confirm you to the end, blameless in the day of our Lord Jesus Christ" (1 Cor. 1:7a-8).

The key terms of this passage are significant. Paul chooses his words carefully. "We" refers to genuine believers, in contrast with "you" in vs. 4 which refers to legalists. "Faith" is used 44 times in this short letter. "Spirit" 18 times, and "flesh" 16 times. These are the major themes of the book. In particular, faith as used here is contrasted with the flesh in 4:23. Living by the flesh does not produce the hope that righteousness by faith produces.

Finally, Paul now speaks of circumcision (referred to 13 times in Galatians) to clarify that the act itself is not significant one way or the other. He does not condemn the act itself, for in Acts 16:3 he had Timothy circumcised (shortly after this letter was penned). His censure had to do rather with circumcision used as a theology of sanctification because then it represents man-made efforts to attain righteousness, rather than depending on God's grace. He asserts that ultimately what really matters is the operation of faith which works through love, not human effort through the Law.

Lord, let Your love so embrace me that my will bends willingly and instinctively to Your Spirit's effort in my life.

Responsibility of Grace

Galatians 5:7-8

⁷ You were running well; who hindered you from obeying the truth? ⁸ This persuasion did not come from Him who calls you.

"**R**unning well" was the best description Paul could use of the Galatians— in the past! But something had changed. They were no longer living in the freedom of the gospel of grace. Interestingly, Paul frequently depicts the Christian life in terms of a sporting competition. In Galatians 2:2, he had already expressed his fear that he "might be running, or had run in vain." In another place, the Christian life and ministry is portrayed as a boxing match: "Therefore I run in such a way, as not without aim; I box in such a way, as not beating the air; but I discipline my body and make it my slave, so that, after I have preached to others, I myself will not be disqualified" (1 Cor. 9:26-27). Paul was motivated, at least in part, by the fear of failure. You see, starting well in the Christian life is important, but a person must finish well also.

"Running" is identified with "obeying the truth." That truth is this: we are no longer obligated to live by the Law, for that is impossible. The truth also includes the fact that we are freed to live for God because of the grace of Christ, something the Law could not accomplish. So, then, to obey the truth means that we order our lives according to grace, not according to Law. That is the "persuasion" God has called people to.

Jesus warned about the problem of starting well but not finishing well. Though not specifically talking about legalism, His parable of the sower and the seed (Luke 8) highlights two scenarios where things begin well, but don't end well. Seed cast on thorny soil represents believers whose spiritual life is choked out by worldly cares. Today, do we not see Christians caught up in all kinds of worldly concerns: movies, media, internet, money, possessions, conflicts and recreation. They have plenty of time for such enticements of the flesh, but little time for things that really matter. They began well, but do not finish well.

Seed cast onto rocky ground represents believers whose spiritual life is shallow, and as a result, they turn spiritually dry and wither away. Those who do not study the word, pray or exercise their faith will eventually be sidelined and proved to be useless for producing spiritual fruit.

We must guard against the flesh's propensity for submitting to the bondage of rules and regulations or to worldly enticements. We cannot blame others for "enforcing" the rules, but we must take responsibility for rooting ourselves in the truth and obeying the truth of God's grace by living in freedom!

Lord, help me recognize the hindrances to spiritual life that so easily become entrenched. You have set me free, and I want to live that freedom unencumbered.

WEEKEND READING

Saturday – Matthew 20
Sunday – Matthew 21

_____
_____
_____
_____
_____
_____
_____
_____
_____
_____
_____
_____
_____
_____
_____
_____
_____
_____
_____
_____
_____
_____
_____
_____
_____
_____
_____
_____
_____

Clear Thinking

⁹ A little leaven leavens the whole lump of dough. ¹⁰ I have confidence in you in the Lord that you will adopt no other view; but the one who is disturbing you will bear his judgment, whoever he is.

One person can influence a whole group. And, the less people think clearly about things, the more easily they are influenced. Few people think well! The causes of this phenomenon are numerous: 1) Lazy minds, accustomed to being entertained with amusement—("a-musement" means without musing or thinking!); 2) Enslavement to poor thinking habits—never trained to engage one's mind; 3) Minds bent by the effects of repeated sin—a person begins to see life differently; 4) Limited natural thinking ability—and no effort to grow in this area; 5) Uncontrolled emotions that neutralize perspective—despair, greed, jealousy, anger, etc.; 6) Building a mental framework for interpreting truth based on distortion that comes through repetition of wrong ideas.

A skilled thinker with a charismatic persona knows how to marshal this insight to manipulate large groups of people to follow in ways that don't make sense to an "outsider." Hitler was a master of this; so have been many powerful influential people, whether political or religious. Paul wrote of leaven (a.k.a. yeast). As moisture and heat are added to the dough, air is formed which permeates throughout and the bread rises. False teachers, likewise, capitalized on people's hindered thinking, adding the right words in a certain way to persuade them to follow a perverted message.

The apostle appealed to this group to consider the original message and how it was inherently superior to the false message that includes the Law. The logic of it stands on its own. Yet, some would not accept this, because the false teachers were influential in keeping their minds confused and hindered. Paul's goal was to help them see that the message of grace actually sets a person free, sets their minds free. The framework for thinking about life and God and spiritual things had changed. There is a new grid—one that brings freedom. The only real hope that satisfies is the hope that comes through Christ alone.

Paul did indeed have confidence that the true believers among the Galatians would not revert to the old message again, and he likewise had the confidence that those harassing them would be judged by God. It doesn't matter who that person is. Anyone, Peter, James, an angel from heaven, or even himself—anyone trying to persuade others that observing the law of Moses was required for justification is to "be accursed" (Gal. 1:8-9).

Lord, help us watch for those who try to bring us into bondage. Thank You for elders who guard the flock of God from spiritual "wolves" (Acts 20:28-29).

An Earthy Argument

Galatians 5:11-12

[11] But I, brethren, if I still preach circumcision, why am I still persecuted? Then the stumbling block of the cross has been abolished. [12] I wish that those who are troubling you would even mutilate themselves.

Paul continued his attack against those who distorted the gospel of grace. This is such a crucial issue, such a go-to-the-wall theme, that he relentlessly pressed his point from all angles. Genuine Christianity rises or falls on getting this right. If circumcision is required (or baptism or any other rite for that matter), Christianity is just another works-based religion, dependent upon a person's ability to meet a pre-set standard. God's standard, though, is perfect holiness, and we all fall short. That is what's wrong with man-centered religious efforts. The grace of Christ is categorically different; it is God-centered. Human efforts are absolutely foolish by comparison. Paul shows this in two ways.

First, his own personal testimony—he does not preach circumcision. The proof of that is in his being persecuted. It was not part of the original message that brought the Galatians to salvation through faith in Christ. That seems to be stating the obvious. The cause of the persecution was that Paul did not preach that circumcision was required of believers. To avoid that persecution, he could have started preaching circumcision. But that would be tantamount to abolishing the teaching of the cross, which would cut the heart out of his message!

Paul extended his objections to the false teachers by appealing to the absurd—they should take their argument to its logical conclusion. Speaking rather crudely, but for maximum effect, he suggested they should "mutilate" themselves. The term literally means "to cut off." What Paul is thinking about here is castration—that would take circumcision to its logical, if ludicrous, conclusion. In essence, if the legalizers are so passionate about keeping the Law and its symbol, circumcision— if this is such a big deal that it is the lightening rod in the discussion about Christ, just how far will they go in the adamant over-intensification of the Law and distortion of God's ways. Since they are completely maligning Scripture and have set their interpretation of it loose from the actual meaning and sense of it, they ought to just go all the way!

Paul was a master of rhetoric, using words, phrases and thought patterns to convey the truth. On the surface, one might detect sarcasm and crudeness, but the real thrust was to show the absurdity of trying to use God's Word for one's own vain purposes. Sometimes, he wrote starkly to his readers, "You foolish Galatians" (Gal. 3:1), and we, too, need to hear the truth in very earthy terms.

Lord, help me not to fall into the absurdity of thinking I can somehow add to Your finished work of grace in making me justified before Your holiness.

Let Freedom Ring

Galatians 5:13-15

13 For you were called to freedom, brethren; only do not turn your freedom into an opportunity for the flesh, but through love serve one another. 14 For the whole Law is fulfilled in one word, in the statement, "YOU SHALL LOVE YOUR NEIGHBOR AS YOURSELF." 15 But if you bite and devour one another, take care that you are not consumed by one another.

In 1832, Samuel F. Smith borrowed a tune from a German hymnal and rewriting the patriotic words, published what became a famous American patriotic song, "My Country, 'Tis of Thee." The last line of the first stanza continues to stir the human heart, "Let freedom ring." While there seems to be something innate in the desire for living free in a free country, the heart yearns for a greater freedom. Not just a freedom from tyranny and bondage, but freedom to live out the purpose for which we were created.

Paul appeals to the Galatians (and to us) that being unshackled from the tyranny of the Law, frees us up to love and serve others. That is what we were made for, and that is the only thing that satisfies the redeemed soul's yearnings. This is the new law written in our hearts (Jer. 31:33). It is the fulfillment, the ultimate objective of the Law of Moses in terms of our relationships. Paul quotes Leviticus 19:18 to demonstrate his point, "You shall love your neighbor as yourself." Jesus Himself listed that as the second greatest commandment, the first being to love the Lord God with your whole being (Matt. 22:39). Jesus gave it a heightened emphasis, "A new commandment I give to you, that you love one another, even as I have loved you, that you also love one another" (John 13:34). Redemption by the grace of God implants this commandment in the soul of each believer. No, it instills the desire for this, and we need to fan it into flames.

Grace is immensely practical. This new commandment is not just a reimaged version of the typical religious approach to God, a kind of Christian-flavored law system. No, it is a transformation—and our responsibility as believers in Christ, who have been set free by His grace, is to cooperate with that grace working in our lives.

The implications are practical, not judicial. Taking our freedom for granted, for selfish purposes, does not put our justification in question. Rather the consequences are a continuation of the very kind of life we have been saved from, namely, the life of the flesh that is characterized by personal conflict and bondage to self-centered desires. We have been saved for something much better than that!

Lord, I do want to cooperate with Your grace in my life. Help me focus on serving others in love, and not live for myself.

Walking By the Spirit

Galatians 5:16-18

16 But I say, walk by the Spirit, and you will not carry out the desire of the flesh. 17 For the flesh sets its desire against the Spirit, and the Spirit against the flesh; for these are in opposition to one another, so that you may not do the things that you please. 18 But if you are led by the Spirit, you are not under the Law.

Freedom in Christ describes the new life a Christian has. But how do we keep experiencing that freedom? On the one hand, it is true that we are free from being judged by the Law. But, since we should not use our freedom as a license to sin, how can the knowledge of this freedom, the knowledge of grace, affect our daily struggle to live holy lives? The desires of the flesh are still strong even after becoming a believer in Christ!

The antidote is not the standard religious fare familiar to all other belief systems in the world. We cannot win the battle against legalism with a set of new laws, albeit Christian ones. Nor, can we win the battle against fleshly desires that way. Rather, we win by what Paul calls walking by the Spirit. This constitutes a different kind of living, a different kind of motivation for living right. Paul spends these and the next few verses filling in the details of this grace-filled lifestyle.

So far in this letter, we have learned that we received the Spirit by faith through hearing (3:2); we, therefore, began by the Spirit. The Spirit works miracles in the lives of Christians (3:5), the greatest of which is salvation. Receiving the Spirit is a direct result of the promise to Abraham (3:14). Our having the Spirit is irrevocably connected to our adoption as sons of God (4:6). The Spirit gives us hope (5:5). Since all this is true of the Spirit in our lives, it follows that we should "walk by the Spirit," that is, we need to live in accordance with what the Spirit wants to accomplish in our lives.

Walking by the Spirit is the remedy to living as though the Law still had effect. This remedy is diametrically opposed to living under the Law. This is because, while the Law has absolutely no value in combating the desires of the flesh, walking by the Spirit produces great results.

Human life in its most elemental form is goal driven—and there are only two goals in view, self-absorbed pleasure or God-centric living. The first rouses the flesh, the second empowers self-denial for the glory of God ("you will not carry out the desire of the flesh"). The question is, which goal do we set for ourselves? Ordering our lives by the Spirit's leading is the only effective way to win the daily battles against the flesh.

Father, help me ever keep the goal for my life clear, that I may walk by Your Spirit and not for the momentary enjoyments of the flesh.

Look Out!

Galatians 5:19-21a

[19] Now the deeds of the flesh are evident, which are: immorality, impurity, sensuality, [20] idolatry, sorcery, enmities, strife, jealousy, outbursts of anger, disputes, dissensions, factions, [21] envying, drunkenness, carousing, and things like these ...

A daily devotion focusing on sin can be depressing, not very uplifting! However, spiritual exercise in our Christian life needs regular assessment of our spiritual walk—and this includes reminding ourselves of some of the more obvious sins into which we can so easily fall. Like a doctor assesses the symptoms in order to diagnose an illness, Christians ought to look for the outward symptoms of fleshliness to determine whether we are walking by (or being led by) the Spirit or not.

Young Christians struggle with what is meant by "the flesh." Paul indicated that it may be known by its symptoms. The first three listed relate to sexual immorality and are somewhat comprehensive, beginning with immorality. (Note: The KJV includes as the first, adultery). This is the general Greek word, pornea, from which the word pornography derives. The word was used for immoral or inappropriate sexual relationships, particularly prostitution or intercourse outside of the marriage relationship. In the Greek and Roman world, it was considered "the most open and shameless vice" (Gabelein). Impurity refers to anything that stimulates the sexual urges in biblically inappropriate ways. Sensuality (also translated debauchery, lewdness or lustful pleasures) describes unrestrained sexual immorality.

The next two symptoms of fleshliness, idolatry and sorcery, have to do with cultic practices. Today, this would include using horoscopes and fortune tellers, and also good luck charms, superstitious practices and the like.

The following eight symptoms (from enmities to envying) could be called social or relational sins and are quite comprehensive. They are all expanded upon elsewhere in Scripture, from the Sermon on the Mount (Matt. 5-7) to James (esp. 4:1-3). Which of these can a Christian say has never been a part of his or her experience? Read them over again and meditate on each one asking the Lord to give you the humility to recognize any and all symptoms in your life.

The last two, drunkenness and carousing (also translated at times orgies) represent the ultimate in self-abasement for the sake of bodily and momentary pleasure. Fleshliness is no more pathetic than when a person gives control over himself to things like shameless drunkenness and unrestrained sexual pleasures.

O Father, help me recognize and confess the self-entitlement, self-justification and self-pleasure that allow for unchecked fleshly behavior in my life.

WEEKEND READING

Saturday – Matthew 22
Sunday – Matthew 23

PERSONAL
REFLECTIONS

Loss of Salvation?

Galatians 5:21b

²¹ ... of which I forewarn you, just as I have forewarned you, that those who practice such things will not inherit the kingdom of God.

Can a Christian lose his salvation? Some think so, based on passages like this one. Is not Paul writing to Christians? Is he not saying that Christians who display the previous list of fifteen symptoms of fleshliness will not be entering into heaven? I do not think that is what this passage is addressing at all.

First, which of us has never failed in some regard concerning these symptoms? Even the most mature of us has disputes with others from time to time or has been jealous. Would we not all, then, be disqualified from entry into heaven? Of course not. Further, Paul is not listing these things as a sort of Christian law system that we must perform in order to merit or keep God's forgiveness. Grace that so freely forgave our sins before we came to Christ is also sufficient to forgive us for any of these fleshly deeds after conversion.

Paul, by his own writing, is not referring to Christians but to those "who will not inherit the kingdom of God." He says elsewhere, "Or do you not know that the unrighteous will not inherit the kingdom of God? Do not be deceived; neither fornicators, nor idolaters, nor adulterers, nor effeminate, nor homosexuals" (1 Cor. 6:9). These are descriptions of people who are not Christians, whose lifestyle and practices give evidence that they are unconverted. They are still under law, and the law will judge them as sinners.

But why, then, would Paul be writing this to the Christians in Galatia? He explicitly says this is a repeated warning, so it is not to be dismissed as irrelevant. The answer is that in all groups of Christians there may be some unbelievers (the tares among the wheat—see Matthew 13). The apostle, as he wrote elsewhere, counsels his readers to, "Test yourselves to see if you are in the faith; examine yourselves! Or do you not recognize this about yourselves, that Jesus Christ is in you—unless indeed you fail the test?" (2 Cor. 13:5).

This does not mean that anyone who lapses into failure in one of these symptoms forfeits what he already has, that is, salvation. The tense of the verb practice indicates the habitual nature of the life style. The person who is characterized by one or more of these symptoms, who has an unrepentant heart, needs to think soberly about his pretentions to faith and fellowship among true believers. The true believer, on the other hand, is motivated not by a fear of losing salvation, but by an abhorrence of that for which the non-believers are judged. He does not want to continue in sin that is condemned by God in the lives of non-believers. Why flirt with that which God detests?

Lord, help me avoid the sins of the flesh and detest them as much as You do.

A Life of Fruitfulness—part 1

Galatians 5:22a

²² But the fruit of the Spirit is love, joy, peace ...

The fruit of the Spirit form a comprehensive and profound picture of the Spirit-controlled life. They are not called "fruit of human effort", which are described in the previous verses as the "deeds of the flesh." The fruit of the Spirit cannot be fabricated or faked without eventually giving way to exposure. One cannot draw pictures of apples on paper, cut them out, then tape them onto a tree with the hopes of creating real fruit. Rather, it is the tree that produces real fruit, which is nourished from the internal life of the tree.

The Christian is like a tree. Simply pinning on a facsimile of spiritual fruit does not make him or her spiritual. That is the picture of someone trying to live spiritually by using the Law. In contrast, the vitality that produces genuine spiritual fruit comes from the Spirit of God working internally, with us responding to Him, not to Law. This is what Paul early referred to as "walking by the Spirit" (Gal. 5:16) and being "led by the Spirit" (5:18).

The obvious contrast is made between the "deeds of the flesh" (vs. 19) and the "fruit of the Spirit." The word "fruit" is used in the collective singular, and this fruit is delineated into nine specific manifestations, all of which are expanded upon in other portions of Scripture. Love, of course, is exalted by Paul as being the first, consistent with his writing in 1 Corinthians 13, particularly that, "Love is the greatest" (vs. 13). He further writes to young Timothy, "But the goal of our instruction is love from a pure heart and a good conscience and a sincere faith" (1 Tim. 1:5). This is God's supreme motivation, and it brings Him great glory when He sees this fruit in the lives of His people.

Joy, of course, is the theme of the letter to the Philippians. If there is anything needed today, it is the joy of the Lord. This is the antidote to spiritual depression that seems so prevalent. Peace was prominent in the Lord's teaching in the upper room, "Peace I leave with you; My peace I give to you; not as the world gives do I give to you. Do not let your heart be troubled, nor let it be fearful" (John 14:27). Genuine inner peace can only come from the Lord Jesus, not through relaxation techniques. This becomes the stake in the ground for controlling our emotions, our interactions with others, and our sense of contentment.

How do we grow this fruit? By walking with the Spirit by faith! This is not mysticism or a matter of "phenomenal manifestations," but simply obeying by faith the Spirit's inner leading in our lives.

Lord, help me learn how to walk with the Spirit by faith. I am not looking for a sensational, super-spiritual experience, but a life of spiritual fruitfulness.

A Life of Fruitfulness—part 2

Galatians 5:22b-23

²² [But the fruit of the Spirit is] ... patience, kindness, goodness, faithfulness, ²³ gentleness, self-control; against such things there is no law.

Fruit of the Spirit is essential evidence in the Christian's life of walking by the Spirit. After love, joy and peace, come another six. These are all found ultimately in the Lord and, thus, should reflect a Christ-centered, Spirit-led life. God's patience allowed His kindness to finally lead us to salvation (Rom. 2:4). He did not give up over our long resistance to the message of grace. He continues to be patient, "The Lord is not slow about His promise, as some count slowness, but is patient toward you, not wishing for any to perish but for all to come to repentance" (2 Peter 3:9).

The goodness fruit is also rooted in God's goodness, for there is only one good and that is God (Mark 10:18). Any goodness we have is a derivative of His. He remains faithful when we are faithless (2 Tim. 2:13). The Lord is gentle, "Take My yoke upon you and learn from Me, for I am gentle and humble in heart, and you will find rest for your souls" (Matt. 11:29). As for self-control, "While being reviled, He did not revile in return; while suffering, He uttered no threats, but kept entrusting Himself to Him who judges righteously" (1 Peter 2:23). This took tremendous self-mastery.

So, the fruit of the Spirit is a reflection of Christ-likeness in our lives. There is a sense where sanctification is a passive sort of thing, in that these traits are produced by the Spirit and not by human flesh. However, as we shall see a few verses later, Paul instructs Timothy and us that we should keep in step with the Spirit. We should be living in every way in cooperation with what the Spirit desires in us. Peter puts it this way, "Now for this very reason also, applying all diligence, in your faith supply moral excellence, and in your moral excellence, knowledge . . . (2 Peter 1:5). We add our efforts to what the Spirit is doing.

This cooperation is not a form of works in keeping with the Law, where we earn God's favor through our efforts. Rather, since the fruit are the results of a grace-filled life, they become the focus of spiritual development for our efforts. They cannot be codified in a law—that is what Paul means when he says, ". . . against such things there is no law" (vs. 23b). Paul uses classical understatement to make his point. The law was given to restrain evil, but it had no control over the qualities that are Christ's. It commanded love of God and neighbor, but it did not provide the means for doing so. The Spirit provides the means, and our role is to cooperate with our efforts.

Lord, thank You for being the source, impetus, and the power for my living in Christ-like ways. May the fruit of the Spirit be evident in my life.

Keeping In Step

Galatians 5:24-25

²⁴ Now those who belong to Christ Jesus have crucified the flesh with its passions and desires. ²⁵ If we live by the Spirit, let us also walk by the Spirit.

Concluding his teaching on sanctification, and before he moves on to practical application of that teaching, Paul gives a concise final comment on the matter in two brief statements.

The first refers to what has already taken place. Notice he refers to "those who belong to Christ Jesus." They are the ones who have become believers in Christ through God's grace. He has just spent two chapters (3 & 4) explaining and defending the doctrine of justification based on grace alone, apart from the works of the Law. Those who embrace this teaching are spoken of here as belonging to Christ Jesus. This is a relationship that was begun in the past, is a present reality and has enduring results. Christians are those who have come to faith in Christ, whose relationship with Him is not in doubt—because it does not depend on their own works of the Law, but on God's grace. Grace removes doubt—thus, one can speak of "belonging to Christ."

If justification were by works of the Law, Paul would speak of Christ Jesus belonging to us. But, since it is by grace, the initiative belongs to Him; we are His to be reclaimed. And we have been reclaimed and given life. It is God who justifies (Rom. 8:33). Our role in justification is always referred to in the passive, we are those who are justified. We belong to Him.

What is our role then? Two things. First, what we have already done, as believers, we "have crucified the flesh with its passions and desires." This does not mean we never sin again, but it means we have abandoned all efforts of attaining righteousness through human efforts at keeping the Law—which only incites the passions and desires. We nailed them to the cross, as it were; we crucified them. Secondly, as those who belong to Christ, we are alive in the Spirit, having been justified. If that is true, and in fact it is true, we should then "walk by the Spirit." The NIV translation captures the idea well, "Since we live by the Spirit, let us keep in step with the Spirit." Our role as believers is not to sit back in a passive way. Just as we nailed our flesh to the cross, in agreement with the message of grace, we live in agreement with what the Spirit desires to do in our life. We walk in newness of life, cooperating with Him.

This is different from keeping in step with the Law: the motivation is different; the enabling power is different, and the results are different. It's all about grace!

Lord, keep reminding me of Your grace as I keep walking in step with Your Spirit. Thank You for owning me as Your very own—that is very assuring.

Grace Living

Galatians 5:26-6:1

26 Let us not become boastful, challenging one another, envying one another. 1 Brethren, even if anyone is caught in any trespass, you who are spiritual, restore such a one in a spirit of gentleness; each one looking to yourself, so that you too will not be tempted.

Though these verses cross the chapter boundaries in our English Bibles, the ancient manuscripts did not divide the New Testament documents into chapters and verses. These divisions were added much later by copyists as a convenient method for consistently identifying Scripture passages. This is one place where the chapter division seems out of place. Thematically, verse 26 of chapter 5 really goes with verse 1 of chapter 6, and begins the application of the truth Paul has been propounding in chapters 3 and 4.

How does the gospel of grace affect relationships in conflict? The fleshly response is one of competition characterized by proud boasting, one-upmanship—external actions motivated by inner envy. Isn't life filled with such relationships? Consider how much of our thought life and conversation is taken up with people and their problems or our problems with them. The person who lives his life in relationship with God based on the legal requirements of spirituality, tends to measure himself by other people—which begs for comparisons. This affects his attitudes and behavior when others oppose him or are perceived to be "better" than him. How often do we see other people's faults and tend to exalt ourselves as being superior? It may be a look, a snide comment, or a judgmental attitude—but the heart of the matter is self-centeredness.

In contrast with such fleshly attitudes and behavior, Paul challenges us to rise above that fray. He strikes a gentle, familial tone with the use of the term "brethren." This is family business! He is talking with fellow Christians, those who have been called to the freedom of grace (Gal. 5:13) from fleshly living by the Law and the comparisons it engenders. Where there is conflict, there is a better way, the way of grace living!

How do we then deal with a Christian who is acting out sub-Christlike behavior, here termed as a trespass? Paul appeals to true spiritual-mindedness. Our goal is not self-centered comparisons or bringing judgment on the fallen brother. Our goal should be to help him regain his spiritual vitality. There is a genuine humbleness in this, recognizing that we all are tempted, and we all can fail. We should have the attitude portrayed by the modern proverb, "There, but for the grace of God, go I."

Father, it is true, I sometimes act out sub-Christlike behavior. Help me to be gracious to others when they fall, so that we can help each other walk in grace.

WEEKEND READING

Saturday – Matthew 24
Sunday – Matthew 25

PERSONAL
REFLECTIONS

_____

_____

_____

_____

_____

_____

_____

_____

_____

_____

_____

_____

_____

_____

_____

_____

_____

_____

_____

_____

_____

_____

_____

_____

_____

_____

_____

_____

_____

On Being a Burden Lifter

Galatians 6:2-5

---

² Bear one another's burdens, and thereby fulfill the law of Christ. ³ For if anyone thinks he is something when he is nothing, he deceives himself. ⁴ But each one must examine his own work, and then he will have reason for boasting in regard to himself alone, and not in regard to another. ⁵ For each one will bear his own load.

Two complementary tasks: bear one another's burdens and bear one's own load. That doesn't sound fair, it's not a 50-50 proposition. But living a life of grace towards others means doing more than one's share. If everyone set a goal of doing no more than their share, much would be left undone, because we all fall short in our abilities to bear our own burdens and others' as well. The only solution is the one of grace, where we don't keep score, and we simply take on the burdens of others as though they were our own. This doesn't relieve us of our responsibility to bear our own load, though, lest grace degenerate into laziness.

What are these burdens and loads? They are anything that weighs us down as believers, the normal struggles of life including relational conflicts and hardships of various sorts. We have been called into a grace community relationship with God through Jesus Christ, where we are not judged by how well we keep the Law. So also, in our grace community with others, we do not judge according to some objective standard—which inevitably leads to favorable judgment of ourselves as compared to others. Is that not the reason we often do not help others with their burdens? We tend to think of ourselves as better than they. We saw earlier that, in restoring a fallen brother, we should do it humbly for we, too, could easily be tempted and fall as well (6:1). So, we also should help with our brother's hardships, because we ourselves are weak.

Self-centered pride is not becoming a Christian who is captured by grace. We need to be reminded of this often, because we can so easily deceive ourselves in this matter. If anything, our self-thoughts must be sober (see Romans 12:3), comparing our own works and efforts with ourselves, what we used to be apart from the grace of our Lord and the ministry of the Holy Spirit in our lives. Then, as we see this growth in grace, we can boast. This is not a boast of comparison with others, but rather a boast in what God has done in us (this anticipates Galatians 6:14 where our boast is in the cross of Christ alone). Thus, the law of Christ is fulfilled as we bear other's burdens and don't demand that others bear our load. This is true community!

Lord, help me move from expecting others to bear my load and instead show me today someone whose burden I can help lift.

Sharing the Good Things

Galatians 6:6

⁶ The one who is taught the word is to share all good things with the one who teaches him.

Teaching in the church is absolutely essential, for knowing the Word of God creates a foundation for everything else. In the Word is truth, and the truth sets us free (John 8:32). The first piece of the Christian's armor is the belt of truth (Eph. 6:14). The Word of God is "a lamp to my feet and a light to my path" (Ps. 119:105). Jesus, quoting Deuteronomy 8:3, taught that, "Man shall not live on bread alone, but on every word that proceeds out of the mouth of God" (Matt. 4:4). And, He later emphasized the importance of His own teachings, "Therefore everyone who hears these words of Mine and acts on them, may be compared to a wise man who built his house on the rock" (Matt. 7:24). In the upper room before He was crucified, he prayed to His Father about His followers, "Sanctify them in the truth; Your word is truth" (John 17:17).

Given the significance of the Word of God, it is no surprise the importance God places on teaching the Word. The early church was founded on the "apostles teaching" (Acts 2:42). The only way we know what Jesus taught is through the teachings of the apostles, because He did not leave for us his own handwritten memoirs. God appointed to the church, "some as apostles, and some as prophets, and some as evangelists, and some as pastors and teachers . . ." (Eph. 4:11). The first two are foundational gifts (Eph. 2:20)—of course, Christ is the foundation, the cornerstone of the church (1 Cor. 3:11; Matt. 16:18). The foundation has been laid, and it is now the evangelists and the pastor-teachers who build on it. While the soul-winners are those who add to the church, the pastor-teachers are those who build up the church through teaching.

In our passage today, we are encouraged to ". . . share all good things with the one who teaches . . ." Teaching is one of the most taken for granted ministries in the church, we come to expect it. We evaluate it, we criticize it, we compare it with other churches' teaching ministries. We run to popular televised preaching. But do we honor the teachers in our own midst. What about the faithful teacher who instructs our children in Sunday School? Or, the nursery worker who teaches infants and toddlers while singing children's hymns to them? What about the small group leader who sacrifices time during his or her week to prepare for the study? The one hour you hear the preacher on Sunday mornings may well represent hours and hours of preparation. With all of these, how can we share "good things?"

Lord, help me to think creatively and sacrificially, so that I can share some of the good things You have given me with those who teach my loved ones and me.

Choosing Where You Sow

Galatians 6:7-8

⁷ Do not be deceived, God is not mocked; for whatever a man sows, this he will also reap. ⁸ For the one who sows to his own flesh will from the flesh reap corruption, but the one who sows to the Spirit will from the Spirit reap eternal life.

C ontinuing on with the application of grace-living as opposed to law-living, the natural question arises: What is our motivation for living right if there is no system of law to live by? Does grace mean we can do anything we want? Just to make it absolutely clear, we are no longer judged by law; it is no longer our master—that kind of living does not produce righteousness. We are declared righteous by grace through faith in Christ. But, certain cause and effect principles are still operable. Just as gravity still works, so also the principle in these two verses still works.

Being made righteous does not mean that we can cleverly find a way around living the kind of life God wants for us or that we can pull the grace trump card to justify our self-centered lifestyle choices. Such behavior carries its own consequences. Both the person justified by grace and the person still under the law may step off a cliff, and they both will suffer when they hit the bottom. So also, being a justified believer does not suspend the consequences of self-serving behavior. We reap what we sow.

There are two ways in which this can be taken. A person's actions prove or disprove his words. Calling oneself a Christian, faking one's behavior to look the Christian part, will not fool God. Such living only feeds the flesh and, in the end, will produce a worthless life devoid of spiritual blessing, that is, it will be shown ultimately to be rotten to the core, corrupt. "God is not mocked."

On the other hand, this can be taken as a genuine Christian who, though being truly justified, lives a self-centered life, believing that how he lives doesn't affect his justification. He will reap a worthless life, receive no rewards, but, as Paul says elsewhere, "will be saved, yet so as by fire." (1 Cor. 3:15).

It is noteworthy that this teaching follows on the heels of giving to those who serve in the teaching of the Word. That would be sowing with our material wealth to the Spirit in the sense of propagating the teaching of God's Word, as opposed to spending our money on self-pleasures. The reaping of eternal life does not refer to justification, but reaping in the sense of enjoyment of that future life even now. Many Christians do not truly experience the blessings of walking in the Spirit, missing the abundance and joy of Christ.

Father, I confess my selfishness in how I use the resources You have blessed me with. Help me do everything I can for the spread of Your Truth.

Don't Give Up—Part 1

Galatians 6:9

⁹ Let us not lose heart in doing good, for in due time we will reap if we do not grow weary.

Cancer of the soul is how someone has described discouragement in the Christian life. Or as this verse puts it, losing heart in doing good. It is a curse that waits in the wings throughout the Christian life, ready to strike at any time—sometimes when it seems eminently justified; other times it surprises us.

A new Christian flies high on the emotion of discovering the love and grace of God and experiences immediate life change and impact on those around him or her. But not long after, discouragement barges in through doubts, resistance to his testimony, falling into an old sinful habit and, to put it generically, failure in actually making good happen. To this person, the Lord says, "Don't lose heart!"

But discouragement is not limited to new believers. Serving in ministry has its cancer as well. The Christian's sacrificial efforts and best intentions at times seem to produce seemingly little results (at best) or adverse consequences (at worse), like resistance from others, criticism or failure. Self-doubts and self-worth intrude uninvited like a SWAT team yelling, "You are a failure" or "This Christian serving thing doesn't work!" God's message is the same, "Don't lose heart!"

Ironically, even after seeming success, the cancer jumps out from behind the spiritual bushes. After a ministry success, a big event attended by many people, a growing ministry, whatever—discouragement grabs hold and says, "This doesn't make you feel any closer to God. You are a hypocrite. You are arrogant. You need this for your self-esteem. Your ministry is not as big or successful as _____." The whispers are many, but they are there.

Sometimes, the cancer feels more like a spiritual malaise. As the psalmist wrote, "Why are you downcast, O my soul?" (Ps. 42:5a). The Christian life was supposed to be more than this, wasn't it. And we resort to doing religious deeds that we hope will somehow kickstart our spiritual motor. We go to spiritual pep-rallies (services designed to charge us up emotionally-spiritually), or we engage in ascetic practices and castigate ourselves, or we vow to do something spiritually-heroic for God. But what is God's answer? "Let us not lose heart in doing good, for in due time we will reap if we do not grow weary!" Notice, the apostle says, "We." It was his struggle as well. We are in good company, to say the least. Let us keep our eyes fixed on Christ, who is our great hope.

Lord, once again, Your words buoy me up in the face of that constant cancer of discouragement. Like the psalmist, I keep hoping in God. (Ps. 42:5b).

Don't Give Up—Part 2

⁹ Let us not lose heart in doing good, for in due time we will reap if we do not grow weary.

M any start well but give up in discouragement. In context, the apostle had just written about sowing to the Spirit and not to the flesh (vs. 7-8) with particular application made to supporting the teaching ministry of the Word. We need to live the grace-filled life and not fall back into fleshly living by religious regulation or self-centered living of the flesh.

God reminds us to keep doing the "good works, which God prepared beforehand so that we would walk in them" (Eph. 2:10). The book of Hebrews is built on the premise that the Jewish believers were being tempted to give up the way of God's rest and to go back to the old way of effort through law and ritual and Old Testament priestly sacrifices. "Do not throw away your confidence, which has a great reward. For you have need of endurance, so that when you have done the will of God, you may receive what was promised" (Heb.10:35-36).

Men and women by the churchload have become demoralized, spiritually desensitized, and soulishly numb to the important things of God. Once they were on fire, enthusiastic about following God as they pressed on "toward the goal for the prize of the upward call of God in Christ Jesus" (Phil. 3:14). They saw God answering prayer in providing financial support for short-term missions trips. They found boldness in their youth to witness at the flag pole with scores of other teens. They discovered the emotional charge of Christian music in their language of song that moved them inwardly.

But now life goes on, they settle down into adulthood and its pressures and responsibilities. Answered prayer seems less frequent, simple faith of youth no longer satisfies, and efforts to rekindle the young vibrancy of life when God seemed so real fall flat. People give up by settling for the religious status quo of "Evangelicalism," seeking out the spiritual-emotional high that continues to be elusive, but for the few elated moments with just the right music, atmosphere and relevant contemporary pop preacher. Yet, they are giving up by giving in to a popularized contemporary "feel good and spiritual" kind of religious experience.

Hebrews complements our passage today, ". . . let us run with endurance the race that is set before us, fixing our eyes on Jesus, the author and perfecter of faith, who for the joy set before Him endured the cross, despising the shame, and has sat down at the right hand of the throne of God" (Heb. 12:1b-2).

Oh Father, You have done so much for me in showering me with grace. I want to "love you more dearly, follow you more nearly, day by day."

WEEKEND READING

Saturday – Matthew 26:1-35
Sunday – Matthew 26:36-75

PERSONAL REFLECTIONS

_____
_____
_____
_____
_____
_____
_____
_____
_____
_____
_____
_____
_____
_____
_____
_____
_____
_____
_____
_____
_____
_____
_____
_____
_____
_____
_____
_____
_____
_____
_____
_____
_____
_____

Opportunity Calling

Galatians 6:10

[10] So then, while we have opportunity, let us do good to all people, and especially to those who are of the household of the faith.

Grace-living means being freed from the fear of judgment and condemnation to live out the life God has designed for us, namely to do good. These last two chapters of Galatians contain the practical outworking of the theology of justification by grace that comes through the Lord Jesus Christ. It comes down to simply doing good. That seems to be a no-brainer, and all religions teach that. The huge difference for the Christian, though, has to do with the basis for doing good and the motivation for it. We Christians do good not because our standing with God is in question or our eternal destiny hangs in the balance. Rather, we are now free from inferior motivations, free from guilt and rejection that the Law brings. So, with a clean slate as it were, we are freed to live a life that is characterized by doing good.

God didn't create us strictly for our own benefit. Likewise, He didn't justify us and save us from the Law for our own benefit. We were created and saved to do "good works" (Eph. 2:10). Therefore, it makes sense that Paul follows his intense doctrinal teaching on justification with an equally intense challenge to do good.

In our passage today, he first gives the general injunction that doing good should be our characteristic lifestyle and reputation. But, the command focuses on the fellowship of believers; we should "especially" do good to one another in the "household of faith." We are part of the same family; we share the most important truth and reality, that of being justified before God by His grace. There is a special benefit in the community of faith, of doing good for one another. Unfortunately, being justified doesn't automatically result in benevolent behavior. We still need to be reminded; no, we need to be commanded to do good to believers.

Anyone who has been part of a church discovers just how difficult this can be. Some give up and quit fellowshipping with believers because they are so fleshly, so immature. But others, along with Paul, see church, the fellowship of Christians in church, as an incubator for growing in love and good deeds. Community is always messy, and a church is a community of believers in the truest sense. Rather than expecting perfection from others, we each need to attend to doing good especially to those whom we call brother and sister in Christ, even those to whom it is difficult to do good!

Lord, help me to do good to my brothers and sisters in Christ, patiently, lovingly and graciously, because that is what You ask them to do to me.

Authentic Communication

Galatians 6:11

11 See with what large letters I am writing to you with my own hand.

Paul is coming to the end of his treatise to the Galatian believers. Scattered throughout his writings are historical and personal tidbits like the one found in our verse today. While seemingly innocuous, statements like this are quite important in understanding the background and context for Paul's writings. Two questions arise. First, why was this verse included in the letter to the Galatians, and second, what insight does this give us into Paul's method of ministry?

Paul often used what scholars call an amanuensis, one who writes from dictation of another. For example, Romans 16:21 indicates that a fellow named Tertius physically wrote Paul's letter to the Romans. He was a secretary who took down the apostle's dictation. Whether an amanuensis wrote the entire letter to the Galatians except for this verse or whether Paul penned the whole letter himself is debated. But, the fact that he includes this line for emphasizing the importance of the letter's content is not debated.

Paul's drawing attention to his handwriting has evoked much discussion among Bible scholars. Clearly, this line acted as his imprimatur validating the authority behind the letter. Why the large letters? Could it be that, as one who worked with his hands in tent making, he was not accustomed to the fine motor-skills of a scribe? Could it be a literary means of emphasis, akin to using bold face or italics, as writers today would? Or, would it be a veiled indication of poor eyesight? After all, Paul had suffered beatings prior to this point in his ministry (see Acts 14:19). And, earlier in this same letter he had written, ". . . For I bear you witness that, if possible, you would have plucked out your eyes and given them to me" (Gal. 4:15), implying, possibly, that the apostle had some sort of eye problem. Why else would the Galatians have been willing to "pluck out your eyes" for him? At best, these are conjectures, but one thing we can say for sure is that Paul wrote this line because of his passion for the Galatians believers. He wanted them to know for sure that this letter was from him and that he felt strongly about its contents. After all, he wrote some pretty strong things in this letter, for example, anyone who preached a different gospel is twice cursed (Gal. 1:8-9).

Of course, we do not have any of the original autographs of the apostle (the original parchment that he wrote), so we cannot observe his actual handwriting. But, the original audience for his letter would have read it and seen it as a mark of authorization.

Lord, thank You for all who served in the transmission of Your Word, from the apostles, to amanuenses, to accurate copyists and to faithful translators.

Stand Firm For the Truth

Galatians 6:12-13

¹² Those who desire to make a good showing in the flesh try to compel you to be circumcised, simply so that they will not be persecuted for the cross of Christ. ¹³ For those who are circumcised do not even keep the Law themselves, but they desire to have you circumcised so that they may boast in your flesh.

Axiomatic is the idea that people who attempt to gain righteousness by keeping the Law, also feel urged to compel others to do likewise. The competitive spirit, or rather, the root issue of pride over others, drives this. If I can coerce someone to live as I live, I will always be one-up then, because I was there first and I got them to follow me. Once they follow me, I am in a more powerful position to continue in that superior role, dictating, as it were, my whims and wishes—of course, all disguised as laws required by God.

The reality, though, is that when a person behaves like that, it is all for show, not for substance. In the case of the false teachers among the Galatians, the motivation was to avoid persecution that comes with espousing the outrageously counter-cultural, counter-religious idea that God became man and died for our sins. The cross of Christ speaks of the helplessness and vanity of humans trying to do the good for which we were created. Those who refuse to believe this are left with trying to "make a good showing in the flesh." They have no other recourse.

The grand irony is that the way of the Law brings failure, because those who try to keep it cannot keep it fully. Being circumcised is not enough for justification. Yet, circumcision is enough for prideful boasting. The tragedy is that those who live by the Law set their boast on something that ultimately will be their undoing.

Why would someone not jump at the opportunity presented in the good news of the gospel? The answer: it is the darkened heart that Jeremiah spoke of, "The heart is more deceitful than all else And is desperately sick; Who can understand it?" (Jer. 17:9). Jesus called it this way in addressing the Pharisees and scribes, "So you, too, outwardly appear righteous to men, but inwardly you are full of hypocrisy and lawlessness" (Matt. 23:28) and "Woe to you, scribes and Pharisees, hypocrites, because you travel around on sea and land to make one proselyte; and when he becomes one, you make him twice as much a son of hell as yourselves" (Matt. 23:15). So, Paul saw the error of pharisaical legalism arising again, which it has continued to do throughout church history. That's why this letter to the Galatians remains relevant even today.

Lord, help me stand firm and uncompromising for the truth of the gospel of grace that comes through the death of Your Son, the Lord Jesus Christ.

A Legitimate Boast

Galatians 6:14-15

[14] But may it never be that I would boast, except in the cross of our Lord Jesus Christ, through which the world has been crucified to me, and I to the world. [15] For neither is circumcision anything, nor uncircumcision, but a new creation.

B oasting, by one definition, is "an act of talking with excessive pride and self-satisfaction." Where the law-based religious person boasts in his fleshly efforts and in the converts he makes to his way of religion, the Christian can boast in something different.

We are so accustomed to thinking that all boasting is un-Christian, an exalting of oneself in comparison to others. But, any validity to that is specious for two reasons: 1) There is always someone who is better at doing whatever we boast about in ourselves; we are somewhat selective concerning to whom we compare ourselves. 2) We assume all other things are equal in the comparison of our lives with others. For example, a person who boasts that he owns the biggest boat, is the most educated person in the group, or the best athlete fails to acknowledge the many advantages he has, not of his own doing. He has been born into a wealthy family that can afford such amenities as sports development camps, elite schooling or inherited fortunes. So in every area of life, boastful comparisons cannot be valid, for no two lives have everything else equal. Especially in the religious area is boasting vain. Even then, what difference does it make to boast that one does more law-keeping than the next, when both fall so woefully short?

But there is something we can validly boast in, something that surpasses all comparisons—and that is "the cross of our Lord Jesus Christ." That is the apostle's boast, and it should be ours as well. All acts of righteousness are completely eclipsed by what Christ has done in sacrificing Himself for our sins. It has brought about in the believer a new creation. Everything changes at the point of salvation. In another place, Paul wrote, "Therefore if anyone is in Christ, he is a new creature; the old things passed away; behold, new things have come" (2 Cor. 5:17).

Paul couldn't stop talking about it, with excessive pride! This was not pride in himself, but in another, the One who provided a perfect sacrifice for sins. This truth, when rightly understood, is so overwhelming that it separates us from the worldly way of religion. Paul describes it as a personal crucifixion of the world to ourselves and ourselves to the world. We are dead to a religious way of thinking, and alive to the freedom that comes through God's grace.

Lord, thank You for my new life in Christ, being freed from a system of laws and regulations, and alive to Your grace.

Fitting Conclusion

Galatians 6:16-18

[16] And those who will walk by this rule, peace and mercy be upon them, and upon the Israel of God. [17] From now on let no one cause trouble for me, for I bear on my body the brand-marks of Jesus. [18] The grace of our Lord Jesus Christ be with your spirit, brethren. Amen.

B elievers walk by the grace found in the cross of our Lord Jesus Christ. That's our life; that's our boast. Paul's letter to the Galatians has been crescendoing to that conclusion, and he concludes that we should "walk by this rule." This does not mean Christians are obligated to follow a new set of rules in a legal sense. The underlying Greek word for "rule" is the Greek word canon. It can be translated "standard" or "measure." Grace through faith is the standard for the Christian life; it is the overriding principle, the modus operandi for life. It is our entry into righteousness and the continuity of our spiritual experience.

The early church of the 2nd-3rd centuries came to use the phrase, "rule (canon) of faith." This concept, which was important for establishing which writings were accepted into the canon, was understood as "a summary of the tenets held in common by the churches of apostolic foundation: it is closely related to what is called 'apostolic tradition.'" As Christianity spread after the demise of the apostles and as new writings appeared, the standard of accepted teachings was that which had been accepted by the churches as a whole. At its core was the doctrine of justification by grace, as asserted in this letter.

To those who live by the principle of grace, Paul wishes peace and mercy, and he likewise wishes that on the true Jewish people who trust in the Messiah. His wish for peace and mercy may find its source in his own struggles and longing for peace and mercy for himself. His life as an apostle was not easy, involving permanent physical scars to his body. He sees them as branding marks identifying him with Christ, and all for the defense of the gospel of grace. So, he appeals to his detractors in Galatia, in essence, to quit striving against the message and to let the truth reign in peace. One can almost hear the sigh of a life of suffering, longing for the day of peace.

Finally, he closes with his signature desire for his readers to experience the grace of our Lord Jesus Christ, at a deeply spiritual level.

In conclusion, we have seen that the letter to the Galatians has involved three main movements. In chapters 1–2, Paul defends his apostleship; in chapters 3–4, he presents the doctrine of justification by grace through faith, and in chapter 5–6, he presents the "duties" of a life walking in grace.

Lord, help me know and defend this great doctrine of justification by grace through faith in the Lord Jesus Christ, for this is foundational to all of life.

WEEKEND READING

Saturday – Matthew 27:1-32
Sunday – 27:33-66

_____

_____

_____

_____

_____

_____

_____

_____

_____

_____

_____

_____

_____

_____

_____

_____

_____

_____

_____

_____

_____

_____

_____

_____

_____

Ephesians

No Higher Praise

Ephesians 1:1-2

¹ Paul, an apostle of Christ Jesus by the will of God, to the saints who are at Ephesus and who are faithful in Christ Jesus: ² Grace to you and peace from God our Father and the Lord Jesus Christ.

Paul saturates his letter to the Ephesians with great doctrinal truth, a primary one being that of Christ's beloved body, the Church. As with his letters to the Romans and Galatians, Paul identifies himself as the sole author and stresses his apostleship—probably reflecting the emphasis on the letter's doctrinal content. His other letters are co-authored by Timothy, Silas, etc., the exceptions being his "personal" letters to Timothy. One might say those letters reflect more the outworking of doctrinal truth in the life of the church and individuals.

He writes to the "saints"—what an elated salutation for believers to hear. The term is never meant to distinguish so-called holy men with halos. It occurs 61 times in the Bible (NASB version) and refers simply to Christians. It means we are "called-out ones" who have been set aside as special to God. Even the carnal Corinthian believers were called "saints" (1 Cor. 1:2)!

In contrast to the Corinthians, the apostle describes the Ephesian believers as "faithful in Christ Jesus." There is no higher praise a Christian can receive, reminiscent of Jesus' comment about the servant's reward, "Well done, my good and faithful servant" (Matt. 25:21 NLT). This letter represents not a reprimand for any major failings, but an encouragement to walk in the solidness of their faithfulness. To be sure, no church is perfect, and the letter does contain some correction. However, the Ephesian believers had a solid foundation of teaching and were doing relatively well in their spiritual walk. They had been favored with over two years of Paul's teaching, extended ministry by Aquila and Priscilla, and the powerful preaching of Apollos (see Acts 18–19).

But, doctrinal truth needs to be combined with love or it stagnates. The Ephesian church began well and continued well in their doctrinal beliefs. But, within 40 years, they began to fade in the outworking of that doctrine. When Jesus addressed the seven churches in the Book of the Revelation, the Ephesian church was the first mentioned and the first castigated. The issue was not doctrinal unfaithfulness, but loss of their first love (Rev. 2:4). Right doctrine is not enough! "If I . . . know all mysteries and all knowledge . . . but do not have love, I am nothing" (1 Cor. 13:2).

Paul includes his signature "grace and peace to you," not merely an idle salutation, but a genuine desire for his readers, including us.

Lord, thank You for calling me to be special to You, to be a saint. This is an undeserved blessing. In You alone, I have grace and peace.

Blessings Overflowing

Ephesians 1:3-5

³ Blessed be the God and Father of our Lord Jesus Christ, who has blessed us with every spiritual blessing in the heavenly places in Christ, ⁴ just as He chose us in Him before the foundation of the world, that we would be holy and blameless before Him. In love ⁵ He predestined us to adoption as sons through Jesus Christ to Himself, according to the kind intention of His will ...

"Riches eternal and blessings supernal from His precious hand I received." It's true, as the hymn goes and as Paul outlines in verses 3-14. His praise is to God for what He has done through the Lord Jesus Christ. And, what is that? Paul begins with the summary statement, "every spiritual blessing." What an all-inclusive statement! There is not just one, but all heavenly blessings that we as His children possess. We may not always see the blessings in our earthly experience, but we apprehend them by faith as though they were ours now—and they are ours; we count on them, by faith as we look to our Lord.

Paul spells out some of the blessings for us. We are chosen in Him. This decision took place long before He created the cosmos (the literal rendition of the Greek word translated "world." You and I are wanted by the Creator of the Universe! He desired you and me. And. His choosing us had a purpose, namely that we would live holy lives, apart from sin, as we live for Him.

This choice was not a sterile one calculated for profit as a commercial transaction for God's benefit. It was not a choice designed to improve things in the spiritual realm, as though by adding us to His family, somehow God is trying to add some value to Himself. Nor is it God carrying out some sterilized unaffected decision in the bowels of the Godhead to fulfill the academic, doctrinal mandates of ecclesiastical theologians.

God was motivated by love. The phrase "in love" in the original language can go with either the preceding phrase or the following phrase. This whole section is actually one long run-on sentence; a thing Paul likes to do on occasion when he is on a roll with a thought. It is best taken as a reflection of the Lord's love being the overriding motivation for blessing us.

This love includes a pre-determining. Calvinist and Armenian theologians have long argued over predestination vs. free will of men. Suffice it to say that both are true. God predestines; humans are responsible for our free choices, and somehow, God has it all figured out without any contradiction. We rather rejoice, though, in being chosen and adopted, by God's choice. How much more blessed can we be?!

Lord, what an amazing God You are for choosing to adopt me as Your child. That represents a blessing that surpasses them all. How kind of You!

His Grace, Our Assurance

Ephesians 1:6

⁶ ... to the praise of the glory of His grace, which He freely bestowed on us in the Beloved.

W hat an exclamation coming from the pen of the apostle Paul,! Every word pregnant with meaning, the sum of which is a high response to deep theological truth. The blessings outlined in verses 3-5 evoke praise. Here is one excited apostle! And, we should be as well, when we consider the blessing of being adopted by the Creator God of the universe.

A figure of speech called a metonymy is used in praising "His grace," where a characteristic of a person is used in place of the person himself. In this case, the praise for God is expressed as a praise for His grace. We are wonderful beneficiaries of His unmerited favor, His simply choosing us by an inward motivation that flows out of His character. He is not gracious because His gracious acts make Him that way, as though He were not gracious before He acted graciously. No, that would mean He became gracious. Rather, He acted graciously toward us because He is by character gracious. So, it is natural that He acts toward us that way, because that is the kind of Deity He is. He didn't become that way, He was and is and will always be that gracious.

Literally speaking, it is the "glory of" His grace that Paul is praising. The term "glory" comes from the idea of solidness, weightiness. It was originally used by the ancient Greeks to describe a weighty structure, like a Corinthian column. It was heavy, substantial. In time, the word came to be used in describing a person's character, and the verb form ("to glorify") was used to reveal or show a person's true character. So, Paul is saying that God showed the weightiness, the real character, of His grace in adopting us as His children. When we consider how unworthy we are, it speaks volumes about His actions and the greatness of His character of grace!

As if that wasn't praise enough, the apostle goes on to write that God's choice was entirely free; He was not compelled by anything outside of Himself, certainly not by any works of righteousness we might have done that would indebt Him to us. He freely blessed us as a pure choice of His sovereign will.

Does this choice of God in predestining us to adoption (as verse 6 puts it) negate our free will? No. Paul is not addressing that topic, which so fascinates and confounds arm-chair theologians today. Elsewhere, he makes clear that we are responsible for our choices, in particular, our choosing to confess Christ (see Romans 10:9-10). However, God's choice is dimensionally different than our choices. Praise God that it is so, for His grace is our assurance!

Lord, I, too, praise You for the glory of Your grace in Christ, the Beloved.

Crazy Grace

Ephesians 1:7-8

⁷ In Him we have redemption through His blood, the forgiveness of our trespasses, according to the riches of His grace ⁸ which He lavished on us. In all wisdom and insight ...

Recurring throughout the section is the phrase or concept, "in Him." This was flagged in verse 3 where we discover that all spiritual blessings in heavenly places are "in Christ." The outline of those blessings in this section won't let us miss this emphasis due to the repetition. In Christ, in Him, before Him, in love, through Christ, according to His will, in the beloved, in Him. It's all about the person of our Lord Jesus Christ. Our blessings are intimately, intricately and irrevocably connected with our relationship to Him!

Here, we see that our redemption happened "through His blood." That involved forgiveness of those things which alienated us from God in the first place. To redeem means to buy back or to free from captivity by payment of a ransom, to release from debt or blame. It is a special kind of purchase. In our case, we belong to God by virtue of being created by Him. But through sin, we have trespassed where we ought not to have gone; we have stepped over the bounds. God paid the ransom to free us from our alienated situation. Paul does not go into further detail here, sufficing to simply state the truth.

How much did this cost Him? On the surface, it cost Him the blood of Christ, meaning His death. But, notice Paul, continuing to use words of high praise, asserts that it was "according to the riches of His grace." He is still extolling God's grace, which before was "freely bestowed on us in the Beloved." His grace is "rich" beyond our comprehension. And out of His wealth, He lavished grace on us! God was not miserly, as though reluctantly giving in to something that He was compelled to do. He was generous to the max.

One woman completely missed the point of God's lavish grace when she said, "I may need God's grace, but I don't need it as much as that man over there." Grace needed must be a lavish grace; there is no other grace. Partial grace or measured grace is not grace at all.

The last phrase of verse 8 can be taken either here or with the next verse, as reflected by the various translations. Paul, in the original Greek text, as we mentioned before wrote what some might call a run-on sentence. In actuality, all of what God has done in Christ reflects His wisdom and insight. His grace is not an emotional whim, but fits within His eternal master plan. He designed, before anything was created (vs. 4), a plan to demonstrate His grace. Young people today might call this crazy grace. It's all about Him and His crazy grace!

Lord, thank You for bringing me into the inner circle of grace, in Christ.

Mystery Solved

Ephesians 1:9-10a

⁹ ... He made known to us the mystery of His will, according to His kind intention which He purposed in Him ¹⁰ with a view to an administration suitable to the fullness of the times, that is, the summing up of all things in Christ, things in the heavens and things on the earth ...

E veryone likes a mystery. In a sense, the entire Old Testament contains clues of a mystery, namely, what God had planned for the world. The sacrifices since the time of Adam and Eve (animals had to be killed for the skin coverings), the promise of blessings to Abraham, and the prophecies pointing toward a Messiah—these were all clues. Albeit, they provided hope for a continuously rebellious people, that someday, somehow God would take care of the sin problem once and for all, both for the Jews and also for the Gentiles.

God finally revealed the mystery, and Paul was the one to receive it and make it known. In the letter to the Ephesians, Paul outlines what that mystery is. It was something not fully understood before, but now it has been made known.

At this point in the letter, Paul only makes reference to it as "an administration." This term could be translated as "stewardship" or "the management of one's household." The mystery had to do with how God was managing things. It was the full revelation of His plan, as it was "the summing up of all things." Keeping with his theme in this opening salvo of truth, the plan is "in Christ." The Lord Jesus Christ was the pinnacle of God's revelation to the fallen world, of all God's character and person. In particular, Christ reflects all the wisdom and insight (vs. 8) of God. In other words, this revelation of God's mystery, this administration of grace, is His "Big Idea," the truth that sums it all up.

Notice, this plan is not just for the Jews, or just for the earth, but it is a plan that encompassed all of creation, including the heavens (notice the term "heavens" is plural, referring not to the abode of God, but to interstellar space, and, thus, the universe). We infer from this that whatever God may be doing throughout the universe is related to what Paul writes about in this letter. If there turns out to be life on other planets, they are affected by this same plan of God.

Now, His plan all along was to reveal the solution to the mystery when it was "suitable to the fullness of the times." The subject of the mystery is found in the Lord Jesus Christ. "But when the fullness of the time came, God sent forth His Son, born of a woman, born under the Law . . ." (Gal. 4:4). The full implications will be set out by Paul in this letter.

Lord, knowing that You have an overriding plan for the universe helps me live my daily life with purpose. Thank You.

WEEKEND READING

Saturday – Matthew 28
Sunday – Mark 1

PERSONAL REFLECTIONS

Prized Possession

Ephesians 1:10b-12

[10] ... In Him [11] also we have obtained an inheritance, having been predestined according to His purpose who works all things after the counsel of His will, [12] to the end that we who were the first to hope in Christ would be to the praise of His glory.

The Ephesian church was noted for their wealth of biblical teaching as we have pointed out before, so Paul's writing takes on a deep theological tone. In this opening salvo from verses 3 to 14, we are taken on a whirlwind of truth concerning our relationship with God. In our passage for today, what we have "in Him" includes an inheritance. We have been "blessed with every spiritual blessing . . . in Christ" (vs. 3), chosen "in Him" (vs. 4), adopted as sons "through Jesus Christ" (vs. 5), and grace "has been freely bestowed on us in the Beloved" (vs. 6)—since all this is true, it follows that "in Him" we have "an inheritance." Everything that belongs to Christ now belongs to us by inheritance as sons of God.

Christ has led the way, provided the way, is the way to our coming to the full experience of God's purpose for creating us (see John 10:10; 14:6). His plan was to bring us into full sonship with all its rights and privileges, as it were. I remember as a young Christian walking down a street and passing a majestic tree, enjoying the truth of this inheritance. My thought at the time was that the tree belonged to me, because it was my heavenly Father's tree. Jesus had said, "The meek will inherit the earth." It was mine, waiting for full possession when Christ returns.

Paul relishes the fact that his generation of Christians was "the first to hope in Christ." These, in particular, would be the Jewish believers. We conclude this because the phrase should literally be rendered "first to hope in *the* Christ," which has a distinctly Messianic flavor that Gentiles would not have been accustomed to hearing. He does include his readers, which means you and me, as well as the believers at Ephesus, in the next verse. The desired result is that our hope in Christ will bring "the praise of His glory."

Our being redeemed to the place of sonship comes by the grace of God and is designed to show how great our heavenly Father is. Adam, in the pre-fall condition, did not know God in this way. But, once sin entered the world, the stage was set for God's glory to be made known through grace by the substitutionary death of Christ for us, to bring us into a place, not just as God's creation made in His image, but now as adopted sons and co-heirs with Christ!

Lord, You see me as Your prize possession. Keep reminding me of the great inheritance that is mine, because of my position of being "in Christ."

The Great Promise Keeper

Ephesians 1:13-14

[13] In Him, you also, after listening to the message of truth, the gospel of your salvation—having also believed, you were sealed in Him with the Holy Spirit of promise, [14] who is given as a pledge of our inheritance, with a view to the redemption of God's own possession, to the praise of His glory.

"In Him" is the repeated emphasis of this introduction to Paul's letter to the Ephesians. He is not absent-mindedly repeating himself. The recurrence is designed to draw our attention to the fact that we are "in Him", and it is there where all the blessings find their fulfillment and ultimate expression. Here Paul reminds us that being "in Him" is a state of being that begins after we responded to the "the message of truth, the gospel of your salvation." In other words, after we believed and were saved.

Of particular note is that we were sealed at that point in time. Faith and salvation are not something that happens gradually over a period of time, just as sealing is not a gradual thing. One is either sealed or not sealed; one cannot be partly sealed, for that is the same as not being sealed at all. Furthermore, who God seals, no one can unseal. So, this speaks to the assurance we have in Christ. Our part in salvation has been completed, namely believing the message. God's response is the sealing.

Making this absolutely clear, Paul says we were sealed with the Holy Spirit of promise. This means that every true believer has received the Holy Spirit at the moment of salvation. He is the promised One (see Joel 2:28; Acts 1:4, 8). And He Himself, the Holy Spirit, is the promise, in that He is the pledge of our inheritance. The working of the Holy Spirit in our lives is a foretaste of when our full redemption is realized, when we as God's possession, come into the full expression and fulfillment of our adopted sonship. What a blessing this promise of inheritance is. It is, as Peter says, "an inheritance which is imperishable and undefiled and will not fade away, reserved in heaven for you . . ." (1 Peter 1:4).

This also speaks to our sanctification. In salvation, we have been made holy: "And by [God's] will we have been sanctified through the offering of the body of Jesus Christ once for all" (Heb. 10:10). This is what theologians call positional sanctification, that is, God has set us aside as His own special people. But, we are also being made progressively holy, "For by one offering He has perfected for all time those who are sanctified." (Heb. 10:14). We begin to experience now in part what we will experience later in whole. That is a promise, a pledge by the Holy Spirit, for God's glory. To Him be praise!

Lord, I praise You for the great promise of an inheritance with Christ. I trust You because You always keep Your word.

What a Reputation!

Ephesians 1:15-16

15 For this reason I too, having heard of the faith in the Lord Jesus which exists among you and your love for all the saints, 16 do not cease giving thanks for you, while making mention of you in my prayers ...

Thankfulness marks the Spirit-filled Christian, and it characterized the apostle Paul. In each of the letters he wrote to the churches, he gave thanks to God for them—except for the Galatian church where he was deeply concerned over their doctrinal drift back to legalism. Being thankless is one of the fateful steps leading away from God (Rom. 1:21). Paul mentions the word 40 times (if you count Hebrews as being written by Paul) and continually calls his readers to be thankful to God.

In our passage today, the apostle has good reason to be thankful for the Ephesian Christians. Their faith and love are exemplary, and word has gotten back to him about the reputation they are building. Paul knew about these things to some degree, based on first hand observation, for he had been among them for over two years teaching and doing many miracles. His ministry had resulted in mass repentance and turning to the Lord by both Jews and Greeks (Acts 19:10-19). The conclusion of his personal ministry there was summarized, "So the word of the Lord continued to increase and prevail mightily" (Acts 19:20).

So, Paul observed the response of faith by the Ephesians to the gospel message. And, word had reached him that their faith continued to grow and that they responded by living out their faith through love toward each other. With Paul, faith by itself was not enough, it needed to be accompanied by or result in active loving actions toward others. The Ephesians were not like seed planted in rocky soil or thorny soil. There was the fruit of love.

The author of the Book of James would enthusiastically agree with Paul here. Faith without works is dead—in particular, works of love. Of course, works of love do not save, but they are the demonstrated evidence of true faith. With the Ephesians, their love had no blinders on; it was lavished on all believers without discrimination—note, there were both Jewish and Gentile believers in the congregation! It is no wonder Paul gave thanks continually. They were, in modern terminology, a success story.

Oh, that the Ephesian church would have stayed that way, but by the end of the first century, the Lord said to them, "But I have this against you, that you have abandoned the love you had at first" (Rev. 2:4).

Lord, help me to be a thankful, loving person, reflecting the genuineness of my faith in You. Today I choose to actively demonstrate my love for You and others.

Growing In Knowledge

Ephesians 1:17-18

[17] ... that the God of our Lord Jesus Christ, the Father of glory, may give to you a spirit of wisdom and of revelation in the knowledge of Him. [18] I pray that the eyes of your heart may be enlightened, so that you will know what is the hope of His calling, what are the riches of the glory of His inheritance in the saints ...

Continuing his prayer, Paul moves from thankfulness to request. It was his practice to let people know how he was praying for them. Further, his pattern was to pray specifically to God the Father. In Scripture, we are encouraged to praise and honor the Son, and to some degree, we may bring our requests to Him (see John 14:14). However, the predominate teaching of the New Testament is that, when we bring our needs and requests, we pray to God the Father in the name of the Lord Jesus Christ. Jesus Himself said, "In that day you will not question Me about anything. Truly, truly, I say to you, if you ask the Father for anything in My name, He will give it to you" (John 16:23).

Paul prays that God would give the Ephesians a deeper wisdom and knowledge of Christ. Peter wrote similarly, ". . . but grow in the grace and knowledge of our Lord and Savior Jesus Christ . . . (2 Peter 3:18). Spiritual maturity comes in the progressive appreciation of the depths of knowing Christ. This is not just superficial awareness of the facts about Christ, but an intimacy of the nuances and depth of Christ as the manifestation of God Himself. Paul writes elsewhere "He is the image of the invisible God, the firstborn of all creation" (Col. 1:15). The author of Hebrews writes, "He is the radiance of His glory and the exact representation of His nature, and upholds all things by the word of His power . . ." (Heb. 1:3). There is so much to learn about the Lord Jesus Christ—we will spend eternity plumbing His depths more and more. Paul asks the Father that his readers would make progress in this very thing.

Further, Christian maturity, as Paul prays for, includes a growing insight into the hope that we have, what we really have to look forward to as believers. He describes the object of our hope, "the riches of the glory of His inheritance in the saints." We Christians have a perspective that in essence is otherworldly. The hopes and goals of this world are temporary and cannot sustain the human spirit. Our inheritance is Christ Himself, who is eternal. Therefore, we look forward to His return. This is what He has called us to, and this is one of the key transformational truths that keep Christians going when, from all human perspective, there is no hope. We have been called to a higher plane of life where Christ is presently seated in glory and we are "in Him" (see 1:3).

Heavenly Father, I want to keep learning more and more about Your Son, and all His glory, for it is in His name I pray.

With Knowledge, Power

Ephesians 1:19-20a

[19] ... and what is the surpassing greatness of His power toward us who believe. These are in accordance with the working of the strength of His might [20] which He brought about in Christ, when He raised Him from the dead ...

With knowledge comes power, as the saying goes. In this case, adding to the knowledge of Christ, the hope of our calling in Him, and the riches of our inheritance (as we saw in the previous two verses), Paul here speaks of knowing God's power. Again, this is not just awareness of the fact that God is almighty. Certainly, we believe God was powerful enough to create the vast universe, and His power is reflected in the so-called "powers of nature," like huge ocean surf, volcanic eruptions, and the like.

But, the knowledge here is about God's "power toward us who believe." This means a personal, intimate, experiential knowledge that comes through salvation. Paul's prayer is that God's power might be seen increasingly in the lives of his readers. This is the same power that raised Jesus from the dead. In his letter to the Romans, the apostle ratified this idea when he wrote that Jesus "was declared [to be] the Son of God with power by the resurrection from the dead, according to the Spirit of holiness" (Rom. 1:4). So to the Ephesians, he writes of that kind of power being our experience. And, he emphasizes it by referring to it as "working," "strength" and "might." All the power of God is at our disposal; we simply need to grow in our understanding of it.

Lest some think this is a watering down of the idea of power, we need to consider what this means. First, we were spiritually dead (in our trespasses and sin), but God has made us alive in Christ. We were lost but now are saved. We had rebellious hearts against God, but He has turned our hearts to Him. We were condemned under the law, but now we are forgiven under grace. We were slaves to sin, but now we have victory through Christ. "I can do all things through Him who strengthens me" (Phil. 3:15). All these speak to God's power.

God's power has accomplished everything that God has purposed to do. We saw in the first part of this chapter all that God has done for us in Christ. To take fallen human beings and make us into children of God requires nothing short of a miracle of the highest order. This same power is at work "toward us who believe." In other words, it is not just the power to raise us up to new life, but also the power to help us live the new life. That is the power we need to know. That is the power we need to understand—the power of God to help us walk as adopted children of God.

Lord, help me move beyond the basic facts and to intimately know the power of the resurrection in my life. Help me today to see Your power at work in my life.

Weekend Reading

Saturday – Mark 2
Sunday – Mark 3

PERSONAL REFLECTIONS

_____

_____

_____

_____

_____

_____

_____

_____

_____

_____

_____

_____

_____

_____

_____

_____

_____

_____

_____

_____

_____

_____

_____

_____

_____

_____

_____

_____

_____

_____

Above All Else

Ephesians 1:20b-22a

20 ... and seated Him at His right hand in the heavenly places, 21 far above all rule and authority and power and dominion, and every name that is named, not only in this age but also in the one to come. 22 He put all things in subjection under His feet ...

Exalted above all, that is, well, an exalted description of the Lord Jesus Christ at the present time. He has been installed in the position of prominence over all creation. The details of this passage are specific and highly instructive. He is "seated," meaning His work is completed. This took place upon His ascension into heaven (see Mark 16:19). Earthly priests offered repeated sacrifices which can never take away sins, and thus, could never sit down with finality from their work (Heb. 10:1). However, Christ's priestly work was completed, having offered for all time one sacrifice for sins, and so, He sat down finally and completely (Heb. 10:11-12).

The locus of His sitting was at the Father's right hand (which is noted 10 times in the book of Hebrews), which is in the heavenly places, where our blessings are also found (Eph. 1:4). Is it any wonder Paul reminds us of this connection, in light of what Jesus said, "Where your treasure is, there your heart will be also" (Matt. 6:21)?

This place where Jesus currently resides and where our blessings are treasured is a place of authority. It is not just a protected place or passively occupied by Jesus. He reigns and nothing exists higher than Him. (We do not at this time enter the theological debate about the relationship of the authority of the Father and the Son. We simply observe here that to be seated at the Father's right hand is to share fully in the Father's authority).

This authority extends to all that exists. That includes every and all governing authorities. Jesus had taught His disciples this truth in seminal form at the time of the great commission when He said, "All authority has been given to me, go therefore and make disciples . . ." (Matt. 28:18-19). There is nothing more compelling and more comforting to know in any circumstance of life than this, that our God is in control. Nothing oversteps His sovereignty. Demons are now, and will be shown to be, nothing more than His footstool (Heb. 1:13; 10:13). Even Satan is subject to God's permission (Job 1-2). And ". . . at the name of Jesus every knee will bow, of those who are in heaven and on earth and under the earth . . ." (Phil. 2:10). And so, with our blessings and our position in Christ, we are compelled to fall before Him as our Lord and obey Him.

Lord Jesus Christ, You are my Sovereign and Master. You have been so good to me, and I worship and adore You, for You alone are worthy.

Practice Reflects Belief

Ephesians 1:22b-23

22 ... *and gave Him as head over all things to the church,* 23 *which is His body, the fullness of Him who fills all in all.*

The Lord Jesus Christ is over all creation, and He is the supreme commander in chief of the church. The Greek word kephale, translated head, refers to authority. It was commonly used as a metaphor for the leader of an organization like a general over an army. Christ is the authority over everything in the church; He holds the position of prominence and is the focal point of the glory.

This is true by virtue of the fact that the church is His body. Of course, this is a metaphor and pictures the relationship of believers to Christ very aptly. We are to Him as a body is to its head. The head is the nerve center, the central processor, which controls the rest of the body. When you hit your thumb with a hammer, the nerves transmit a signal to the brain in your head, which interprets this as pain. The head in turn sends a signal to the other hand to drop the hammer and hold the hurting thumb tightly. It all works together, under the control of the brain. In the same way, Christ is the head of the body.

Crucial at this juncture is to ask what is His goal as head of the church? Paul states it simply, God desires the church to be the fullness of Christ. Tomes have been written about this through the writings and in the lives of Christians in church history. But, the fullness of Christ has also, and more fully, been made known as Christians live, learn, worship and fellowship together today. Christ is made known as we minister Him to one another, when we become the channels of the grace God has promised us. In some ways, the saying is right, that the church is God's incubator for Christian growth and service.

There are corollaries to the truth that Christ is the head of the church. No man should dare take on that role! The pervasive practice today, sad to say, is for churches to have a hierarchy type of authority structure with the pastor or "senior" pastor ruling and ministering over all. One man is at the pinnacle of the organization. This is simply unbiblical and dishonoring to Christ who is the Head of the church. Lip-service may be given that Christ is the "invisible" head, but actions reveal true beliefs. For too many, the real leadership of the church requires an organizational head, like a spiritual CEO. But, we have no New Testament teaching of an earthly head to the Church universal or the church local. The standard of governance is a plurality of godly men called elders, who are very clear about their position as under-shepherds, with Jesus Christ being "The Chief Shepherd" (1 Peter 5:4).

Lord, help me keep focused on You only as my spiritual head. While I thank You for the spiritual teachers and leaders in the church, no one takes Your place.

Spiritual Hindsight

Ephesians 2:1-3

¹ And you were dead in your trespasses and sins, ² in which you formerly walked according to the course of this world, according to the prince of the power of the air, of the spirit that is now working in the sons of disobedience. ³ Among them we too all formerly lived in the lusts of our flesh, indulging the desires of the flesh and of the mind, and were by nature children of wrath, even as the rest.

"Stark" describes the contrast between our present life as believers and our past life as unbelievers. We "were dead in our trespasses and sins!" After Paul digresses to shape out what that death looked like, he completes the thought in verse five where he writes that God, "made us alive with Christ." The difference is huge, not to be minimized as though believers have only turned over a new leaf, or have improved their lives with a religious overlay. We were dead, but now we are alive. This reminds us of the man healed by Jesus who said, ". . . one thing I do know, that though I was blind, now I see" (John 9:25). The difference is a quantum distinction of epoch proportions. Just imagine today if a long dead relative came walking into your room. The implications would be no less than that of which takes place at spiritual conversion, when a spiritually dead sinner places faith in the crucified, risen Savior!

The deadness needs to be stressed, though, because it provides the necessary contrast for appreciating the brilliance of the new life. Some teach that there is a spark of goodness in all and that, therefore, faith in Christ is a good option for improving one's life. But, that is not what the Bible teaches. Our deadness was exhibited in behavior which fit right into this world. Like a fish in the water may not feel wet, our behavior seemed normal to us—but we were dead spiritually. Our spiritual deadness, what we used to be as unbelievers, is described in verses 2-3, in rapid fire succession. It was in keeping with the influence of Satan, "the prince of the power of the air," and we were his "sons of disobedience." Paul further describes it as including the lusts of the flesh and the desires of the mind. We lived with no higher standard than ourselves, namely what's good for me, what's in it for me—a self-centered way of life. We need to remind ourselves of what we were, so that we are motivated to avoid falling back into living like that. Peter rejoins, "For the time already past is sufficient for you to have carried out the desire of the Gentiles, having pursued a course of sensuality, lusts, drunkenness, carousing, drinking parties and abominable idolatries" (1 Peter 4:3).

Lord, when I think back of what I was, I am ashamed. But, I don't want the shame of continuing in that way. I praise You for Your grace and forgiveness.

Not My Love, But His

Ephesians 2:4-7

⁴ But God, being rich in mercy, because of His great love with which He loved us, ⁵ even when we were dead in our transgressions, made us alive together with Christ (by grace you have been saved), ⁶ and raised us up with Him, and seated us with Him in the heavenly places in Christ Jesus, ⁷ so that in the ages to come He might show the surpassing riches of His grace in kindness toward us in Christ Jesus.

Mercy is mentioned only once in Paul's letter to the Ephesians. Often repetition is used to emphasize something, for example, "grace" is mentioned twelve times in this letter. However, the singular use of a term can bring a poignant, startling emphasis, highlighting something through understatement. We who were dead in sin deserved judgment and condemnation because we were "sons of disobedience" who lived in step with God's arch enemy, "the prince of the power of the air" (vs. 2). God owed us nothing but rejection for eternity. We have even more reason than Isaiah had who, when he saw the vision of the Lord on His throne, said, "Woe is me, for I am undone" (Isaiah 6:5 NKJV). The NLT translates that anguished cry, "It's all over, I am doomed."

But, Mercy! Rich mercy! Great love with which He loved us. Not just a little. He made us alive! We couldn't do it ourselves because we were totally incapable. The very nature of our condition rendered us condemned and unable to remedy the situation. God acted in mercy, grace and love, and saved us from our predicament.

Paul is on a roll, and the believer's heart rejoices with him. We have been raised up "with Him." Our new life is connected with the resurrection of Jesus. Further, we are seated "in the heavenly places in Christ Jesus," which is also where we experience all the blessings in Christ (see 1:4). It's now a done deal, our salvation, and we can rest in Christ, secure for eternity, for we are already made alive, already raised, already seated and already blessed with every spiritual blessing we will ever have. And, God will continue to show just how great His grace is to us. As we live for Him and grow in our understanding of what we are and have in Christ, though we will never come to fully understand, we will continue for eternity constantly being amazed in the increasing awareness and appreciation for who He is and what He has done.

Someone asked a group of Christians to think about when they came to love Christ in a deeper way and how that changed them. One person responded, "When I came to love Christ is not the issue for me. But, when I came to realize how much He loved me, that's when things began to change in my life."

Lord, thank You for saving me from a lost, dead eternity without You. I want to learn more of Your love, mercy and grace for me.

A Done Deal

Ephesians 2:8-9

⁸ For by grace you have been saved through faith; and that not of yourselves, it is the gift of God; ⁹ not as a result of works, so that no one may boast.

Longtime staple of evangelism, this passage provides a concise statement about the gospel of grace and faith as opposed to a merit-based religion. And, that is good news, indeed. All religions of the world are, in some sense, meritorious, that is, they teach that salvation or attainment of the ultimate spiritual objective is based at least in part on the individual's own efforts. In other words, standard human spirituality agrees that a person must be good in order to attain salvation (whatever that might mean in a given religion). However, in contrast to that false thinking, the good news from God is that, as these verses point out, nothing a person can do will merit salvation.

Paul carefully chose his words. First, grace is the cause of our salvation. He again (see Ephesians 1:6) uses "grace" as a metonymy (a literary figure of speech), where the word is used for "the God who acts in a gracious way." Salvation is first and foremost an act of God that is unmerited and undeserved by the recipient. Second, faith is the means by which God has saved us. Faith is not a "work" as though it merits for us salvation. Rather, it is simply the avenue by which God has determined grace to become operative in a person's life.

Third, salvation is a done deal with present results. The tense of the verb is very specific. The believer "has been saved." That means an action that took place in the past and has enduring effects. We are in the state of "saved-ness" as a result of being saved in the past.

Paul follows with four terse inferences to this truth. First, the salvation by grace through faith that he speaks of is "not of yourselves." Technically, this phrase could be translated, "not out of yourselves." Salvation does not originate with the individual, and it is not caused by the individual. Let the reader take careful note of this. Second, it is God's gift to us. While the Greek word for "grace" (charis) earlier in the verse is related to another Greek word for "gift" (charisma), Paul uses a different word here for gift, "doron," to remove any possibility of ambiguity. This salvation is a gift freely given by God to us, with no cost on our part. To suggest that a person can earn salvation by his good works is to insult God. As if that is not clear enough, the apostle adds, "not a result of works." Finally, the end game of his reasoning is that no one can boast that he has done anything of merit to earn salvation, all are on an absolutely equal footing.

Lord, thank You for Your lavish gift of salvation. I commit to serving You, not in order to gain salvation, but in response of gratitude for what You have done.

WEEKEND READING

Saturday – Mark 4
Sunday – Mark 5

_____
_____
_____
_____
_____
_____
_____
_____
_____
_____
_____
_____
_____
_____
_____
_____
_____
_____
_____
_____
_____
_____
_____
_____
_____
_____
_____
_____
_____
_____
_____
_____
_____
_____
_____
_____
_____
_____

Original Craftsmanship

Ephesians 2:10

¹⁰ For we are His workmanship, created in Christ Jesus for good works, which God prepared beforehand so that we would walk in them.

Doing good is what we were made for, that's the point of this verse. We should do good works. In our zeal to stress that good works is not a requirement of salvation, we fail to realize that our need of salvation is precisely because we failed to do the good works that we were created for. But, this concept needs unpacking, lest we miss the important message of this pericope, or short collection of verses (8-10).

We were created with God's exquisite craftsmanship, where He used Himself as the blueprint for our design. In biblical terms, we were created in His image (Gen. 1:26). While we share certain physical characteristics with other creatures, like arms, legs, heads, etc., we share certain characteristics with God. Classically, theologians tell us these include having emotion, intellect and will. But, also included are the ability to have a personal relationship with God, to have both soulish and spiritual self-awareness, and to have the capacity to willfully share in God's creativeness. In other words, we were created to reflect Him in our lives. Our creation was "in Christ," as our verses today say, meaning the second person of the trinity was intricately involved in our creation and is involved in the outworking of God's purpose in our lives.

Now, God's purpose was well thought out before we were even created and was not just some afterthought. We were created with God's purpose in mind in accordance with His image, representing Him in life. Our problem came when we failed to live up to the purpose for which we were created. Our failure to do good works is merely symptomatic of our failure to obey Him. But, His purpose for us has never changed, namely to live our lives reflecting Him, that is, to do good things in this world.

It stands to reason that salvation (with all that means, including forgiveness, redemption and restoration) cannot be attained through human efforts of good works because, simply put, we have proven ourselves incapable of doing it. In fact, one failure is sufficient to reveal us as sinners, spiritual failures. It is written, "For whoever keeps the whole law and yet stumbles in one point, he has become guilty of all" (James 1:20). God's solution is the gift of grace which we receive not by works, but through faith. And as saved believers, we are now back on track to do what we were created to do, reflect the image of God in the works He created for us to accomplish in our lives. Salvation apart from good works is precisely a salvation that restores us to doing good works.

Lord, fan the flame of desire in me to do the good works You created me to do.

The Blood Connection

Ephesians 2:11-13

[11] Therefore remember that formerly you, the Gentiles in the flesh, who are called "Uncircumcision" by the so-called "Circumcision," which is performed in the flesh by human hands— [12] remember that you were at that time separate from Christ, excluded from the commonwealth of Israel, and strangers to the covenants of promise, having no hope and without God in the world. [13] But now in Christ Jesus you who formerly were far off have been brought near by the blood of Christ.

Gentile believers were Paul's primary audience in this letter. And, he calls attention to the fact that prior to faith they did not enjoy the benefits of God's promises that the Jews enjoyed. They had no hope and were alienated from God, the One who created them. The Jews, for their part, despised the Gentiles and used what amounted to a racial slur in calling them the "Uncircumcision." They took great pride in their own "Circumcision." These terms referred to the outward "surgical" sign that God had given to Israel which marks them out as a people separated to God, special. However, the Jews were nationally arrogant about holding to the outward form but were lacking in the faith necessary for an authentic relationship with God.

Gentile believers do well to remember this. Apart from Christ, non-believers have no promises from God to hope in; they are without Him. They are strangers to all that God was doing in the world. However, though we were like that, now that we have believed, we have been brought into an intimate relationship ("brought near") with God. We are "in Christ," as Paul has repeated throughout the letter. And, it is on account of "the blood of Christ."

Sometimes, Christians like to speak of the blood as though there was something different about the physical properties of Christ's literal blood, something almost magical—as though if one could have captured a few drops of it at the time of Christ's crucifixion, it could be enshrined as a holy relic. However, the blood is used simply as representing the sacrifice required for our salvation, just like the blood of animals in the Old Testament represented the life of the animal (Gen. 9:4; Lev. 17:11, 14). Blood was so associated with an animal's life that it became synonymous with the life itself. Jesus, therefore, left behind a memorial for us to repeatedly practice, namely taking the bread and wine as symbols of His body and blood. So, the blood of Christ has become entrenched in our minds as the enduring representation of Christ's giving of His life for our salvation. How important it is for Christians to continually remind ourselves of the blood shed for us through the practice of the Lord's Supper!

Lord, thank You so much for the death of Your son, the Lord Jesus Christ who shed His blood for our redemption. And, thank You for the weekly reminder.

The Mystery Plan—Part 1

Ephesians 2:14

¹⁴ For He Himself is our peace, who made both groups into one and broke down the barrier of the dividing wall ...

This is the mystery Paul referred to earlier, captured in three verses (14-16), that was hitherto unknown anywhere before. Certainly, it was known that God would bless all the nations through Abraham, not just the Jews. It was also known that the blessings would somehow come through the Jewish people, God's chosen ones, the descendants of Abraham, Isaac and Jacob. What was not known until this time, certainly not as clearly as Paul writes it, was that God would not require the Gentiles to become Jewish in order to receive the blessings, and furthermore, that God would treat the Gentiles and the Jews identically, in terms of the blessings. The Gentiles would not be second class citizens in the kingdom.

In Christ, Jews and Gentiles, are no longer two groups, but one. Paul writes elsewhere, that, "There is neither Jew nor Greek, there is neither slave nor free man, there is neither male nor female; for you are all one in Christ Jesus" (Gal. 3:28). Our peace with God does not depend on any distinctions, whether gender, economic or ethnic. All that matters is grace on God's part and faith on our part (see Ephesians 2:8-9).

We have seen hints of this truth in the historical unfolding and propagation of the gospel, particularly in the story of the conversion of Cornelius, the Roman centurion, and the question whether the Gentiles could receive the faith and the gift of the Holy Spirit (Acts 10-11). The fledgling church wrestled with this and finally accepted Gentiles into the fold. And, of course, the Jerusalem counsel of Acts 15 struggled with and finally accepted that Gentiles were not required to be circumcised. It was at that time Paul wrote his treatise to the Galatian churches where he made this point clear—circumcision was not required for salvation because faith preceded and grace superseded the Law. Paul is the one, however, who lays out this full truth, explained clearly!

That which divided Jews and Greeks, namely the Law, has been broken down. August 13, 1961 marked the beginning of the construction of the Berlin Wall that divided West Berlin from East Berlin and the surrounding East Germany countryside. It came to represent what was known as the Iron Curtain, the ideological divide between the east and the west during the Cold War. But, November 9, 1989, destruction of the wall commenced and free flow of movement began again. The Iron Curtain, as it were, came down. So also in Christ, the dividing wall between Jews and Gentiles came down.

Lord, thank You for tearing down that wall!

The Mystery Plan—Part 2

Ephesians 2:15-16

15 ... by abolishing in His flesh the enmity, which is the Law of commandments contained in ordinances, so that in Himself He might make the two into one new man, thus establishing peace, 16 and might reconcile them both in one body to God through the cross, by it having put to death the enmity.

The dividing wall was torn down between the Gentiles and the Jews; the two have been made into one group, as the previous verse declared. Now, Paul continues by explaining how that came to be. That dividing wall was the Law of Moses, and it distinguished the Jews from all others. They were unique, set apart from the rest of the world. The Law was the sticking point for Gentiles. Prior to Christ coming, in order for Gentiles to experience the full blessing of God, they had to embrace the Law of Moses, that is, they had to become Jews. They had to become, as it were, proselytes, converts to Judaism. So, in that sense, the Law was "enmity," or the cause of friction, between Gentiles and Jews. Contemporary Judaism made a big deal of this distinction.

In Christ, now, the sticking point is neutralized, it is no longer the barrier to Gentile blessing as it once was. Note particularly that this took place through a physical event, "in His flesh . . . through the cross." Christ's death removed the division. His death fulfilled the Abrahamic covenant of blessing to the nations of the earth (that is, Gentiles) by removing the distinction of Jew/Gentile in terms of receiving the blessing. This was a complete surprise! It had been so ingrained in the Jewish mindset that they were a special people to God, that their ethnicity became a source of enormous pride. The Jews by and large had difficulty with the notion Paul writes of here, as can be seen by their constant harassment of him in his travels.

God's plan to reach the world was through the Jews first (Rom. 1:16). The message and promises come through the Jews (Rom. 3:2). Jesus, the ultimate message, was a Jew. But, that didn't mean Gentiles had to become Jews to be rightly related to God. God brought the two together not by Gentiles becoming Jews, but by both being made into one new group. God reconciled that new group to Himself, re-establishing peace with His image-bearers.

In coming to faith, Jewish people must accept the fact that, just like Gentiles, they must come to God by grace through faith (Eph. 2:8-9). To be sure, God still has a unique plan for the Jewish people, played out in the prophetic future. But, in terms of salvation and the spiritual life, there is no difference now between Jew and Gentile. There are not two churches, one for believing Jews and one for believing Gentiles. There is one Church and one faith (see Ephesians 4:5).

Lord, thank You for making peace for us by Your grace!

Open Access to God

Ephesians 2:17-18

[17] And He came and preached peace to you who were far away, and peace to those who were near; [18] for through Him we both have our access in one Spirit to the Father.

The "One Church" doctrine is so important; Paul gives detailed teaching to drill the point home. By this we are not referring to modern ecumenism where all the denominations of so-called Christendom unite and set aside their differences. Right biblical doctrine is never to be compromised for the sake of an outward show of unity. There are serious differences between biblical Christianity and many forms of religious "Christendom." Certainly, the claim of Roman Catholicism to be the mother church, to which all derivatives should ultimately return, is scripturally unfounded. Many down through the centuries charge that it has long departed from biblical Christianity. Any unity today must center around apostolic doctrine as presented in Scripture which holds the ultimate authority for spiritual life and practice for all Christians everywhere.

Paul's concern with unity addressed the issue of how Gentile converts were to relate to Jewish believers. He wrote of this unity as being a great mystery revealed to him through the inspiration of the Holy Spirit. Christ's goal was to bring peace with God to humanity, both Gentiles and Jews. Did not the angels at Christ's birth proclaim to the shepherds, "Peace on earth, good will toward men." That peace certainly has to do with peace among people, but more importantly, it has to do with our relationship with God. Christ came preaching a peace with the Creator God against whom people have rebelled. God sends the dove with an olive branch.

Notice, specifically in our passage today, that Christ's message was intended for two groups of people. The first group of which he writes are his readers, the Ephesians. He says, "to you who were far away." The Ephesian congregation was largely Gentile in character, and as Gentiles, they previously had been far away because of the "dividing wall of enmity," the Law. Then, Paul writes of "those who are near." He uses the third person pronoun, referring not to his readers, but to others. In this case, those who are near refers not to a geographical nearness, but a spiritual nearness to God. The Jews were near to God because they had the oracles, or the written revelation of God, in the Law, the prophets and the other Old Testament writings, "But the word is very near you, in your mouth and in your heart, that you may observe it" (Deut. 30:14).

Now, in Christ and through Christ, the living Word, we have access to the Father in one Spirit. Both Jews and Gentiles have the same access.

Lord, thank You for the completely open access we have in and through Christ.

WEEKEND READING

Saturday – Mark 6:1-32
Sunday – Mark 6:33-56

_____
_____
_____
_____
_____
_____
_____
_____
_____
_____
_____
_____
_____
_____
_____
_____
_____
_____
_____
_____
_____
_____
_____
_____
_____
_____
_____

A Firm Foundation

Ephesians 2:19-20a

19 So then you are no longer strangers and aliens, but you are fellow citizens with the saints, and are of God's household, 20 having been built on the foundation of the apostles and prophets,

S ince Jews and Gentiles are now one people in our standing before God, we all have a privileged status. We Gentile believers are not on the outside but are "fellow citizens" and members of God's household through faith.

This new "one group" is like a building; the apostle uses this metaphor to picture the ramifications of the mystery of one church that includes both Jews and Gentiles. There is a common foundation, that being the teachings of the apostles and prophets. The apostles were crucial because they were Christ's authorized representatives of what He taught. The early believers in Jerusalem following Pentecost "were continually devoting themselves to the apostles' teaching" (Acts 2:42). As Christianity spread, apostolic authority was the supreme test of orthodox teaching, that is, the standard of truth. All teaching had to agree with what the apostles taught and represented as Christ's teachings.

The prophets' ministry was supplemental to the apostles' ministry because the apostles could not be everywhere. Both gifts, apostles and prophets, formed the foundation of the growing church movement. These gifts are no longer operational in the sense of being present day giftings. However, the foundation endured through the testament of Scriptures and "is inspired by God and profitable for teaching, for reproof, for correction, for training in righteousness" (2 Tim. 3:16). All teaching and spiritual life today must be built squarely on that foundation.

This truth has enormous implications. The so-called teaching of "apostolic succession" is unapostolic! That is the erroneous teaching that present day bishops are part of a succession of authority traced back to and carrying the same authoritative role as the first apostles. First, nowhere does Scripture teach that the gift of apostleship is transferrable to others. Second, if apostles still existed today, the foundation would be continually being built. The image of a building with a foundation would lose its metaphorical value. Once a foundation is built and finished, the building itself is constructed. To change the foundation would render the building unstable. We now have the apostolic and prophetic writings of the New Testament as our infallible, unchanging, authoritative and foundational guide. Authority today resides not in a church magisterium of bishops, but in the Word of God.

Lord, thank You for giving us Your word that records the foundational teachings. We know we can build our lives and ministries on a sure footing.

A Welcome Dwelling

Ephesians 2:20b-22

20b ... Christ Jesus Himself being the corner stone, 21 in whom the whole building, being fitted together, is growing into a holy temple in the Lord, 22 in whom you also are being built together into a dwelling of God in the Spirit.

Metaphorically speaking, the apostles and prophets are the foundation of the church, and our passage today indicates that Christ is the cornerstone. This image is different than the image Jesus gave, "I also say to you that you are Peter, and upon this rock I will build My church; and the gates of Hades will not overpower it" (Matt. 16:18). There is no difficulty in admitting that Scripture uses different metaphors to describe similar but slightly different things. Jesus was speaking of the rock-like faith that Peter expressed (the Greek word for "rock" and the word for "Peter" are related but different words, one meaning "rock," the other meaning "stone"). The existence of the church is dependent upon faith in Christ, a faith which Peter so eloquently expressed.

In terms of building up the church, the process began with apostolic teaching. The twelve apostles were the first to teach the faith. Everything else builds on that foundation. In other words, the work of helping the church to grow is rooted in and connected to what the apostles originally taught. The church began at Pentecost with the apostles' ministry and continued to grow on their active ministry through their lifetimes. Today, we have their teachings in the written New Testament, and we continue to build on that foundation.

Our passage expands the metaphor to say that Christ Jesus is the cornerstone. The word actually refers to the capstone of a building, the uppermost stone that finished it off and held it altogether. It was somewhat like the middle piece in an arch or the top piece that bound two walls together like a modern day framing plate. Christ is in that position in the image.

This in no way contradicts Paul's teaching elsewhere, "For no man can lay a foundation other than the one which is laid, which is Jesus Christ" (1 Cor. 3:11). Apostolic teaching embodied the truth of Christ and His teachings, so both passages say the same thing. The emphasis here, though, is on the building up of the Church, and Christ is involved at every step of the process. Paul uses the phrase, "in Him." The growth of the church is "in" Christ. We are being built up, fitted together, growing together. God is preparing us as a residence for Himself. This is the church, not just a social organization, or a religious institution. We are the very dwelling place of God in this world! This is the place where He finds Himself at home in this world.

Lord, I want to be part of that great building up of the people of God, so that You will find Yourself welcomed as You live through our community of faith.

The Mystery of Grace

Ephesians 3:1-3

¹ For this reason I, Paul, the prisoner of Christ Jesus for the sake of you Gentiles— ² if indeed you have heard of the stewardship of God's grace which was given to me for you; ³ that by revelation there was made known to me the mystery, as I wrote before in brief.

P aul begins an idea in verse 1, then digresses to another related thought before recommencing his first thought in verse 14. The intervening verses have proved difficult for translators to punctuate. Verses 2-7, for example, comprise one long sentence in the Greek. This freeform movement of his writing indicates a heightened excitement over the truth about which he writes.

The thought Paul begins in verse 1and continues on with in verse 14 can be summarized this way, "Because of this truth of the mystery, namely, God has reconciled both Jew and Gentile, as one group of people to Himself, we should pray for a deepening love for His people and a greater understanding of God's love for us. After all, we are part of the same body." But, the thought gets interrupted with a further, excited commentary on the mystery he has revealed.

Notice here, Paul identifies himself as the "prisoner of Christ" (see also 4:1; 6:20). He wore that title proudly. This reminds us of Peter and John who rejoiced "that they had been considered worthy to suffer shame for His name" (Acts 5:41). He wrote this letter from jail. The usual word people would use here would be that he languished. However, it is difficult to describe Paul as ever languishing. He carried on quite an active writing ministry while there.

He makes clear that he was given the unique stewardship of this truth. He did not arrive at it through human reasoning; it came by revelation from God. Now, we don't know exactly when this happened. Possibly, it came in rudimentary form during the days after his conversion. He was told by God, through Ananias, "Go, for he is a chosen instrument of Mine, to bear My name before the Gentiles and kings and the sons of Israel" (Acts 9:15). He was privileged to preach the gospel primarily to the Gentiles. Peter affirmed this when he acknowledged that Paul " had been entrusted with the gospel to the uncircumcised, just as Peter had been to the circumcised" (Gal. 2:7).

The full mystery was that God's grace extended not just to the Gentiles, but it extended equally to the Gentiles as to the Jews. This was a huge truth that Paul could not speak about enough. It was his major contribution to the cause of Christ. Grace fully extended to both Jew and Gentile alike. That is why he breaks out from his thought to extol this great truth once more.

Lord, Your grace is so wonderful, because it reached even me.
I praise You for bringing me into Your heavenly family.

A Great Truth Extolled

Ephesians 3:4-7

⁴ By referring to this, when you read you can understand my insight into the mystery of Christ, ⁵ which in other generations was not made known to the sons of men, as it has now been revealed to His holy apostles and prophets in the Spirit; ⁶ to be specific, that the Gentiles are fellow heirs and fellow members of the body, and fellow partakers of the promise in Christ Jesus through the gospel, ⁷ of which I was made a minister, according to the gift of God's grace which was given to me according to the working of His power.

Continuing to extol the revealing of the great mystery, Paul gives more details. In calling Gentile believers "fellow-heirs," he refers to their equal standing with the Jewish believers. Again, he reiterates the underlying truth that there is only one church; it is not a Jewish church, and it is not a Gentile church. It is one church, one "body," one "fellowship," and we are all partakers of the one "promise," that is the promise of Christ Jesus.

The basic concept here is that Christ's death brought salvation to all who believe. What an amazing act that was on God's part. However, it is a bigger story that has enamored the apostle. It is the way God brought about this salvation. It was no longer just a Jewish thing. Christ's death removed the distinction that had been so long in effect, a distinction in which the Jews had too great a pride and which Gentiles had to accept if they were to relate to God.

While earlier Paul emphasized his unique role in communicating this "mystery," he makes clear now that this was revealed to the other apostles and prophets. In particular, Acts 11–12 shows, for example, how Peter learned of this truth in his dealings with Cornelius, the Roman centurion who came to faith and received the baptism of the Spirit. Nevertheless, the truth that God would remove the Jew/Gentile distinction in bringing about salvation was something that was not previously known. In fact, Peter explains it this way, "As to this salvation, the prophets who prophesied of the grace that would come to you made careful searches and inquiries, seeking to know what person or time the Spirit of Christ within them was indicating . . . It was revealed to them that they were not serving themselves, but you, in these things which now have been announced to you through those who preached the gospel to you . . . things into which angels long to look" (1 Peter 1:11-13). This has come about only through God's work in bringing the Church together. The Church is a direct result of God's mystery being revealed. Old Testament prophecies of salvation find their fulfillment in the Church. And God wants us to understand this truth, this insight into the mystery.

Lord, apart from Christ's death on the cross, the only access to You would have been through the Law. Thank You for making the way of grace through faith.

Least Of All Saints

Ephesians 3:8-10

⁸ To me, the very least of all saints, this grace was given, to preach to the Gentiles the unfathomable riches of Christ, ⁹ and to bring to light what is the administration of the mystery which for ages has been hidden in God who created all things; ¹⁰ so that the manifold wisdom of God might now be made known through the church to the rulers and the authorities in the heavenly places.

Overwhelmed, the apostle Paul gushes with the amazing privilege and blessing of being God's servant for the message of the mystery of grace. Yet, humility is the instinctive response of a heart embraced by grace. While he can confidently write with great logic and clarity about the mystery of grace, he is overcome with the thought that God would use him, of all people!

Paul, when he contemplates the greatness of the truth of God's mystery of the church, sees himself as the most unworthy person to be its messenger. He considers himself "the very least of all saints." One might be tempted to think Paul was simply speaking with rhetorical flourish to emphasis his point. But, we rather think he actually believed this self-assessment. In another place, he wrote, "I was formerly a blasphemer and a persecutor and a violent aggressor . . . It is a trustworthy statement, deserving full acceptance, that Christ Jesus came into the world to save sinners, among whom I am foremost of all" (1 Tim. 1:13, 15). The apostle was not given to isolated self-abasement during times of depression. This was a common refrain, "For I am the least of the apostles, and not fit to be called an apostle, because I persecuted the church of God" (1 Cor. 15:9).

Paul understood grace. Paul was overwhelmed by grace. His self-denigration did not drag him into the morass of depression but positioned him to rejoice that he had not only been accepted by grace but also had been graced to be a servant of God to spread the news of that grace. He understood that the grace He experienced was great enough to reach the Gentiles as well. It was the same grace, and it would be overwhelming for the Gentiles as well.

For Paul, this was unfathomably rich! In the Old Testament, God was known as gracious, but that understanding was infinitesimally small compared to what Paul had learned from God and what he was spreading to the whole world. In the church, God is gathering all people who come by grace through faith—it is not a Jewish thing, but a grace thing. The unseen world stands by as the truth unfolds. The Church's existence serves as God's object lesson to the angels who longed to understand these things. They are finally having their "aha" moment. Now, it all makes sense to them (see 1 Peter 1:12).

Lord, I stand with the apostle Paul as "the least of all saints", and I also join him in praising You for wanting to use me . . . of all people!

WEEKEND READING

Saturday – Mark 7
Sunday – Mark 8

PERSONAL REFLECTIONS

_____
_____
_____
_____
_____
_____
_____
_____
_____
_____
_____
_____
_____
_____
_____
_____
_____
_____
_____
_____
_____
_____
_____
_____
_____
_____
_____
_____
_____
_____

Bold and Confident

Ephesians 3:11-13

¹¹ This was in accordance with the eternal purpose which He carried out in Christ Jesus our Lord, ¹² in whom we have boldness and confident access through faith in Him. ¹³ Therefore I ask you not to lose heart at my tribulations on your behalf, for they are your glory.

The mystery of God's grace in bringing together Jews and Gentiles into one body, the church, was His divine plan all along. And, Jesus Christ, His Son and our Lord, is at the center of this magnificent truth. We today have a hard time appreciating the significance of this. The divide was so deep in the Jewish mind of that day that, without this emphasis, the real danger existed of having two separate churches, two separate peoples of God. In speaking of the Gentiles, Jesus had said, "I have other sheep, which are not of this fold; I must bring them also, and they will hear My voice; and they will become one flock with one shepherd" (John 10:16). Then, Jesus prayed in the upper room, "that they may all be one; even as You, Father, are in Me and I in You, that they also may be in Us, so that the world may believe that You sent Me" (John 17:21).

The oneness of His people was a big issue for the Lord! This was to be neither a Jewish oneness nor a rejection of Jewishness. It was to be a oneness that incorporated both Jew and Gentile in such a way that the distinction between the two is irrelevant. What matters now is that we all "have boldness and confident access through faith in Him." How much better can it get! The good news is a message for everyone, an invitation to relationship with God! This comes by God's gracious provision for us in Christ, through simple faith.

Think of that for a moment. We mere creatures, among millions and millions of human beings, like specks, ants on the huge piece of earth floating in an immense universe of billions and billions of stars—we simple, minute creatures are made in the image of God. Though we are fallen, having sinned against an infinitely holy God, we now have access to God, unfettered and unhindered! That is an impossibility for us humans, but not for God. We not only have access, but He wants us to come to Him boldly and confidently. What a privilege and honor. What a grace! Therefore, the apostle writes, his readers should not be overly concerned about his incarceration and suffering, for the believers are the huge beneficiaries and it is Paul's privilege and joy to suffer so that they and others can hear the message of the mystery of God. Yes, being a messenger of God's grace can and often does result in persecution and hardship. But, it is all worth it for the sake of God being glorified for His great grace.

Lord, help me not to shrink back from suffering for the grace of the gospel message. In that message, others hear about the access to God they can have.

Wildly Powerful

Ephesians 3:14-16

[14] For this reason I bow my knees before the Father, [15] from whom every family in heaven and on earth derives its name, [16] that He would grant you, according to the riches of His glory, to be strengthened with power through His Spirit in the inner man ...

Connecting everything he has said about the revelation of the great mystery of God in the church, Paul breaks out into prayer. And, his prayer is instructive. The truth is one thing; living it out is another—he prays for strength.

Like many things in the Christian life, there is an "already" and a "not yet." In God's eyes, the church is already a unity; in practice, we need to live up to that unity. We are already one in Christ, but we are not yet fully experiencing that oneness. This oneness is humanly impossible for we are self-driven individuals with our own highest good motivating our behavior. Divine truth and empowering are required to overcome this self-ward inertia. So, Paul's prayer comes at a very propitious time in his letter. The rest of the letter will be dealing with application of the truth of one church—this prayer forms the bridge from doctrine to practice. In fact, divine help is always the connector between the mind and the feet, what we know and how we walk, what we think and how we live. We need God's help.

The first thing we notice in this passage is that we need to focus on the family nature of the church. This is the predominant metaphor used of the assembly of God's people in the New Testament. We are a family, whose head is God the Father. Churches today get caught up in the organizational structure, the hierarchy, the professionalism of pastoral staff. They identify with a prominent preacher, the size of their building and the multiplicity of programs so that they miss the truth—namely, that the church is first and foremost a family. This should affect every aspect of church life. And, following Paul's example in this prayer, we should take every problem and every situation to the Father.

Our primary identity as a church is not with a specific denomination or movement. Further, we need His strength and power, not just the latest church growth gimmick, high-tech, multi-media Sunday technologies or latest cultural-spiritual lingo. We need genuine Holy Spirit power and inner strength that takes root deep in our lives, that reflects the riches of His glory. God is able to make us wildly powerful to live the Christian life of unity. It takes that kind of strength to experience the fullness of our unity in Christ. This is the gift of God's blessing in unveiling the great mystery of the Church.

Lord, I need the strength of Your power to live in unity with other Christians. This both reflects Your glory and reveals Your glory.

What the Church Needs Now

Ephesians 3:17-19

[17] ... so that Christ may dwell in your hearts through faith; and that you, being rooted and grounded in love, [18] may be able to comprehend with all the saints what is the breadth and length and height and depth, [19] and to know the love of Christ which surpasses knowledge, that you may be filled up to all the fullness of God.

"What the world needs now, is love, sweet love." So goes the popular song from the 1960's. It is true, but not in the worldly sense. In particular, what the church needs is love; that's for certain. The unity that God has established must be nurtured with sacrificial behavior for the benefit of each other. It is no mistake that Paul mentions the word "love" twenty times in this letter on the doctrine of the church. Fellowship and unity cannot be experienced apart from active love among believers.

So, Paul's prayer is fourfold: 1) that Christ may dwell in our hearts through faith, 2) that we would be able to comprehend the love of Christ, 3) that we would be able to know the love of Christ, and 4) that we would be filled up with the fullness of God.

It is true that Christ has come "into" every believer, in the sense that we have "received Him" (see John 1:12; Galatians 2:20; Romans 8:10), though this is ultimately metaphorical language that pictures Christ as being physically inside of us in some spiritual-spatial sort of way. The concept in our passage today has more to do with Christ being at home in our lives as a welcome resident. It speaks of a familial relationship, and it happens as we live by faith, believing it to be so, but also living consciously with the sense of His welcomed presence in our lives.

This dwelling of Christ in us is what gives a foundation for reaching out in love toward others, in a way that expands beyond our human capacity. No man has yet to discover the full extent of the love of Christ. But, we delve deeper as we build upon the love foundation of Christ. In loving, with all the difficulty that entails, we increasingly appreciate His love for us, with all the difficulty that entails for Him —the sacrifice on the cross.

Notice that this discovery comes in the context of the community of believers, whom Paul calls "saints." We are called out "in love," founded upon His love, so that we might grow "in love" by reaching out "in love" to others. This is what sets Christians apart from the world. Did not Jesus Himself say, "By this all men will know that you are My disciples, if you have love for one another" (John 13:35)? That is the fullness of what God is all about!

Lord, teach me more of Your love that I might grow in Your love as it works in me and works through me in loving others.

God At His Best

Ephesians 3:20-21

20 Now to Him who is able to do far more abundantly beyond all that we ask or think, according to the power that works within us, 21 to Him be the glory in the church and in Christ Jesus to all generations forever and ever. Amen.

Overflowing with exuberance, the apostle gushes with praise for God. This was his pattern of writing—no dry, academic dissertation here. See Paul's monumental work on the doctrine of Justification (we call it the Epistle to the Romans) where he lays out in eleven chapters, painstakingly tight, logical detail, the foundational truth of Christianity, the gospel of grace in all its glory. There the apostle can no longer contain an academic theologian demeanor, and breaks out in doxology: "Oh, the depth of the riches both of the wisdom and knowledge of God! How unsearchable are His judgments and unfathomable His ways! . . . For from Him and through Him and to Him are all things. To Him be the glory forever. Amen." (Rom. 11:33-36). Likewise in other places, Paul becomes overwhelmed with the greatness of the truth about which he writes.

So here, the truth of the mystery that the Jew and Gentile have been brought together in one body by the grace of God in Jesus Christ sends Paul into a moment of spiritual reflection and effervescent praise. It's almost like, from human perspective, God has outdone Himself; as when an artist produces a piece of work that completely surpasses all his other works, in quality, design, color and nuance. He has outdone himself, and the piece is far and away better in every way than anything he has done before.

In God's case, all His work is excellent: "O LORD, our Lord, how excellent is Your name in all the earth" (Ps. 8:1 NKJV). "The whole earth is full of His glory" (Isa. 6:3). So, God can't really "outdo" Himself because all His ways are perfect (Deut. 32:4). But, from our perspective, new discoveries of God's truth leave us in amazed wonder whether anything God does could get any better than what we have just comprehended. It's like one preacher who asked, "When was God at His best?" and then going through the major events of God's working in this world, beginning with creation *ex nihilo,* (out of nothing). Just when you think you have contemplated God at His best, you discover something newer and greater. Surely that thing must reflect the pinnacle of His greatness. In the end, God is at His best when He is able to do "beyond all we ask or think according to the power that works within us." He is changing us, revealing Himself to us, loving us and loving through us. That is when God is at His best (from our humble, astonished perspective).

Lord, I praise You for Your greatest work in my life, namely, Your grace in the Lord Jesus Christ that has worked and continues to work in my life.

Walking Worthy

¹ Therefore I, the prisoner of the Lord, implore you to walk in a manner worthy of the calling with which you have been called ...

Of all the New Testament writers, Paul uses the phrase "I therefore" (or similar) the most frequently. This reflects his tight logical reasoning. Certain truths result in certain logical inferences or corollaries. Paul was a master thinker and communicator, and the Lord used his intellectual gift of insight and deduction to convey what is called propositional truth. By propositional truth, we mean truth that is arrived at through the logical connection of propositions or factual statements. This is distinguished for experiential truth. For example, gravity is true because when you step off the cliff you fall to the ground; you know it by experience. It can also be contrasted with revelatory truth, where God speaks directly, therefore, by definition, what He says is true.

Paul, of course, conveys revealed truth, but notice that much of what he says does not begin or end with, "Thus says the Lord," as happens with so many of the prophets. There are certain revelations that Paul has indeed received in this letter to the Ephesians. For example, the mystery of the one church. However, God used Paul's logical abilities to build on and to elaborate the revealed truth. Further, these teachings, we believe, are also revelations with the same authority as the "Thus saith the Lord . . ." statements in other portions of Scriptures—the method of revelation is simply different.

Often, these elaborations of Paul's come in the form of admonishments to his particular audience, in this case the Ephesians. However, these admonishments extend to all believers everywhere, for we see by the illumination of the Holy Spirit the truth as it applies to each of us. So, from a prison cell some 2000 year ago comes the challenge to walk worthy (the same as is echoed in Colossians 1:10; 1 Thessalonians 2:12). From his incarcerated, limited confines, Paul knows the value of walking free. But, it is not just freedom of physical movement, but the manner of life he speaks of.

The controlling standard for the Christian's behavior is the "calling with which you have been called." This calling doesn't change, "for the gifts and the calling of God are irrevocable" (Rom. 11:29). While Paul goes on to describe the manner of the calling, the calling itself is to preserve the unity of the Spirit (verse 3). Prejudice is set aside, whether Jew or Gentile. Hardly would it be a stretch of inference to set aside all other prejudices, whether black, white, male or female, wealthy or poor (Gal. 3:28). We are one body in Christ!

---

*Lord, thank You for making us one. Let there not be
any partiality, racism, or bigotry in my life.*

WEEKEND READING

Saturday – Mark 9
Sunday – Mark 10

PERSONAL REFLECTIONS

_____
_____
_____
_____
_____
_____
_____
_____
_____
_____
_____
_____
_____
_____
_____
_____
_____
_____
_____
_____
_____
_____
_____
_____
_____
_____

Resemblance of Christ

Ephesians 4:2-3

² ... with all humility and gentleness, with patience, showing tolerance for one another in love, ³ being diligent to preserve the unity of the Spirit in the bond of peace.

Walking worthy has the look of six descriptors, Paul writes. These quiet, unsung characteristics of the Christian life do not get the fanfare of great prophecies, fantastic healings, or great oratory. Yet, these comprise a worthy life more than moving mountains, giving vast sums to the poor or establishing large religious organizations. They cannot be faked; they cannot be manufactured, and they cannot be mimicked for personal benefit. They are qualities of none-other than the Lord Jesus Christ, and the apostle calls upon us to set these as the focus of worthiness. (See Colossians 3:12 for a list of similar characteristics).

Humility begins the list and is reflected in many other places in Scripture (see Philippians 2:1-11; Romans 12:3, etc.), but especially in Jesus, "Take My yoke upon you and learn from Me, for I am gentle and humble in heart, and you will find rest for your souls" (Matt. 11:29). Contrary to our fallen human nature, humility is the antidote to prideful self-centeredness. I am not the center of the universe—that must be set straight before anything else.

Gentleness joins humility in Christ as well. There is no need for forcefulness in relationships with others since my agenda does not include asserting my rights and security. Christlikeness is focused on others.

Humbleness also leads to patience. By lead, I don't mean that one naturally results in the next. Rather, these are spiritually linked and feed off one another. It is difficult to be patient when one is self-centered, but the inner ego demands, however so subtly, that all others do our bidding and do it in our timetable. Patience means relinquishing my grip on time. It is not mine; ultimately, it belongs to God—and He loves the people who "take up space" in my timeline.

Tolerance, seen in this light, becomes understandably the outworking of patience. Tolerance means I make allowance for the differences between how I think things ought to be done versus how others do things. It allows others to share my space in life, and I relax my grip on my time-line and enjoy their presences regardless.

All these things can only be motivated by selfless love, agape love. This will give us a good foothold for preserving true unity, which Paul has regaled as being the great mystery of the Church, namely, we are one in Christ. This is what brings genuine "peace on earth, good will toward all men."

Lord, help me to walk in the image of Christ, displaying a close resemblance.

Trilogies of Unity

Ephesians 4:4-6

⁴ There is one body and one Spirit, just as also you were called in one hope of your calling; ⁵ one Lord, one faith, one baptism, ⁶ one God and Father of all who is over all and through all and in all.

Unity in the Church where the division between Jew and Gentile is broken down now gets further explanation. The body metaphor, one of the common images we are given of the Church, is singular. While it is true that each individual Christian is a "temple of the Holy Spirit who is in you, whom you have from God . . ." (1 Cor. 6:19), the Church as a whole also is in possession of the Holy Spirit in a unique way. It is not just a human organization, but it is seen as one body, having one Spirit. We must not lose sight of this truth!

Churches today that are often run like businesses, that are headed by pastor-CEO's and that see leadership simply as technique for efficiency miss the whole idea of "church." Collectively, we are not primarily an organization or an institution, and certainly not manmade, no matter how much the human failing may be. The church is an organism, alive, related to God as a whole.

Further, all Christians, whether Jew, Gentile or any other human distinction, are brought together by a common calling, namely the forward anticipation of "hope." We are a called out people with a common future. We are forgiven and eagerly look forward to being fully united with Christ when He returns. The apostle Peter put it this way, "His great mercy has caused us to be born again to a living hope through the resurrection of Jesus Christ from the dead, to obtain an inheritance which is imperishable and undefiled and will not fade away, reserved in heaven for you . . ." (1 Peter 1:3b-4). As believers, we anticipate the same destination, and by faith, we live that heavenly life now.

So, we have one body, one Spirit and one hope. This trilogy is followed by two more threesomes, each emphasizing the unity of the Church. There is not a Jewish Church and a Gentile Church, but one Church. There is not a white Church and a black Church. To be sure, local churches have their "flavors" and "personalities" that may reflect cultural differences. But, the primary Lordship of Christ, the doctrines of the faith, and the discipline of baptism are the same. That is because the God we Christians worship and see as our common Father is "over all and through all and in all." This last trilogy ties it all together, so there is no room for any theology that divides the church or differences in practices that should alienate one church from another. This is the outworking of our Lord's prayer, "that they may all be one" (John 17:21).

Lord, I don't pray that You would make us one, for we already are one in Christ. Help us to live the truth of this unity, for that glorifies You.

Diverse Grace

⁷ But to each one of us grace was given according to the measure of Christ's gift.

Diversity in unity. Sameness is not the point of Paul's message to the Ephesians; don't be mistaken. Unity does not mean identicalness. The beauty of the Church is that we are a kaleidoscope of giftedness all working toward the same goal, as one body in harmony. Paul turns the corner in his teaching. For three chapters, the emphasis has been on the unity we have in the Church. That foundation is absolutely essential before teaching about our individuality in the Church. Having established the foundation, it is now "safe" to speak of diversity within that unity.

Our distinctiveness as believers in the church is not set aside; in fact, each of us makes a unique contribution to the whole. This is not like the teaching of some eastern religions where the individual is absorbed into the cosmic whole, like a drop of water in the ocean loses its individuality. Our personhood is not lost to the ultimate consciousness of the universe. On the contrary, we remain individuals both here and in eternity. And, it is our specific uniqueness that adds to the color and functioning of the body of Christ, of which we are now members.

Notice, the emphasis on "to each one of us." Every Christian has received grace from God. Now, this grace is an extension of the grace of salvation, talked about in Ephesians 2:8-9, which is saving grace. For the saved Christian continues to "be graced" by God. That means, God continues to act toward and in the believer in ways the believer does not deserve. It is God at work energizing and gifting us—what a privilege that we are instruments of God in this world and in the Church!

Our grace from God speaks of His gifting (see verse 8 and 11). Now, this grace is "according to the measure of Christ's gift." In other words, each of us is given gifts in some measure. We know from other places in Scripture that our gifts are different (see 1 Corinthians 12:4-7). But, the standard for the gift has nothing to do with our merits or natural abilities, but it has everything to do with God's grace. His grace is a gift. Although the underlying Greek word for grace (charis) can at times be translated as "gift," another word (dorea) is used here for gift. The point is that the focus is on God's grace as the gift. The gift is the grace. This looks different in each believer, but the grace is the same—it all comes from God, and it is dispensed at His pleasure.

Lord, I am overwhelmed by Your graciousness in giving me a part in Your wonderful Body. Let me live out Your grace through my giftedness to others.

Ascended Gift Giver

Ephesians 4:8-10

⁸ Therefore it says, "WHEN HE ASCENDED ON HIGH, HE LED CAPTIVE A HOST OF CAPTIVES, AND HE GAVE GIFTS TO MEN." ⁹ (Now this expression, "He ascended," what does it mean except that He also had descended into the lower parts of the earth? ¹⁰ He who descended is Himself also He who ascended far above all the heavens, so that He might fill all things.)

Pivoting from the doctrine of the unity of the Church, Paul turns to the diversity of giftedness. Amidst this cantata of gifts working together for the goal of growing into the fullness of Christ (Eph. 4:7-16), we find inserted this somewhat cryptic passage. If this is an allusion to Old Testament prophecy, Psalm 68:18, as some commentator's think, then Paul would be charged with changing the text from "you have received gifts among men" (Ps. 68:18) to "he gave gifts to men." Thus, Paul would then be making an allusion to the prophecy and, therefore, adapting it, but not actually quoting it. In this view, Paul was expanding the meaning of the Psalm, under inspiration of the Holy Spirit. However, other commentators think he quoted a contemporary hymn that was familiar to the readers. This last view is supported by the way Paul introduces the thought with, "Therefore it says." This is not the usual way of prefacing Old Testament references. It is identical to Ephesians 5:14 where the phrase introduces not a Scripture quote, but most likely a verse from an ancient hymn.

In either case, the One who gives the gifts (which is the subject of Ephesians 4:7-16) is One with authority, by virtue of His victory over the spiritual enemies of God ("He led captive a host of captives," see also Colossians 2:15) and His ascension into glory. Ascension implies a descension. Jesus stated this clearly, "No one has ascended into heaven, but He who descended from heaven: the Son of Man" (John 3:13). Christendom has argued over what this means, that Jesus "descended into the lower parts of the earth." On the one hand, some believe this refers to hell, as most renditions of the Apostle's Creed state. In support of this, see 1 Peter 3:19, 20; 4:6. A variation of this is simply that God the Son descended not just to the lowliness of becoming a man, but also went to death and the grave.

However, others interpret "the lower parts of the earth" to mean earth itself, which is lower when compared to heaven. This phrase is used this way by Isaiah, "Shout for joy, O heavens, for the LORD has done it! Shout joyfully, you lower parts of the earth; Break forth into a shout of joy, you mountains, O forest, and every tree in It . . ." (Isa. 44:23). When Christ ascended, the church was formed, and God then gave the spiritual gifts to the Church.

Lord, thank You for humbling Yourself, so that You could be exalted and then distribute gifts to Your family.

Equipping—Part 1

Ephesians 4:11-12

[11] And He gave some as apostles, and some as prophets, and some as evangelists, and some as pastors and teachers, [12] for the equipping of the saints for the work of service, to the building up of the body of Christ ...

Gift giving comes by God's nature, the inherent outflow to the His image-bearers. Spiritual gifts, of which we have four mentioned in our passage (for other spiritual gifts see Romans 12:6-8; 1 Corinthians 12:8-10; 1 Peter 4:10-11) are planned by God as essential to the Church. They are part of the design, the blueprint. They are essential to all else in the church, like wings are to an airplane or air to a balloon.

We can see this more clearly when we realize that spiritual gifts are not only supernatural abilities, but the gifts are also the people God raises up to do specific things. The person becomes the gift! The gift is only of value when the person so gifted uses their gift in a way that is a gifting of themselves to the church. That is grace in full operation, building up the Church. We each are God's gift to each other!

The four gifts in our passage today are the equipping gifts. The underlying Greek word for equip means "to make someone completely adequate or sufficient for something." These four gifted kinds of people are designed to make all the other believers adequate or sufficient for doing the ministry of the local church. "The work of service" (NASB, NIV) is translated as "ministry" (NKJV, ESV, NET). Unfortunately, in modern Christendom, ministry is thought of as being what the paid, professional staff does. However, it is something all Christians are to be involved in. The four gifts here are necessary only insofar as they equip others to do the actual work of ministry. All gifts are ministry, not just these four. In a very true sense, these four gifts are really support services, not "The Ministry" of the church. The real ministry is what everyone else does.

Too much emphasis is given today to the preacher or teacher or the paid staff of the church. The four gifts are like the personnel trainers in the company, the swing coach for a professional golfer, a psychologist for marital counseling. The real work is done by the personnel of the company, the golfer and the married couple. So also in the church, these gifts support the real work being done by the rank and file who are the real workers, the true ministers of the church.

Having said all this, blessed is that church with equippers who are committed to building up others and not receiving glory for themselves.

Lord, You are the master builder of the Church. Help me to humble myself to serve others. But also let me exult in the truth that I am Your gift to others.

WEEKEND READING

Saturday – Mark 11
Sunday – Mark 12

PERSONAL REFLECTIONS

Equipping—Part 2

[11] And He gave some as apostles, and some as prophets, and some as evangelists, and some as pastors and teachers, [12] for the equipping of the saints for the work of service, to the building up of the body of Christ ...

Four spiritual enablings or gifts are listed separately from other ministries in the church. Their role is to equip ("to make someone completely adequate or sufficient for something"). Paul rewords this as "building up of the body of Christ." These gifts are like the machinery used to construct a building. Their purpose is not for their own glory and benefit; the glory belongs to the Church, the bride of Christ, which reflects the glory of Christ.

The first two, as we mentioned before, are foundational and no longer in immediate operation today now that the cannon of Scripture is closed (see comments on Ephesians 2:20). However, we benefit from the equipping ministry of the apostles and prophets in that they built up the first century church directly, and their disciples built up the next generation, and so on through the ages to the present day. Also, we are being equipped today by the writings of those apostles and first century prophets as recorded in the Word.

The third equipping gift, the evangelist, builds up the church in two ways. First, he adds to the church numerically through bringing people to salvation. Second, he teaches, trains and prompts people in evangelism. What would our outreach efforts be like without evangelists who are constantly prodding the rest of us to reach out? They are not the "paid salesman" for a product called "Christianity," but they are those who lead the way and bring others along.

The last gift, though it may look like two gifts, is really one: the pastor-teacher. The Greek grammatical structure makes a distinction in listing the last two words "pastors" and "teachers" differently than the first three. The various English translations try to account for this by the use of "the" (NIV, NLT, ESV) or "some" (NASB, NET) in front of the first four terms but not in front of "teachers." The word "teachers" goes together with the term "pastors," thus, pastor-teachers. This gift combines two abilities for equipping believers. It is a teaching ministry that has as its primary goal to shepherd other believers toward maturity and service.

Pastor-teachers are not offices of the church, like elders or deacons. This gift does not refer to the presiding clergy or "Pastor" of the church. It is simply a spiritual gift. Certainly, an elder may be a pastor-teacher, and a woman may be a pastor-teacher over other women and children. Praise God for those who give themselves to training, discipling, and mentoring others toward godly maturity.

Lord, thank You for all those whom You have raised up to help equip me to walk in a manner worthy of Christ, toward godly maturity.

Communal Maturity

Ephesians 4:13-14

[13]... until we all attain to the unity of the faith, and of the knowledge of the Son of God, to a mature man, to the measure of the stature which belongs to the fullness of Christ. [14] As a result, we are no longer to be children, tossed here and there by waves and carried about by every wind of doctrine, by the trickery of men, by craftiness in deceitful scheming ...

A lready, not yet—that is the way of describing the intersection of eternity with time. From God's perspective, the body of believers is one body; there is unity—this is the "already" aspect of the truth. As we go through time, this is being worked out daily in the life of the Church—this is the "not yet" side of things. Both are true. From the perspective of Him who dwells in eternity (Deut. 33:27; 1 Tim. 1:17; 6:16), we are a Church united, perfect and sanctified. As we go through time, we are moving toward that goal.

The task in front of us is the unity of faith. The Lord knows the constant divisions among Christians. The multiplicity of denominations and disunity within denominations and movements grieves Him. However, the answer is not found in an ecumenism based the lowest common denominator around which to unify. Unity must focus on truth (knowledge) and maturity that leads to the "fullness of Christ." Paul emphasized sound doctrine repeatedly. The truth is absolutely central.

Division in the church is inevitable if outward Christendom or organizational structures are involved. The truth may result in, indeed justify, division if the alternative is compromise. Paul was adamant to the Ephesian elders in his farewell speech, "Be on guard for yourselves and for all the flock, among which the Holy Spirit has made you overseers, to shepherd the church of God which He purchased with His own blood. I know that after my departure savage wolves will come in among you, not sparing the flock; and from among your own selves men will arise, speaking perverse things, to draw away the disciples after them." (Acts 20:28-30). Unity does not trump sound doctrine.

Maturity means not being wishy-washy in one's core beliefs. But, believers working together, as directed by the Holy Spirit, being equipped by the evangelists and pastor-teachers, help each other grow to maturity in Christlikeness as we all use our spiritual gifts. We are committed to the Lord and to each other—this is essential to become all that Christ saves us to be.

We need to know and understand sound doctrine, so that we may know Christ more intimately, growing into maturity in Him—together in unity.

Lord, thank You for making us one. Now, let us act out the truth of that so we may be considered to be walking worthy of our calling in Christ.

Growing Joints

Ephesians 4:15-16

15 ... but speaking the truth in love, we are to grow up in all aspects into Him who is the head, even Christ, 16 from whom the whole body, being fitted and held together by what every joint supplies, according to the proper working of each individual part, causes the growth of the body for the building up of itself in love.

Coming full circle back to the idea of Ephesians 4:1-3, the focus on unity is encompassed in love. It is "in love" that we are to walk in a manner worthy of our calling. And, it is "in love" that we are to speak the truth that enables the fitting of everyone together in the body of Christ. At its most basic understanding, love is sacrificing oneself for another. The ultimate statement of this, of course, is, "Greater love has no one than this, that one lay down his life for his friends" (John 15:13). Every effort in serving people is to be a self-sacrificing act of love, even to the point of what we speak to others.

Now, this is a difficult thing to do. Maybe on occasion, one could act in love. But, to act in love in everything? Yes, it may sound extreme in our narcissistic culture, but this is key to body life in the Church. We need to keep the metaphor in focus to help us see the big picture here: we Christians are like a body, whose head is Jesus Christ. The body grows under the direction of the Head. Each believer is considered a part of the body.

The apostle points out one particular part of the body for special mention, the joints. This emphasizes that which holds things together, a subtle reference to the importance of love, which is the adhesive that keeps Christians of widely disparate likes, preferences, personalities and temperaments in fellowship with one another. But, notice that every person ("every joint") is needed for the growth of the whole body (see 1 Corinthians 12).

God fits us all together, He knows what each individual local church needs and can provide. Outside the church, we can choose our friendships, neighbors and work environment. But in the church, God makes the choices for us. He has brought together just the ones He wants in the local church. If left to myself, I might not have chosen the one who has a personality clash with me, but that person's presence forces me to grow in my ability to love. I learn not to flee difficulties with people, but to work through them in a manner worthy of my calling (Eph. 4:1). In the local church, I learn the sufficiency of God's grace and the perfection of His power (2 Cor. 12:9) to change me and to mature me in Christ. And in the process, I grow to be more like Him.

Lord, thank You for the exact composition of the people in my church. You are using each one of us to bring maturity to the whole church.

Put Your Behind in the Past

Ephesians 4:17-19

[17] So this I say, and affirm together with the Lord, that you walk no longer just as the Gentiles also walk, in the futility of their mind, [18] being darkened in their understanding, excluded from the life of God because of the ignorance that is in them, because of the hardness of their heart; [19] and they, having become callous, have given themselves over to sensuality for the practice of every kind of impurity with greediness.

"**P**ut your behind in the past" is a humorous saying today that reflects the apostle's sentiment. We have already been encouraged to walk in a positive way, in the good works for which we were created (Eph. 2:10) and in a manner worthy of our calling in Christ (4:1). Now, Paul warns against walking in the ways of our pre-conversion past.

Here, the word "Gentile" is being contrasted with the people of God. Remember, the dividing wall has been broken down, and Jew and Gentile are made into one new entity, the Church. God no longer sees them as "Gentiles" (see Galatians 3:28). Our pre-Christ days are described as being "Gentile" in character—what does that mean?

In Paul's day, Greek culture predominated in the ancient Near East, having spawned the great intellectual and philosophical centers of Athens and Alexandria. Few today have not heard of philosophers Socrates and Plato. The Gentile world resonated with all things intellectual. "For indeed Jews ask for signs and Greeks search for wisdom . . ." (1 Cor. 1:22-23). Paul was very conversant in such Gentile learning, as is obvious from his writings. Yet, rather than characterizing their pre-conversion "Gentile" days as being wise and intellectual, Paul says those days are more aptly labeled "futility of the mind." Despite the elevation of human reasoning, non-believers are ironically "darkened in their understanding." He uses other terms like "ignorance" and "hardness of their heart." Clearly, a life of intellectual stimulation and acquisition without Christ renders a person spiritually callous, morally sensual and impure, and never satisfied.

Paul strongly challenges us to avoid that way of living at all costs. Peter writes similarly, "For the time already past is sufficient for you to have carried out the desire of the Gentiles, having pursued a course of sensuality, lusts, drunkenness, carousing, drinking parties and abominable idolatries" (1 Peter 4:3). Why live like unregenerate unbelievers? What a waste of time! No amount of that kind of living will ever satisfy the flesh; it only excludes people from the life God has created us for.

Lord, thank You for saving me from such a self-centered, immoral, narcissistic life style. I want to make the most of my time living in Your ways.

A New Education

Ephesians 4:20-21

²⁰ But you did not learn Christ in this way, ²¹ if indeed you have heard Him and have been taught in Him, just as truth is in Jesus ...

Contrasting with the self-centered, passion-controlled, Gentile-kind of living, Paul turns to the Ephesian readers (and all Christians everywhere) and writes, "But you." Their conversion to Christ rendered them completely dissimilar to what they were before faith in Christ. They had come to "learn Christ"—they didn't just hear about Christ. It was not simply knowledge concerning who Christ was. They learned Him; that is, they came to know Him personally. They became true disciples who not only followed their master's teachings, but committed to being like Him.

Disciples of Christ, or more simply, followers of Christ, ought not, therefore, to live like unregenerate Gentiles. Coming to Christ is a not a matter of self-centered, pleasure seeking. Christ is not the object of those lusts and desires. Christ is the antithesis of all that Paul had described Gentiles to be. He was self-sacrificing, loving, patient and disciplined. He had changed their lives.

"If indeed" does not introduce doubt about their salvation. This is what might be called an "if of certainty" or "if of contingency." The truth of the statement depends on the truth of an antecedent truth. In this case, what Paul is saying is , "If you have heard Him—and we are assuming this to be true in your case . . . you certainly did not learn Christ that way!" This is a frequent literary method Paul uses to convey truth in a logical manner.

The connection here between knowing Christ and salvation is important. "Truth is in Jesus" (vs. 21). Truth is not a philosophical perspective on life; it is not a collection of truth claims that "correspond to reality." Nor is truth the territory of mystics and monks who contemplate the universe. Jesus Himself told us about truth, "I am the way, the truth and the life . . ." (John 14:6). He is the truth; the truth is Christ. "This is eternal life, that they may know You, the only true God, and Jesus Christ whom You have sent" (John 17:3). He is the logos of John chapter one, who became a human individual. When Pilate asked, "What is truth?" (John 18:38), little did he realize the answer was literally and physically staring him in the face!

As those who know the truth, that is, who know and follow Jesus, we should avoid falling back into the old non-Christian ways of behaving but rather live the life of Christ, which Paul is now about to address. Is it any wonder that we should fix our eyes on Jesus the author and perfecter of our faith (Heb. 12:1).

Lord, thank You for the knowledge of the Lord Jesus Christ. Help me to know Him better, for living His life is far better than living the old, non-Christian life.

WEEKEND READING

Saturday – Mark 13
Sunday – Mark 14:1-31

PERSONAL REFLECTIONS

Put Off, Put On

Ephesians 4:22-24

[22] ... that, in reference to your former manner of life, you lay aside the old self, which is being corrupted in accordance with the lusts of deceit, [23] and that you be renewed in the spirit of your mind, [24] and put on the new self, which in the likeness of God has been created in righteousness and holiness of the truth.

The dichotomy between the old, pre-conversion life and the new life in Christ is stark. And, it should be. There is an element of passivity that often happens when a person first comes to Christ. It seems to the new believer that changes are happening to him, with no effort on his part. In actuality, he is making efforts, but the sense of God's presence, the working of the Holy Spirit, the exhilaration of forgiveness and the new awareness of eternal life, all serve up an overwhelming experience. New commitments along with a new hope energize the person to make changes in his life that were impossible before.

In time, the newness and exhilaration of new life are tempered and a challenge surfaces. That which came easily at our conversion to Christ, in time becomes difficult. God hasn't changed, nor have His promises. What has changed is the believer. Paul's call in the passage to "put off" and "put on" is really no different than what we did when coming to Christ in the first place. This is a reminder.

These three verses summarize the task: put off the old, put on the new. The old way of life is one that spirals downward despite the hollow promises of lust. The passions of the old self hold out for satiation, but it never completely happens. Desires of the sinful flesh lead to increased want, because the desire is to fulfill (or relieve) the inner self, the inner compulsion, the inner desires of the heart. It is a constant carrot on the stick leading the poor mule along, never attaining what he is really after.

The "new self" refers to the new life in Christ. It begins in the mind—we are to be "renewed in the spirit of your mind." With this, other Scripture agrees (see Romans 12:1-2; 2 Corinthians 10:5; 1 Peter 1:13). Walking worthy of our calling (vs. 1) means a change of mind, a renewal in how we perceive life circumstances. It is bringing our thoughts in line with the image of God in us. Grace has renewed in us His likeness in which we were created and to which salvation is intended to restore us. We were created to be righteous and holy, and now, in Christ, we are returned to that. Our role is to not revert back to our unsaved life style but to consciously live in accordance with that likeness of God. That is the true way of living.

*Lord, thank You for saving me from the spiritually
dead treadmill of lustful living.*

Anger Management

Ephesians 4:25-27

25 Therefore, laying aside falsehood, SPEAK TRUTH EACH ONE of you WITH HIS NEIGHBOR, for we are members of one another. 26 BE ANGRY, AND yet DO NOT SIN; do not let the sun go down on your anger, 27 and do not give the devil an opportunity.

Devils need no help. In this case, the Devil is none other than Satan himself. Elsewhere, we are told to stand against him (Eph. 6:11), resist him (James 4:7) and be alert for him (1 Peter 5:8). In regard to him, we need to identify things to do and things not to do. Here we see just how this can happen, namely, with a proactive game plan.

Details of the putting off and on now emerge. First, comes dealing with truth in personal relationships. Avoid lies, and speak the truth. We have seen this already earlier in this chapter (Ephesians 4:15, see also Colossians 3:9). This should be nothing new, for one of the ten commandments is to not bear false witness. Much of the moral code of the Old Testament carries over to and is reinforced in the New Testament. What is new here is the reason, "for we are members of one another." It makes no sense to misrepresent, distort or otherwise falsify the truth, or in any way misrepresent reality in our dealings with other people, and with Christians in particular.

Yet, today we live in an image-falsifying society, where people feel they can photoshop their way through life, altering what really is and replacing it with what they want it to be. Life, it seems, is better when depicted on the video screen, airbrushed and with music added. Lying happens when we misrepresent ourselves, trying to project on to others an image of ourselves that does not correspond to reality, but is fed by our self-exalting bent. We do this for various reasons, one of which is the futile attempt to gain advantage or standing. At the heart is the desire to please oneself (aka "living like Gentiles") rather than walking worthy of our calling.

Relationships also involve anger, a natural response in certain circumstances. Here, Paul does not say, "Don't get angry." Trying to eliminate emotions is not possible, for even God gets angry. The trouble is when anger is unjustified or not adequately expressed or dealt with. Anger is not the problem, but sinning while angry is. This well quoted verse today speaks of limiting the extent of your anger. Deal with it; don't let it fester or engender bitterness. Don't take revenge against or stop loving those with whom you get angry. Satan's goal is to cause division. Don't give him a foothold!

Lord, search me and know me, and see if there be any angry way about me. Help me rather to speak truth and resolve my issues.

More Than Your Own Load

²⁸ He who steals must steal no longer; but rather he must labor, performing with his own hands what is good, so that he will have something to share with one who has need.

In His epic speech which we refer to as the Sermon on the Mount, Jesus gave authoritative commentary on many of the Old Testament teachings as well as correcting some of the conventional perspectives of contemporary rabbis. One teaching had to do with the eighth commandment, "You shall not steal." The Lord added some corollaries to the basic axiom. Paul does the same thing in this letter to the Ephesians. The way to obtain what you want is not by stealing, but by working hard for it. For his present audience, Paul recognizes that work in most cases involved manual labor of some sort, or as we would say today, blue-collar work. Businesses usually involved selling something one made or grew. The service industry was largely manned by slave labor. There were few, if any, "office" jobs. For most people, one's work was tied to one's hands.

Physical work is good. After all, in the perfect environment of the Garden of Eden, God gave Adam and Eve work to do in tending to the garden. Ecclesiastes tells us that, in spite of the vanity of life, there is a potential that ". . . every man who eats and drinks sees good in all his labor—it is the gift of God" (Eccl. 3:13). Paul practiced what he preached. In his final address to the Ephesian elders, he said, "I have coveted no one's silver or gold or clothes. You yourselves know that these hands ministered to my own needs and to the men who were with me. In everything I showed you that by working hard in this manner you must help the weak and remember the words of the Lord Jesus, that He Himself said, 'It is more blessed to give than to receive'" (Acts 20:33-35).

So, we followers of Christ should work hard for three reasons: 1) there is satisfaction in work, 2) working provides for our needs and 3) working provides for the needs of others. Work is not an evil task of a fallen world. Certainly, sin has made it more difficult, but the problem is not with work. But rather, the problem has to do with our own sinfulness that has turned work into a drudgery, a means to selfishly accumulate money for ourselves, a path to power and control over others, or a desperate attempt to fulfill our need for significance. Stealing is a way to obtain things without working for them. That's being a taker, rather than a giver. The unity of the church depends upon everyone being a giver.

Lord, help me remember the purpose of work, so that I can learn to be more generous with the things You have provided me through work.

Mouth Guard

Ephesians 4:29-30

29 Let no unwholesome word proceed from your mouth, but only such a word as is good for edification according to the need of the moment, so that it will give grace to those who hear. 30 Do not grieve the Holy Spirit of God, by whom you were sealed for the day of redemption.

Controlling one's words is one of the most difficult things for us mere humans. James spoke of this, "So also the tongue is a small part of the body, and yet it boasts of great things. See how great a forest is set aflame by such a small fire!" (James 3:5). So, even though we believers are indwelt and sealed by the Holy Spirit, the difficulty of this must none-the-less be addressed directly. Paul presents a positive alternative to "unwholesome words." We should focus the effort of our words on building up others as the need arises. "Edification" means to build up; such efforts are in short supply today. People hear enough things in this world that tear them down one way or the other.

What would our fellowship be like if each person was committed to using his words to build others up, rather than criticize, chastise or gossip. To be certain, there is a time for confronting or saying difficult things. But, even those efforts should have the goal of ultimately building the other person, not destroy them: "Faithful are the wounds of a friend, But deceitful are the kisses of an enemy" (Prov. 27:6). This is grace.

To do this is tantamount to coming along side of the Holy Spirit, for it is His desire to build up the body, and in particular, to build up individuals in the body. Tearing down others through our careless or calculated, cutting words grieves the Spirit, because that effectively undermines His desire to unify us.

This is not a small or isolated problem for a few people. Scripture deals with this repeatedly. To the Pharisees and other religious leaders, for example, Jesus thundered, "You brood of vipers, how can you, being evil, speak what is good? For the mouth speaks out of that which fills the heart" (Matt. 12:34). It is a heart issue as much as a discipline issue. We guard our mouths as a way of confronting our hearts.

Later in this letter, Paul gives some specific examples of what to avoid in our conversations (Eph. 5:4). For now, suffice it to say, we should avoid working against the Spirit's work by bad-mouthing others. Let us keep our conversations positive and uplifting. Let us build up one another rather than tearing each other down.

Lord, thank You for securing me until my promotion to heaven. Until then I want to keep in step with Your Spirit and use my words to buildup others.

The Key to Harmony

Ephesians 4:31-32

[31] Let all bitterness and wrath and anger and clamor and slander be put away from you, along with all malice. [32] Be kind to one another, tender-hearted, forgiving each other, just as God in Christ also has forgiven you.

Itemizing a list of applications, Paul continues to expound on what it means to walk worth of our calling (Eph. 4:1). Bitterness, the first in our section today, acts like a soul-destroying cancer. Often, it lurks below the surface only to arise when provoked by a memory, a slight or a past or present injustice. It can lead to either spiritual depression or excessive assertiveness (in the form of criticism, cynicism, resentment). It can grab hold of a person's mind and emotions, imprisoning them in the thoughts and pains of the past. It is, to use the next two terms in verse 31, wrath or anger covered over but still seething inside like the inner rumblings of a volcano, ready to explode without warning. Attempting to suppress anger never works; it only drives the emotion underground where it simmers. That is not victory over the sin nature; rather, it is simply redirecting it inward where the damage is much more subtle.

Bitterness must be dealt with along with the wrath and anger that feed it. There is a relationship between bitterness, wrath, anger, clamor, slander and malice—they are all of the same substance, with varying degrees of action. Bitterness is inward, malice at the other end of the spectrum is outward. We are to put them all "away," lay them aside like dirty, stinking clothes.

Preventative measures are always best. "See to it that no one comes short of the grace of God; that no root of bitterness springing up causes trouble, and by it many be defiled" (Heb. 12:15). Bitterness, when it takes hold, is a difficult weed to get rid of. Grace is the key and is mentioned twelve times in the letter to the Ephesians. The positive antidote of grace is being proactive in our Christlikeness toward others. The action items come to the fore: being kind is the first. This is the opposite of malice. Malice is when I do something to hurt another. Kindness is when I do something good for another. The second is "tenderhearted," which gives integrity to our actions of kindness.

Finally, there is forgiveness. We need to willingly forgive one another because we all fail from time to time in laying aside the old "Gentile" ways, and we don't always act in ways that are "putting on Christ." Forgiveness is the basis of a sinner's relationship to God, and it is also the basis of a sinner's relationship to other sinners. This grace is key to Christian unity and harmony.

Lord, help me to walk in a manner worthy of my calling in Christ, who came to unify people in the Church.

WEEKEND READING

Saturday – Mark 14:32-72
Sunday – Mark 15

PERSONAL REFLECTIONS

_____

_____

_____

_____

_____

_____

_____

_____

_____

_____

_____

_____

_____

_____

_____

_____

_____

_____

_____

_____

_____

_____

_____

_____

_____

_____

_____

_____

An "Incensed" Life

Ephesians 5:1-2

¹ Therefore be imitators of God, as beloved children; ² and walk in love, just as Christ also loved you and gave Himself up for us, an offering and a sacrifice to God as a fragrant aroma.

Who on earth would attempt such a thing as trying to act like God? Sounds absurd, doesn't it? We are so accustomed to such phrases as, "Who are you to try acting like God?" However, such notions reflect poor efforts at acting like God, rather than good efforts. We are not to "be God" to people, like sitting in judgment over others (James 4:11). Yet, we are to imitate the way God loves. As the saying goes, "Like Father, like son."

We are to excel at loving people as God loves them, because there should be a family likeness. It does no good to say, "Well, I am only human, you know. No one is perfect." But, Jesus said, "Therefore you are to be perfect, as your heavenly Father is perfect." (Matt. 5:48).

So how does God love us? Paul switches to speaking of Christ's love—which incidentally points to the deity of Christ. Jesus' love is demonstration of God's love. This is what the Gospel of John means when it says, "No one has seen God at any time; the only begotten God who is in the bosom of the Father, He has explained Him" (John 1:18). The term "explained" means to exegete, explain, bring out the full meaning of something. Jesus was the full exegesis of God's love. This is epitomized in His sacrifice on the cross. He gave Himself up for us; His very life was substituted for ours. He died in our place, so that we might have life. The author of Hebrews writes, "He, having offered one sacrifice for sins for all time, sat down at the right hand of God." (Heb. 10:12).

Christ's sacrifice is described as having an aromatic bouquet. The metaphor here is rich and reflects the Old Testament sacrificial system (see for example Exodus 29:18). Bible students recognize in this a literary device called "anthropomorphism," where God is pictured as having human characteristics. God is said to enjoy the sacrifice of Christ the way a human would enjoy the fragrance of incense or some other pleasing smell. The imagery of what the Old Testament called a "burnt offering" (Lev. 1:4, et. al.) giving off a pleasing odor is hard to miss here.

Paul's point here is that we followers of Christ, as sons and daughters, should likewise provide God the pleasurable fragrance of our actions of love. When we sacrifice for others this is like offering a "burnt offering" to God. He takes a deep inhale and finds it very, very pleasing.

Lord, I want my life to be a pleasure to You. Show me today whom I may demonstrate Your love toward, even if it means sacrificing something great.

Avoiding the Vices

Ephesians 5:3-4

³ But immorality or any impurity or greed must not even be named among you, as is proper among saints; ⁴ and there must be no filthiness and silly talk, or coarse jesting, which are not fitting, but rather giving of thanks.

Common vices are these in the world—the life of non-Christians can be quite crude and lacking in moral virtues. That Paul takes time to warn us testifies to the fact that they continue to be temptations for Christians. Not only should we avoid these things, we should stay so far away from them both individually and as a community of believers that there should be not even a hint of them in our midst.

Immorality is the English translation of the Greek word pornea and refers to the general idea of sexual sin. Any sexual activity outside of a husband-wife relationship is considered in Scripture to be pornea, or sexual sin. Behavior outside of marriage that incites the sexual passions is dangerous to the Christian who desires to "walk worthy of your calling" (Eph. 4:1). While clearly this has to do with behavior, Jesus made clear that sexual sin includes thoughts of the mind and heart (Matt. 5:28). This includes indulging in sexual fantasies or visualizations through reading, magazines and the internet. Today, internet pornography is epidemic. So, the Holy Spirit tells us to "consider the members of our earthly body as dead to immorality, impurity, passion, evil desire, and greed . . ." (Col. 3:5).

Paul adds impurity and greed to the list of things to avoid. Impurity has to do with sexual impurity. Greed is the uncontrolled desire to obtain something. In contrast, there is nothing so pure and good and giving as the sexual relationship in marriage. God created this in the Garden of Eden to be enjoyed. Sexuality is core to who we are as created beings. Like magnetism, it draws male and female together. God's guidelines are for it to be expressed and experienced in the committed relationship of marriage where it can be fully enjoyed, encouraged and protected.

A person who is self-centered desires the blessing without the commitment and that is where it goes wrong with sex outside of marriage. The world in its arrogant selfishness wants full freedom to experience sex without restraint, but in so doing, enslaves itself to the passions it seeks. In Christ, there is freedom to enjoy sexuality as God intended, under control and in the right relationship. Anything else is just not "proper." Finally, our talk should also show a respect for the sanctity of sex, rather than to demean it with crude sexual jokes.

Lord, help me in both behavior and language to walk in purity of body and mind. "Lead me not into temptation, but deliver me from evil. Amen."

A Secure Obedience

Ephesians 5:5-6

5 For this you know with certainty, that no immoral or impure person or covetous man, who is an idolater, has an inheritance in the kingdom of Christ and God. 6 Let no one deceive you with empty words, for because of these things the wrath of God comes upon the sons of disobedience.

Many Christians have stumbled on this verse (and others like it). The warning is severe. Paul cautioned against any specious argument that renders the warning ineffective. A common teaching imposed on this passage is that if Christians sin badly enough in the area of sexual immorality or greed, they could lose their salvation. I don't think that is what the apostle had in mind.

It is true that eternal destiny is in view, for "inheritance" is often used biblically in connection with eternal life. "His great mercy has caused us to be born again to a living hope . . . to obtain an inheritance which is imperishable and undefiled and will not fade away, reserved in heaven for you" (1 Peter 1:3-4). Paul previously wrote, "[the Holy Spirit] is given as a pledge of our inheritance, with a view to the redemption of God's own possession . . ." (Eph. 1:14). However, Paul, in our passage today, refers to the future status of those who are not genuine believers. Earlier, he warned the Ephesians to "walk no longer just as the Gentiles walk" (4:17). Make no mistake about it, "Gentile walking" was the way they used to live when they were under the condemnation of God. And, that life renders non-believing Gentiles without any hope for future inheritance in God's eternal kingdom. Unbelieving people given over completely to immorality and greed (which are forms of idolatry—see other translations which capture this better than NASB) will not be saved.

Christians, on the other hand, are already forgiven (Eph. 4:32). Paul has written that the Holy Spirit is our guarantee (1:13-14) and also, "by [the Holy Spirit] you were sealed for the day of redemption" (Eph. 4:30). Nothing can separate us from the love of Christ (Rom,8:38-39). We are secure.

Paul is not trying to motivate the Ephesians by hanging their eternal destiny over their heads. Fear is a rather poor motivator. Rather, he is saying this: now that Christians have an inheritance that is secure, they should not go on living like Gentiles who will not receive a spiritual inheritance! Why live as though you did not know Christ? This is a re-emphasis of what he wrote earlier, that "you be renewed in the spirit of your mind, and put on the new self, which in the likeness of God has been created in righteousness and holiness of the truth" (Eph. 4:23-24)

Lord, I don't want to live like I used to live. Your word motivates me now, not by fear, but by the security of the inheritance that is already mine.

Children of the Light

Ephesians 5:7-10

⁷ Therefore do not be partakers with them; ⁸ for you were formerly darkness, but now you are Light in the Lord; walk as children of Light ⁹ (for the fruit of the Light consists in all goodness and righteousness and truth), ¹⁰ trying to learn what is pleasing to the Lord.

Distinction is clearly made between Paul's readers and those whom they should "know with certainty" will not have "an inheritance in the kingdom of Christ and God" (vs. 5, see yesterday's reading). Christians do have this inheritance, that is, eternal life, so, therefore, should not share in the activities and life style of the lost. That lifestyle is best described as darkness, Paul says. They were formerly darkness personified, but now they are a light source in the world. Using this strong metaphor, he says they were not "in the darkness," nor that they are like darkness, but they were darkness. That is what they used to be, but they aren't that now.

Believers, however, are described as Light in the Lord. Notice the apostle doesn't say the Ephesian believers are "in" the Light, nor that they are like light, but that they are light. This light, of course, is sourced in the Lord; it is reflective rather than original. Paul is simply echoing what Jesus had taught His disciples, "You are the light of the world" (Matt. 5:14).

This contrast is a repeated theme in Paul's letter (see Ephesians 2:1-3 and 4:17-24). Believers and unbelievers are in two completely separate camps, as different as light and darkness, day and night. And, the goal of the two kinds of life is stark. For believers, it means walking as children of the Light, not just resting on our status as believers. Paul pictures, as he does elsewhere (Gal. 5:22-23), the Christian life as a fruit-bearing tree. Here, the fruit is depicted as "goodness and righteousness and truth," the opposite of the Gentile kind of living. The Christian has as his goal, or should have, the desire to please God. While the accomplishing of this in perfect form may be elusive, the desire ("trying to learn") has the sense of "determining to learn," not a half-hearted effort in the least. This is absent from the non-believer, who lives to please himself.

Pleasing God is the ultimate endeavor of the Christian, and it involves obedience, worship and praise. Indeed, when a human desires these things for himself, we understand this to be sinful self-centeredness. But, when God desires these, it is only fitting, for He is in fact the center of the universe! It pleases Him greatly when we walk as children of the light.

Lord, Your pleasure is my goal; not my pleasure of You, but Your pleasure from my life. There is no better life or motivation than this.

Avoiding the Darkness

Ephesians 5:11-12

¹¹ Do not participate in the unfruitful deeds of darkness, but instead even expose them; ¹² for it is disgraceful even to speak of the things which are done by them in secret.

Avoidance of the old, sinful practices is a common theme in this letter of Paul to the Ephesians. Their doctrine was not assailed, for they had an excellent foundation in the teaching of Paul (over two years), the powerful preaching of Apollos, and the personal ministry of Aquila and Priscilla. But, their faithfulness to the Lord was tenuous, judging from the amount of space Paul gives to warning them against falling back into old practices.

Here, the readers (including us) are instructed not to partner in any way with the sinful life. The term "participate" has the sense of sharing in, together with. This means to not become actively involved in sinful acts (which we have outlined previously), nor take advantage of the results of sinful acts. Elsewhere, Paul speaks of multiple levels of participating in sinfulness, ". . . although they know the ordinance of God, that those who practice such things are worthy of death, they not only do the same, but also give hearty approval to those who practice them" (Rom. 1:32). Giving approval of someone's sin is just as blameworthy as doing the sin itself. Being an accessory to the act is included in this judgment, as does paying money to be entertained by sinful activities, as can often be the case when watching movies or reading stories. When one attends a movie, one supports the making of the movie and, thereby, supports the activities portrayed in that movie.

Paul says we should rather expose those activities, that is, expose them for the sin that they are, so that we are warned and can avoid them. We should bring them out into the light and judge them in the light of God's Word, for we are light and should walk as children of Light (5:8). We should promote "goodness and righteousness and truth" (5:9), rather than the fruit of darkness. To even speak of these activities as though they are normal things of life should be shameful for Christians. How could a Christian even think about participating? That is the logic of it, yet, as is all too apparent, it is ever so easy to fall back into the dark side of life. We need to be vigilant, and this means seeing the old "Gentile" way of life the way God sees it—as darkness.

The battle between the new-self and the old-self continues throughout life. Christians, secure as we are, need continual reminders against embracing any of the sinful practices of the non-Christian lifestyle.

Lord, help me to live my life as a light and not to live in the darkness of the old way of life, so that I might bear good fruit for Your enjoyment.

WEEKEND READING

Saturday – Mark 16
Sunday – Luke 1

PERSONAL REFLECTIONS

_____
_____
_____
_____
_____
_____
_____
_____
_____
_____
_____
_____
_____
_____
_____
_____
_____
_____
_____
_____
_____
_____
_____
_____

Sleeper Cell Awaken

Ephesians 5:13-14

¹³ But all things become visible when they are exposed by the light, for everything that becomes visible is light. ¹⁴ For this reason it says, "Awake, sleeper, and arise from the dead, and Christ will shine on you."

Exposure of sinful living is no small thing, either in terms of frequency of reference in Scripture, nor in terms of weightiness. We so easily fall to the unconscious (or even conscious) idea that God ignores our less than spiritual behavior. Determination to sin puts the Lord on the shelf in the back room of our spiritual lives. To use a different metaphor, more appropriate to our text today, we just turn out the light and hope God doesn't see or at least He won't really care.

However, Scripture repeatedly warns us that we can't hide from God, nor conceal our sin from Him:

"And there is no creature hidden from His sight, but all things are open and laid bare to the eyes of Him with whom we have to do" (Heb. 4:13).

"If I say, 'Surely the darkness will overwhelm me, And the light around me will be night,' even the darkness is not dark to You, and the night is as bright as the day. Darkness and light are alike to You" (Ps. 139:11-12).

"For My eyes are on all their ways; they are not hidden from My face, nor is their iniquity concealed from My eyes" (Jer. 16:17).

"It is He who reveals the profound and hidden things; He knows what is in the darkness, And the light dwells with Him." (Dan. 2:22).

In the context of our passage today, this exposure to light comes through the holy lives of Christ's followers. Their mere presence provides light that exposes sin. What behavior once seemed innocuous, often in the presence of a Christian, becomes seen for what it is, namely, sinfulness. It is like someone turning on a flashlight in a darkened room. And, those who are sinners become "light" themselves through the exposure to the light through other believers. While a bit cryptic, the idea is that through the testimony of believers (spoken and lived), others come to see their sin in the light of holiness, leading to their repentance and faith. Light, as a general rule, has a way of reproducing itself (MacDonald). Therefore, Paul quotes a saying that was in common circulation at that time (possibly loosely based on Psalm 60:1), encouraging the Ephesian believers (and us as well) to take the message of salvation to unbelievers who live in the darkness, in order to awaken them from spiritual deadness.

Lord, shine the light of Your truth and holiness in my life, search me and know me and see if there is any sinful way in me (Ps. 139:23-24).

Wasting Time—Not!

Ephesians 5:15-17

[15] Therefore be careful how you walk, not as unwise men but as wise, [16] making the most of your time, because the days are evil. [17] So then do not be foolish, but understand what the will of the Lord is.

Wasting time constitutes a monumental sin, for once it is spent it is completely gone, never to be re-spent. We have only one opportunity to use each moment that comes our way. The struggle with sin is not something to be put off for another day, for today is the day. There is no moment to lose.

This admonition finds fertile soil only among the faithful who fully realize that they ". . . have been bought with a price," and, therefore, desire "to glorify God in your body" (1 Cor. 6:20). In the NKJV, the phrase "bought with a price" is translated with the familiar "redeemed," which that translation also uses in our text today, "redeeming the time" for "making the most of your time." The underlying Greek word can be translated, to buy something out for one's personal use, to take something away with a purchase price.

We need to take each moment of each day and make the most of it—that only makes sense, when we consider that evil never takes a break. Considered from a godly, spiritual perspective, evil confronts us every day in some form or another, whether selfishness as an inward attitude, or as an outward manifestation of prideful interactions. The wise thing is to be continuously vigilant, to be walking wisely, keeping our spiritual eyes open and aware.

To redeem the time, what a concept! It means taking ownership of the moment in which I am currently living. I may not always choose my circumstances or control what other people do. But, I can choose how I respond to the time that is given me. Redeeming the time means not seeing myself as floating passively along like a cork on the stream of time. Neither does it mean responding with knee jerk reactions to the events in my life. Rather, I choose to respond with wisdom to make the most of my circumstances. Foolishness focuses on how I can make it from one minute to the next and stay intact. But ,wisdom sees time as a commodity to be used for a greater purpose.

The will of God for us is found in using every moment in service to the glory of God. Even those moments when all hell breaks loose to drag us down into spiritual discouragement or depression or fear. We can still choose to redeem the time. Every day can be our downfall from the forces of the enemy, or in Christ, we can make the most of what is given us, even in the best of times and the worst of times (Dickens).

Lord, thank You for the time You have given me. I want to use it all for Your glory and purposes. Help me resist temptations to use my time foolishly.

Spirit-filled Control

Ephesians 5:18-19

18 And do not get drunk with wine, for that is dissipation, but be filled with the Spirit, 19 speaking to one another in psalms and hymns and spiritual songs, singing and making melody with your heart to the Lord ...

The quest for unity, the common theme of this letter to the Ephesians, continues in a picturesque, yet tangible, way. There are certain things we can actively do to promote unity in the church. The positive summation is to "be filled with the Spirit." Some teach we are to allow the Holy Spirit to fill us up with Himself, like one would fill up a glass of water, and therefore, becoming a spiritual Christian means we need more of the Spirit. However, this cannot be the case, for Jesus said, "He gives the Spirit without measure" (John 3:34b).

The more likely interpretation of this filling of the Spirit is by contrasting it as Paul does with being drunk. One who is inebriated has given himself over to being controlled by wine. Likewise, a person who is filled with the Spirit is one who gives himself over to being controlled by the Spirit. Do we not use similar language when we say things like, "George is full of anger" or "Debbie is full of envy." By these, we mean the person is controlled by their anger or envy. So, being Spirit-filled is simply another way of saying a person is spirit-controlled. Thus, we view Paul's command as submitting oneself to be controlled by the Spirit.

What does this look like in action, then? This is not an esoteric experience of spiritual euphoria or wellbeing; in other words, it is not an emotional feeling as one feels when singing a sentimental hymn. Rather, Paul lays out for us what this looks like. Our conversation with others is characterized by music. There is a joyful overlay to our relationships that can only be expressed musically. As we submit to the Lord, the tension of sinfulness that corrupts peaceful relationships fades. Our focus is on the Lord rather than being intoxicated with ourselves.

A few observations are in order: there seem to be three kinds of music represented here. Psalms would refer to the inspired music of the Old Testament Book of Psalms (along with other assorted psalms of scripture). Hymns refers to music that is composed and sung in worship and praise to God. These are God centered—not speaking of God, but speaking to God. Spiritual songs are those tunes and lyrics which speak of spiritual life in general. All three kinds of music are evident in the Spirit-filled life and congregation, for these are things we use outwardly to speak to one another and to worship and praise the Lord.

Father, thank You for the gift of music. I submit to Your authority in my life, so that my heart is set free to worship and praise You, and to rejoice with others.

Lifestyle Gratitude

Ephesians 5:20-21

[20] ... always giving thanks for all things in the name of our Lord Jesus Christ to God, even the Father; [21] and be subject to one another in the fear of Christ.

S pirit-filled living is interesting for its non-spectacular restraint. Unfortunately, in some circles, the work of the Holy Spirit is assumed to be demonstrated in eccentric, unbridled, wild manifestations. Things like speaking in tongues and fantastic healings are considered to be the new normal for Christians enlivened by the Spirit. However, Paul presents a different picture.

In verses 18-19, we saw Spirit-filled living was contrasted with being under the control of alcohol. It is manifested in a song-filled life. In verse 20, the Spirit-filled life is experienced as a grateful life. Gratitude is a profound core demonstration of a heart given over to the control of God. Why is that? Because there is submission to God in all that He either brings or allows in our lives. He is at work, and we willingly accept everything as guided by His gracious hand. Romans 8:28 is the mantra of their heart, "And we know that God causes all things to work together for good to those who love God, to those who are called according to His purpose." Paul built on this, "In everything give thanks; for this is God's will for you in Christ Jesus" (1 Thess. 5:18).

When we consider that the first step away from God in the spiral down in sin is lack of gratefulness along with dishonoring God (Rom. 1:21), it makes sense that the return to the Lordship of God finds a certain wholeness in gratitude. Spirit-filled gratitude exudes from the inner man. And, this can only be a reality when we live not for the free expression of ourselves through the activities and attitudes of the old nature, but through a commitment to "the Lord Jesus Christ" (vs. 20). When He is on the throne of our lives, our outlook on even the worst of circumstances is transformed. Rather than complaining, bitterness and self-assertion (all the things that destroy unity among God's people), the Spirit-filled Christian sees the negative things as opportunities for God's glory.

So, with this kind of attitude, Paul's admonition in verse 21 comes much more easily, "be subject to one another in the fear of Christ." Because Christ is truly at the center of our universe as spirit-filled Christians and we have placed ourselves under His loving and sovereign rule (the word for "subject" means "to take one's place under someone else"), we can willingly submit to other Christians, when we are called to place ourselves under them, for the good of the unity of the body.

Lord, help me to submit, even when it is not easy—for the sake of the unity of Your body, the church.

An Unlikely Submission

Ephesians 5:22-24

22 Wives, be subject to your own husbands, as to the Lord. 23 For the husband is the head of the wife, as Christ also is the head of the church, He Himself being the Savior of the body. 24 But as the church is subject to Christ, so also the wives ought to be to their husbands in everything.

Submission today, in some circles, constitutes a four-letter word; not the count of letters, but the social repulsiveness of the concept. On this point, of wives being subject to their husbands, contemporary, conservative Christianity has received a black eye. Women are now CEO's of large blue-chip companies like Xerox and IBM, and more women earn college and post-graduate degrees than men. Hard fought suffrage rights are now entrenched in our western society. So, how can Christians be so "archaic" to believe that in marriage wives should submit to their husbands?

For many Christians, this is a hard pill to swallow and creates a formidable barrier to the gospel. One common solution is to develop a clever hermeneutic (i.e. method of interpretation) to get around these verses: Paul was only speaking to a different culture. Other approaches point out that the original Greek does not even include the word "be subject" in verse 22. Further, in fact, the previous verse (21) does use the word "be subject," and there it refers to everyone in the church, not just to wives or women in general.

In response, it must be pointed out that the beginning Greek student is not unfamiliar with the "missing verb" phenomenon. In fact, it is quite common; the context makes clear what verb intended, and that is why all modern translations include the word in verse 22. This verb "be subject" is implied from the previous verse, and therefore, its absence in the Greek is not problematic.

The cultural argument, on the other hand, is a slippery slope at best and dangerous at worst. It says that the NT writers addressed a different culture at a different time than what we live in today, and therefore, we need to adapt the broad principles and ignore the cultural specifics. In other words, if it doesn't fit with today, just principle-ize it enough until you can make it fit. The problem with that approach is the lack of controls for the interpreter in deciding what biblical teaching is universal in application versus what is limited in application. For example, do we limit baptism or the Lord's Supper to the first century where many religions had a similar practices? Does our culture allow for one person to pay for the crime of another? What does that mean for the substitutionary death of Christ for us? One must be careful in relegating Biblical assertions to cultural irrelevance.

Lord, help me understand how Your word cuts through the relativeness of our culture, so that I can see clearly the way to serving others.

WEEKEND READING

Saturday – Luke 2:1-38
Sunday – Luke 2:39-80

_____

_____

_____

_____

_____

_____

_____

_____

_____

_____

_____

_____

_____

_____

_____

_____

_____

_____

_____

_____

_____

_____

_____

_____

A Biblical Submission

Ephesians 5:22-24

22 Wives, be subject to your own husbands, as to the Lord. 23 For the husband is the head of the wife, as Christ also is the head of the church, He Himself being the Savior of the body. 24 But as the church is subject to Christ, so also the wives ought to be to their husbands in everything.

Substitutionary payment of prison time will not fly in today's culture. Yet, when it comes to biblical truth, substitutionary atonement is not a culturally limited concept—this doctrine applies for all time. Only the coldest anti-biblicist would mock the idea as an artifact of an ignorant, unliberal religion. Yet, many today deride the scriptural concept of submission in marriage as being hopelessly archaic. The emotional backlash is remarkably telling. Disagree maybe, but why such venom? Could it be our popular, western culture has echoed in the hearts of many otherwise Bible-committed Christians? The idea of group-think seems rather pervasive in this case.

Aren't women equal to men (see Galatians 3:28)? Are they not as smart as men, as responsible? In some cases, are not women physically stronger, and can they sometimes run faster than men? In all these cases, yes. Yes, that is, speaking generally from our human perspective. Interestingly, we cannot avoid differences, try as we might to find cases to prove otherwise. Even in athletic competition, the exceptions don't sway the obvious "rule" that men are generally faster and stronger than women. The Olympics separate men from competing with women. Western societies still maintain separate public restrooms. So, who decides which differences are legitimate and which are "cultural?"

A case can be made that our current generation is trying to force a "sameness" of the sexes but in reality is proving the exception to the rule, that is, as defined by God. In the Bible, we find that God sees a difference, and this can be traced back to creation. At the genesis of human life, the record shows that God didn't create a generic human being and then distinguish this un-sexual being into two sexes. No, the first human was created as a man, the second as a woman (see Genesis 1–2). Sexuality is inherent to creation itself. The differences can be seen in the rest of the biblical story of humankind. (for a fuller discussion of this, see "A Cosmic Drama," by Chuck Gianotti).

So, we can't so easily dismiss the Holy Spirit's teaching here through Paul as being culturally limited and, therefore, irrelevant to our present day situation. Admittedly, the teaching of this passage is radical, but it is not to be dismissed. Marriage today is proving to be a disaster, and sexual confusion is rampant. It makes sense to give God's way a better look.

Lord, help me see the beauty and wisdom of a radical standard for marriage.

A Complementary Submission

Ephesians 5:23-24

[23] For the husband is the head of the wife, as Christ also is the head of the church, He Himself being the Savior of the body. [24] But as the church is subject to Christ, so also the wives ought to be to their husbands in everything.

W e are spending multiple days on this passage for a reason. Not that we are obsessed with the subject, but because the world has got it so wrong and erroneous thinking has almost completely eclipsed the beauty of marriage as God intended it. It has infected many Christian minds as well. The result has not been better marriages. In fact, at the time of this writing, it is being reported that more children in the US are being born out of wedlock than in wedlock. Marriage itself is being marginalized today.

God invented marriage, and He has given us instruction through the Bible on how best marriage should work. His ways are higher than our ways (Isa. 55:9), so His plan for marriage is far superior to any other. It is true that all believers are called to be subject to one another (vs. 21). That is what Spirit-filled living is all about. We submit to one another out of a grateful heart, in a Spirit-controlled way, out of respect for ("fear" of) the Lord. Our commitment to unity in the body, the theme of Ephesians, means the Christian will readily set aside his own needs and desires and live so as to build others up as he or she serves them. However, submission looks different in different relationships. And, this is true in the context of the husband/wife relationship.

Paul describes what submission looks like for the wives, using the church's submission to Christ as the analogy. Then, he goes on to show what submission looks like for the husband. Just as the unstated verb submission is supplied in verse 22 by the general principle of verse 21, so also the concept of submission carries into verse 25 for the husband. It is true; in vs. 25, a verb is already there; husbands are to love their wives. However, love is not a different word or concept than submission, it is a greater word. There is no greater submission than to love another person. Jesus defined love this way, "Greater love has no one than this, that one lay down his life for his friends" (John 15:13). Love is submitting one's life in totality for the wellbeing of another.

For the wife (we will address the husband later), the standard of her submission is connected to her husband being the "head." The underlying Greek word, kephale, when used metaphorically, refers to one in authority. For example, a CEO is the head of the corporation. Christ is the head of the church (1 Cor. 11:3). So also, the husband is the head of the wife. The wife should respond to her husband's leadership as the church ought to respond to Christ, its head.

Lord, help me learn to sacrifice my life for my spouse, for Christ's sake.

A Modeled Submission

Ephesians 5:23-24

23 For the husband is the head of the wife, as Christ also is the head of the church, He Himself being the Savior of the body. 24 But as the church is subject to Christ, so also the wives ought to be to their husbands in everything.

Submission is a good thing, once we get past the abrasive, self-centered individualism of our western culture. It provides a key to all relationships. This can be found even within God Himself. Jesus, who was perfect in every way, submitted Himself to His Father, "Not my will be done, but yours." Lest we interpret that to refer to His human nature only, Paul makes it clear that His submissive attitude will remain for all eternity, "When all things are subjected to Him, then the Son Himself also will be subjected to the One who subjected all things to Him, so that God may be all in all" (1 Cor. 15:28).

Submission is a way of life for Christians. "Remind them to be subject to rulers, to authorities, to be obedient, to be ready for every good deed" (Titus 3:1, see also 1 Peter 2:13). The younger should be submissive to those who are older, "You younger men, likewise, be subject to your elders; and all of you, clothe yourselves with humility toward one another, for God is opposed to the proud, but gives grace to the humble" (1 Peter 5:5).

Notice that submissiveness correlates with humbleness. This is a voluntary thing, not a coerced submission. True biblical submission is the act and attitude of giving preference to another's leadership. Submission that is forced, or manipulated, or guilted is not biblical submission.

In marriage, wives base their relational submission to their husbands on the model of the church submitting to Christ. That means she will follow the husband's lead willingly, not just by the letter of the law. The church (that is, the people of God), ideally follows the lead of Christ joyfully. When we don't understand or we may at times disagree with God (I am not speaking audaciously), being a believer means we know that His ways are above our ways, His thoughts higher than our thoughts. So, we still follow Him faithfully.

Now, there is a difference with following the lead of a husband. Christ is perfect; a husband is not. Christ never makes mistakes; husbands do—and they sin. This is not an isolated teaching that can be used to establish male sovereignty where a wife submits like a slave. No! Christ doesn't force submission, neither should a husband. Remember biblical submission only has meaning when there is freedom to act otherwise, not dictated by the letter of the law. There is a greater submission that God requires of the husband, which we shall see next.

Lord, help me in whatever situation I am in to have a submissive attitude so that the world doesn't always revolve around me and my desires.

A Loving Submission

Ephesians 5:25

25 Husbands, love your wives, just as Christ also loved the church and gave Himself up for her.

As we have written earlier, there is no greater submission than to submit one's entire life for the sake of another. A husband may put down the newspaper and take out the garbage for his wife. That is loving submission to her needs. He will sacrifice his sports time to encourage his wife with some quality time with her. He will be sensitive to her emotional, spiritual and intellectual needs. The things concerning her will be concerns of his.

Now, there is a difference in how this submission looks. But, make no mistake, submission is a two-way street. The wife submits to the husband for leadership and ultimate responsibility for the relationship, for he is the "head." He, on the other hand, submits to her needs, not to her leadership. But, it is precisely at this point so many men fail. They feel a personal right, selfishly (or if they desire pseudo-biblical justification, a biblical right) to do as they please, making decisions and acting like the master of the house. That is not how Christ loved the church. He submitted Himself, in love to the Father and in love for us, to the cross. His ultimate statement of love, His ultimate sacrifice, His ultimate submission to our wellbeing—He died for us, for our salvation, for our eternity, saving us from punishment of hell. His whole life, living as He did in obedience to the Father, was lived for our benefit.

So, likewise, a husband should love his wife in the same way, sacrificially. This means more than taking the garbage out. It means the husband leads his wife (and family) with the goal of doing what is best for them, sacrificing his own wants and desires. It may mean passing up on a job promotion that would require more stress and time away from home. It may mean listening to his wife when they get home from work, rather than spending time in his own selfish pursuits. Women can see this clearly as simply the way men ought to be in a relationship. For men, these things seem like huge sacrifices—just as Christ made a huge sacrifice. Most men fancy throwing themselves in front of a speeding truck while pushing their woman out of the way—a momentary demonstration of heroism. But, as the saying goes, it is easy for a man to shed his last drop of blood—however, it is the first drop that is the most difficult. So with a man, the greatest sacrifices of love may indeed be the small ones. Time spent listening, seeking her counsel, talking, sharing, encouraging, leading with her best interests in mind. This is true submission of one's own desires for the good of another—this is love that God commands of the husband for his wife.

Lord, help me submit to You, so that submission to my spouse will seem easier.

A Beautifying Submission

Ephesians 5:26-27

26 ... so that He might sanctify her, having cleansed her by the washing of water with the word, 27 that He might present to Himself the church in all her glory, having no spot or wrinkle or any such thing; but that she would be holy and blameless.

Though Paul addressed wives first, he spent more time instructing the husbands. The standard for a husband's behavior toward his wife is clear, namely, the way Christ treats the Church. We saw yesterday that men are to sacrifice for their wives. In our passage today, Paul dresses up this idea with the imagery of a groom and his bride.

A husband should have as his goal to "sanctify" his wife. The word can also be translated "to make holy." It means he should treat his wife as special, set apart from all other women. She is not his servant or second class resident in the home. She is like fine china, not throw-away paper plates. His behavior toward her makes her feel special, not taking advantage of her for his own benefit.

Unfortunately, many men focus on "women's submission," yet never give any thought to their responsibility to meet her unique feminine needs. The story of creation shows that if God was intending for Adam to simply have a servant, then animals would have sufficed. Man, however, needed a valued partner, someone like him. The two, male and female, were both made in the image of God (Gen. 1:27). And, in our passage today, we are told she needs him to treat her as special, different than all other women. The questions every husband needs to ask himself are, "Does my wife know that I think she is special?" and "Does she understand my behavior as reflecting that I think she is special?"

The husband's role also includes helping her become beautiful ("in all her glory, having no spot or wrinkle or any such thing"). To be sure, there is an outward beauty that even the writers of Scripture recognize (e.g. Gen. 29:17, Job 42:15). More importantly is the beauty of the inner woman: "Your adornment must not be merely external . . . but let it be the hidden person of the heart, with the imperishable quality of a gentle and quiet spirit, which is precious in the sight of God" (1 Peter 3:3-4). While compliments concerning external beauty are appropriate and valued in building up one's wife, the more important effort should be to build up the inner beauty, in helping his wife become more like Christ, indeed, holy and blameless, resting in the security of her husband's love. There is a unique quality in femininity that responds well to the masculine affirmation of her beauty, not just the outer appearance, but also the inner woman.

Lord, You created beauty. Help us to encourage that inner beauty that is so easily assaulted and abused in our fallen world.

WEEKEND READING

Saturday – Luke 3
Sunday – Luke 4

A Golden Submission

Ephesians 5:28-30

[28] So husbands ought also to love their own wives as their own bodies. He who loves his own wife loves himself; [29] for no one ever hated his own flesh, but nourishes and cherishes it, just as Christ also does the church, [30] because we are members of His body.

The so-called "Golden Rule" says, "Do unto others what you would have them do unto you" (based on Matthew 7:12, although the concept is also found in Judaism and other religions). Paul applies that principle to the husband's behavior towards his wife. Rather than abusing his "headship," that is, his authority, he should accept responsibility for his wife's well-being, just as much as he would for his own. Paul argues from the greater to the lesser. He first wrote about husbands sacrificing themselves for their wives, just as Christ died for the church. Now, if that is right, husbands should at least put their wives on an equal footing with how they treat themselves.

The assumption is that a man already loves his body. He takes care of it and does not intentionally hurt it. He gives his body pleasurable experiences. When he is tired, he rests it; when he is hungry, he feeds it. When he has a weakness, as in a sprained ankle, he favors that side of his body. So too, the husband should provide these things for his wife. His goal as the head of the wife is not only his own enjoyment as "king of his castle."

Paul gives more instruction here to the men than to the women—more is required of the husbands. Peter puts it this way, "You husbands . . . live with your wives in an understanding way, as with someone weaker, since she is a woman; and show her honor as a fellow heir of the grace of life . . ." (1 Peter 3:7). A man cannot look to his wife to be of equal strength, someone to be competed with—for he will end up dominating her, which is not at all Christ-like. In the fall of Adam and Eve, the curse included Adam's tendency to "rule" over the woman like he would rule over the animal world (see Genesis 3:16). But, with a Christian marriage, that should not be so. The husband provides leadership that treats his wife well—just like he would treat himself. Not in dominion over her, but loving her and looking out for her best interests. For a man, this is nothing short of submitting his fallen nature for the good of his wife.

Once again, the analogy of Christ and church is made. Christ "nourishes and cherishes" his body, the Church, of which we are all members. So, men should not be passive but do everything in their power to ensure that their wives grow in all areas of life.

Lord, I pray for the marriages around me, that they would live according to the model You have given us of Christ and the Church.

A United Submission

Ephesians 5:31-33

[31] FOR THIS REASON A MAN SHALL LEAVE HIS FATHER AND MOTHER AND SHALL BE JOINED TO HIS WIFE, AND THE TWO SHALL BECOME ONE FLESH. [32] This mystery is great; but I am speaking with reference to Christ and the church. [33] Nevertheless, each individual among you also is to love his own wife even as himself, and the wife must see to it that she respects her husband.

Submission is the theme of this series of meditations from Ephesians 5:21-33, beginning with the concept, ". . . and be subject to one another in the fear of Christ." A wife shows her submission by following her husband's lead the way the church responds to Christ. The husband submits his natural tendency to live selfishly and instead exercises godly, sacrificial leadership to help his wife become all God created her to be. Both are submissive, though differently.

Paul now appeals to the creation narrative about the husband and wife becoming one flesh—this is a rationale for a man treating his wife as he would treat his own flesh (vss. 28-30). The idea that the two are one flesh profoundly captures the imagination. The two are one flesh, a sort of physically separate unity, as though one body co-existing in two spatial locations at the same time. Most picturesquely, at the time of conjugal relationships, the one flesh is a graphic reality, with the oneness being not just physical, but for a brief time an experience of intense emotional and sexual unity—a unity of the souls in a most sensuous, "earthly" sense. But, the one flesh at that moment goes beyond the simply physical union to include a true union of two human beings.

What a beautiful experience and profound picture! And, God has placed within the human being an inexplicable magnetism from the beginning to draw male and female together. Even the writer of Proverbs sees this as a mystery, "There are three things which are too wonderful for me, four which I do not understand: . . . the way of a man with a maid" (Prov. 30:18-19).

Paul takes this mystery of the oneness of male and female in marriage and turns it around to apply to Christ and the Church (vs. 32). This is the greater mystery, which is the theme of the first part of the letter to the Ephesians. The one new entity called the Church (composed of both Jewish and Gentile believers) has been brought into unity with the head, namely Christ. So closely does the marriage relationship mirror the relationship of Christ and the Church, that the imagery goes both ways.

Paul finally summarizes the topic of marital relationships in verse 33. A man should love his wife as himself, and the wife should respect her husband!

Lord, I pray that my marriage would model the relationship of Christ and the Church. What a beautiful picture!

A Command and Promise

Ephesians 6:1-3

¹ Children, obey your parents in the Lord, for this is right. ² HONOR YOUR FATHER AND MOTHER (which is the first commandment with a promise), ³ SO THAT IT MAY BE WELL WITH YOU, AND THAT YOU MAY LIVE LONG ON THE EARTH.

Six times in the New Testament, God reiterates this command to honor parents, many times through the words of Jesus. The activity of honoring someone is common in Scripture. Jesus honored His Father; the Father honored the Son; we are to honor God; God honors us; the church is to honor widows, etc. So, what does it mean to honor someone, seeing that this is an important topic, especially for children? The underlying idea means "to estimate value, assess." One lexicon puts it this way: "To attribute high status to or respect someone." To honor someone is to treat them as of great value and significance.

Our passage today focuses on children's behavior and attitude toward parents. Certainly, parents everywhere know the basic command well. In children, "honoring" is equated with "obeying." This word "obey" is to be contrasted with the word "submit" that was emphasized in the previous chapter of Ephesians. Submission is to be a general attitude of all Christians toward each other (Eph. 5:21). This, we saw, characterizes the marriage relationship. However, with children a different word is used. They are to "obey" their parents.

This is not a blind, legalistic obedience separate from a relationship with the parents. A child must learn to view his or her parents with great respect. Whether the parent is worthy of that respect is dealt with in the next verse. Suffice it to say, the first responsibility of a child is to honor the parent.

Why is this so important? Verse three gives us the answer. It is a wise, practical answer. Honoring parents comes with a promise from God—there is a benefit to the child. Inherently, all the commands of God entail the promise of blessing as opposed to cursing. His laws are not capricious. But, the command to honor parents has the promise clearly stated (see Exodus 20:12), "so that it may be well with you and that you may live long on the earth." Thus, for children, the emphasis on the results is clearly laid out.

Everything else is affected by how well they learn this principle: a good and long life. We may question whether this is the case in every single circumstance. However, in learning to obey parents, a child is saved from serious consequence of foolish, self-centered behavior that has a detrimental effect on the length and quality of his life. For example, a child obeying his father not to ride his bike in the street is less likely to be hit by a car than one who disobeys.

Lord, help me be not so self-centered that I cannot honor those who brought me into this world and have nurtured me to adulthood.

Keeping the Lid On It

Ephesians 6:4

⁴ Fathers, do not provoke your children to anger, but bring them up in the discipline and instruction of the Lord.

Often neglected, this instruction to the fathers may be the most crucial influence in a child's life. First, it is to be noticed that Paul addresses fathers, not parents. There is another word he could have used had he intended this for both mother and father, but he didn't. Second, of all the things he could address to fathers, this rises to the top in Paul's mind. He only uses this term provoke to anger one other time, in Romans 10:19, where he quotes a prophecy of God provoking Israel to anger using another nation invading them. Fathers, however, are not to do that to their children.

There are many ways a father can provoke a child to anger: being unduly harsh, expecting behavior beyond what a child is capable of, excessive discipline, unrelenting teasing, sexual or physical abuse, emotional manipulation and even continuous neglect. Of course, different children have different temperaments and express their anger differently. Some children out of fear, suppress their anger, only to have it boil over during the teenage years or later. It is difficult for them, as children, to learn how to "be angry, and yet do not sin" (Eph. 4:26). That is something the parents need to teach children, but it becomes extremely difficult, if not impossible, to learn that if the father is provoking them to anger! Growing up with provoked anger makes for an inadequate preparation for the conflicts and tensions that are the normal part of life.

Fathers should, rather, invest the time, energy and interest into their children, focusing on discipline and godly instruction. Discipline is not synonymous with punishment. It is much more than that. It is teaching the child through positive example, instructions, training in all aspects of life. From helping them to learn to play baseball, to handling rejection and failure, to helping those less fortunate (and a myriad of other things indispensable to godly living). This is more than occasionally showing up to bark out instructions. "Bring them up" implies time spent with them, going through life together. Moses wrote it this way, "These words, which I am commanding you today, shall be on your heart. You shall teach them diligently to your sons and shall talk of them when you sit in your house and when you walk by the way and when you lie down and when you rise up" (Deut. 6:7). To be sure a man must work to support his family, and this may involve large amounts of time away from home. However, it is the rest of his time that makes the difference.

Lord, I pray for fathers, that they will give priority to their children over their hobbies and sports and even their own comfort and leisure.

Recognizing My True Boss

Ephesians 6:5-6

⁵ Slaves, be obedient to those who are your masters according to the flesh, with fear and trembling, in the sincerity of your heart, as to Christ; ⁶ not by way of eye-service, as men-pleasers, but as slaves of Christ, doing the will of God from the heart.

Cultural interpretation and adaptation are essential in understanding Scripture. This passage begs an explanation which does not justify slavery. Was Paul somewhat less than inspired, being a child of his age? Should he not have instructed slaves to rise up in non-violent civil disobedience? Why does Paul not speak out on their behalf? We in North America are particularly sensitive to this because of our history of racial oppression and strife.

Actually, the apostle does address the subject more specifically in the book of Philemon where he essentially revolutionizes the institution of slavery, particularly when it involves a Christian master and a Christian slave. Even in this letter, a few verses later, he does address the behavior of slave masters.

However, slavery was an embedded political and economic institution and was not based specifically on race. There were probably considerably more slaves who came to Christ in Ephesus than slave-masters, so he addresses his audience. Paul is not endorsing slavery but regulating behavior within slavery. In fact, his instructions to slaves renders them really no different than subordinates in any social or employment situations. There will always be some sort of hierarchy of authority and responsibility, whether in slavery, employment, society or family. If these instructions here apply to the most difficult of situations, that of being a slave, they then would apply to all lesser difficult situations.

The primary instruction is "to obey," the same word for children "to obey" their parents. That means to place oneself under the authority of another. In the case of slaves, notice that Paul says this is a relationship "according to the flesh." It has no spiritual significance—it is purely a human invention. But, within that human situation, there is hierarchy. Subordinates should set as their goal to be the best subordinate possible; to do so "with fear and trembling, in the sincerity of your heart." This means with an open face, not conniving, resisting or manipulating. They should act in the best interest of their employer or master. The key is to recognize that their real master is the Lord Jesus Christ. As one preacher put it to a Christian in the workplace, "You are on assignment from Christ as his ambassador, secretly disguised as a factory worker." With this in view, we can serve God whole heartedly no matter how demanding our earthly master, employer, or parent is.

Lord, I accept my position with joy, for it is You that I serve in all situations.

WEEKEND READING

Saturday – Luke 5
Sunday – Luke 6

PERSONAL REFLECTIONS

Transformation Within

Ephesians 6:7-9

⁷ With good will render service, as to the Lord, and not to men, ⁸ knowing that whatever good thing each one does, this he will receive back from the Lord, whether slave or free. ⁹ And masters, do the same things to them, and give up threatening, knowing that both their Master and yours is in heaven, and there is no partiality with Him.

Doulos is the Greek word translated "slave." In most cases in ancient Greek culture (which was the predominant culture of New Testament times), slavery was held in distain. This came from the Greeks' strong sense of freedom. So, Paul's comments go completely against the grain of his times. His was not a movement to violently overthrow slavery but to transform it from within. And, transformation, in his estimation (and as inspired by the Holy Spirit), was a matter for both slave and master.

He continues from the previous verse to address slaves, but at the same time, segues to the masters. He says in verse 9, "And masters, do the same things to them." There is a commonality between the two, particularly in light of Christian community. Note that Paul directly addresses both in the second person. Both slave and master need to see themselves as servants (or slaves) of the Lord! The master is to the Lord Jesus Christ what the slaves are to their earthly masters. The Greek term for "render service" in verse 7 is the verb form of the noun "slave." There is a great leveling in Christianity of all authority relationships, no partiality (vs. 9). We all have the same heavenly Master. This doesn't remove authority, as various kinds of authority are affirmed in Scripture. But, it does revolutionize the use or practice of authority. In the case of slavery, Paul's teaching would transform slavery into a more present-day kind of employment (see the book of Philemon for an example of how this worked in the case of a runaway slave).

To be sure, Paul doesn't specify the details of labor relationships, but the principle stands (apart from the instruction to not threaten). In all we do, regardless of our earthly position, we are to "render service, as to the Lord, and not to men." Our motivation is not our earthly reward or even our paycheck. As Christians, we are compelled by the knowledge that our heavenly Lord is the one who will reward us for the good things and the good work we do.

If these things are true for the "institution" of slavery, they are also true for any other kind of authority relationship. Christians should transform their work place with the sense of service to a high authority, the Lord Jesus.

*Lord, help me today to serve You as I go to my workplace.
I am Your representative on assignment to show the
good deeds for which I have been created.*

Super-human Strength

Ephesians 6:10

¹⁰ Finally, be strong in the Lord and in the strength of His might.

Spiritual strength resides high on the list of necessities for the Christian. Without it, the Christian faith is impotent, and Christian teaching falls useless. To be sure, there is no lack of teaching today, considering the plethora of radio, TV and internet resources. The Ephesians had probably the best teaching in the early church (from the ministry of Paul, Apollos, Aquila & Priscilla). But, we know from Paul's teaching that knowledge without love is useless (1 Cor. 13:2). Yet, without strength, love is mere sentiment. Strength is what is needed to take the knowledge and love and act upon it. Strength is needed in the face of sacrifice. Many Christians know the right thing to do, but they shrink back because of the cost. They have no spiritual strength.

Yes, there is a place for asking the Lord for strength when we are weak and believing what He has already given us. "For God has not given us a spirit of timidity, but of power and love and discipline" (2 Tim. 1:7). But, our passage today tells us that it is we who are to "be strong." There is a part that God will not do for us, which we have to do ourselves. We need to summon the strength that God has given us, and it is we that need to use that strength and "be strong."

Let me be very clear. It is God's strength that enables us; it is His might that gives us power. But, what God does in us will lie stagnate and ineffective if we don't do something about it. And, that is Paul's point here. He has just taken aim at Christian slave masters, hitting them in the pocketbook, so to speak. Slavery was an economic institution as much as it was a human rights issue in those days. For these new Christians to change the way they treated their slaves would have serious financial and social repercussions. To treat them as fellow-servants of the Lord would be scandalous as well as financially disrupting. It may have meant letting go of debts and grievances. This would not be easy.

Many things God instructs Christians are impossible in mere human strength. When Jesus taught, "Turn the other cheek," we realize that the life of someone who follows Jesus will require what he doesn't have in himself. So, we must get our strength from the Lord. But, it is we who must get it.

Worn out slogans like, "Let go and let God," are nice, but we need to be careful. They may provide a good reminder when we are at wits' end that we can't do anything apart from Christ. But, the fuller truth is that, "I can do all things through Him who strengthens me" (Phil. 4:13). It is "I" who can do all things, and I can do them because of His strength. So, Christians, be strong!

Lord, help me not take a passive cop-out with misguided
slogans. Thank You for giving me the power to be strong.

Know Thy Enemy

Ephesians 6:11-12

[11] Put on the full armor of God, so that you will be able to stand firm against the schemes of the devil. [12] For our struggle is not against flesh and blood, but against the rulers, against the powers, against the world forces of this darkness, against the spiritual forces of wickedness in the heavenly places.

L ike a general preparing his troops for the big battle, Paul stirs up the field-soldiers of faith with a vision of the larger picture. This is what the real battle is about, the true enemy. So often Christians struggle against the wrong thing, or we stand firmly against the lesser things. Not that they are bad things, but we need to see clearly who or what is trying to destroy our faith.

Putting on the full armor of God begins with understanding what is really going on. Nothing worse than putting on your sports equipment before asking which game we are going to play. That hockey equipment is not much help if you are entering a swimming contest. We need to understand the nature of the ultimate enemy, and let that knowledge determine the kind of defenses we need.

For Christians, the enemy is the devil, a real, personal entity. He goes by many names: Lucifer, Satan, the father of lies, the accuser of the brethren, Beelzebub. The enemy is not a neighbor who plays loud music, or the member of the board who always wants his own way. It is not cancer, or diabetes, or MS, or a congenital abnormality. It is not the drunk driver who takes your child's life; the boss who fires you, or the Christian who opposes you.

Your sworn enemy is Satan and the forces at his disposal, and he has declared war on the people of God. His armies are not physical like an earthly army. Although some Christian authors paint fanciful images of demonic figures complete with sulfur-breath and stereotypical evil features, Paul describes them simply as "rulers . . . powers . . . world forces of this darkness . . . spiritual forces of wickedness in the heavenly places." Apparently, in the spiritual non-physical realm (here called heavenly places), there is structured ordering of evil beings. We have seen these before in Ephesians (see 1:21; 2:2; 3:10).

These are formidable foes, and we cannot afford to treat their existence lightly. As any general would know, the more you know about your enemy and his ways, the more you are able to counter-act his offensives. However, we must remember verse 10, to be strong in the might of the Lord. We must stand firm and not shrink back. Fears must be overcome, the fear of failure, criticism, doubts, weakness, insignificance. We need to train ourselves to understand the darts and shots of our enemy.

Lord, You are the General of my life. I stand strong in You as I face the onslaught of the devil, even in the daily skirmishes of life.

Armed for Battle

Ephesians 6:13-14a

¹³ Therefore, take up the full armor of God, so that you will be able to resist in the evil day, and having done everything, to stand firm. ¹⁴ Stand firm therefore, HAVING GIRDED YOUR LOINS WITH TRUTH ...

Preparation is key to any battle, whether it be military wars, sports competition, interpersonal conflict or spiritual temptations. In verse 11, we were instructed to put on the full armor of God as a defense against the devil's attempts to influence us. Now, Paul begins to break this preparation for temptation into distinct steps, corresponding to military armor of his day.

We are to "take up" the various parts of the armor, one by one, understanding each so that we can use them to maximum effectiveness. Our goal is to resist in the "evil day." While this surely has some prophetic value in reference to difficult times ahead for the Christians of the first century, it also has anticipatory value for all Christians. Satan continues to prowl around looking for Christians who are ill-prepared for him. He is way more powerful than we are. However, we can resist and stand firm, but we must use all the armor.

Three times now Paul has said to stand firmly against the devil. The picture is of an enemy onslaught trying to knock you back from your position of advance. Satan continually attempts to beat us back from what we have already obtained. Of course, we stand on the Rock, who is Jesus Christ, and the gates of hell will not prevail against the church. However, the enemy continues his assault against our faith. Though he may not affect our security, he may weaken our assurance and influence us to doubt our Savior.

Obviously, armor is a metaphor for the different spiritual actions we must take in order to be successful in resisting temptation. The first action is "having girded your loins with truth." This refers to a belt used for gathering in the tunic, and was the place where the breastplate was attached and from which the sword and other instruments of battle hung. It was the first piece of battle equipment put on. (The phrasing of this actually alludes to the Old Testament; the NASB translators indicate this by using caps in the verse, in this case Isaiah 11:5).

If there is no foundation of truth, there is no basis for confidence in any other defenses (see Psalm 11:3). Satan knows and attacks this. In the Garden of Eden, he subtly asked, "Has God said . . .?" (Gen. 3:1). He always brings truth into question, planting seeds of doubt. So, as Christians, we must know and study the truth, for it sets us free from the deceptions of God's enemy (John 8:32). We must make it our daily practice to be in the Word and for the Word to be in us.

Lord, help me know Your Word, so my life is solidly built on Your truth.

Complete Outfitting

Ephesians 6:14b-16

[14] ... HAVING PUT ON THE BREASTPLATE OF RIGHTEOUSNESS, [15] and having shod YOUR FEET WITH THE PREPARATION OF THE GOSPEL OF PEACE; [16] in addition to all, taking up the shield of faith with which you will be able to extinguish all the flaming arrows of the evil one.

Equipping oneself for spiritual battle is critical to the Christian life. The goal is not to enjoy the spiritual lazy-boy chair with feet up sipping a cool drink. A battle rages on all around us. Temptations, doubts, conflicts, insecurities and a whole host of other spiritual skirmishes flood around us. The Bible refers to these collectively as a battle, whose ultimate foe is none other than Satan himself. God could easily have taken him out long ago, but because of His own superior reasons, He has left him here allowing him to do battle against Christians.

But, God has not left us defenseless, for ". . . His divine power has granted to us everything pertaining to life and godliness, through the true knowledge of Him who called us by His own glory and excellence" (2 Peter 1:3). So, using personal armor language, Paul encourages us to use what we have been given. So, after the belt of truth is put on, we are to affix the "breastplate of righteousness." A confident embracing of the truth of righteousness through faith by grace (Eph. 2:8-9) is an absolute must. Without a breastplate, we are unprotected from mortal wounds to the heart. We stand forgiven and accepted in Christ, and we now have His righteousness, which at the core affects everything else.

Next listed is "spiritual" footwear. Imagine entering physical battle barefoot or with sneakers! War requires solid footwear for moving forward. Being prepared to share the good news is likened to having good footwear, bringing us forward on task, on mission to reach the world (Matt. 28:18-20).

Next comes the "shield of faith." Our enemy is on the lookout for gaps in our armor. The shield of faith is impenetrable; its only weakness is in being used improperly. Satan continually attacks our faith in order to stop us in our tracks and to prevent the spread of the gospel. He is a master of subtlety and nuance when it comes to derailing our trust in God. When we are strong, we begin to doubt ourselves; when we are weak, we doubt God's strength; when we are sick, we question God's ability; when we are victorious, we can feel defeated. We have opportunity to share the gospel, but we are paralyzed by fear of failure, questions, futility. Our mind begins to rationalize or question. Let us keep sight of the mission for which we have been equipped. The objective is nothing less than the spread of the good news. Let's use what God has given us for the battle!

Lord, help me keep on mission by sharing the gospel with someone today.

WEEKEND READING

Saturday – Luke 7
Sunday – Luke 8

PERSONAL REFLECTIONS

Ready for Conflict

Ephesians 6:17-18

[17] And take THE HELMET OF SALVATION, and the sword of the Spirit, which is the word of God. [18] With all prayer and petition pray at all times in the Spirit, and with this in view, be on the alert with all perseverance and petition for all the saints ...

Imagery of battle armor includes two more pieces. The helmet protects the head, the control center of the body. The brain orchestrates things on more than one level. Physically, the nerves all connect back to it. When the toe suffers injury, an electronic signal travels through the nerve pathways back to the brain which interprets the signal as pain.

But, also residing in the brain is the will power that determines what the rest of the body will do, where it will go, how it will move. In this latter sense, the head is the field marshal controlling the members of the body. So, the head and the brain must be protected in battle by a helmet.

The analogy is that the helmet is security of salvation. If the enemy could destroy the knowledge of salvation, everything else would change—how the Christian deals with temptation, conflicts, and failures are all affected and overlayed with the terror of God. The helmet represents the constant reminder that our salvation is secure. This is different than the shield of faith mentioned earlier. While faith is involved, the helmet of salvation has more to do with the knowledge and certainty of salvation. If this be in doubt, everything else is then in doubt. If we aren't sure of our relationship with God, we can't be sure of our faith, our purpose for evangelism, or even how to stand firm in the face of Satan's onslaught. So, crucial to standing firm is being sure of our salvation.

Finally comes "the sword of the Spirit, which is the Word of God." This is the offensive weapon. The feet prepared for the gospel bring us to our objective in the spiritual battle, but the sword is what forges the way through the barriers and oppositions of Satan. In the wilderness temptation (see Matthew 4), this was the instrument of battle Jesus used against Satan's temptation. Jesus quoted Scripture. The writer of Hebrews put it this way, "For the word of God is living and active and sharper than any two-edged sword, and piercing as far as the division of soul and spirit, of both joints and marrow, and able to judge the thoughts and intentions of the heart " (Heb. 4:12).

All these implementations of spiritual warfare are needed for success in our Christian walk. Above all, everything should be bathed in prayer, the universal, spiritual overlay. Having armored ourselves, we need spiritual awareness so we can be alert and not drowsy.

Lord, thank You for equipping me for battle. Help me be alert in prayer to You.

Join the Battle

Ephesians 6:19-20

[19] ... and pray on my behalf, that utterance may be given to me in the opening of my mouth, to make known with boldness the mystery of the gospel, [20] for which I am an ambassador in chains; that in proclaiming it I may speak boldly, as I ought to speak.

S egueing from prayer as the armament overlay for spiritual battle, Paul transitions to a personal prayer request. He is beginning to wind down his letter to the Ephesians, and as is his custom, he closes with a few personal remarks. In these few comments, though, we gain significant insight into his ministry.

Paul sees his ministry as something coming from the Lord. Peter echoes this idea when he wrote, ". . . Whoever speaks, is to do so as one who is speaking the utterances of God" (1 Peter 4:11a). Paul was very aware that he could not preach the gospel apart from God's enabling. And, he recognizes the need for others to pray for him in this regard. The temptation is strong to preach the words of man and not the words of God.

And, he was very aware of his weakness. When you consider how much he suffered for the gospel, several beatings, shipwreck, hunger, ridicule (see 2 Corinthians 4:7-11; 7:5; 11:23-27), it is no wonder he asks for prayer! Even as he wrote, he was in chains (vs. 20)! It was not easy being an apostle. But, the good news of the mystery was worth sacrificing for. Remember—the mystery which he had the privilege of sharing is that all people can come to the God of Israel, without having to go through the Mosaic Law. The way is by grace through faith (Eph. 2:8-9).

Clearly, Paul sets for us an example of the Christian's self-identity. He was never confused about his role. He was Christ's ambassador. He lived his life as a representative of another. He wrote to the Corinthians, "We are ambassadors for Christ, as though God were making an appeal through us; we beg you on behalf of Christ, be reconciled to God" (2 Cor. 5:20). Whatever we do, we represent Christ, whether at our work place, with extended family or in our neighborhoods.

The gospel is not just for telling but for boldly proclaiming. The armor of God is not so that we huddle together in a defensive posture to protect ourselves. The armor is there to prevent any hindrances to our going forward with great courage with the gospel message to the lost. This means actively sharing the message even when people resist it and we suffer social tensions and spiritual barriers. We are equipped to take the offensive in this battle!

Lord, help me like Paul not be a passive bystander, but to join the battle with the goal of victory of lost souls coming to faith.

Beloved and Faithful

Ephesians 6:21-22

²¹ But that you also may know about my circumstances, how I am doing, Tychicus, the beloved brother and faithful minister in the Lord, will make everything known to you. ²² I have sent him to you for this very purpose, so that you may know about us, and that he may comfort your hearts.

Companions of Paul were numerous, but some rise to the surface. Tychicus was one of seven (which also included Timothy) who accompanied the well-traveled apostle on his third missions tour, particularly mentioned in Acts 20:4. Paul had come from what we would today call Asia Minor, specifically the city of Ephesus, where a near riot had taken place over his preaching of the gospel. Tychicus hailed from Asia Minor.

From there, Paul traveled west to Macedonia and then south to Greece, presumably visiting the troubled church in Corinth where he spent three months, only to get in trouble with the local Jewish population. Then, he embarked on his return trip to his "home church" in Antioch of Syria, but first going back through Macedonia. It was during this leg of his tour that Tychicus is mentioned along with six others as accompanying Paul. Once in Macedonia, the companions went ahead to Troas while Paul stayed back in Philippi.

Meeting up again in Troas, we find the famous story of Paul's long sermon into the night, and a young man falling asleep in the window, falling to his death—but Paul raised him up alive. Tychicus was a witness to this event. Following this, he would presumably be still with Paul as he gave his farewell speech to the Ephesian elders (Acts 20:15-38).

We mention this bit of history to give background to Paul's comment about Tychicus in our present passage in his letter to the Ephesians. The Christians in Ephesus were concerned about him being one of their own. He was apparently well known also to the Colossian church (see Colossians 4:7). Paul considered him a "beloved brother and faithful minister." It was not just that Tychicus was efficient and effective in the Lord's work, but that he was "beloved." He connected with people at a deep, relational level.

It is this one whom Paul sends back to the Ephesians to inform them of his current situation. Many Bible interpreters believe Tychicus was the courier bringing this letter to the Ephesians. Notice Paul's concern for the Ephesian anxiety over both himself and Tychicus (vs. 22). What faithfulness and what love among God's people! This was true Christian fellowship.

Lord, help me to have a growing, deep love for my fellow workers in the Lord's service. And, help me to be faithful in my service to them.

Beloved and Faithful

Ephesians 6:23-24

[23] Peace be to the brethren, and love with faith, from God the Father and the Lord Jesus Christ. [24] Grace be with all those who love our Lord Jesus Christ with incorruptible love.

Closing his letter to the Ephesians, Paul turns to familiar themes: peace, love and grace. He mentions all three in every one of his writings, and ends every one with "Grace be with . . ." These were not just idle salutations but were evidence of the overriding reflection of what was most operative in his life.

"Peace be to the brethren," reflects his particular theme in this letter, the peace between believers, regardless of the Jewish or Gentile backgrounds. The Christian faith trumps nationalism, ethnicity, and racial backgrounds. Our unity in Christ is one of the main goals of the Holy Spirit, who has sealed us in Christ (Eph. 1:13). We have all been "bought" and are now Christ's possession. We are equally possessed and owned by Him.

"Love with faith" captures the heart of the Christian walk. Paul wrote much on the subject of love (see 1 Corinthians 13). "Now faith, hope, love, abide these three, but the greatest of these is love" (1 Cor. 13:13). It is the first listed of the "fruit of the Spirit" (Gal. 5:22). This love, though, is closely associated with faith, for one cannot love truly without an unreserved faith that God loves first. And, both peace and love find their source in God.

Finally, grace. This is considered by many to be Paul's trademark teaching. "For by grace you have been saved through faith; and that not of yourselves, it is the gift of God; not as a result of works, so that no one may boast" (Eph. 2:8-9).

When the apostle ends his letters this way, these are the things he desires for his readers—that these may be their experience. His hope is that these qualities that are true of God (He is a God of peace, love and grace) may become our defining qualities, that our experience of growing in God's peace would be reflected in how we handle conflict with other Christians, that our growing experience of God's love toward to us, who once were enemies of the cross and now can be quite selfish in our behaviors, might be reflected in our sacrificial love for others, that our experience of God's continual grace in our lives when we deserve nothing good from Him might result in our gracious acceptance and deference to others.

The standard is the Lord Jesus Christ whose love is unchanging and untarnished. Let us take Paul's teaching and focus on Christ, the one who loves us.

Lord, help me to live up to the standard of Christ, that
I might be a person of peace, love and grace.

Philippians

Savory Salutation

Philippians 1:1-2

¹ Paul and Timothy, bond-servants of Christ Jesus, to all the saints in Christ Jesus who are in Philippi, including the overseers and deacons: ² Grace to you and peace from God our Father and the Lord Jesus Christ.

Co-authors, Paul and Timothy, together penned this letter to the Philippians with a sense of joy, reflecting a close relationship with their readers and a maturity in their faith. How much of this letter was actually written by Timothy, we don't know. Possibly, the two had conversations about what the Philippians needed, which led to the writing. Nevertheless, being the effective discipler that he was, Paul includes Timothy as co-author of this work which ultimately found its way into the canon of Scripture.

Their humble introduction of themselves as "bond-servants" (in the Greek "doulos") reflects the teaching of chapter two on the humbleness of Christ. This otherwise despised word in the ancient world became an appellation of honor when depicting the service of our Lord Christ Jesus. Though he was a powerful apostle in the hands of God, he was, in his own mind, simply a servant. Likewise, early Christians adopted "bond-servant" as their self-identification.

In contrast, when he refers to the Philippians, he does not call them servants, but saints or "holy." They have, as do all believers, the exalted privilege of being set aside out of the world to be treated special by God, as one would treat fine china in contrast to paper plates. While Paul used this designation for the Corinthians as well (1 Cor. 1:2), the Philippians had more to be commended for in their behavior than the Corinthians. Yet, both are holy in God's sight.

Notice that Paul writes to the whole congregation, though he mentions the overseers and deacons. This was not a communication to be filtered through the ecclesiastical hierarchy to the common people of the pew. The leadership is addressed in the context of the whole church—nothing secret here. "Overseers" is the Greek word episkopos, from which we get our word "bishop." However, this word is used of elders interchangeably. When Paul gave his farewell speech to the Ephesian elders, he said, "Be on guard for yourselves and for all the flock, among which the Holy Spirit has made you overseers, to shepherd the church of God which He purchased with His own blood" (Acts 20:28, see also Acts 20:17). Elders are overseers and shepherds over the local church. There is no biblical evidence of bishops ruling over an area of churches.

Finally, with his usual flourish, he desires for his readers to experience grace and peace from God. He gives full berth to deity, namely the Fatherhood of God, and Lordship of Jesus with his title of Christ, the hoped-for one.

Lord, I humbly set aside my life in service of You, for You are my Master.

Weekend Reading

Saturday – Luke 9:1-27
Sunday – Luke 9:28-62

Personal Reflections

Of Gratitude and Grace

³ I thank my God in all my remembrance of you, ⁴ always offering prayer with joy in my every prayer for you all, ⁵ in view of your participation in the gospel from the first day until now.

Gratitude becomes the Christian, and so it is true of the apostle Paul. He considered it a high privilege to be a servant of the Lord. At another time, he wrote to his co-author Timothy (vs. 1), "I thank Christ Jesus our Lord, who has strengthened me, because He considered me faithful, putting me into service . . ." (1 Tim. 1:12). But, blessing upon blessing, he saw good fruit in the Philippians, and this is cause for greater thanks to God. Serving is a grace from God, and seeing results is also a grace. Think of Jeremiah who was called to serve but would not see the desired result: "You shall speak all these words to them, but they will not listen to you; and you shall call to them, but they will not answer you" (Jer. 7:27). A true servant of God faithfully serves and leaves the results to God—and is thankful for the privilege of serving even if results are not obvious.

Whereas with the Corinthians Paul was thankful for the grace given to them (1 Cor. 1:4), in the case of the Philippians, he was thankful for their consistent and faithful participation in the gospel. He was doubly grateful. It is true that we are to be appreciative in all things (Eph. 5:20), but for some things, we can be more so.

Such joy is a good reward considering what Paul went through in serving God and His people. He suffered many beatings, stonings, imprisonments, shipwrecks, hunger, fatigue, sleepless nights, discouragement, etc. (2 Cor. 11:25). It has been said that the greater one suffers for something, the greater he appreciates what he suffered for. So true for the apostle!

So, the Philippians were a highlight of Paul's ministry. His letter to them reveals very little in the way of rebuke or admonishment. Primarily, he encouraged them to higher living, building on what they were already doing well. This is reflected in his opening prayer, for every thought of the Philippians was saturated with joy and gratitude.

Notice the implication of this. Paul doesn't see the good results in the Philippians as a credit to himself; otherwise, there would be no basis for thankfulness. Rather, his gratitude speaks to the acknowledgement that God was at work in the Philippians (see for example the next verse, 1:6). Grace and gratitude are interchangeably intertwined.

Lord, help me to grow in my understanding and appreciation of Your grace in my life, so that I will have a heart of thankfulness.

Confident Prognosis

Philippians 1:6

⁶ For I am confident of this very thing, that He who began a good work in you will perfect it until the day of Christ Jesus.

Discipleship courses at some point all emphasize this verse and encourage the assurance of sanctification in the young believer's life. What a promise; that no matter how discouraged or defeated the Christian is, he has the assurance that God is at work and, like a master artist, the Lord will finish His masterpiece! The disorganized threads or, at best, a picture with very jagged edges or reversed coloring—that is the way our lives sometimes look. Not much beauty—until the picture is turned around and finally seen in its completion. That is like the work of the Master in our lives. In the end, we will finally see the exquisite masterpiece, made up of the many dark-lines, jagged edges woven into a smooth-flowing, beautiful image of Christ.

We must ask some hard questions of this passage. Was Paul giving his opinion and only speaking of the Philippians? Would he say the same to the Corinthians? To be sure, at times, he does seem to give an opinion, for example, "Now concerning virgins I have no command of the Lord, but I give an opinion as one who by the mercy of the Lord is trustworthy" (1 Cor. 7:25). But, what he was saying there is that the Lord Jesus, while on earth, did not teach on the subject Paul was addressing to the Corinthians. So, also in writing to the Philippians, he was speaking as the inspired Scripture writer when he says, "I am confident . . ." in our verse. If Paul is confident, we can be also.

But, is he talking only of the Philippians or only to faithful Christians? He just got through commending them for their faithful participation in the gospel. So, is this "promise" perhaps conditional on a Christian's faithfulness? Three things militate against this. First, the entire book is written to the Philippians, and we surely don't discount the entire book as being only for them. Secondly, he called the Corinthians "saints" (1 Cor. 1:2). So, comments about sanctification cannot be limited to the believers' faithfulness. Third, if the Philippians' faithfulness was something Paul thanks God for (as opposed to thanking the Philippians), their progress in the faith is credited to God, not to them.

Therefore, the promise of this verse is not limited to just the Philippians or just to faithful Christians. God, in His grace, began a good work in each Christian, including you and me, and He will finish His work. He will graciously combine the dark lines of our failures with many blessings, to produce a wonderful picture of Christ in us.

Lord, I commit to working in concert with Your design for my life.
My greatest goal is to be like my Lord and Savior, Jesus Christ.

More Than Amazing

Philippians 1:7-8

⁷ For it is only right for me to feel this way about you all, because I have you in my heart, since both in my imprisonment and in the defense and confirmation of the gospel, you all are partakers of grace with me. ⁸ For God is my witness, how I long for you all with the affection of Christ Jesus.

Paul's confidence is justified. It seems odd, though, that he would speak of this confidence so obviously. Such sentiment is notably absent in his letters to the Corinthians or the Galatians; both of which were having serious struggles in basic areas of faith and Christian life. With the first, there was a great abuse of the practice of grace, and with the second, a struggle with the doctrine of grace. But, for the Philippians, there was an enjoyment of grace, and Paul seemed to have a special regard for them.

Keep in mind, this relative affection is of a high order. It is not that he did not have regard for the Corinthians—in fact, he thanked God for the grace given to them (1 Cor. 1:1-9). He even expressed confidence that the Lord, ". . . will also confirm you to the end, blameless in the day of our Lord Jesus Christ" (1 Cor. 1:8). But, the affection Paul had for the Philippians was so much more notable that he needed to explain himself.

His explanation referred to their partnership in the gospel efforts. They stood with Paul when he was in prison. They assisted him while he was defending the gospel from attack, as well as when the gospel was having its good effect in changed lives. They were not fair-weather supporters of Paul, only showing concern when it was in their best interest.

Paul describes it in terms of grace. Just as he saw it a high privilege to be a servant of the gospel and even a higher privilege to be seeing good results of his efforts in the Philippians' lives, the Philippians now entered into that grace. They, too, saw the privilege of sharing in the sacrifice of the gospel effort. In addition, they would share in the joy of the results as they stood with Paul as he defended the faith and as his efforts produced results. The Greek word for "partakers" is related to the word "koinonia," and means "to share with." They truly were sharers in the grace of God with Paul. This was a real partnership.

The bond between Paul and the Philippians, therefore, was affectionate. No greater partnership exists than when people work together in the gospel effort; there is no greater work to share in. Both the effort and the results are a privilege because all are working for the same goal—to share the grace of God with others. Grace is absolutely central to the message, and it is absolutely central to life the way God intended.

Lord, thank You for Your overabundant grace. I am wonderfully blessed!

Turbo Love

Philippians 1:9-11

⁹ And this I pray, that your love may abound still more and more in real knowledge 3and all discernment, ¹⁰ so that you may approve the things that are excellent, in order to be sincere and blameless until the day of Christ; ¹¹ having been filled with the fruit of righteousness which comes through Jesus Christ, to the glory and praise of God.

Spiritual complacency has no place in the life of a growing and maturing Christian. We never arrive at the place where we can say, "Ah, now I have made it; I am spiritual and don't need to grow anymore." The Philippians were doing well, so Paul stirs them on to do better.

In particular, love needs to continually "abound." If love is the greatest of all virtues (1 Cor. 13:13), it can easily become the greatest to stagnate. But, love is not mere sentiment or a feeling. It needs to grow in a knowledgeable and discerning way. An immature believer may see love in stark terms, like throwing oneself in harm's way to save another. A maturing believer sees the daily nuances of love, for example, in patiently listening to the deep hurts of others, or giving up the need to say, "I" and learning to say, "you" more often, or even allowing others to receive the glory instead of oneself. Love increasingly may be seen in the willingness to warn another of harmful behavior, to use one's gift for the sake of others or to take a risk in living as a model of righteousness.

It is this growing, maturing love that puts to the test (i.e. "proves") what God considers excellent. Is living a Christ-like life really as great as it is made out to be? Paul here is saying that the way to find out is by living a growing life of love. That life brings its own confirmation. This is echoed in Romans 12:2, where Paul challenges us to live the committed life as a way to ". . . prove what the will of God is, that which is good and acceptable and perfect."

The maturing believer continues growing until Christ returns (that's what the phrase "the day of Christ" refers to). In the end, and only then, can it be said that they will be "sincere and blameless" (vs. 10). They will have lived a life that has proven God true. It will have been more excellent to live the life of grace than any other way of living. Only in that way can the believer's life be described as righteous. Not just a "little" righteous, but "filled." Not just acknowledging the truth of the doctrine of righteousness, but living a life that manifests the "fruit of righteousness," that is, deeds of right living under the grace of God.

Oh Lord, help me never stray from Your grace. I want my life to be a living demonstration that Your way is the most excellent way to live.

Who's the Captive?

Philippians 1:12-14

12 Now I want you to know, brethren, that my circumstances have turned out for the greater progress of the gospel, 13 so that my imprisonment in the cause of Christ has become well known throughout the whole praetorian guard and to everyone else, 14 and that most of the brethren, trusting in the Lord because of my imprisonment, have far more courage to speak the word of God without fear.

Ever the optimist, Paul knew his God was in control, no matter what the circumstances. Prison was a mere stepping-stone to the progress of sharing the gospel. He got great mileage out of every experience. On a personal level, the apostle had learned that suffering was a means to spiritual growth (Rom. 5:3-5). He had learned to live beyond his own life.

On the immediate level, his imprisonment gave unprecedented access to an otherwise unreached audience. Imagine being the soldiers assigned to guard Paul! It is commonly thought that imprisonment often involved Paul being chained to a guard. Talk about a captive audience! Word spread through the whole palace guard. This reminds me of a godly, old evangelist who often went snow skiing by himself, riding up the chairlift with a captive audience for the gospel!

Word had gotten around that Paul was not your usual prisoner. He continued to live out his mission when others would give in to overwhelming despair. He will extol more on this later in this letter.

But, there was a second and equally important benefit in his present incarceration. Other Christians were becoming emboldened to witness for Christ. Specifically, Paul's imprisonment encouraged others to fearlessly "speak the word of God." Why was this? They could see Paul's example, that jail time was not an over-ruling experience; he didn't give in to fear and despair. The apostle kept on mission; the message of the truth really was more important and more powerful than even prison. So, others were strengthened in their resolve to keep on mission and not to give way to fear.

Over the years, Christians have been emboldened by the stories of God's servants who suffered, yet never gave up the faith, even rejoicing in the midst of their sufferings. There is something about those tales that stirs up the spirit of the believer. A classic collection of such stories is "Foxe's Book of Martyrs. A more recent one is, "Jesus Freaks." Yet, a story of faith in the midst of struggle is no farther away than the nearby cancer hospital where a Christian may be dying, but sees his or her predicament as an assignment from God to help others in the hospital come to know the glory of Christ.

*Lord, help me to speak the Word of God fearlessly
in the circumstance You have placed me.*

WEEKEND READING

Saturday – Luke 10
Sunday – Luke 11

PERSONAL REFLECTIONS

_____
_____
_____
_____
_____
_____
_____
_____
_____
_____
_____
_____
_____
_____
_____
_____
_____
_____
_____
_____
_____
_____
_____
_____
_____
_____
_____
_____
_____
_____
_____
_____

Market-share Preaching

Philippians 1:15-17

15 Some, to be sure, are preaching Christ even from envy and strife, but some also from good will; 16 the latter do it out of love, knowing that I am appointed for the defense of the gospel; 17 the former proclaim Christ out of selfish ambition rather than from pure motives, thinking to cause me distress in my imprisonment.

It can be a heady, self-promoting experience to command the attention of many people with a message so compelling, namely the gospel. This doesn't take away from the many who minister for the right motivation, love. Praise the Lord for those who at great personal sacrifice dedicate their lives to preaching the Word of God so that others might know His grace.

Yet, the preaching of the gospel can be a tool of manipulation. Indeed, some people will use any means available to exalt themselves or carry out their selfish goals. The prophet warned, "The heart is more deceitful than all else and is desperately sick; Who can understand it?" (Jer. 17:9).

During Paul's imprisonment, some saw the opportunity to advance themselves unopposed, all while taunting Paul and attempting to rub his face in the dirt, so to speak. Why would anyone want to do that? One can understand the Jews resisting the entire message of Christ, because of their misguided belief that the Gospel undercut the Law of Moses. But, to take the same message as Paul and to preach it to the same audiences with a goal to "distress" Paul is almost inconceivable. This constitutes one of the most egregious actions of the fallen nature—taking something that is absolutely good and pure, the gospel of grace, and using it for nefarious purposes.

One can't help but think of the huge "Christian" enterprises today with their finely clad, photogenic preachers strutting before immense crowds of worshipping fans. Millions of dollars exchange hands for Christian entertainment. Pastors negotiate increasing salaries as they think of the ministry as "a job," rather than a passion for Christ and His message. When church leaders gather, they often inquire about the size of each other's churches. Why is that important? Christian publishers have been bought by secular media conglomerates because lots of money can be made. "Commercial competition" is indeed rife in the Christian world. One Bible translation is marketed as being, "The most widely used translation today." What's that all about? Selling one successful Christian book with its speaking circuit spin-offs can set up an author financially for life. Yes, and all the while, servants of the gospel struggle with persecution around the world, simply to get the message out to needy, lost souls.

Lord, search me and see if there is any wicked thing in me (Ps. 139:23-24).

The Message's the Thing

Philippians 1:18-20

18 What then? Only that in every way, whether in pretense or in truth, Christ is proclaimed; and in this I rejoice. Yes, and I will rejoice, 19 for I know that this will turn out for my deliverance through your prayers and the provision of the Spirit of Jesus Christ, 20 according to my earnest expectation and hope, that I will not be put to shame in anything, but that with all boldness, Christ will even now, as always, be exalted in my body, whether by life or by death.

Succumbing not under pressure to compete, Paul took the high road and rejoiced that the message was in fact still getting out there, even though he was not out there, but in prison. Most of us would denounce those who preach the message with false motives. But. the apostle had a larger view in mind.

First, he recognized that Christ was being proclaimed. In his time, that was an attention-getter. I remember during my pre-Christian college days an eccentric, toothless evangelist came once a year and preached from the university quadrangle where all campus paths seemed to cross. He was crass, uneducated, and always ridiculed as he called down hell fire and damnation on students. He was a joke to most of us worldly non-believers. However, quietly on the side were individual members of a campus Christian group who were engaging students in small group conversations. They were not specifically identified with the backwards preacher, but they took advantage of the spectacle to ask other students, "What do you think of Jesus?" Paul could have been doing likewise, making the most of the situation in which others were taking advantage of his incarceration. He saw that God was higher than those with false motivation, and in fact, the "Spirit of Jesus Christ" could indeed use their actions, complete with their selfish reasons, to advance the kingdom program. So, Paul could rejoice!

Additionally, the apostle recognized that this state of affairs resulted in true believers stepping up their prayer for him. We note that in Acts 12 there is no record of prayer concerning James the apostle's incarceration in prison and beheading. After that event, prayer began in earnest for Peter who was also in prison. Persecution has a wonderful way of focusing God's people in prayer.

Paul had experienced enough hardships and difficulties that he knew his God, and therefore, always had high "expectations and hope." His bottom line was that, even if he were to rot in prison and die, he fully expected God would somehow come out of that situation glorified—"Christ will even now, as always, be exalted in my body, whether by life or by death" (vs. 20)

Lord, that is my prayer, that You would be exalted in both my life and my death. Help me to die daily to my own selfish motivations.

A Personal Mission Statement

Philippians 1:21

²¹ For to me, to live is Christ and to die is gain.

Poetic language, concise and memorable. Startling in its core thought, a personal mission statement that is at once remarkable and, at the same time, not so unexpected from a man like Paul. He had given up everything that was important to him, all that he once held dear (his family pedigree, his standing in the Hebrew community, his academic successes and his prominence as an up and coming bright star among the religious elite), to become a follower of the Lord Jesus Christ, He did not lose it all as though it were taken from him; rather, he gave it all up. More about this in chapter three of this letter.

Paul had discovered a better way of living, namely to live for Christ. He was all about the Lord of grace. He understood the words of Jesus, "The thief comes only to steal and kill and destroy; I came that they may have life, and have it abundantly" (John 10:10). His old way of life was like the thief that stole the peace of God from people. But, the new life was all about people finding life in Christ. "This is eternal life, that they may know You, the only true God, and Jesus Christ whom You have sent" (John 17:3).

So, everything he did, every thought he had, every motivation that moved him, was all about Christ. His words were not superfluous when he wrote, "For from Him and through Him and to Him are all things. To Him be the glory forever. Amen" (Rom. 11:36). Or, "May it never be that I would boast, except in the cross of our Lord Jesus Christ, through which the world has been crucified to me, and I to the world" (Gal. 6:14). Life for Paul was Christ!

Death, that big non-negotiable of life, most people are resigned to—not Paul. Rather than resignation, it was anticipation for him. Now, he was often, especially as he wrote this letter from prison, living with death close by. But, rather than striking fear, it excited him, because death would bring gain for him. He would finally arrive at his reward (which he talks about in more depth in chapter 3). But more so, he would be with his Savior and Lord forever. No more suffering, beatings or various other kinds of hardships. The battle would be over, and he would enter into eternity with the Master. All when he died.

His life was transformed, and no difficulty on earth could take away the eternal life he had with Christ. Death could not hold sway over him, because that would be even better than life. Just as Satan tried to disparage Job, he also tried to deter Paul through his sufferings, to get him to abandon the cause of Christ. But, Paul stayed the course—with a clear vision.

Lord, give me clear vision of Christ, so that He alone will fill my life now as I joyfully serve Him. For to me, to live is Christ, and to die is gain.

Tough Choice

Philippians 1:22-24

²² But if I am to live on in the flesh, this will mean fruitful labor for me; and I do not know which to choose. ²³ But I am hard-pressed from both directions, having the desire to depart and be with Christ, for that is very much better; ²⁴ yet to remain on in the flesh is more necessary for your sake.

Paul's personal mission statement presented a quandary known only by those fully committed to Christ. The desire to be with the Lord in eternity is overwhelmingly compelling. That is the driving force, like that of a lover who desperately desires to see the one he loves. It is sometimes said there is nothing more distracting than being around a young man separated from his fiancée. So, Paul had a constant anticipation of his betrothal (though he didn't specifically use the language of John's "marriage supper of the Lamb," Revelation 19:9, yet he wrote of the husband/wife relationship of Christ and the church in Ephesians 5). For him personally, nothing would be better than to die and finally be united forever with the Lord whom he had served and whom he loved.

But, here is the rub. What was for him the greatest thing, would result in deprivation for the believers. His mission on earth was not yet complete. The pull toward heaven was counteracted by his pull toward earth. He had a real love for the believers whom he had won to Christ and whom he had discipled—and for the churches he had planted. His ministry was of continuing great value. For him personally, it would be better to be done with this life and to be with the Lord forever. But, for the believers, it would be better for him to remain among them, ministering as he had always done.

It is not as though Paul had a real choice here, but he does state his quandary as though it were. It is possible that, being in prison (not his first time by any means) and with advancing age, the easy thing would be to just give in and stop trying to serve people so much. Many Christians do go into "cruising" mode as they get older, where they stop pursuing Christ and His love for people. They become so "heavenly minded" that they are no longer any "earthly" good. For Paul, his primary motivation was not ultimately what was good for himself—whether that be enjoying the Lord's immediate company or even the rewards awaiting him in heaven. In fact, his love for people led him to write, "For I could wish that I myself were accursed, separated from Christ for the sake of my brethren, my kinsmen according to the flesh . . . (Rom. 9:3). Does that not sound like Christ portrayed on the cross? He did become a curse for us (Gal. 3:13). Paul was willing to live and to die for the sake of helping people find life.

Lord, help me to understand that You have left me here on earth so that I can be of service in helping others find new life in Christ.

The Right Choice

Philippians 1:25-26

25 Convinced of this, I know that I will remain and continue with you all for your progress and joy in the faith, 26 so that your proud confidence in me may abound in Christ Jesus through my coming to you again.

So, Paul's choice was to remain on the earth in this life, rather than to die and be with the Lord. The irony is that there was probably no one who wanted to be with the Lord more than Paul. He had personally met Christ on the road to Damascus (Acts 9), and his life was radically and unalterably changed through that encounter. Consider also that he had had a glimpse of heaven already, ". . . I will go on to visions and revelations of the Lord. I know a man in Christ who fourteen years ago . . . was caught up to the third heaven. And I know how such a man . . . was caught up into Paradise and heard inexpressible words, which a man is not permitted to speak" (2 Corinthians 12:1-4 Paul refers to himself in the 3rd person in his defense to the Corinthians). He wrote of ". . . the surpassing greatness of the revelations given to him" (2 Cor. 12:7). He was constantly pressing on "toward the goal for the prize of the upward call of God in Christ Jesus" (Phil. 3:14).

So, Paul was highly motivated to be with the Lord. Yet, he was "taking every thought captive to the obedience of Christ" (2 Cor. 10:5). Jesus had taught that we should serve others in the way that He served us. So, Paul was willing to set aside his own desires just like Christ did, for the sake of the Philippians "progress and joy in the faith." He had a heart for the Lord's people, who the Lord "purchased by His own blood" (Acts 20:28).

The apostle wanted them (as well as us present day readers) to have a proud confidence in him, and that such confidence would springboard into confidence in the Lord Jesus Christ. He was very aware that he was modeling Christlikeness for them. In this letter alone, he twice instructed the Philippians to follow his example (see 3:17; 4:9). However, his modeling of Christian behavior was not designed to win accolades or rewards for himself, but was intended to help the Philippians join him in following Christ: "Have this attitude in yourselves which was also in Christ Jesus . . ." (Phil. 2:5). He said it succinctly, when he wrote, "Be imitators of me, just as I also am of Christ" (1 Cor. 11:1). He was all about Christ; he looked forward to being with Christ for eternity, and he wanted others to join him in that great outlook in life. Therefore, he looked forward to another visit with the Philippians so that he might continue to help them along in becoming Christlike.

Lord, help me to grow in Christlikeness, so that I can be an example to others, and so help them become more like my Savior.

WEEKEND READING

Saturday – Luke 12:1-34
Sunday – Luke 12:35-59

PERSONAL REFLECTIONS

_____

_____

_____

_____

_____

_____

_____

_____

_____

_____

_____

_____

_____

_____

_____

_____

_____

_____

_____

_____

_____

_____

_____

_____

_____

_____

_____

_____

_____

Herd Worthiness

Philippians 1:27-28

* Only conduct yourselves in a manner worthy of the gospel of Christ, so that whether I come and see you or remain absent, I will hear of you that you are standing firm in one spirit, with one mind striving together for the faith of the gospel; in no way alarmed by your opponents—which is a sign of destruction for them, but of salvation for you, and that too, from God.*

Christian belief means little if is not reflected in Christian behavior, a recurring theme of Paul's (Eph. 4:1; Col. 1:10; 1 Thess. 2:12). God is concerned about our deeds as well as our doctrine. To be sure, our deeds do not save us, but our deeds reflect the reality of what we believe, namely God's grace working through faith. So, Paul's message was holistic in that sense.

The manner in which we behave ought to be consistent with the gospel of Christ; in fact, it should reflect well on the gospel. In other words, our life witness must demonstrate the excellence of the message just as much as our words explain the truth of the message. Now, the message is not a social gospel, but a gospel of grace, where God has wonderfully saved us through no merit of our own, but freely through His love for us. This message is wonderful, because it not only saves us, but changes us as well, giving us a new purpose and mission in life (this message saturates Paul's letter to the Philippians).

The apostle's admonition is that this behavior he asks of them becomes intrinsic (motivated from within), rather than extrinsic (motivated by Paul's presence). It is not Paul who judges in the end, but the Lord whom we ought to please, for unlike Paul, the Lord is always with us.

In particular, Paul was thinking of the unity in life and witness for the gospel. Those familiar with this letter can see the anticipation of chapter two in these words, "standing firm in one spirit, with one mind . . ." Maturing faith remind us of our Lord in the upper room where He prayed, ". . . that they may all be one; even as You, Father, are in Me and I in You, that they also may be in Us, so that the world may believe that You sent Me." (John 17:21). Oh, that this would be more apparent among believers today!

This kind of unity among believers, staying together as a herd, provides two things for the believers. First, unity is a sign that their enemies are defeated, for their persecution cannot divide the Christian community. Indeed, a common attack principle of the enemy is to divide the opponent, and then, it is easier to conquer. Second, unity confirms salvation to the church, a community confirmation. As Christians, we stand more strongly together than we do apart.

Lord, thank You for like-minded brothers and sisters in Christ. The strength from living and growing together encourages me to walk worthy of the gospel.

Redeem Your Suffering

Philippians 1:29-30

[29] For to you it has been granted for Christ's sake, not only to believe in Him, but also to suffer for His sake, [30] experiencing the same conflict which you saw in me, and now hear to be in me.

Opposition will come in the Christian life. Paul hinted at this in the last verse (28), that we don't need to be alarmed by those who oppose our faith. Unity of the believers is our protection. This seems odd on the surface of it. The Greek word "granted" is charizomai which means to bestow something freely. It is related to the word "charis," grace. Here, Paul encourages his readers that not only is faith a gift from God, but suffering is as well.

Suffering is the big "Why?" question that plagues human existence. The problem of pain has been the screaming issue for untold millions who suffer from physical, relational and emotional pain. Sickness and death are unfortunate facts of life. Yet, Paul wrote that suffering is "granted" or "bestowed" on us. How in the world can all this be a gift? Isn't suffering a symptom of living in a broken world, a result of sin in the world?

Of course, this question begs a much larger answer than we can adequately address here, but suffice it to say that Paul is speaking of suffering that comes in opposition to faithfulness. It is all of one package, faith and suffering, common to Paul and to the Lord Jesus Christ. When faith penetrates the darkness, there is disruption and stress. The darkness reacts. And, a point of entry forms every time faith is expressed, for it is precisely at that point eternity penetrates the membrane that engulfs the world. The Philippians, and all faithful believers, are God's chosen vessels for this penetration. We continue to walk in His image as we believe and as we accept the suffering of opposition as a necessary attendant to being light in the world.

Notice, the suffering is not a stand-alone experience without purpose. God does not call us to "enjoy" or even to embrace suffering as though by itself there is some spiritual value. Suffering is indeed a result of living in a broken world, but suffering is redeemed through faith and given value and purpose. Did not God do this at the cross? He redeemed mankind through the suffering caused by mankind's rejection of Christ. So also, though our spiritual opponent Satan can use any kind of suffering to knock us off our faithful pathway of trusting God, faith turns suffering into an opportunity to trust Christ and share in suffering like He experienced. So, in this sense, suffering of any kind can be redeemed and thought of as "bestowed" or "granted" to use for Christ's sake.

Lord, help me see the purpose in suffering as an opportunity to show Your glory in this dark and broken world.

Realized Unity

Philippians 2:1-2

¹ Therefore if there is any encouragement in Christ, if there is any consolation of love, if there is any fellowship of the Spirit, if any affection and compassion, ² make my joy complete by being of the same mind, maintaining the same love, united in spirit, intent on one purpose.

How can Christians experience genuine unity in authentic relationships? Paul gives us the answer, beginning with our passage today. Five "givens" are laid out and assumed to be true—in Greek, this is called a first class conditional statement. If these things are true of the Christian community, what follows comes naturally. These then lead to a number of action items.

First, in Christian community, there is (or should be) encouragement in Christ. This could also be translated "comfort." It is the same word used to describe the Holy Spirit elsewhere, the Comforter. Paul has in mind the inner strengthening in Christ that comes from the community of believers. As individuals are strengthened, they have the where-withal to strengthen each other, fleshing out God's activity of encouragement.

Second, the consolation of love. This is the assuagement that comes from the self-sacrificing attitude and actions among God's people. Christians know inherently that love is to override everything, because the love of God has so overwhelmed our own souls. We set a high standard for this in others, and we castigate ourselves when we give in to our own selfishness. Third, fellowship of the Spirit. Christians have been brought into a deep, personal relationship with the God of the universe, the author of grace and mercy. We long for and expect that kind of relationship with other believers.

Finally, affection and compassion make up the last two "givens" of Christian community, which deepen the intimacy of fellowship on an emotional level. These five things, variously related to Christ, love and the Spirit, are the deep desire of all Christians in community with each other. We desire them; we expect them; we fret over the lack of them.

So, Paul built on such thinking (it is the joy that compels him to prompt the Philippians to a higher standard) and wrote that if these things are the true ideal that we all agree upon, what can we do to make genuine fellowship happen? In a word, work toward unity: same mind, same love, united in spirit, intent on one purpose. To be sure, there is diversity among Christians, but we must work toward a comprehensive unity and be satisfied with nothing less. The one thing standing in the way is an unrelenting selfishness. That is why the apostle next reminds us of what is true about Christian fellowship.

Lord, You desire unity, so help me to see past my selfishness.

Of Humility and Vainglory

Philippians 2:3-4

³ Do nothing from selfishness or empty conceit, but with humility of mind regard one another as more important than yourselves; ⁴ do not merely look out for your own personal interests, but also for the interests of others.

The crux of the unity matter comes down to this: the only way God's people can have any semblance of unity is found in adopting a "humility of mind." So simple to state, so difficult to do. Partial humility is not enough. Occasional humility won't do. Selective humility is insufficient. In the original language, the word "nothing" is in the position of emphasis. We are to do absolutely "nothing" out of "selfishness or empty conceit." One moment of prideful acts or words can set in place a rift between believers that can last a long time.

The word translated "selfishness" has the sense of strife caused by personal ambition. This is when conflict arises because of self-promotion. It is followed by "empty conceit," which could be literally translated "vainglory." A person who is vain is one who seeks after his own glory, narcissism at whatever level is important to him. It is vain, because any glory achieved this way is superficial, self-made (which ironically is utterly empty) and temporary. It is like singing to an empty auditorium, then when finished, running down to the front row seat and giving yourself a standing ovation. This attitude does not bring about the unity of God's people.

The Philippians had a good example of such wrong behavior in the people who preached while Paul was in prison, ". . . the[y] proclaim Christ out of selfish ambition rather than from pure motives . . ." (Phil. 1:17). Yes, it is possible to preach God's word for one's own personal glory. But, this comes with a consequence. James tells us, "For where jealousy and selfish ambition exist, there is disorder and every evil thing" (James 3:16). Paul was glad the gospel was at least being preached, but such preaching would not bring about unity.

The upside to this conversation, though, is simple: we need to embrace an attitude and take an action. The attitude is humility; the action is to look out for the interest of others. Inner thinking breeds outward behavior. Humility is not a matter of putting down and thinking negatively about oneself. Rather, it is to think soberly of oneself (Romans 12:3) and to think highly of others. Humble interest is not for self-aggrandizing curiosity to satisfy our "need to know." Rather, it is to show concern for others for their good, with the goal to make oneself available to the other. If everyone in the Christian community were to act this way, it would cover all the times that each of us individually falls short of genuine humility.

Lord, help me take the first step of humility in my Christian community.

Imitation of Christ

Philippians 2:5

⁵ Have this attitude in yourselves which was also in Christ Jesus ...

Thomas a Kempis' book, "The Imitation of Christ," written in the 15th century, is considered the classic of Christian devotionals. The title alone captures the central theme of the Christian life. Is there any higher aspiration than to be like Christ? In the context of our passage today, does not the example of Christ help us in our quest for unity through selfless humility, for the Lord Jesus was always thinking of others? His death on the cross was the ultimate statement of putting others before Himself.

Many scholars view verses 5-11 as an ancient hymn recorded by the apostle (due to the literary structure). It certainly captures in a most poetic way an image of Christ's humility that led to His exaltation.

Yet, imitating Christ's attitude is not a mercenary humility, intended primarily as a path to glory. Such efforts in time fail. There is always a mixture in this life of fallen motivations due to self-centeredness and the aspiration of the inner spirit to glorify God. The goal of Christ's humility was to obtain a self-promoted glory. True humility will not seek its own. The reward, though, is inherent in the thing itself. There is another glory in true humility, a glory that is not sought for oneself, but which ultimately accompanies the humble other-glory. For God, the most natural thing is His own glory because He is truly the center of the universe and is essentially glorious in His nature. For humans, the glory comes to us when we realize and act upon the reality that He alone is glorious and we are not, which is the essence of humility. That which we obtain is reflection of His glory, but then when we see Him, it will be a true sharing in His glory: ". . . We know that when He appears, we will be like Him, because we will see Him just as He is" (1 John 3:2).

Scripture is replete with the challenge to model our lives after Him. "Take My yoke upon you and learn from Me, for I am gentle and humble in heart, and you will find rest for your souls" (Matt. 11:29). "If I then, the Lord and the Teacher, washed your feet, you also ought to wash one another's feet" (John 13:14). "Greater love has no one than this, that one lay down his life for his friends" (John 15:13). "For even Christ did not please Himself . . ." (Rom. 15:3). "For you have been called for this purpose, since Christ also suffered for you, leaving you an example for you to follow in His steps . . ." (1 Peter 2:21). "Husbands, love your wives, just as Christ also loved the church and gave Himself up for her . . ." (Eph. 5:25).

Lord, today I want to be like Jesus Christ, help me take every step with the same attitude of humility that He has had, being humble to serve others.

WEEKEND READING

Saturday – Luke 13
Sunday – Luke 14

PERSONAL
REFLECTIONS

_____
_____
_____
_____
_____
_____
_____
_____
_____
_____
_____
_____
_____
_____
_____
_____
_____
_____
_____
_____
_____
_____
_____
_____
_____
_____

A Form of Humbleness

Philippians 2:6-8

⁶ ... who, although He existed in the form of God, did not regard equality with God a thing to be grasped, ⁷ but emptied Himself, taking the form of a bond-servant, and being made in the likeness of men. ⁸ Being found in appearance as a man, He humbled Himself by becoming obedient to the point of death, even death on a cross.

Modeling Christ's life does not mean having a superficial sentimentalism or a "treating everyone nice" mentality. The substance of His humbleness is monumental. He is God who became a man. No commentary could ever capture the full import and beauty of this passage.

A few simple observations, though, are in order. Jesus existed in the form of God. This is not a statement that places Christ at a status of somewhat less than God, being "only" a form of God. Hebrews 1:3 tells us He is the "radiance of His glory, the exact representation of His nature." John 1:1 informs us that He was in the beginning with God and "was God" (see also Colossians 1:19, 2:9). The point here is that Jesus set aside the outward appearances or form of Deity and entered the world looking like a mere man. There was nothing God-like about Him in terms of the usual imagery of Deity. He "emptied" Himself of the outward manifestation of being God. His mission on earth did not require proving His deity through self-declarations of divine authority. He behaved like God, to be sure, but He behaved like God would behave in human form.

His life as a man was one of the humbler sort, not as an exalted earthly king or ruler, with the trappings of worldly acclaim. He came to experience the more common strata of mankind, of those most aptly described as "servants." And furthermore, He came to experience the most creaturely experience of death. What a huge step down, a condescension from the outward "form of God" to the depths of the fallen human condition—death.

It has been said that death represents separation. Jesus experienced physical death, obviously, the separation of the soul from the body. He experienced soul death, the separation of the soul from the spirit, on the cross, as prophetically anticipated, "My heart is poured out like wax . . ." (Ps. 22:14). The emotional toll was terrible. Finally, He experienced spiritual death, the separation from God His father. "My God, my God, why have you forsaken me . . ." (Ps. 22:1; Matt. 27:46). In death, though, He shared in the expectation God had for humans created in His image, obedience: "Although He was a Son, He learned obedience from the things which He suffered" (Heb. 5:8).

Lord Jesus, when I consider how You humbled Yourself, help me to set aside my futile attempts for personal glory and strive to humbly serve others.

Well Deserved Greatness

Philippians 2:9-11

⁹ For this reason also, God highly exalted Him, and bestowed on Him the name which is above every name, ¹⁰ so that at the name of Jesus EVERY KNEE WILL BOW, of those who are in heaven and on earth and under the earth, ¹¹ and that every tongue will confess that Jesus Christ is Lord, to the glory of God the Father.

Exaltation and humbleness—what a difficult combination. Human nature sees an inherent value in humbleness and exalts it in principle. It takes, however, a great person to be truly humble. In fact, only God can truly be humble. When humans attempt humbleness, mixed motives rule. There is a human limit because true humbleness happens when a great person does not grasp hold of or jealously guard his greatness. But, mere humans are not all that great, except when comparing themselves with other humans. The greatness of being humble is directly proportional to the greatness of being. Thus, it is relative in human terms.

Conversely, God is absolutely great, so therefore, His humbleness in becoming a man is an absolute humbleness. He didn't need to grasp hold of His greatness as God. Therefore, His humbleness is not just greater than human examples of humbleness, but it is of a completely different kind, of a higher order. And, it is that humbleness that we are to emulate.

Jesus Christ was exalted before and after His incarnation. Before—which gives substance to humbleness in becoming a man. After—to demonstrate that this humble man is the Lord of eternity. Just as He bowed in humility by becoming a man, every human that has ever lived or will live "will bow" in humbleness to His greatness. Not just humans, but every member of the spiritual realm, including angels and demons. There is none greater than Christ! All will eventually acknowledge His Lordship.

At the mere mention of His name, this humbling of humanity will take place. Christ is not just a nebulous concept like the Absolute in eastern religions. "There is salvation in no one else; for there is no other name under heaven that has been given among men by which we must be saved" (Acts 4:12). God's ultimate plan has been and is to exalt Christ among all of His creation. He is the perfect union of the Creator with creation. The incarnation, humbleness and exaltation show just how great our God really is. In no other religion, do we find a God who is so intimate with His creation. No wonder Christ will be exalted when we all see with unveiled eyes who He really is. The exalted Lord garbed in human flesh. How better could God have possibly shown Himself to be great!

Lord, right now I bow my heart and will before You as my Lord and my Savior. No one can compare to You either in humbleness or greatness.

A Good Work Out

^{12} So then, my beloved, just as you have always obeyed, not as in my presence only, but now much more in my absence, work out your salvation with fear and trembling ...

Subject of much theological debate, the question cannot be relegated to intramural academics to be decided by the scholars and the ecclesiastical courts. Eternity hangs in the balance for each individual as to how the question is answered. Our text is addressing individuals, not the collective. In the end, we each will stand before the Creator and Judge of all the earth and have to answer for ourselves. Too many rely on their pastor, their church, their denomination to answer this question, "How do I work out my salvation?"

Does this passage mean, as some would teach, that we must work for our salvation, in some way earn it through our good works? That can't possibly be the case, for we are told elsewhere in Scripture that, "All have sinned and come short of the glory of God" (Rom. 3:23). We have already failed in trying to work for our salvation! What we have earned, what we have worked for has resulted in failure: "The wages of sin is death" (Rom. 6:23). So, how can we possibly work for and earn our salvation through living righteously? We can't—it's impossible.

But notice, our passage does not say, "Work for your salvation." Rather, it says, "Work out your salvation." There is an eternity of difference in meaning. Many commentators have interpreted it this way, "Work out the implications of your salvation." Paul had given them the gospel teaching, the good news of the new life in relationship to God, one that comes about by grace, a gift from God. Now (at time of writing), he is no longer with them and, therefore, unable to help them work out all the ramifications of that foundational truth. He defers to them to think through and to put into practice all that the gospel means for living the Christ-centered life. Salvation itself is not in question for them. What is in question is the quality of life they will live now that they are saved. Will they live like saved people, walking in the grace of God?

God is at work in us and will perfect the work He began (Phil. 1:3). The Christian's "work" is to keep in step with what God wants to accomplish in us. That is what He has saved us for (Eph. 2:20). And, that takes effort on our part; it takes work. Lazy Christianity is not what Christ died for. But, neither did He die so that we would spend our lives trying to win salvation. It's a done deal; now live out the truth of that, live up to it!

Lord, thank You for Your wonderful salvation. I renew my efforts to live in a way that honors what You have done in my life.

A Pleasurable Work

Philippians 2:13

[13] ... for it is God who is at work in you, both to will and to work for His good pleasure.

The primary "work" of our salvation is done by God, not by us. But, we do our work by keeping in step with His work. In the previous verse (Phil. 2:12), we learned that we are to "work out" our salvation. Here, we are given the reason. Our working out of the implications of salvation in our daily lives can only happen because God is working it out in us.

Think of this for a moment; don't let the verse make a perfunctory appearance in your thoughts and then morph into a platitude. The infinite, holy and transcendent Creator God of the Universe, the One who spoke the cosmos into existence with a mere word, He who controls the storms and the earthquakes, the One before whom every knee will someday bend—this One is operating, making things happen in our finite, little lives. Comparatively, we are like specks of dust in the galaxy of humongous stars and planets. And, God is energizing His plan and purpose for our lives!

What is it that He is doing in our lives? He has a specific will, that is, a purpose and a plan. God accomplishes what He desires, and that means we have a destiny. What about our will? That is an age-old debate: the will of God versus the will of man. Whatever the answer, we can be assured of one thing: God is at work and will complete what He has begun (Phil. 1:3). We can also be assured that we are responsible to keep in step with His desires. In the end, when we see Christ in all His glory, the tension will be resolved: "For now we see in a mirror dimly, but then face to face; now I know in part, but then I will know fully just as I also have been fully known" (1 Cor. 13:12).

Notice, finally, God is at work "for His good pleasure." He enjoys working in and through us. It gives Him immense pleasure to carry out His handiwork forming us into His masterpiece, both individually and as a community of His people.

Reconciliation and unity of God's people brings Him pleasure. That is why at the birth of Christ, angels announced, "Glory to God in the highest, and on earth peace among men with whom He is pleased" (Luke 2:14). His pleasure was not in a select group of men, which He then saved. Rather, His pleasure is in those whom He saved through the coming of His Son. They are the ones who experience peace with God and with each other. Thus, He enjoys bringing unity among His followers in Philippi and among all His believers.

Lord, thanks for doing in us what we cannot do without You—live in unity with other believers. Help me live like Christ, the One in whom You are well pleased.

Lighting the World

Philippians 2:14-15

[14] Do all things without grumbling or disputing; [15] so that you will prove yourselves to be blameless and innocent, children of God above reproach in the midst of a crooked and perverse generation, among whom you appear as lights in the world ...

Glass half-empty, negative attitude, or in the words of our passage today, "grumbling or complaining"—this kind of behavior does not portray a family resemblance to God. But, what is so wrong with being like that? After all, none of us is above such tactics.

Well, first off, Paul indicates that this resembles a "crooked and perverse" lifestyle. Strong words! The trouble is that complainers and grumblers don't see themselves that way. They are just "speaking their minds" or "setting the record straight." But, all along Paul has been admonishing the Philippians to not act like Gentiles, that is, like the unsaved world. While complaining and grumbling may characterize the unsaved world, it should not be normative for Christians. We have changed family allegiances and now belong to the family of God. Thus, there should be a godly family resemblance. Christians should reflect Christ in the world; we should act like lights. Grumbling and complaining darkens the world; it hides Christ from view. When people see Christians acting like that, they don't see Christ; they see people like themselves. What good is that? Further, when we grumble and complain before each other, we don't help each other become like Christ or learn about His grace. We need to model Christ-like behavior.

Interestingly, this teaching is not original with Paul. Jesus said, "Blessed are the peacemakers, for they shall be called sons of God" (Matt. 5:9). Grumbling and complaining do not bring conflicting people together. Peacemakers don't inherently act like that. Peacemakers, whose words build up and bring together, show the family resemblance of God; hence, they are "called sons of God." (In biblical times, to call someone "the son of . . ." someone or something meant that they had the characteristics of that person or thing).

A grumbler or complainer is a person who, knowing he cannot change something, reverts to words designed not to change anything, but to let his displeasure be known. It is classic passive-aggressive behavior, to resist with words without necessarily resisting physically. God did not look very leniently on the "rabble" during the Exodus period of Israel (see for example the sons of Korah in Exodus 16), nor does He look favorably on it today.

Lord, I don't want to be a grumbler. Convict me
when I do it, and I will confess it as sin.

WEEKEND READING

Saturday – Luke 15
Sunday – Luke 16

PERSONAL REFLECTIONS

Boasting to Live For

Philippians 2:16

16 ... holding fast the word of life, so that in the day of Christ I will have reason to glory because I did not run in vain nor toil in vain.

B oasting was actually not uncommon for the apostle Paul, as odd as that may seem. To understand this, we must unpack the use of this word ("to glory" in the NASB version can be translated "to boast" as rendered in other translations) and the concept as used in the Scriptures.

There can be good boasting and bad boasting. To be sure, certain kinds of boasting at times were censured. For example, in 1 Corinthians 5:6, Paul tells the carnal Christians in Corinth that their prideful tolerance of gross immoral sin was absolutely reprehensible. In classical understatement, he wrote, "Your boasting is not good." They were arrogant in their attitude toward sin.

However, using the same underlying Greek word, Paul wrote to the Philippians, earlier in the book, that he was planning to stay on in service of the Lord, ". . . so that your proud confidence in me may abound in Christ Jesus through my coming to you again" (Phil. 1:26). The words, "proud confidence," are rendered from the same Greek word for "boasting." But, the cause of the boasting is different. In the first case, the Corinthians' boast was in their own religious "sophistication" in tolerating sin. In the second case, Paul was encouraging the kind of boasting that focused on what God was doing through him in the lives of the Philippians. It was a boasting that would abound in Christ.

This is a far cry from boasting before God about any meritorious works we might do that could earn us favor with God. Paul wrote to the Romans, "For if Abraham was justified by works, he has something to boast about, but not before God" (Rom. 4:2). Obviously, we cannot boast about ourselves independently from God as though something we do might impress Him. Our salvation is "not a result of works, so that no one should boast" (Eph. 2:8).

So, what is Paul boasting about in our passage today? He is speaking of a future boast, when the Lord returns. He wants to be able to look back from eternity future and see that all his labors here in this life produced something of worth. His prayer or desire is simply that his life will not have been in vain, and he will, in the end, have proven to be a useful tool in the hands of the Lord. It is a simple desire, a singular one, and in fact, a humble one. For, it is propelled by his ultimate boast, "But may it never be that I would boast, except in the cross of our Lord Jesus Christ, through which the world has been crucified to me, and I to the world" (Gal. 6:14).

Oh Lord, I pray that the cross of Christ may so permeate my life that I may be of some use to You in this world.

Camaraderie of Serving

Philippians 2:17-18

[17] But even if I am being poured out as a drink offering upon the sacrifice and service of your faith, I rejoice and share my joy with you all. [18] You too, I urge you, rejoice in the same way and share your joy with me.

Paul gave everything in his service to the Philippians . . . and to all the other churches he served. In fact using the same metaphor in communicating to Timothy, he summed up his life, "For I am already being poured out as a drink offering, and the time of my departure has come" (2 Tim. 4:6).

The apostle anticipated the soon-coming end of his life and ministry (as seen from the context of Philippians 2:16), and he viewed the totality of it as an offering to the Lord, the One who alone is worthy of Paul's complete and ultimate sacrifice. The imagery of the Old Testament ritual of pouring out a drink offering before the Lord is instructive. The drink offering accompanied the other sacrifices routinely offered at the altar; it was somewhat of a secondary offering. The idea was that the animals or grain offered were pictured as food for Deity, and thus, drink would go along it. Obviously, God didn't need physical food, but symbolism involved the people sacrificing what was essential for their own physical well-being. Some of the food was burned up completely (for example, the whole-burnt offering), but a portion of some sacrifices was given to the priests and Levites for their personal use.

Paul pictures his sacrifice of a lifetime in ministry as being secondary to the "sacrifice and service of your faith," which was a greater sacrifice, in his estimation. The Philippians were repeatedly facing persecution and were standing firm. Paul found great joy in helping in their spiritual progress. He was not focused on his own ministry, as though it were simply a career choice with its own goals and rewards. He was all about people. He rejoiced to see that his efforts were being fruitful in encouraging the sacrificial faith of the Philippians.

So, the Philippians shouldn't grieve, but rejoice with Paul as he anticipates his departure. Giving one's self for the Lord and his people either in life or death is the greatest service and the greatest joy one can experience. Such a life is contagious, for as Paul served them, they also served each other (and they served Paul in their financial support, as we will see later in the letter). The camaraderie of serving was enlarging, having such notables as not just the apostle and the Philippians, but also the Lord Jesus Christ who came not to be served, but to serve (Matt. 20:28). This camaraderie includes all who dedicate their lives to pouring out themselves as a drink offering in the service for others.

Lord, help me be a servant like the Lord Jesus Christ who washed others' feet.

Team Ministry

Philippians 2:19

¹⁹ But I hope in the Lord Jesus to send Timothy to you shortly, so that I also may be encouraged when I learn of your condition.

Paul was not a loner; he believed in and practiced team ministry. He had a penchant for developing young leaders, and he mentions two by name in his letter to the Philippians. Timothy was the better known of the two. On his second missionary tour, Paul picked him up in a place called Lystra (Acts 16:1). Timothy had apparently become a "disciple" during Paul's first trip through that area of Galatia (an area now known as the country of Turkey) in the eastern Mediterranean area. His background was of mixed ethnicity, half-Jewish and half-Gentile. The godly influence came from his mother's and grandmother's Jewish side (2 Tim. 1:5).

Paul spent considerable time mentoring this young man, taking him along on his extensive travels, as can be seen in the book of Acts. Timothy co-authored five of Paul's canonical letters (epistles)—one can imagine the interaction between the two as Paul set thoughts to paper.

In later years, Paul wrote two "personal" correspondences specifically to Timothy, which became recognized by the early church as authoritative for the whole Christian movement. Fortunately for us, these two letters contain much instruction for how the church (locally) should function: ". . . I write so that you will know how one ought to conduct himself in the household of God, which is the church of the living God, the pillar and support of the truth" (1 Tim. 3:15).

In Paul's interaction with Timothy, we see a model of what he taught Timothy to pass on, "The things which you have heard from me in the presence of many witnesses, entrust these to faithful men who will be able to teach others also" (2 Tim. 2:2). Timothy, in turn, presumably, passed it forward (so to speak). Since he himself was faithful, he would most certainly have found other faithful men to teach and to train, who would do likewise with other faithful individuals.

So, it is this Timothy that Paul planned to send to the Philippians in order to touch base, see how they are doing, and then report back to Paul. The apostle had a passion for the Philippians' spiritual growth and needed a faithful disciple to send—Timothy was the one. Oh, that more faithful Christians would step up to being disciples, servants of the Lord and His people—young men and women in particular, who are willing to serve where needed, willing to be mentored by godly older believers—who in turn will mentor and disciple others.

Lord, count me in as one of Your faithful servants. Use me, send me, empower me. That is my desire, Lord. Guide me, Lord, in Your grace.

Kindred Spirit

Philippians 2:20-22

[20] For I have no one else of kindred spirit who will genuinely be concerned for your welfare. [21] For they all seek after their own interests, not those of Christ Jesus. [22] But you know of his proven worth, that he served with me in the furtherance of the gospel like a child serving his father.

Love for the Philippians ran deep with the apostle Paul, and he was very particular about who to send as his emissary. The task of finding out how the Philippians were doing spiritually required a depth of spirituality. So here, we see a glimpse of how his mind worked in choosing his protégés. And since, in these meditations we have encouraged in a number of places to follow Paul's example, we do well to examine this mental process carefully. This will help leaders to establish wise and godly patterns for choosing others to lead. It will help each of us know the characteristics that are essential in the Lord's work.

First, a servant of God must have a genuine interest in the spiritual welfare of others. This is the humble characteristic emphasized in the first part of the chapter, ". . . do not merely look out for your own personal interests, but also for the interests of others" (Phil. 2:4). Christ is the prime example here, for His deep interest in us led Him to His sacrifice and service of redemption.

Second, a servant of God must be of proven worth (this phrase can be translated "proven character"). His life must demonstrate an interest in others. Serving the Lord and His people requires a genuineness, a solidness that can only be seen over time. "Do not lay hands upon anyone too hastily and thereby share responsibility for the sins of others . . ." (1 Tim. 5:22). Much damage has been wreaked in the Lord's work when great responsibilities have been placed on untested shoulders.

Paul recognized there were many unsuitable candidates for the task, men who simply were unproven or whose lives had been shown to be self-centered. This must have been one of the discouragements of his ministry, that there were so few who really had the character to be servants of God. He identified Timothy as an exceptional young man. He had a genuine interest in the Philippians, and he had proven his worth (or character) in his demonstrated efforts with Paul in the work of the gospel. Timothy was a great understudy, teachable and submissive to Paul's mentoring. He was exactly what was needed to connect with the Philippians about their spiritual wellbeing.

It is faithful, proven people that God uses for His work—for it is they who seek the interests of Christ, not their own.

Lord, I pray that You will raise up more young men and women who are able to move beyond self-centeredness and become other-centered.

Circumstantial Confidence

Philippians 2:23-24

²³ Therefore I hope to send him [Timothy] immediately, as soon as I see how things go with me; ²⁴ and I trust in the Lord that I myself also will be coming shortly.

S omething was burdening Paul's mind about the Philippians, but his attention first had to be with his current situation. He was imprisoned in Rome at the time of his writing and was apparently awaiting a legal decision. Remember in Acts 21-26, Paul had returned from his third missionary tour and had gone to Jerusalem where he was apprehended by the Jewish authorities. While being interrogated before the Roman authorities, he claimed his right as a Roman citizen to appeal to Rome. So in Acts 27-28, he was shipped to Rome under guard. The last we hear of him in the historical account of Acts, he was under house arrest in Rome awaiting the verdict (Rom. 28:16). During this time, we believe he wrote some of his so-called prison epistles.

Timothy would be dispatched once the outcome was made known, and he would inform the Philippians of Paul's wellbeing and doings. His hopes were that he himself would be also able to visit the Philippians subsequently. These small details give insights into the close relationship the apostle had with the Philippians. They had followed his ministry closely, being supporters of him from the earliest days (as we will see in later chapters of this letter).

A few observations are in order. Paul, although walking spiritually, being astute theologically and at times functioning prophetically, did not pretend to know his personal future with certainty. Not presuming upon God's will, he used words like "hope" in reference to what was ahead for him. Yet, at the same time, he had a confidence in how things would turn out, for he said, "I trust in the Lord . . ." which could also be translated, "I am convinced in the Lord . . ."

Also, we see, he used normal human wisdom in laying out his plans. He took pains to communicate them clearly, so there would be no second guessing why he was not going to the Philippians right away. Although he walked with the Lord, he still operated in the earthly realm and was subject to the normal affairs of the world, in this case, the deliberations of Caesar.

We have no record of Paul's having actually visited Philippi again, although the likelihood of that happening is not out of the question. That he was released from Roman incarceration is attested by many, but subsequent to that, his travel itinerary is somewhat sketchy to the historian. We do know that his plan was eventually to go to Spain (Rom. 15:28).

Lord, help me make the most of circumstances,
knowing that the future is in Your hands.

WEEKEND READING

Saturday – Luke 17
Sunday – Luke 18

PERSONAL REFLECTIONS

Fellowship the Way It Should Be

Philippians 2:25-26

25 But I thought it necessary to send to you Epaphroditus, my brother and fellow worker and fellow soldier, who is also your messenger and minister to my need; 26 because he was longing for you all and was distressed because you had heard that he was sick.

Highly esteemed in Paul's eyes are those who are other-centered. He really did believe what he wrote in the early part of the chapter, where he said, "Do nothing from selfishness or empty conceit, but with humility of mind regard one another as more important than yourselves; do not merely look out for your own personal interests, but also for the interests of others" (Phil. 2:3-4). He mentioned Timothy as an example and now Epaphroditus. Both had "this attitude . . . which was also in Christ Jesus" (vs. 5).

Epaphroditus apparently had been sent by the Philippians to Paul with a love-gift of financial support (see Phil. 4:18). Interestingly, the text says he was their messenger, which translates the word "apostolos," meaning "one who is sent on behalf of another." Whereas Paul was an apostle sent by the Lord to minister the Word to the Philippians, Epaphroditus was an "apostle" or "sent-one" commissioned by the Philippians to minister financial support to Paul. Now, Paul is sending him back, presumably with this letter.

Paul laid out high accolades in his threefold praise of Epaphroditus. First, he was a brother, obviously referring to their relationship as part of the family of God. Indeed, as a brother, Epaphroditus was more important to him than his earthly family, of whom we hear little in Paul's writings (see Acts 23:16). Second, this brother was Paul's fellow-worker. Epaphroditus was not a freeloader but served at great personal expense and with much energy. Finally, Paul calls him a "fellow soldier." He was one who saw his ministry as a war against the principalities and powers of the unseen world (Eph. 6:12). I pray that the Lord would send forth more workers like Epaphroditus, who are willing to sacrifice and work hard for the Lord and His people (Matt. 9:38).

He had apparently become quite ill and almost died. His fellow Christians back home heard about it and were very concerned. Possibly, he became homesick as well. Further, he was worried about their reaction to his illness, and this caused him additional stress. What an tremendous example of Philippians 2:1 where Christian fellowship is described: "Therefore if there is any encouragement in Christ, if there is any consolation of love, if there is any fellowship of the Spirit, if any affection and compassion . . ."

Lord, help me and my fellow Christians in my local church develop this same kind of affection and compassion for each other.

Honoring Missionaries—part 1

Philippians 2:27-30

[27] For indeed he was sick to the point of death, but God had mercy on him, and not on him only but also on me, so that I would not have sorrow upon sorrow. [28] Therefore I have sent him all the more eagerly so that when you see him again you may rejoice and I may be less concerned about you. [29] Receive him then in the Lord with all joy, and hold men like him in high regard; [30] because he came close to death for the work of Christ, risking his life to complete what was deficient in your service to me.

Not one to give up easily, Epaphroditus continued in his service alongside Paul even when sick. Another disciple, John Mark, bailed out on an earlier mission (Acts 13:13), and Paul refused to take him along on the next one: "But Paul kept insisting that they should not take him [John] along who had deserted them . . . and had not gone with them to the work" (Acts 15:38). But, Epaphroditus was called by Paul, "my brother and fellow worker and fellow soldier" (Phil. 2:25). He would have stayed on task, except that Paul insisted he go back to the Christians who had sent him to work with the apostle.

Obviously, Epaphroditus was healed of his ailment, and Paul saw this as a tremendous mercy on both Epaphroditus and himself. Had he died, Paul would have been plunged into deep grief. Therefore, upon his healing, he sent Epaphroditus back home, so that his sending church could rejoice with him. It may be that convalescence was in mind as well.

Lest they think Epaphroditus was a quitter, Paul wrote them the reason he was sending him back: 1) that the Philippians might rejoice over him 2) that Paul would be relieved of his concern over the Philippians' anxiety for Epaphroditus, and 3) that they would take the occasion to highly regard Epaphroditus and others like him who risked their lives in service of the Lord.

One thinks of the many who have left all to serve the Lord around the world. They have suffered illness and even death due to lack of adequate medical care. Some have died alone at the hands of persecutors. All have abandoned the comforts of home and warm support of family. Most are unsung and have had no books written about their lives. Many are forgotten, except in the annals of God's mind.

We should make every effort to honor men and women like that. We so easily recognize when a young person makes the huge step of faith and leaves a promising career to serve as a missionary. But, don't forget the senior missionaries who are often long forgotten and living out their days in a sub-standard nursing home. They should be honored as well!

Lord, thank You for the example of the many saints who have gone out and given everything to serve You. Help me to follow in their footsteps.

Honoring Missionaries—part 2

Philippians 2:29-30

²⁹ Receive him then in the Lord with all joy, and hold men like him in high regard;
³⁰ because he came close to death for the work of Christ, risking his life to complete
what was deficient in your service to me.

Receive them back—that is the message from our passage—one of the clearest, most succinct teachings on treatment of returning missionaries. In Epaphroditus' case, he had become sick to the point of dying, but God had healed him. The human tendency would be to see Epaphroditus' mission tour as over, illness having cut it short, and now, life would go back to "normal." While details are lacking, enough is said to indicate a great sacrifice had been made; nothing would ever be normal again.

When missionaries leave home today, the sacrifices are greater than most realize. Leaving careers behind is no small thing. Even those who serve short term (a few years) are set back enormously in their financial prospects. Consider missionaries who have served their entire life at great deprivation of things that everyone else so easily takes for granted and return home at an advanced age with health issues. Their work has not been of the sort that makes for "cutting edge" missions promo campaigns. How many are forgotten in nursing homes or are being looked after by a few younger relatives who see them as a burden?

Paul says to "receive" them back and to "hold them in high regard." This latter idea could be translated to "honor them." Interestingly, a closely related word was used in 1 Timothy 5:17 and translated "honor" in reference to financial support for those who teach and rule well in the local church. Churches should financially support their sick and elderly missionaries, especially those unable to continue serving "in the field."

Behind this emphasis is the "sending" and "receiving" that takes place with mission work. Epaphroditus was sent out by the Philippians as their "messenger and minister" to Paul's needs (Phil. 2:25). His work was "to complete what was deficient" in their service to Paul (vs. 30). This is at the root of New Testament missions work. A missionary is one who serves as a representative, an extension of the church. As such, the sending church should fully receive the missionary back with great honor and respect, for he was serving in their place. Every missionary effort requires both those who send and support, and those who go! Even Paul had the church at Antioch, which was God's vessel for sending him and Barnabas out on the first missionary tour (Acts 13:1-4). In the greatest sense, mission work is a team effort.

Lord, I confess my lack of honoring retired missionaries who are no longer able to serve as they did in younger years. Thank You for their sacrificial service.

Reinforcing Reiteration

Philippians 3:1

¹ Finally, my brethren, rejoice in the Lord. To write the same things again is no trouble to me, and it is a safeguard for you.

Writing was a significant part of Paul's ministry, in addition to being a traveling evangelist. Because God had appointed him to be an apostle to the Gentiles, he travelled from place to place, establishing the truth of the gospel. As a result, he did not spend much time in any one place. The longest period he stayed was one and a half years in Corinth (Acts 18:11) and three years in Ephesus (Acts 20:31). But, his practice was to write back to the churches he had visited.

From the earliest times, Paul's letters were recognized as authoritative. He himself fully accepted that responsibility. He did not hesitate to identify himself as an "apostle" and to wield his authority in writing. His written ministry carried such weight that others forged his name in circulating their own false teaching. For example, he wrote the Thessalonians to ". . . not be quickly shaken from your composure or be disturbed either by a spirit or a message or a letter as if from us, to the effect that the day of the Lord has come" (2 Thess. 2:2).

Peter, one of the original twelve, also one of the "inner circle" of three with James and John, recognized the authority of Paul's writings in referring to them on the same level as Scriptures: ". . . our beloved brother Paul . . . wrote to you, as also in all his letters, speaking in them of these things, in which are some things hard to understand, which the untaught and unstable distort, as they do also the rest of the Scriptures, to their own destruction" (2 Peter 3:15-16).

Paul himself was conscious of the effect his letters had and encouraged the Christians to circulate his writings. To the Colossians he wrote, "When this letter is read among you, have it also read in the church of the Laodiceans; and you, for your part read my letter that is coming from Laodicea" (Col. 4:16). His written ministry would go far beyond his "in person" ministry. In fact, his letters are continually used by the Lord to the present day, though Paul is long dead.

Here in this letter to the Philippian church, Paul reminded them of the basic things he taught them in person. The truth was so delightful to him, rehearsing it over and over was not drudgery, but a real joy. He never tired of his task of spreading the Word of God, nor of emphasizing it repeatedly. Truth needs to be constantly reinforced, lest our joy dissipate. In the case of the Philippians, he was now about to remind them of the lofty goal that had captured his heart for a life of service: the prize of the high calling in Christ.

Lord, thank You for preserving Your word through the teaching of the apostle Paul. I rejoice in all that he taught along with the rest of Scripture.

Threefold Beware

Philippians 3:2

² Beware of the dogs, beware of the evil workers, beware of the false circumcision ...

A cerbic language is what Paul used to describe false teachers. But, not just any false teachers. He had in mind a certain kind that was trying to mix the law with grace. They taught that faith in Jesus was important, but Gentile converts also needed to keep the law of Moses and its most celebrated symbol, circumcision. We call those people Judaizers. When he wrote to the Galatians, the apostle addressed them and that issue very pointedly.

With the Philippians, he addressed this issue in passing, really as a segue into his own testimony. But, he used the strongest possible pejoratives, the most cutting invectives to covey his contempt for people who teach such a false gospel. It is not that those men were ignorant. They knowingly determined to undermine the truth. The essence of their teaching still pervades the religions of the world, that God can only save people who become good enough by keeping the rules and, thereby, merit a favorable place before deity. Paul calls the purveyors of such teaching "dogs." It is the height of arrogance, that somehow a mere mortal can act in such a way the God is somehow beholden to him.

In the ancient world, this kind of language was about as harsh as it could get. Even today, in the middle-east, calling someone a dog is the worst possible insult. Paul also called them "evil workers" and "the false circumcision." This was not simply an intramural skirmish among like-minded theologians. The two views simply cannot co-exist. The core message is at issue.

The Jews of that day often referred to themselves as people of the circumcision, as in "We are the circumcision." Paul throws this back in their faces by saying they are in fact the "false circumcision." They have completely missed the point of the Law of Moses. It was designed to show the absolute holiness of God and His requirement of holiness on the part of His people. What the Jews failed to realize was that the Law brought condemnation, because as Paul wrote in another place, "All fall short of the glory of God" (Rom. 3:23). So, Paul reminds the Philippians to beware of those false teachers.

Today, in the effort to reach the "unchurched," the temptation is to not confront people with their sinfulness, but to simply present people "a better way to live, the way Jesus lived." The reality is that we are all sinners in need of forgiveness and salvation. Paul next shows that, despite all his former efforts at keeping the law, he now considers that all worthless.

Lord, help me constantly remind myself and others that the true Gospel of God is all about grace, not about meriting salvation through keeping the rules.

WEEKEND READING

Saturday – Luke 19
Sunday – Luke 20

A True Confidence

Philippians 3:3-4

³ ... for we are the true circumcision, who worship in the Spirit of God and glory in Christ Jesus and put no confidence in the flesh, ⁴ although I myself might have confidence even in the flesh. If anyone else has a mind to put confidence in the flesh, I far more ...

False circumcision—that is what Paul called the false teachers who tried to sway the Christians to submit to the Law of Moses and circumcision. Those teachers prided themselves in their ability to keep the Law. But, Paul in verse 2 dismissed them as "dogs" and "the uncircumcision."

Now, the apostle counters that "we" (meaning himself and those who follow his teachings) are the "true circumcision." His message was more true to historical Judaism than the Judaizers' outward adherence to the Law.

He wrote that true believers are characterized by three things: 1) They "worship in the Spirit of God." Jesus Himself had said, "An hour is coming, and now is, when the true worshipers will worship the Father in spirit and truth; for such people the Father seeks to be His worshipers" (John 4:23). This worship contrasts with fleshly worship which prides itself in keeping the Law. 2) True believers "glory in Christ Jesus." They are all about Him. He is the focus of their worship; they are ultimately concerned with His reputation. He is the One they fix their eyes on and make known in the world. The Judaizers had rendered Jesus Christ as being a good rabbi, but He was not central to their life's purpose. For the Christian, Jesus is the beginning and the end. He is everything. He is the message of the gospel. 3) True believers do not put any confidence in their human abilities (i.e. flesh) to attain standing with God. The Judaizers, on the other hand, promoted adherence to the Law which breeds a false pride of accomplishment.

Paul digresses into a personal testimony about his former life under the Law. If anyone could find satisfaction in that way of life, he was the one. To the casual reader of Scripture, Paul may seem to be bragging, which would of course be sub-Christian. However, he is looking back on his attitude before his conversion. He was not just your typical Jew, promoting the law of Moses, but he was one of the most advanced practitioners of the Jewish religion. Of everyone, he had the most to boast in. And, he had the most to lose in coming to faith in Christ. It was certainly not his failure in comparison with others that led him to true faith in Christ. In the next few verses, he outlines his major credentials and gives us an insight into his former pride.

Lord, You have called us to worship in spirit the Lord Jesus Christ and give Him all the glory. Help me to never glory in myself or my abilities.

A Faded Pedigree

Philippians 3:5-6

⁵ ... circumcised the eighth day, of the nation of Israel, of the tribe of Benjamin, a Hebrew of Hebrews; as to the Law, a Pharisee; ⁶ as to zeal, a persecutor of the church; as to the righteousness which is in the Law, found blameless.

Credentials are important . . . and no less so to Paul—although the importance of them changed for Paul. Here, he substantiated his previous claim that if anyone could boast in the flesh (that is, their ability to keep the Law of Moses, see verse 4), he would have a far better resume to do so. His list of accomplishments or fortunate life situations is noteworthy.

His Jewish pedigree was impeccable (see Galatians 1:8), beginning from his early childhood. His parents had him circumcised in strict accordance with the command to Moses, on the eighth day (Gen. 17:12). Thus, he was a Jew by birth, not a proselyte (i.e. convert). As such, he was a covenant member of the nation of Israel. His standing as a Jew might have been questioned by some who were natives of the land of Israel. They may have thought that since Paul was born in Tarsus, a Gentile city, and not born in Israel that maybe his Jewishness was suspect. After all, he was thoroughly conversant in the Greek culture. But, Paul insisted that he was as Hebrew as one can get ("a Hebrew of Hebrews"). He was a member of the tribe of Benjamin, the only tribe to side with Judah during the divided Monarchy. That tribe was considered an aristocratic leader among the others and, in fact, was the tribe of the first king of Israel, Saul.

Paul had been a Pharisee and, as such, had a reputation for strict adherence to the Law. No one could question his passion for defending the Law of Moses and harassing any who would dare to contravene it. Particularly well known was his persecution of the new movement, called the church. Then, in a startling statement of former self-righteousness, he claims that, when measured by the Law, he saw himself as being without sin, blameless. At the least, he felt that others saw him that way, and probably they did.

If ever there was an individual who had made a good case for becoming righteous by living a righteous life, it was Paul in his pre-conversion days. But, why is he saying all this? Is he trying to make himself look good in the eyes of others, to prove he is better? No, not at all! Remember, he had been addressing the teachings of those who urged believers to adopt the Law of Moses and be circumcised. Paul was saying that he went that route of keeping the Law, and he presented himself as the finest specimen of that way of living. But, this is a lead-in to his main point— how worthless it all really was.

Lord, help me not to look to my own religious efforts to add value to what Christ has done for me. Works of the Law add nothing to Christ's work.

A Loss For Knowing

Philippians 3:7-8

---

⁷ But whatever things were gain to me, those things I have counted as loss for the sake of Christ. ⁸ More than that, I count all things to be loss in view of the surpassing value of knowing Christ Jesus my Lord, for whom I have suffered the loss of all things, and count them but rubbish so that I may gain Christ ...

Pile up all the awards, accolades, academic accomplishments and praise of others, and they don't even come close to what Paul had come to discover. At one time, his past life was a source of pride, but no more. What made the change? It was that fateful encounter on the road to Damascus (Acts 9), when he was confronted by One whose glory blinded Paul's eyes to everything worldly. He walked away from all his former accomplishments to follow Christ. Only one thing mattered.

Paul didn't just walk away, as though the things of his past were neutral. No, he eschewed them; he counted them to be a loss. He even went as far as calling them rubbish. In the world's eye, that is backward. People that follow Christ give up so much; they suffer loss of the good and pleasant things of the world. Yes, it is true, being a Christian, a genuine one, means walking away from things once enjoyed, things from which one receives much pride.

How can a person do that? The only way to walk away from something considered of value is by moving toward something of greater value. For Paul, and for all Christians, that would be the Lord Jesus Christ. Because of Him, Christians have forsaken all. They have turned their backs on the things that once gave them significance or security. One young man, on the day he was saved, rushed home and threw out all his athletic trophies. Another took down his award certificates. Their significance now lay in something greater.

Knowing Christ is of surpassing value, says the apostle. There is nothing greater in all of life. No longer did his past give him satisfaction; there was now only one source of satisfaction, and that is Jesus Christ.

Paul had in view not just his old life in Judaism, but he also included anything else that a Christian could aspire to. To be sure, there is knowledge of many things that are helpful in both this life and in the spiritual realm. And, it's possible to seek after promotion in Christian circles, to seek after fame, positions of influence and significance. But, as a life pursuit, they all fall short of the greatest possible knowledge, namely knowing Christ. Paul's desire was to "gain Christ." In some respects, he already had Christ, but for him, it was a constant striving, a continual gaining Christ.

Lord, I confess that I have held too tightly to my accomplishments and my trophies. There is only one thing I desire now, and that is to know You better.

A Righteousness To Lose For

⁹ ... and may be found in Him, not having a righteousness of my own derived from the Law, but that which is through faith in Christ, the righteousness which comes from God on the basis of faith ...

The Christian leaves all behind, walking away from his trophies, his worldly achievements, his self-centered life, so that he might gain Christ (3:8). There is something compelling about that. What does he lose? Nothing in comparison to what he obtains, namely, Christ! But, not only has the Christian gained Christ; he is now "found in Him."

This is one of the greatest truths in all of Scripture, to be "in Christ." While Ephesians chapter one expands on all the benefits to us for being "in Christ," here Paul propounds one aspect of that pervasive topic: we now have a new kind of righteousness. He now lists six truths about this righteousness.

First, this righteousness comes only by being "in Him." Second, it is not our own righteousness. Third, it does not come through keeping the Law, Fourth, it comes through believing in Christ. Fifth, this righteousness comes from God. Sixth, it is based on faith.

The error of Paul before coming to Christ was that he saw righteousness as connected to him, within him. It was his righteousness that came through his meticulous law-keeping. It had nothing to do with Christ, the perfect sacrifice, the one who alone kept the Law perfectly. Of course, God was righteous, and Paul's determined effort had been to develop that godly righteousness through his own merits, based on the measurement of the Law. However, now that he had found Christ, this new righteousness completely eclipses the old kind of righteousness, which is really not righteousness at all. That is why Paul considered it rubbish (3:7-8), it was worthless in attaining to true righteousness.

Consider today, how many religions of the world teach a man-centered, law-enforced righteousness. In that sense, all religions are the same, only the rituals differ—a man becomes righteous by the things he does. Biblical Christianity, in contrast, teaches that a man is proven to be unrighteous by the things he does; he cannot possibly become righteous on his own. But, that which he cannot do for himself, God can and does do. He provides His own righteousness, and this is simply by His grace. Each of us is left to simply acknowledge his failure (confession), turn (repentance) and believe (faith) in the Lord Jesus Christ. As someone said, this is too good to be true. Yet, it is true!

*Lord, thanks for Your gracious love in giving me
Your Righteousness, which came by faith.*

Knowing Him in Power

Philippians 3:10

10 ... that I may know Him and the power of His resurrection ...

Paul's greatest aspiration in life was to "know Christ." All else was a corollary to this axiom of life. Nothing surpassed the knowledge of Him who is God personified in human flesh. Paul and Jeremiah were of the same cloth: "Thus says the Lord, 'Let not a wise man boast of his wisdom, and let not the mighty man boast of his might, let not a rich man boast of his riches; but let him who boasts boast of this, that he understands and knows Me, that I am the Lord who exercises lovingkindness, justice and righteousness on earth; for I delight in these things,' declares the Lord" (Jer. 9:23-24).

In his letter to the Romans, Paul finished his doctrinal treatise on justification with this exalted doxology: "For from Him and through Him and to Him are all things. To Him be the glory forever. Amen." (Rom. 11:36). His praise for Christ is threaded throughout his writings. For example, in writing to Timothy, he breaks out: "Now to the King eternal, immortal, invisible, the only God, be honor and glory forever and ever. Amen" (1 Tim. 1:17).

As one "untimely born" (1 Cor. 15:8), not having seen the Lord in his pre-resurrection days, Paul was driven to learn more of Christ. Of course, he was not talking about elementary knowledge of the facts of Christ. Rather, he desired the kind of knowing that comes only through prolonged experiences together with someone. He wanted to eat, drink, sleep and think Christ.

He wanted to know the power of His resurrection. But for Paul, this was not an infatuation with the supernatural. To be sure, it is exciting to see a bona-fide miraculous event, first hand! But, Paul knew the stories of the Old Testament, that the miracles of God were mimicked by the magicians of Egypt. He knew that Satan could pose as an angel of light, performing amazing feats. Today, there are charlatans abounding, portraying the supposedly miraculous to gullible, naïve people desperately wanting proof to bolster their lacking faith. That is not the kind of power Paul sought. He knew that God is there (as writer Francis Schaefer would say) and didn't need the miraculous to prove it.

Rather, Paul wanted to know the power that transforms lives from spiritual death to eternal life and liveliness—that is truly miraculous, something only God can do. Spiritual transformation can't be faked. Paul wanted to know the power over conquered sin, both in the lives of others and himself. To be sure, God worked miracles at Paul's hand. But, the greater knowledge he sought was Christ Himself. The manifestations of power were simply icing on the cake.

Lord, help me to know You and not become infatuated with signs and wonders. Please work Your real power in my life to conquer my self-centered attitude.

WEEKEND READING

Saturday – Luke 21
Sunday – Luke 22:1-38

Knowing Him in Suffering

Philippians 3:10

[10] ... that I may know Him and ... and the fellowship of His sufferings, being conformed to His death ...

K nowing Christ in the power of his resurrection is one thing. But, many Christians are satisfied with a message where they are well-fed, like the multitudes of John 6 that followed Christ. "Jesus answered them and said, 'Truly, truly, I say to you, you seek Me, not because you saw signs, but because you ate of the loaves and were filled'" (John 6:26). When the Lord's teaching turned difficult, "many of His disciples withdrew and were not walking with Him anymore" (John 6:66). Miraculous powers and signs do attract attention to a miraculous working God. If that, however, is the only thing people are looking for, they will be sorely disappointed in Christ.

Paul also wanted to know Christ in the "fellowship of his sufferings, being conformed to his death." But, who really wants suffering? Is Paul super-human or super-spiritual? No. It was not the suffering that he desired, but he wanted to experience the depth of fellowship that only suffering can uncover. Think of Peter and John when they had been imprisoned for the first time in the early days of the church. After being flogged and released, "They went on their way from the presence of the Council, rejoicing that they had been considered worthy to suffer shame for His name" (Acts 5:41).

Could it be that Paul, as one untimely born (1 Cor. 15:8), was reflecting on the fact that he was not there when Christ went through his suffering and death? Like a builder who wants to see his structure put to the ultimate stress test, Paul desired to see Christ's ability to see him through the ultimate stress test of life—suffering and persecution. But, can a Christian experience the very presence of Christ and His comfort in the middle of vexing circumstances? Can there be intimate fellowship with the God who cares when our suffering tempts us to scream out that He doesn't care? Can we have confident fellowship with the mighty God of the universe when our weakened soul is tempted to think He is unable to do anything with our situation?

Precisely in times of suffering we can begin to understand that He is in fact greater than we are. His mystery overwhelms us—but in a most excellent way. In suffering, we cling to truths like, "The secret things belong to the LORD our God, but the things revealed belong to us and to our sons forever, that we may observe all the words of this law" (Deut. 29:29). Even in the ultimate suffering of death, God speaks to us: "Precious in the sight of the LORD is the death of His godly ones" (Ps. 116:15).

Lord, it is not suffering I desire, but to know You in ways only suffering allows.

Excitement for the Soul

Philippians 3:11

11 ... in order that I may attain to the resurrection from the dead.

Paul wanted to know Christ, His power and His companionship during suffering, but how is that related to his hope of resurrection? Was his eternal destiny hanging in the balance, depending on the level of his commitment to know Christ? If only the immediate verse is considered, that would seem to be the case. However, the connection is found in the trilogy of purposes that the apostle had for leaving his old way of life behind (vs. 8). He did this "... that I may gain Christ" (8), "and may be found in him" (9) and "I may attain to the resurrection from the dead" (11). He clearly understood the "stakes" when he became a follower of Christ.

As a Pharisee in his former life, Paul would have believed there would be a resurrection, as opposed to the Sadducees who did not believe in a resurrection (Mark 12:18). However, it is clear from his testimony in Philippians that it had been only an academic adherence to the concept of a resurrection. He had not had personal assurance of it, for he listed his desire to have that as one of the reasons for leaving the old way behind.

What point is there in being a follower of Christ if there will be no resurrection? Paul makes that point in his letter to the Corinthians: "If we have hoped in Christ in this life only, we are of all men most to be pitied" (1 Cor. 15:19). Why is that put on the level of significance with knowing Christ? It seems so self-serving. For Paul, the resurrection meant spending eternity with Christ, the One he loved and faithfully served! He looked forward to no longer seeing "in a mirror dimly, but then face to face; now I know in part, but then I will know fully just as I also have been fully known" (1 Cor. 13:12). The struggle with the flesh will be finally over (Rom. 7). As part of the beloved church, he surely looked forward to that day when Christ would, "present to Himself the church in all her glory, having no spot or wrinkle or any such thing; but that she would be holy and blameless" (Eph. 5:27). Eternity for Paul would be unending fellowship with the lover of his soul.

The prospect of resurrection is what keeps the Christian going during times of struggle and suffering. "For momentary, light affliction is producing for us an eternal weight of glory far beyond all comparison ..." (2 Cor. 4:17). It is the final graduation from this life, promotion to glory, a complete transformation into the full realization of the likeness of God in Christ. We rejoice now, "knowing that He who raised the Lord Jesus will raise us also with Jesus and will present us with you" (2 Cor. 4:14).

Lord, the thought of being raised to be with you excites my soul!

Getting a Grip

Philippians 3:12-13a

12 Not that I have already obtained it or have already become perfect, but I press on so that I may lay hold of that for which also I was laid hold of by Christ Jesus. 13 Brethren, I do not regard myself as having laid hold of it yet ...

Paul was very clear about his ultimate mission in life. It was not reaching people for Christ! This is probably one of the most misunderstood things among Christians today. As radical as this may sound, the church is not ultimately all about winning souls.

True, helping people (we call this evangelism) come to Christ in repentance to receive forgiveness of sins is absolutely important. God himself sent His son into the world to save sinners. And, the Lord challenged all Christians of all time with the Great Commission (Matt. 28:18-20). But, that was not Paul's ultimate goal, nor should it be ours; it was not the thing that helped him arise in the morning after a beating or shipwreck and continue going on in his ministry. He was reaching higher. Evangelism was a means to an end. His real goal wasn't even the thing that he himself set as a goal. It was a goal God had given him, and he was compelled by it.

Paul's goal was to know to know Christ (vs. 10). Here, he put it, "that I may lay hold of that for which also I was laid hold of by Christ Jesus" (vs. 12). He wanted to line up his life with God's purposes for him. Nothing more, nothing less. Yes, God wanted him to be the apostle to the Gentiles (Gal. 2:7-9). But, it was not apostleship that Paul coveted, but rather, he desired the relationship with God whereby he obeyed what God wanted him to do. In his case, it was being obedient as an apostle to reach the Gentiles. But, the specific task was not the ultimate issue. Just as Christ was obedient to His father, so also Paul wanted to be obedient to God. But, even Christ had a goal higher than that.

The humble reality of Paul was remarkable. If his goal was just winning people to Christ, he could rest assured that he was quite successful (from human perspectives). However, he had not yet fully attained the real goal for which he was called. A godly, older woman once told me as I was about to embark into ministry fulltime, "Remember, you are not going out to serve people . . . you are going out to serve the Lord." Our passion to help people comes out of our commitment to serve God. He is our master, our leader, the head of the church. A devoted child focuses on the gift giver, and then, the gift is so much more enjoyable. The servant focuses on the master, and task assignment comes into better focus . . . because it is tied to the master. Paul set his sights on more and more laying hold of God's purpose in his life. He was always pressing ahead.

Lord, I set You before my eyes, for You are my goal and my purpose in life.

Greater Motivation

Philippians 3:13b-14

[13] ... but one thing I do: forgetting what lies behind and reaching forward to what lies ahead, [14] I press on toward the goal for the prize of the upward call of God in Christ Jesus.

This is the ultimate, worthy goal of the Christian. It is like the E=mc2 formula for the theory of relativity: simple to state, but profound in its implications. Paul simplifies his life's mission to "one thing I do." This sums it all up. And, it would serve every Christian well to contemplate this thought.

There are myriad of experiences in our past lives that have potential to keep us from this goal, though. Regrets, painful memories, bitterness or failures may thwart us. But like Paul, we need to forget what lies behind us. In financial investing terms, past results are no guarantee of future returns. In spiritual terms, however, dwelling on the past can guarantee future failure! We cannot move forward by living in reverse. We cannot change the past.

True, we need to learn from our experiences, but we cannot dwell on them in negative ways and become debilitated by them. To be sure, there is a place for sorting through issues that paralyze us. But, we must be careful that such efforts don't become a way of life, keeping us stuck in the past. The reality is that we may not be able to resolve all those issues. Our faces and thoughts must be turned forward. But to what?

Paul was forward thinking, a forward mover. He describes this as looking toward the goal of winning a prize. There will be an award for his labors. He is not talking here about salvation—that is already his. Romans 8:1 says, "Therefore there is now no condemnation for those who are in Christ Jesus." Paul models for us a motivation in the Christian life that comes from his relationship with the Lord Jesus Christ. This is not about winning spiritual trinkets that we will proudly boast about through eternity. Rather, the prize he has in mind is the "upward call of God."

The apostle saw his ultimate destiny as a "promotion to glory." It will be a graduation from this testing experience we call life into the ultimate life we were made for, called eternity. "He who is faithful in a very little thing is faithful also in much; *and he who is unrighteous in a very little thing is unrighteous also in much*" (Luke 16:10). It is what Peter wrote about when he said, "for in this way the entrance into the eternal kingdom of our Lord and Savior Jesus Christ will be abundantly supplied to you" (2 Peter 1:11). Imagine such a welcome into eternity!

Lord, help me keep Christ in view, with the eternal prospects of the much greater life with Him when I am received into Your presence for eternity.

Attitude Aspiration

Philippians 3:15-16

¹⁵ Let us therefore, as many as are perfect, have this attitude; and if in anything you have a different attitude, God will reveal that also to you; ¹⁶ however, let us keep living by that same standard to which we have attained.

Twice now, we are challenged to have an attitude. In Philippians 2:5, the attitude of Christ is the goal, humbleness. Here, the mindset of Paul is to be imitated, having a clear focus on the "prize of the upward call of God in Christ" (vs. 14). This is something worth dying for—to know Christ.

Now, Paul addressed those who are "perfect", and he includes himself in the "us." What's that all about? Earlier on, he had written that he had not already become "perfect" (vs. 12). Lest Paul is blatantly contradicting himself, which is highly unlikely on a number of fronts, then he is using these words differently in the two verses. Previously, he was stressing that he had not yet come to completely know Christ (vs. 10), and he was still striving for that intimacy and depth of knowing. Here in our passage for today, he refers to those who are mature (which is one of the meanings of the underlying Greek word translated "perfect" in the NASB—in fact, some other translations render the word as "mature"). Some Christians will be mature enough to not only understand Paul's commitment to an all out pursuit of knowing Christ, but they will accept the challenge to adopt the same "attitude."

However, some will not accept this challenge, or may not have sufficiently grown in their faith to appreciate the significance of it. This is not a tiered level of Christian faith, but simply a continuum of growth in faith. Paul is not pressing the issue, but laying out the gauntlet for those "who have ears to hear."

At the very minimum, whether we "get" Paul's attitude or not, we should at least hold our ground at the level of faith that we have attained. This is not the same as putting your life in neutral. He means for us to keep on actively walking in faith at the level of understanding you are at. Keep living up to the commitment and the standard of faith-walking to which we have already reached, to what God has revealed to you already. Don't go into "cruising" mode, neutral or falling back.

Paul's was not a ministry of complacency; for when Christians coast in their spiritual walk, they will end up falling backwards. There is a difference between actively living and growing as a Christian over 30 years versus living one year as a Christian repeated 30 times over! We should continue living up to what we have attained, and pursue Christ even more.

Lord, help me to always move forward, with the same attitude as the apostle Paul, never content to coast. I want to go all out for Christ!

WEEKEND READING

Saturday – Luke 22:39-71
Sunday – Luke 23:1-25

_____
_____
_____
_____
_____
_____
_____
_____
_____
_____
_____
_____
_____
_____
_____
_____
_____
_____
_____
_____
_____
_____
_____

To Model Or Not

[17] Brethren, join in following my example, and observe those who walk according to the pattern you have in us.

Integrity was his confidence, yet without arrogance. Very few would dare tread where Paul goes in his teaching. He is actually using himself as an example of how to live the Christian life! Paul would never have said, "Do as I say, not as I do." His life was an extension of his teaching.

There is nothing more powerful in conveying truth than when a person lives the truth he propagates and invites imitation. When a parent teaches a child to tie his or her shoes, he will often say, "Here, watch me do it." Nothing arrogant or hypocritical about that. And then, the child imitates the motions of the parent. So, also, in discipling or mentoring other Christians, there is a place for the more mature believer saying, "Here, watch me do it." However, in doing this, we need to avoid the attitude that we are "better" than others in our Christian walk. Paul's model was not that of one who has arrived, but of one who was striving to move ahead (see 3:12-15). He invites us to join him in the struggle to know Christ.

The apostle was intentional about modeling his teaching. He wrote to the Corinthians that he was their tutor "Therefore I exhort you, be imitators of me" (1 Cor. 4:16). He kept this modeling in humble perspective when he later wrote, "Be imitators of me, just as I also am of Christ" (1 Cor. 11:1). In other words, his example was not perfect, but we should follow him as he reflects Christlikeness. Peter also emphasized this when he instructed elders to "be examples to the flock" (1 Peter 5:3).

Modeling fleshes out the teachings of Scripture in human form. The example of those who are more mature acts like a surrogate, standing us in good stead until we reach that level of maturity and conviction for ourselves. For example, as a young believer I adopted the view and application of biblical teachings on end times prophesy (eschatology) held by those who were discipling me. I was not ready at that time nor equipped to give this topic the thorough study needed to gain personal conviction. But in time, I came to a place and understanding of Scripture to be able to study that topic in depth and arrive at my own convictions. A great part of the Christian life is learned this way. First, following others' example and then personal conviction.

All the more reason we need good models of Christ-like living; those who have set their focus on pressing toward the mark of the upward call in Christ.

Lord, I want to be a model of the Christian life for others. Help me so live that others will see and follow my example, as I follow Christ.

A Model To Not Follow

Philippians 3:18-19

[18] For many walk, of whom I often told you, and now tell you even weeping, that they are enemies of the cross of Christ, [19] whose end is destruction, whose god is their appetite, and whose glory is in their shame, who set their minds on earthly things.

What a tragic statement for Paul to have written, such a complete, final declaration. Maybe the weight of this kind of assessment was a part of what he meant earlier when he wrote: "Apart from such external things, there is the daily pressure on me of concern for all the churches" (2 Cor. 11:28). Of all the concerns he had, this one must have been one of the heaviest. And, Paul was warning the Philippians that in following his example and others like him (Phil. 3:17), they should avoid following the example of these "enemies of the cross of Christ." But, who were the people to whom Paul was referring?

He was probably not referring to pagans in general, because exemplary living would not be expected of them. Neither would these be from the rank and file of the Philippians, for the whole tenor of the letter would then have been different. They could have been the Judaizers who frequently posed as Christians but attempted to bring believers under the Law—yet in reality were self-exalting. Another possibility is that they were "antinomians," that is, people who went to the other extreme from legalists and lived a life "free" from all laws and restraints. Certainly, Christians should avoid both extremes. At any rate, the warning seems to be about "professing" Christian teachers who were trying to gain a following among the Philippians.

Paul describes them in five ways: 1) They are enemies of the cross of Christ, completely opposed to everything He is about. Christianity is not simply about following the teachings of Jesus; it is about His propitiatory, substitutionary death for sinners. To minimize or ignore this is tantamount to being an enemy of God Himself. 2) Their destiny is destruction. This refers to judgment in hell forever. 3) "Their god is their appetite;" they worshiped at the altar of unrestrained self-indulgence. Their lives were focused supremely on their own desires. 4) Their glory is their shame. The very things they were proud of will bring them enormous shame for eternity, though they may not yet realize it. 5) Their minds were set on earthly things. There was absolutely no hint of any kind of spiritual sensitivity or concern.

The thought of "professing Christians" like that is what makes Paul weep, and the Philippians should avoid their life style.

Father, thank You for regenerating me into a new creation in Christ. I affirm to You that Jesus and His death on the cross is central to my salvation and my life.

Finally Perfect

²⁰ For our citizenship is in heaven, from which also we eagerly wait for a Savior, the Lord Jesus Christ; ²¹ who will transform the body of our humble state into conformity with the body of His glory, by the exertion of the power that He has even to subject all things to Himself.

What a wonderful truth! There is coming a time when the struggle to live rightly will be over, and we will all be transformed. Up until now in his letter to the Philippians, Paul had been encouraging them to press onward, following his example, in the struggle for keeping the focus on Christ and knowing Him. But, that struggle will not go on forever. Though we have not arrived yet at perfection, one day we will attain that goal, God will see to it!

Our hope begins with the fact we are citizens of the heavenly realm. Our time on earth is temporary, as ex-patriots of God's nation. We are on assignment as ambassadors, but our true home is with God. Further, our hope is fanned by the desire to know Christ, the power of His resurrection and the fellowship of His sufferings—all themes of this letter. When a Christian desires to know Christ, he will eagerly look forward to the Savior's return.

Beside the prospect of His actualized presence, we will enjoy a complete change in our lives. This body of mine that carries my soul and spirit will be revolutionized. This will take place at the resurrection (or rapture, whichever comes first). The details of this transformation are kept secret (for example, will our new bodies have age appearance?). But, we do know that our bodies will become like Jesus' body. The apostle John corroborates this: "Beloved, now we are children of God, and it has not appeared as yet what we will be. We know that when He appears, we will be like Him, because we will see Him just as He is" (1 John 3:2). We also know our new bodies will be glorious, perfect in every way, no more temptation to sin, no more pain or fear of any kind.

God will finally take complete charge of the change process. Certainly, He has been sovereign all along, and the Spirit is involved in our "progressive" sanctification, enabling us to grow to be more like Christ. And, it is true that we are already "positionally" sanctified, that is, set apart for God's purposes. But, God will "perfect the work" (Phil. 1:6) that is not fully accomplished on earth, and it will be an instantaneous work at His coming. His power and sovereignty will be seen plainly in the complete change He accomplishes in us. Is it any wonder that Christians eagerly wait for His coming? It is part of His plan to bring all things, including our bodies, into subjection to Himself.

Lord, what an exciting promise You have given us. Help me to be patient and to continue pressing onward until that day when I see the Lord Jesus face to face.

Joy of Fellowship

Philippians 4:1

¹ Therefore, my beloved brethren whom I long to see, my joy and crown, in this way stand firm in the Lord, my beloved.

S tand firm! That is the instruction to Christians who are doing well, as were the Philippians. Paul had given as examples Timothy, Epaphroditus and himself. Now, as teacher and discipler, he summarized this exhortation: it is left up to the Philippians and to us to simply stand firm.

However, Paul's relationship with them was more than just being a teacher-discipler. He expressed close relationship with them in five ways, and in these, we can see how we ought to strive for relationships with other Christians.

First, Christian fellowship and service is defined by love. Paul, twice in this verse, called the Philippians "my beloved." Love is the primary motivator in Christian community. Whether our service to others is to teach or to disciple, or to serve or to show acts of mercy, our ministry needs to be motivated and saturated with love. People are not just numbers to be written down on an "accountability" sheet. They are beloved of God; are they beloved of us?

Second, we are all part of the same family, a spiritual one, building each other up. Paul calls the Philippians "brethren," a term used eight times in this small letter. Spiritual family, to him, was more important than earthly family or relationships.

Third, ministry with people needs human contact. Paul longed to be with the Philippians. In this day of internet communication, ministry can become very impersonal. Sending email is not the same as talking in person. Genuine Christian fellowship needs physical presence.

Fourth, the old saying is true, there is joy in serving others. Paul thought of the Philippians as his joy. Joy, of course, is the theme of the book of Philippians. He had prayed for them in joy (Phil. 1:4). He asked that they would "make my joy complete by being of the same mind . . ." (Phil. 2:2), and in his letter, he wanted to share his joy with them (2:17).

Fifth, when we serve others, they become our crown, the fruit of our labor. Our rewards are inseparable from serving others in love and joy. What could be better than knowing your gifts are being used by God to build up others?

Do you see the imitation of Christ here? We are beloved by God (John 15:12); He longed to be with us and so become a man (Phil. 2:6-7); He is not ashamed to call us brethren (Heb. 2:11); we were the joy set before Him (Heb. 12:2); He has been crowned with glory because of His sacrifice (Heb. 2:7).

Lord, thank You for the community of fellowship with You and Your saints!

The Urge of Fellowship

Philippians 4:2-3

² I urge Euodia and I urge Syntyche to live in harmony in the Lord. ³ Indeed, true companion, I ask you also to help these women who have shared my struggle in the cause of the gospel, together with Clement also and the rest of my fellow workers, whose names are in the book of life.

Fourteen times Paul "urges" (the Greek word is "parakaleo") the readers of his various epistles. He urges, for example, a sacrificial life for Christ (Rom. 12:1) and unity of the believers (1 Cor. 1:10). Here in our passage, Paul breaks from speaking to the church as a whole to address two women by name. And, he exhorts them equally by the repetition of the word "urge." Clearly, he was not taking sides in the dispute.

These two women must have been quite prominent, and their disharmony must have been making quite the negative impact on the fellowship of an otherwise joyful assembly of believers at Philippi. The nature of the dispute is not revealed, and it is probably just as well! It was certainly not a doctrinal issue, for Paul would have urged fidelity to the truth, rather than commitment to fellowship. Most likely, the conflict had to do with personal issues, for which there needs to be harmony in the fellowship (see Philippians 2:1-4).

Much has been written about the identity of the individual referred to as "true companion." Suggestions include Timothy or Epaphroditus (who were mentioned in chapter 2). Another suggestion sees in the underlying Greek word an actual name, Syzygus, whose name means "true companion." Regardless, the idea is that intervention was needed; someone to come alongside to help them work through their differences. Is not interpersonal conflict a frequent occurrence in the family of God, where two believers simply have a difficult time getting along? Likewise, it should also be normal for others to care enough for their brothers and sisters in Christ to become involved in being peacemakers or arbiters in such disputes.

Paul had a particular interest in these women, for they had apparently been part of a ministry team with Paul and Clement. Possibly, they were among the first group of believers in Philippi along with Lydia, the Philippian jailer and others (see Acts 15:12-40). The fellowship among them may have been particularly deep because of the persecution Paul and Silas (and possibly others) endured in Philippi. Indeed, camaraderie borne out of shared adversity runs at a different level than that which knows of no hardship. These women had demonstrated the genuineness of their faith, so that Paul can safely say their "names are in the book of life."

Lord, help me to get along with my co-workers in the service of the Lord.

WEEKEND READING

Saturday – Luke 23:26-56
Sunday – Luke 24

PERSONAL REFLECTIONS

Joy Twice Over

Philippians 4:4

⁴ Rejoice in the Lord always; again I will say, rejoice!

Joy is the theme of this book, as many have pointed out. Rejoicing is a word used to describe the act of expressing joy. This should characterize all Christians, so Paul repeats himself on this. We can never be reminded enough.

Why is it so difficult to rejoice when we have so much to be joyful about? We have been redeemed and assured of salvation (Phil. 1:6). For us, the Creator God of the universe humbled Himself, and despite the present circumstances of evil in the world, He has been exalted and one day will be seen as exalted (Phil. 2:5-11). Yet, daily difficulties so easily overwhelm us and rob the joy from our experiences. We fret; we worry; we dwell on slights and innuendoes. We become angry, frustrated, fearful, vengeful and unforgiving. None of these brings joy, so they rob us of life.

If only, we think, the things that cause these behaviors or feelings could be eliminated, then and only then, we could experience joy. However, true joy is not contingent upon our outward circumstances, but on our commitment to being joyful. Otherwise, joy could not be commanded.

We can look for no better example than that of our Lord on the night in which He was betrayed. In the upper room, just ahead of the greatest tragedy this world has ever known, when darkness attempted to extinguish the Light, the world which He made and in which He came to dwell rejected Him. It was during this time that Jesus made these remarkable statements:

"These things I have spoken to you so that My joy may be in you, and that your joy may be made full" (John 15:11).

"Until now you have asked for nothing in My name; ask and you will receive, so that your joy may be made full" (John 16:24).

"But now I come to You; and these things I speak in the world so that they may have My joy made full in themselves" (John 17:13).

So, we see that our Lord experienced joy in the midst of the worst circumstances and taught His disciples about that joy. Further, the writer of Hebrews tells us to, "[fix] our eyes on Jesus, the author and perfecter of faith, who for the joy set before Him endured the cross, despising the shame, and has sat down at the right hand of the throne of God" (Heb. 12:2). Joy rises above our circumstances, for it ascends to the source of all joy: "Splendor and majesty are before Him, strength and joy are in His place" (1 Chron. 16:27). Let us rejoice as an act of our will.

Lord, You have given me much to rejoice in. And, it gives me great joy to live and to walk in Your presence, where there is fullness of joy (Ps. 16:11).

An Unrelenting Requirement

Philippians 4:5

⁵ Let your gentle spirit be known to all men. The Lord is near.

Gentleness is incumbent upon all Christians. This instruction carries all the more significance after Paul's chastising of Euodia and Syntyche in verse 2-3 for their disharmony. It is difficult to be gentle and disagreeable at the same time. Because the Lord's coming is near, we need to take this to heart.

Gentleness is a quality easily overlooked on the list of priorities for Christian growth. In a world of changing theologies and philosophies, including post-modern thinking which questions the very nature of truth itself, there seems to be far more important things to be concerned with. If ever there was a time for Christians to assertively stand up in the public square to proclaim in no uncertain terms the truth of God, that time is now. Gentleness could get steamrolled by aggressive debate and by the cacophony of voices.

Gentleness as used in our passage is the translation of the Greek word epiekeio, which conveys "the quality of gracious forbearing." It is similar to the word used by Jesus to describe Himself: "Come to Me, all who are weary and heavy-laden, and I will give you rest. Take My yoke upon you and learn from Me, for I am *gentle* and humble in heart, and you will find rest for your souls. For My yoke is easy and My burden is light." (Matt. 11:28-30 emphasis mine). Some translations render the word as "meek." So, this is characteristic of the Lord Jesus Christ.

In addition, gentleness takes its place in the fruit of the Spirit (Gal. 5:23), an essential aspect of the Spirit-filled life. It may seem counter-intuitive, but God places a high premium on this understated quality of personal character.

What good does it do us to be gentle in a world that says that you must look out for yourself because no one else will? Won't we get run over by those who are more aggressive, who are willing to take advantage of any and all people weak enough to give way to their superior force? This is where the power of the living God comes into play. Jesus said, "These things I have spoken to you, so that in Me you may have peace. In the world you have tribulation, but take courage; I have overcome the world" (John 16:33). The Lord has already won! He is waiting until the world will be seen as His footstool (Heb. 1:13; 10:13), but it is as good as done now. We can be gentle because we know the ultimate outcome of everything—the Lord has overcome.

Acting in gentleness is a way to step aside and allow God to supernaturally intervene. It means setting aside revenge. It means learning what Proverbs teaches, "A gentle answer turns away wrath" (Prov. 15:1).

Lord, teach me how to be gentle, not out of weakness but strength.

Peace Or Anxiety

Philippians 4:6-7

⁶ Be anxious for nothing, but in everything by prayer and supplication with thanksgiving let your requests be made known to God. ⁷ And the peace of God, which surpasses all comprehension, will guard your hearts and your minds in Christ Jesus.

Peace or anxiety, polar opposites, comprise the choice every Christian makes. Neither is a given, determined by the consequences of birth or of circumstances. God cannot command that which is intrinsically impossible for us to do, so it must be within our ability to resist anxiety. So in a universal appeal, the inspired writer simply instructs, "Be anxious for nothing"—no matter the events that happen to you, however difficult they may seem. Cancer, loss of a loved one, uncertainty about the future, threats, dangers of any sort—the choice for either anxiety or peace remains yours to make.

Now, this is not the psycho-mumbo-jumbo of positive thinking as though you have it within yourself to will into a state of peacefulness. This has no ultimate effect because it is not grounded in anything other than yourself. It's like throwing the anchor overboard, only to have it land on the lower deck—not much help! Rather, the antidote to anxiety is prayer.

What a wonderful promise is laid out. The God of peace will give us the peace of God—and that peace exceeds our rational comprehension. In some ways, God's peace makes no sense. How can we face the ultimate tragedies of life (to put the matter to the extreme) or any lesser stress, with an inner peace that really does guard us from irrational thoughts and actions or emotions out of control?

The key, though, is confident prayer in the God of peace. It is the kind of prayer where we bring our pleas for help to God with a sense of thankful anticipation of supernatural working in our inner person. This is confidence not only in God's ability to bring us peace, but also in God's willingness to do so.

The point here is not the occasional experience where we cast ourselves upon God in the face of some particularly difficult circumstance. Rather, it is a lifestyle of dependence upon Him in everything; it is a way of life trusting Him even in the smaller stressors of life. What an antidote to the stress and anxieties of life! For some, this is a completely foreign way of living. For others, it is the Christian norm. Some completely disintegrate in the face of life's difficulties. Others, through trusting the Lord, walk vigorously and confidently with the peace of God, even in the most trying times of life.

Lord, I ask that You would remind me when anxiety creeps into my life experience that this is Your flag signaling me to trust in You.

From the Inside Out

Philippians 4:8

⁸ Finally, brethren, whatever is true, whatever is honorable, whatever is right, whatever is pure, whatever is lovely, whatever is of good repute, if there is any excellence and if anything worthy of praise, dwell on these things.

Many admonitions Paul gave to the Philippians, that group of Christians who simply needed prodding to continue doing well. The Philippian church was remarkable in its lack of serious problems. To be sure, there were some interpersonal skirmishes, but overall the church was harmonious, and Paul's letter to them was a relatively easy read.

So, Paul now enters into his final exhortation, to focus one's inner thoughts on things higher than the mundane issues of this world. Scripture says, "For as he thinks within himself, so he is" (Prov. 23:7). What a person thinks, controls his behavior. Behavior does not change the real person inside, but rather, the real person inside, what he really thinks, controls his outward behavior. God is interested in change from the inside out, not the outside in. "For the mouth speaks out of that which fills the heart. The good man brings out of his good treasure what is good; and the evil man brings out of his evil treasure what is evil" (Matt. 12:34b-35).

So, how does one go about changing his thinking? Paul gives the prescription in eight parts. We need to "dwell on these things." That means to ponder, consider deeply and meditate on them. What are they? Rather than define them, Paul simply describes them. Things that are true, honorable, right, pure, lovely, good repute, excellent, worthy of praise. These defy exhaustive exegesis. They simply are. And, they speak to the inner, new man. Like recognizing the color blue when you see it, these are qualities that are recognizable to the spiritual man (though they are invisible to the carnal man).

Christian maturity is aided by the training of our minds to look for these things. Like a pianist trains by studying the musical score and practicing it repeatedly, so the Christian trains his mind by studying what is true, honorable, etc. and practicing these things in his outward behavior. Does a list of eight things to dwell on sound overwhelming? These can be thought of, though, as the perfections of God Himself. Therefore, "[God will] keep him in perfect peace whose mind is stayed on you, because he trusts in you" (Isa. 26:3).

Is this not the context leading up to our verse, "Do not be anxious, for the peace of God will guard your hearts and mind?" For our victory is found in focusing our thoughts on God Himself, the locus of all good things.

Lord, I commit to focusing on those things which reflect Your character. I don't want my life to be consumed with inferior thoughts of this world.

An Imitation Based Growth

Philippians 4:9

⁹ The things you have learned and received and heard and seen in me, practice these things, and the God of peace will be with you.

Imitation has long been a primary form of learning. It begins with an infant who copies his parents, from waving "bye, bye" or taking his first steps. God placed something inside each human to make order out of life's experiences and stimuli—we call that learning. Very little is learned from scratch, though. Behavior is the sum total of all that we take in from around us, sorted through and then adapted by our own internal decision making and evaluative processes to the actions we take that then affect the outer world. Imitation is the shortcut. We do something simply because we have seen someone else do it, because we judge (however quickly or thoughtfully) it to be the correct way to behave.

One can set upon to only act according to what one has thoroughly thought through himself. However, life is not long enough to figure it all out for oneself. So, in the Christian world, imitation is a good thing; it is based on trust. We trust someone else enough that we deem his or her behavior worthy of our imitation, and we build from there. Paul consciously invited his readers, the Philippians and us, to imitate him—like a parent teaching the child how to tie his shoe, saying, "Here, watch me." He laid his whole life out there for them as a model: the things he taught, what they have received, heard and seen in Paul's life.

What are needed today are mentors and disciplers like the apostle Paul. One of the things we should imitate about him is his ministry of discipling others. There is only so much that can be conveyed through pulpit preaching on Sunday mornings. What is needed for Christian growth and maturity are models to be followed. Models of mature Christian men and women who are not afraid to say, "Yes, imitate me as you grow in your Christian life."

Is it arrogant for a person to make such a statement; does it imply that he has arrived at perfection? Of course not. Paul already said that he himself had not yet arrived to complete maturity (Phil. 3:13). Rather, it means a Christian at some point ought to be able to say, "Yes, I have grown and matured in my walk with Christ. I am not perfectly mature yet, but I can show to younger Christians by my life and teaching how it works for me."

There is a particular insight here, though, in Paul's ministry. God had given him as an inspired, biblical model to follow, and when we imitate his sacrificial life, we will experience the presence of peace from the God of peace.

Lord, thank You for the godly examples in my life, and especially that of Paul the apostle, who have given me a standard to live up to.

WEEKEND READING

Saturday – John 1
Sunday – John 2

PERSONAL REFLECTIONS

_____
_____
_____
_____
_____
_____
_____
_____
_____
_____
_____
_____
_____
_____
_____
_____
_____
_____
_____
_____
_____
_____
_____
_____
_____
_____
_____
_____
_____

No Fund Raising Here

Philippians 4:10

[10] But I rejoiced in the Lord greatly, that now at last you have revived your concern for me; indeed, you were concerned before, but you lacked opportunity.

Overjoyed with the Philippians' renewed financial support for him in his ministry, the apostle effuses with commendation for them. Apparently, they had previously helped him with his expenses and travel needs, but a hiatus for an undetermined amount of time had interfered with their otherwise faithful support for him. Maybe it was a logistical problem, or possibly the Philippians had some temporary financial setback. It is even possible their interest had lagged; as the old saying goes, "Out of sight, out of mind." Whatever the case, their interest in supporting Paul was restored.

Paul doesn't chastise them or in any way make them feel guilty. He simply commends them for their support and lets them in on his inner joy in the Lord. One application here might go like this: when we give to support people serving in ministry, we not only allow God to use us to support them in their work, but we also cause their joy in the Lord to abound. And, if our hearts are knit together with the Lord's, we rejoice in the Lord as well, knowing we are used by God.

While his thankfulness to them is implicit, Paul rejoiced "in the Lord greatly." The Philippians were simply the conduit of God's provisions. Paul knew that their monetary support was ultimately from God. In fact, he trusted the Lord to supply, and he recognized God's hand in providing for him.

There is a subtle but profound point to be made here. When a minister of the gospel looks to people as the source of his support rather than to God, a whole host of difficulties arise. Will they stop giving support if he preaches a message they don't like or if they don't think he is working hard or long enough? Do salaries and benefit packages become negotiable? Does the giver (or giving institution) become master to the receiver? The temptation can arise to preach to the source of the support and neglect those who cannot "pay" as much. Then, there can be bitterness because of low incomes or pay scales as compared to worldly careers or selecting ministry opportunities based on pay.

One is reminded of Mr. Bill Bright (founder of Campus Crusade) who insisted on living at the same income level as the rest of the Crusade staffers. Or, George Mueller, who, following Paul's pattern, never asked for money for his orphanage ministry or for himself. One cannot serve God wholeheartedly while trusting in people to provide his needs. Only God can do that.

Lord, help me not trust in the human instruments of Your blessing (whether gifts or salary), but to look only to You—for You are able to meet all my needs.

Contentment—part 1

Philippians 4:11-12

[11] Not that I speak from want, for I have learned to be content in whatever circumstances I am. [12] I know how to get along with humble means, and I also know how to live in prosperity; in any and every circumstance I have learned the secret of being filled and going hungry, both of having abundance and suffering need.

Tempting is the thought that Paul had ulterior motives for his praise of the Philippians' renewed support for him—that it really was all about his getting more financial support from them. However, that interpretation goes against everything we know about Paul.

He makes clear that he was not writing these things because he had a particular need at the time of writing. Nor is he making provision for a steadier or higher life style, if only he (I speak tongue-in-cheek) can get his monthly commitments up to the stipulated level set by headquarters. No, Paul was not fund raising, even subtly or secondarily, for himself. It meant nothing to him whether they supported him or not. He was content with what he had.

For Paul, that sometimes meant hunger and sometimes abundance. He knew that God was aware of his needs. That is why he could write so freely about these things. Paul was in it for the ministry, not for the money. And, the Philippians were giving because of love for Paul and fellowship in the gospel.

To be sure, a servant of the Lord is worthy of support. In 1 Corinthians 9, Paul makes a case for the need of and right to support for people serving the Lord in fulltime vocational ministry. He concluded, "So also the Lord directed those who proclaim the gospel to get their living from the gospel" (1 Cor. 9:14). We should support those who have left behind secular work to serve the Lord. But, Paul added (verses 15-18) that he set aside that benefit so that he could maintain his boast that he was service "without charge" to preach the gospel, so as "not to make full use of my right in the gospel" (vs. 18). It meant at times poverty, and other times it meant enough.

There is no evidence to suggest that Paul or anyone else ever asked for financial support for himself. Biblical teaching on this subject is confined to the believers' responsibility to support the workers, not to the workers to engage in personal fund-raising or deputation. Paul was not averse to asking for other people's benefit (1 Cor. 16:3; 2 Cor. 8-9). But, he never asked for himself.

How does this all work in practical terms? Faith is exercised by the workers and obedience by all other Christians!

Lord, help me walk by faith and obedience, trusting in You only for my needs, and walking in obedience as I support others in Your service.

Contentment —part 2

Philippians 4:11-12

* Not that I speak from want, for I have learned to be content in whatever circumstances I am. I know how to get along with humble means, and I also know how to live in prosperity; in any and every circumstance I have learned the secret of being filled and going hungry, both of having abundance and suffering need.*

So much of our lives is controlled by money, or should I say resources. Money is often seen as simply the currency controlling our resources. Life has its necessities: food, clothing, transportation, shelter, health care and many other things. Is it possible to live our lives without money being the final controlling or arbitrating factor?

Paul would answer, "Yes." He settled that early in his Christian walk. He had learned contentment. One would need to study his life to see how this developed, but it is clear that this contentment that he discovered was directly related to his faith in taking the promises of God seriously. He dared to believe what he was about to tell the Philippians that, "my God will supply all your needs according to His riches in glory in Christ Jesus" (Phil. 4:19).

But, is this way of living only for the super-spiritual ones, those who have a larger measure of faith, who are called to missionary work? That would be an easy out for the average Christian who punches the time clock five days a week. But, God has called all Christians to a life of faith. That paycheck at the end of the week is God's supply coming through the hands of your employer. The reality is that we are all called into missionary work, to walk by faith in order to reach a lost world. Some have been assigned by God to leave their homes and secular employment to give more of their time to the specific work of the Lord. Others are on assignment by God, being placed in secular jobs to reach people where they work. To be sure, much of their time is spent "working" their jobs, but their faith transforms their work. As one person said, "I am an ambassador for God, cleverly disguised as an assembly line worker!" Indeed, we are all called into fulltime service for the Lord as His ambassadors.

But, we must become content in whatever situation we find ourselves, so that our work and the money it produces does not become the goal, but a means to an end—to glorify God where He has put us. He is in control, and we must see our status of life, whether humble or prosperous, as His calling in our lives at this moment. Then, and only then, can we be content. The secret to having enough in life is to be content with what we already have.

Lord, thank You for what You have given me and where You have placed me. I want the controlling force of my life to be the goal of living for You.

Confident, Expectant Strength

Philippians 4:13

¹³ I can do all things through Him who strengthens me.

Well quoted verse as this may be, the Lord's strengthening defies simple caricature. The Samson story immediately surfaces; he who in his final moments cried out, "O Lord God, please remember me and please strengthen me just this time, O God . . ." (Judg. 16:28). One would expect God to be able to do as Samson pled, for after all He spoke the cosmos into creation. But, can He help those who need moral or spiritual strength?

Paul instructed the Ephesians, "Finally, be strong in the Lord and in the strength of His might" (Eph. 6:10). He himself accepted the mantle of this teaching when the Lord supernaturally spoke to him, "And He has said to me, 'My grace is sufficient for you, for power is perfected in weakness.' Most gladly, therefore, I will rather boast about my weaknesses, so that the power of Christ may dwell in me. " (2 Cor. 12:9). So, the correct answer is, "Yes, the Lord can help us with strength."

But, do we really believe it? Is this only for the super-spiritual, the Christian mystics who walk all day long in a spiritual aura? No! This strengthening of the Lord is within reach of all Christians. Scripture does not limit this to those who already are spiritually strong, but it extends the promise to those who are morally or spiritually weak. That includes the sub-grouping of humanity that includes the apostle himself. Even the Lord Jesus was strengthened in Gethsemane (Luke 22:43). Although the Greek word there is different than the word for "strength" in our passage today, they both convey the same idea of "giving strength." Thus, the sub-group of humanity that needs strengthening from God is co-extensive with all of humanity!

So, we are all in need, and God is the same God for all of us. Why then do we not believe this promise? Indeed, is it not a promise and not just the personal musings of the apostle? He speaks for all the faithful; can you join him in faith? Do you dare believe it? When faced with temptation, do you, do I, believe that God will not allow anything beyond what we are capable of handling (1 Cor. 10:13)? Do we believe that God will strengthen our faith when everything precious in our lives is ripped from us, and we are tempted to question whether God is good or whether He is sovereign, but not both? If He is good, He is powerless then to prevent a certain tragedy. If He is sovereign, He is not good then for "allowing" that tragedy. Faith is strengthened when we conclude that it may not make sense to me, but I trust in Him. That is spiritual and moral strength.

*Lord, though at times Your acts are incomprehensible, I can
face all things because of Your strength working in me.*

Non-Solicited Funding

Philippians 4:14-16

¹⁴ Nevertheless, you have done well to share with me in my affliction. ¹⁵ You yourselves also know, Philippians, that at the first preaching of the gospel, after I left Macedonia, no church shared with me in the matter of giving and receiving but you alone; ¹⁶ for even in Thessalonica you sent a gift more than once for my needs.

O f all the churches Paul founded, the one in Philippi was exemplary in their support for him. They had sacrificially help meet his practical needs in the work of the gospel by their financial gifts. In the previous verses, he had made clear that his enthusiasm over their renewed support was not because of the benefit to him, but it was an indicator of their spiritual maturity. This can be difficult for modern day readers to accept at face value. We are so accustomed to hearing slick pulpiteers and "missionary" presentations asking desperately for prayer, or "prayer letters" pleading for partners, but which, in reality, are fund raising efforts in disguise. Evangelicals have become quite adept at fundraising. Whole organizations exist to guide ministry leaders in how to get constituents to give more money, either openly as "capital campaigns" or under the not so subtle guise of "stewardship." There must have been those in Paul's day who subscribed to such tactics, for he felt it necessary with the Philippians to make his motives clear. (Caveat: yes, there is a place for "prayer" letters for keeping people up to date on what their prayers have been accomplishing, but every effort should be made not to use such things as a cover for money appeals).

Having made that clear, the apostle affectionately commended the Philippian believers for their part in his ministry. They go a long way back in Paul's ministry, to the "first preaching of the gospel." Remember, the initial believers there, the women he met by the river outside of Philippi (Acts 16:13), the wealthy woman, Lydia, who was identified as the "seller of purple fabrics" (Acts 16:14) and the Philippian jailer (Acts 16:30-40). From those early days, this young church supported Paul in his missionary tour. In fact, they stood out for their generosity, and at times, their support was all Paul had received from anywhere! And, while he was at the next missionary stop, while in the city of Thessalonica, the Philippians sent him support there.

Do you get the picture? Paul served sacrificially, traveling around the eastern Mediterranean, and Christians, moved by the Spirit, supported him. When necessary, he worked as a tent maker (Acts 18:3), but he never engaged in fundraising for his own needs.

Lord, help me to be generous, like the Philippians, in my support of those who have committed their lives to serving You and the gospel.

WEEKEND READING

Saturday – John 3
Sunday – John 4

PERSONAL
REFLECTIONS

_____

_____

_____

_____

_____

_____

_____

_____

_____

_____

_____

_____

_____

_____

_____

_____

_____

_____

_____

_____

_____

_____

_____

_____

_____

_____

_____

_____

Mmmmm, Smells Good

Philippians 4:17-18

[17] Not that I seek the gift itself, but I seek for the profit which increases to your account. [18] But I have received everything in full and have an abundance; I am amply supplied, having received from Epaphroditus what you have sent, a fragrant aroma, an acceptable sacrifice, well-pleasing to God.

Motive is essential, as Paul makes very clear the cause of his enthusiasm over the Philippians' renewed support for the gospel. The actual gift is not the point; a statement that requires significant integrity to make. On the one hand, the words are easy to say, in a sort of false humility sort of way. But, Paul's attitude toward money was that if the Lord supplied through gifts from the believers, praise the Lord. If not, he would gladly work with his hands to provide for his own needs. It really did not matter to him. Either way, he was fully engaged in serving the Lord.

So, he could honestly write that he saw the renewal of the Philippians' support as a benefit to them; it was a credit to them. But, in what sense? Certainly, Paul would not have in mind a merit system for salvation. Neither would he be suggesting an incentive method for obtaining God's favor, as though sanctifying grace needed to be earned. Eternal rewards are not in mind, then. God's grace always remains freely given, otherwise it would not be grace.

We may be better served by asking, what does the phrase "profit which increases to your account" mean? First, Paul noted their participation in the gospel, which resulted in his prayer of thanks to God for them (Phil. 1:3-4). This was credited to their account. Then, Paul said there was evidence of God's perfecting the work in them that He began (1:6), such that Paul was confident that the Lord's work would be completed. Then, in verse 1:10, he points out that the Philippians were approving the things which are excellent. He, thus, credits them with spiritual maturity and insight. They are experiencing the excellence of God's grace working in and through them.

As they gave out of the abundance which God had given them, their account of grace experienced increases. This isn't a health and wealth gospel, but rather a grace and grace message. The more grace you show, the larger your capacity for grace grows. The more you allow God to work grace through you, the greater facility you have to appreciate God's grace toward you.

So, the gift they sent Paul was more than enough for him, because he was overflowing with the joy of seeing God's grace at work in them. Their gift was not just to him, but was also a fragrant offering acceptable to God.

Lord, help me to see my financial support for missions as a sacrificial offering to You, and not just a response to the most effective fund raiser.

An Amazing Promise

Philippians 4:19-20

¹⁹ And my God will supply all your needs according to His riches in glory in Christ Jesus. ²⁰Now to our God and Father be the glory forever and ever. Amen.

Well-quoted verse this is, a great and precious promise. Whatever our need, God stands ready to meet it. We must consider the context of this verse so that we understand the scope of the promise. The better we understand it, the more confidence we have to believe it. We don't want to treat this as a "Christian" platitude or a catch phrase that diminishes its value.

Paul had been talking about his personal financial situation, being content in whatever state he was in, either having abundance or having little. He saw everything he possessed as being God's supply for his needs. It came through either his own hard work (making tents) or through gifts from God's people. His goal was not to become rich, but to make his life useful for God's purpose. Therefore, his needs were not "wants." They were practical, we suppose, for sustenance and travel expenses. His "wants," if he had them, were in line with his "needs," making his way toward God's plan for his life.

The Philippians had rejoined Paul's mission as financial partners. We can safely assume their gifts to Paul meant their sacrifice in areas of need, not just areas of want, because Paul was instructing them to look to God to meet their needs. Their giving placed them in the same arena of faith as Paul. Their fellowship with Paul went to a deeper level, sharing in helping to meet the needs of others, and in so doing, placing themselves "voluntarily" in the same position of needs—and, thus, looking to God in faith to supply that need! No wonder Paul rejoiced that they had truly joined in the mission.

Missionary work is clearly a team effort: there are those who give up a lot to go to the "front lines" physically. There are others who give up much money, to send it to the "front lines." But, all go to the front lines spiritually, serving together in fellowship of the work of the Lord. The Philippians got it. This truly is teamwork in action.

Now, the promise makes better sense. When we sacrifice greatly to provide for others in the Lord's work, God, then, provides for us in support of the "team." And, His supply is "according to His riches in glory in Christ Jesus." Spiritual wealth comes through sacrificial giving. Nothing helps us to delineate more clearly between wants and needs than sacrifice. And, nothing helps us experience God's overwhelming resources more than a sacrificial heart for promoting His kingdom here on earth. Paul concludes, therefore, that it is all about God's glory. And, all God's people echo, "Amen!"

Lord, thank You for being the One who can and does supply all of my needs.

Grace Greetings

Philippians 4:21-23

²¹ Greet every saint in Christ Jesus. The brethren who are with me greet you. ²² All the saints greet you, especially those of Caesar's household. ²³ The grace of the Lord Jesus Christ be with your spirit.

Personal notes accompany most of Paul's writings, although this one to the Philippians is a bit shorter than others. Obviously, he had a close relationship with them by the tone of his words. He calls them saints, as he did at the beginning (1:1). They are the "sanctified ones," as are all Christians. Contrary to popular religious culture, the Bible never uses the term "saint" to refer to exemplary individuals that have been beatified by the church, complete with halos. When a person comes to Christ in faith, a number of things happen, one of which is that they are now set apart for God as special. That is what the word "holy" means. The English word "saint" comes from the same Greek word "holy." Believers are "holy" ones. That is how God sees us, all of us! Even the carnal Christians in Corinth are called "saints." (1 Cor. 1:2).

Paul, then, mentions that the saints with him, even some believers from Caesar's own household, send their greetings. His incarceration in Rome had the effect that "my imprisonment in the cause of Christ has become well known throughout the whole praetorian guard and to everyone else" (Phil. 1:13). The fact is that some within the intimate circles of the Roman emperor had come to faith in Christ and were now considered part of the church.

It was important that the various churches around the Mediterranean Sea maintain contact and fellowship. Though the movement of faith in Christ had been growing, with the number of local gatherings increasing, Paul continually stressed the unity of all believers. We might safely assume that, as Christians travelled, the camaraderie would have been evident as they visited the different gatherings. As a minority group, such visitations would have been refreshing and encouraging. The church today has become so populous and diverse, that unfortunately, fellowship is often lost between Christians of different churches and denominations.

Finally, grace! Paul begins every letter with "grace to you" and closes every letter with a salutation near the end which includes grace. Paul was all about the "grace of God." Salvation is by grace, and the Christian life is by grace. As believers, it is God's grace that is sufficient. We become partakers of His grace as we participate in the gospel mission, as the Philippians had with Paul (1:17). We become channels of grace, conduits for God's grace through us to others. And in so doing, we don't stagnate but grow in grace.

Father, may the grace of my Lord Jesus Christ be with my spirit.

Grace Greetings

Philippians 4:21-23

Paul notes ceremony, most of Paul's writings, although this one is the shortest...

Colossians

Greetings to the Faithful

Colossians 1:1-2

¹ Paul, an apostle of Jesus Christ by the will of God, and Timothy our brother, ² To the saints and faithful brethren in Christ who are at Colossae: Grace to you and peace from God our Father.

The letter to the Colossian Christians is part of the so-called "prison epistles," being written while Paul was incarcerated (see Colossians 4:10) and was written probably around the same time and with similar content as the letter to the Ephesians. The city of Colossae was located about 100 miles east of Ephesus in Asia Minor. As a Roman city, it was unremarkable at the time of Paul's writing for it had "seen its better day" in previous times. Yet, the letter contains remarkable teaching.

One of the major themes of the letter has to do with a particular false teaching which later, in its full-blown manifestation, came to be known as Gnosticism. Present day interest in this cultic persuasion has been revived in popular film and book culture. It is still as false today as it was in its beginning forms in Paul's day.

The apostle begins the letter in his usual way, identifying himself as author. There had been no serious question of his authorship until the 19th century with the rise of higher criticism. But, from the earliest times and by virtually all early Christian writers, Paul the apostle was believed to be the genuine author of this letter (as opposed another "Paul" or someone falsely using his name). He identified Timothy as his co-author, the one to whom he later penned two letters which we call 1 and 2 Timothy in the New Testament.

Continuing his introduction, he identifies his audience, the members of the church in Colossae. He describes as "Saints"—this word comes from the root word meaning those who are called out as special. A saint, in Paul's usage, is not someone who has been canonized by an ecclesiastical council. Rather, all people who believe in Jesus Christ, who have been redeemed by the grace of God, are saints. There is no division between "ordinary" Christians and a special class called "saints." We are all special to God! Paul was probably infused with the attitude of the Psalmist who wrote, "As for the saints who are in the earth, they are the majestic ones in whom is all my delight" (Ps. 16:3).

He also calls the Colossian believers "faithful brethren," a high commendation. If there is one thing God requires and values in us, it is faithfulness (see Colossians 4:2). The Colossians were doing well in that area, and Paul encourages them to build on their faithfulness to God as they confront false teaching.

Lord, help me to remain faithful to You as I grow in my understanding of truth.

A Great Three

Colossians 1:3-5

> *³ We give thanks to God, the Father of our Lord Jesus Christ, praying always for you, ⁴ since we heard of your faith in Christ Jesus and the love which you have for all the saints; ⁵ because of the hope laid up for you in heaven, of which you previously heard in the word of truth, the gospel ...*

Good reputation ranks high on most people's "want to have" list. One can have a reputation for being a good athlete, scholar or writer. Or, for being generous, fun or hardworking. One can have a good reputation or not-so good reputation. The Colossians are commended for their good reputation in the vital areas of Christian virtue.

In light of this very positive report, Paul and Timothy are grateful to God. Why? Because even though they themselves had not visited Colossae in person, their work of the gospel had affected them and produced good fruit in Colossae and the surrounding area. The word had spread during their travels throughout the nearby area during the second missionary tour (see Acts 16:1-11) and possibly from the extended teaching in Ephesus. The Colossians must have heard about the gospel from those who had heard Paul directly.

Thankfulness was expressed in frequent prayer for the Colossian believers. Paul and Timothy prayed not because they were "committed" to a spiritual discipline. Rather, prayer came as the expression of what they valued and wanted for others. What they highly regarded energized their thankfulness to God for seeing those things come to fruit in the Colossians' lives.

So, what are these Christian virtues so highly regarded? First, there is "faith in Christ Jesus." Christians need a solid foundation of believing in Christ (for salvation) and believing His word (for guidance); this is what God looks for above all else. "And without faith it is impossible to please Him . . ." (Heb. 11:6).

Next, Paul speaks of their reputation of "love which you have for all the saints." The word for love, agape, was not common in the ancient world, until the Christians brought widespread use of it. It had the connotation of being "unconditional" giving, that is, totally other-person centered. It is not a feeling or an emotion, but an action. What is unique about the word is the pervasive use of it among Christians to describe the heart of the Gospel and of their behavior toward others. The Colossians had a reputation of selfless generosity in all areas of life toward all believers. They were not partial to socio-economic or any other kind of class distinctions. Lastly, the Colossians' hope for the future was well known. What a reputation they had. Oh, that we would all have these three characteristics!

Lord, I want to grow in faith, love and hope, not just for the reputation it gives me, but because You value those things in me. I want to value them as well.

WEEKEND READING

Saturday – John 5
Sunday – John 6:1-25

_____

_____

_____

_____

_____

_____

_____

_____

_____

_____

_____

_____

_____

_____

_____

_____

_____

_____

_____

_____

_____

_____

_____

_____

_____

_____

_____

Pray For More Workers

Colossians 1:6-8

⁶ ... [the gospel] has come to you, just as in all the world also it is constantly bearing fruit and increasing, even as it has been doing in you also since the day you heard of it and understood the grace of God in truth; ⁷ just as you learned it from Epaphras, our beloved fellow bond-servant, who is a faithful servant of Christ on our behalf, ⁸ and he also informed us of your love in the Spirit.

Gospel spreading—that is normal New Testament Christianity. The Colossians were examples of what was happening throughout the Roman Empire. The message of the gospel, "the good news," conveys the truth that God has brought redemption to all people by grace through faith in the Lord Jesus Christ to all who believe. And, it had produced results, "constantly bearing fruit and increasing." That is bible-speak for many people coming to Christ and leading others to Him.

The Colossians themselves had experienced the expansion of the gospel. Notice, they had heard about it from Epaphras, not from Paul directly. We don't know how Epaphras came to faith, but it is entirely possible that it happened during Paul's second missionary tour when he was redirected from the Galatian area, where he was reinforcing the churches established on the first tour. Paul had traveled through the general area of Colossae, though not apparently visiting the city itself. Epaphras may have met Paul at that time, then taken the message to Colossae.

He originally hailed from Colossae, but he was with Paul at the time of writing, as indicated later in the letter, "Epaphras, who is one of your number, a bondslave of Jesus Christ, sends you his greetings, always laboring earnestly for you in his prayers, that you may stand perfect and fully assured in all the will of God" (Col. 4:12). Notice the apostle's description of him: a bondslave of Jesus Christ, a term he also used of Tychicus (Col. 4:7). Paul always had a cadre of younger men whom he was discipling. They were not just students but co-workers in the labor for the Lord, partners in sacrificing everything to follow their Lord and Master Jesus Christ. They were men who had proved themselves to be "faithful" (vs. 7) and to be servants.

There is a connection between the spread of the gospel and the dedication of workers willing to tell others and to sacrifice everything to get the message out. Oh that the Lord would raise up more workers for the harvest; those willing to explain the gospel in a way that people "understand" "Therefore beseech the Lord of the harvest to send out workers into His harvest" (Matt. 9:38).

Lord, please raise up more workers to fearlessly share the message with others, so that the gospel would continue to bear fruit and increase.

To Know You More

Colossians 1:9-10

⁹ For this reason also, since the day we heard of it, we have not ceased to pray for you and to ask that you may be filled with the knowledge of His will in all spiritual wisdom and understanding, ¹⁰ so that you will walk in a manner worthy of the Lord, to please Him in all respects, bearing fruit in every good work and increasing in the knowledge of God ...

Prayer was vital to the life and ministry of the apostle Paul. His letters to the churches usually included an opening prayer. These were not perfunctory, but reflected his intimate, spiritual dependence on the Lord for everything he did. In this letter to the Colossians, he begins with a heart of gratitude, thanking God for the Colossians' fruitful growth in faith, love and hope (vs. 3-8). Now, he continues with his requests to God for them.

We cannot escape noticing the intensity and frequency of his prayer for them—"we have not ceased to pray for you." When he thought of the Colossians, it was in the form of a continual discussion with the Lord about them. His thoughts were not just idle recollections or simply fond memories of them; rather, the apostle disciplined his mind to "take every thought captive to the obedience of Christ" (2 Cor. 10:5).

Now, it would be impossible to pray this intensely and often about every person he met or concerning every report he received from every church. But, this prayer of Paul's has a reason, "for this reason." That is, he prayed this way because the Colossians were being particularly fruitful in their spiritual walk—therefore, Paul was particularly thankful for the work of God in their lives, and he was particularly interceding for them. It was not like they were doing well so they didn't need prayer. Rather, it was because they were doing well that they very specifically needed prayer, so that they would continue on and not lose ground. The mistake we often make is to assume that people who are doing well spiritually don't need as much prayer. If things get really bad, we will pray then. This is clearly a mistake. Every step of the way, we are and need to be completely dependent upon the Lord's grace and strength.

The things Paul prayed for are not mundane, although we are certainly encouraged to pray for our every need, including our "daily bread." Paul had a heart for the larger, spiritual needs. And, he asked for two areas: 1) that they "may be filled with the knowledge of His will" and 2) that they "will walk in a manner worthy of the Lord," with the end result that they would continue bearing spiritual fruit.

O Lord, this is my desire to know You more, to please You in my spiritual walk so that there would be much fruit for Your enjoyment.

The Great Qualifier

Colossians 1:11-12

11 ... strengthened with all power, according to His glorious might, for the attaining of all steadfastness and patience; joyously 12 giving thanks to the Father, who has qualified us to share in the inheritance of the saints in Light.

Continuing his prayer for the Colossian believers, Paul asks that they would be "strengthened." Not with personal resolve, but with spiritual ability on the level of "His glorious might." In the Colossians' case, false teaching was encroaching on the church which over the decades turned into a full-blown religious system which we now call "Gnosticism." This insidious teaching threatened the believers' understanding of truth about Christ and the universe. Now, the Colossians had been known to be faithful, loving and hopeful, and they "understood the grace of God in truth" (Col. 1:6). But, they also needed spiritual strength from God to confront the error.

We cannot fight only in the flesh or with just our personal resolve. We will be easily felled by the weakness of the flesh. This happens when we give in to pride of doctrine, argumentativeness or unnecessary harshness of attitude. Weakness is revealed also when we fear or ignore conflict in hopes it will go away. We need to avoid extremes: 1) Not confronting falsehoods because of fear or laziness or a false sense of unity, 2) over-reacting with a negative spirit of the flesh and 3) fighting the wrong battles, for instance, treating relatively minor issues as major doctrinal errors.

The goal of this strengthening is "steadfastness and patience." Being consistent in our doctrinal beliefs and faithfulness to the Lord is key here. Patience has to do with being steadfast over the long haul. It is noteworthy when a person comes to a conviction of Scripture and is willing to take a stand in defense of sound doctrine. But, the real question addresses whether he will be able to continue being firm for the truth five, ten, twenty-five years down the road. Many, thinking they were strong, have strayed because of weakness in the relentless onslaught of the world's philosophy or religions.

Finally, Paul expresses together with them joyful gratitude to God. He begins his prayer with thankfulness and ends it that way. And why not? He is praying to the One "who has qualified us to share in the inheritance of the saints in Light." What an amazing thing that we who are sinners saved by grace would also inherit God's eternal riches! We have not earned this nor have we merited it. He is the qualifier, and we are the qualified. He is the saver; we are the saved. He is the lover; we are the loved ones. He is the forgiver; we are the forgiven. He is the praise-worthy One; we are the praise-giving ones!

Lord, You are wonderful in all You have done for us. I thank You eternally.

The Great Rescue

Colossians 1:13-14

¹³ For He rescued us from the domain of darkness, and transferred us to the kingdom of His beloved Son, ¹⁴ in whom we have redemption, the forgiveness of sins.

Good news is described in Scripture in many different ways. Christians are saved, redeemed, regenerated, forgiven, justified, adopted, sanctified, and secured. In our passage today, we are "rescued." To be distinguished from the more general word, "saved," the word "rescued" refers to deliverance from a dire circumstance. In this case, we have been delivered from the "domain of darkness."

Darkness in Scripture has long been the analogy of life without God. In fact, the Scripture, in referring to Jesus says, "The Light shines in the darkness, and the darkness did not comprehend it" (John 1:5). He came because the world was plunged into spiritual blackness. He is the fulcrum between light and darkness: those who reject Him will be permanently cast into "outer darkness" (Matt. 8:12). This is the judgment on all of us. But God has provided a solution.

That solution is the Lord Jesus Christ. The Sovereign of the universe has "rescued" us out of that spiritual darkness, those who have dared to put the weight of our eternity on Him in faith. He whisked us away to a new kingdom that is not of darkness. This is the kingdom of "His beloved Son." We are citizens of a new and different country, one that is diametrically different, completely unlike the "domain of darkness." As one person said, "Once I was blind, but now I see" (John 9:25). It's the difference between day and night.

However, at just the mention of the Son of God, Paul launches into a brief exaltation of some of the aspects of what this means. First, because we have been rescued, we have also been redeemed. This means God has exchanged something of great value to Him to obtain that which was of great desire to Him. We have been "purchased with His [Christ's] own blood" (Acts 20:28). He sacrificed His Son "in whom I am well-pleased" (Matt. 17:5) to obtain you and me. Is that not the greatest thing to praise Him for? Scripture provides us words of praise, "Worthy are You . . . for You were slain, and purchased for God with Your blood men from every tribe and tongue and people and nation" (Rev. 5:9).

Our praise expands because we have "the forgiveness of sins." Our sin problem is solved—not that we will never again sin or that no one will ever sin against us. But, we have been forgiven! All because of God's love in reaching out to us lost image-bearers.

Lord, I can't praise You enough for what You have done for me. You are so great; I am so looking forward to learning more about You and Your glory.

The Image of God

Colossians 1:15a

¹⁵ He is the image of the invisible God ...

Christ is exalted in all of Scripture, either through prophecy, symbolism, story, teaching or direct exclamation and praise. For Paul, exaltation of Christ overlaps the boundaries between all of these. His prayer now morphs into an expansion of who Christ is. In light of the issues he will be dealing with, the apostle first establishes a high view of the person of the Lord Jesus Christ, for everything else depends on this core truth of Christianity. But at the core of all false teaching is an inadequate view of Christ.

In verses 13-14, we saw what God has done in Christ, but now, we are directed to see who Christ Himself is. First, "He is the image of the invisible God." Now, no man can see God at anytime, or he will die. When Moses asked to see God's glory, he was granted a mitigated view of God's "back" for God made it clear, "You cannot see My face, for no man can see Me and live!" (Ex. 33:20). God simply could not be seen in all His glory. Of course, we are dealing with limitations of human language. Jacob was under the impression that he had seen God face to face (Gen. 32:30). Many believe he saw a pre-incarnate manifestation of Christ, with whom he had been wrestling. Yet, the Scripture is clear that "The LORD used to speak to Moses face to face, just as a man speaks to his friend" (Ex. 33:11). Yet, Paul speaks of God's invisible attributes in Romans 1:20.

So, does God show Himself visibly or not? However perplexing that can be, in Christ the confusion is cleared up. He is the "image of the invisible God" (see also 2 Corinthians 4:4b where Christ is again referred to as the "image of God"). That which could not be known about God before is now revealed in Jesus. Jesus is Deity, because He perfectly reflects God. Paul elaborates this further in verses 1:19 and 2:9. God is no longer invisible.

The word translated "image" is the Greek word "*eikon*," from which we get "icon." This term is often used interchangeably for "idol" or "statue of an idol." Scripture is unequivocal that God will not tolerate false gods or idols before Him. "You shall have no other gods before Me. You shall not make for yourself an idol, or any likeness of what is in heaven above or on the earth beneath or in the water under the earth" (Ex. 20:3-4). Only God can represent Himself accurately, and no inferior imitation will do. Jesus is that perfect representation of the essence of God. The writer of Hebrews says, "He is . . . the exact representation of His nature" (Heb. 1:3b). Only those blinded by Satan (2 Cor. 4:4a), who love darkness rather than light (John 3:19), cannot see it.

Lord Jesus, I praise You that You are the perfect expression of God!

WEEKEND READING

Saturday – John 6:26-71
Sunday – John 7

PERSONAL REFLECTIONS

_____

_____

_____

_____

_____

_____

_____

_____

_____

_____

_____

_____

_____

_____

_____

_____

_____

_____

_____

_____

_____

_____

_____

_____

_____

_____

Priority One

[15] He is ... the firstborn of all creation.

The Lord Jesus Christ was not a created being—although some erroneously claim our verse today asserts that very thing. We want to unpack this very carefully, because of the enormity of this truth. Genuine Christianity is completely contingent upon the deity of Christ. If He was only a creation, His death on the cross was not sufficient to take away sins. Liberal theologians would then be right; His untimely death was simply a model of love, a sacrifice made for a greater cause. If Christ was a created being, He could not be the Savior of the world.

It is true; the body of Jesus came into being some 2000 years ago, but the 2nd person of the Godhead pre-existed eternally. In context, Paul refers to Him as "Christ," not to Jesus. So, he is talking not just of the man Jesus, but of the Messiah, the one sent by God. Yes, the body of Jesus was created in the womb of Mary, albeit through miraculous circumstances, who had been impregnated by the Holy Spirit. The biblical record clearly points to a virgin birth. But Christ, the One to whom Paul refers in our passage today, existed before the conception of His physical body.

But, what about this verse calling Him the "firstborn of all creation?" First, notice that the verse does not say nor does it imply that Jesus Christ was the first-created being. Nothing could be further from the truth. Read the wording carefully. He is the "firstborn" of creation. Second, He was obviously not the very first person ever to be born, so the term must mean something else.

So, what does this mean then? In the Jewish mindset, the firstborn referred to the eldest son, who became the head of the family in the absence of the father. The firstborn would receive the greater inheritance from the father than the other sons. The firstborn had the status of the family member with priority over the others. In some cases, that position could be bought and sold (see the story of Esau selling his birthright to his brother Jacob). Israel (the descendants of Jacob) was called by God, "my firstborn" (Ex. 4:22), even though Esau was literally born first. And, clearly the people of Israel were not the first created nation on the earth.

Christ is the "firstborn of all creation" in the sense that He is God's pre-eminent One over all creation. He has the priority. He is in creation; He is over creation, but He Himself is not a created being. There is nothing greater in all creation than the man who was God. Paul continues with this theme of exalting Christ in the upcoming verses.

Lord, I worship You as the pre-eminent One in my life.

The Pre-Eminent One

Colossians 1:16-18

[16] For by Him all things were created, both in the heavens and on earth, visible and invisible, whether thrones or dominions or rulers or authorities—all things have been created through Him and for Him. [17] He is before all things, and in Him all things hold together. [18] He is also head of the body, the church; and He is the beginning, the firstborn from the dead, so that He Himself will come to have first place in everything.

Firstborn status comes from His role in creation. "For" gives the reason. The Lord Jesus Christ is the creator of everything that exists. Since Genesis 1 clearly teaches that God created everything, we irresistibly deduce that Jesus must, therefore, be the Creator God of the Universe. John corroborated this, "All things came into being through Him, and apart from Him nothing came into being that has come into being" (John 1:3). Lest anyone want to minimize this in any way, Paul described the extent of His creation role: All things were created 1) "by" Him—He is the direct cause of creation, 2) "through Him"—He is the agent of creation and 3) "for Him"—He is the purpose for which all things were created. It's all about Him! Nothing escapes His sovereignty; nothing is beyond His reach; nothing is outside of His purposes. If anything exists, He is the one who caused its existence for His reasons.

Furthermore, nothing can continue to exist without the Lord's divine work in maintaining its existence: "in Him all things hold together" (vs. 17). He is the glue that holds the molecules and the atoms together. Without His active thought, all would fly apart and disintegrate into total chaos.

Emphasizing Christ's role in the creation of all things flies directly in the face of the budding false teaching. In that false worldview, the ultimate God of the universe is too holy, too pure to have created the physical world. But, there were, according to that teaching, a succession of "emanations" propagating out from the Ultimate, Holy Truth—and the farther these emanations flowed out from Absolute Holiness, the less holy they became. In time, one of these emanations became the God of the Bible who created all things. But, Paul here says that Christ is essentially greater than all things that exist, whether "visible or invisible, whether thrones or dominions or rulers or authorities." The creator God over all is none other than Jesus Christ. He is absolute truth and holiness.

Paul applies this to the church when he points out that Christ is the "head of the church." "He is the firstborn from the dead," which means He has the "first place in everything." There is no authority higher than Christ for believers. He is pre-eminent over all there is.

O Lord, Pre-eminent One, I surrender first place in my life to You!

Joyful Incarnation

Colossians 1:19-20

19 For it was the Father's good pleasure for all the fullness to dwell in Him, 20 and through Him to reconcile all things to Himself, having made peace through the blood of His cross; through Him, I say, whether things on earth or things in heaven.

Incarnation brought pleasure to God; there is no other way to see it. God becoming a man was not a burden but a delight. True, He was burdened for our sin, but it was done because of the "joy set before him" (Heb. 12:2). Now, properly speaking, one could make the point that this does not refer to the incarnation, per se, but to the idea that the Father fully dwells in the Son, the second person of the trinity, apart from taking on human form. But, notice the verse states clearly that it was the "fullness" of God that dwelt in Christ. Later, Paul clarifies this when he writes, "For in Him all the fullness of Deity dwells in bodily form" (Col. 2:9). Clearly God becoming a man is in view.

Note also that the saying, "the fullness to dwell in Him" indicates the full deity of Jesus. There is nothing about God that is not true about Jesus. He is not just a man who was inspired by God, nor was He a man who became God. The fullness of God includes pre-existence, in fact, eternal pre-existence. Further, Jesus was no less God than God Himself. In other words, the verse (along with Colossians 2:9) presents very strong proof from Scripture that Jesus was fully God!

As God, the Lord Jesus Christ accomplished restoration of our relationship with God. The passage describes this in two ways: 1) He reconciled us to God (see Romans 5:10), 2) He made peace between God and us. That was the whole point of the incarnation, and it results in great pleasure for God to do it.

Now, about whom does Paul write? Reconciliation does not include things "under the earth," that is, the demonic world. That realm will be subject to the Lord in the end (Phil. 2:10), but it will not be reconciled. However, things "on earth or things in heaven" will be reconciled to God. As MacDonald says, His death is "sufficient" for mankind, but is "effective" only for those who believe.

This truth cuts across the false teaching influencing the Colossians. For us Christians, there is no striving to attain Absolute Truth or Holiness. The work has already been done. The Creator God of the Universe has personally interacted with the world to bring about human reconciliation. This work was not assigned to some created emanation far distant from God. God took great pleasure in making this happen through the Lord Jesus Christ, God in the flesh.

*Lord, You are the great God of the Universe who was pleased
to send Jesus to reconcile me to You. Thank You!*

Reconciled Forever

Colossians 1:21-23

²¹ And although you were formerly alienated and hostile in mind, engaged in evil deeds, ²² yet He has now reconciled you in His fleshly body through death, in order to present you before Him holy and blameless and beyond reproach— ²³ if indeed you continue in the faith firmly established and steadfast, and not moved away from the hope of the gospel that you have heard, which was proclaimed in all creation under heaven, and of which I, Paul, was made a minister.

Universal to the particular—the sufficient to the effective. God's work in Jesus Christ was adequate to reconcile all things to Himself (vs. 20), but now He has worked effectively in reconciling "you," that is, the Colossian believers (and by extension all believers). Reconciliation means restoring a broken relationship to its previous, unbroken state. In our case, we were completely separated from God. The Scripture cuts us no slack—we were hostile in mind. That is God's assessment. When David sinned by committing adultery with Bathsheba and had murdered her husband Uriah, he confesses his sin as, "against You (Lord) only have I sinned" (Ps. 51:4). All sin is an affront to God; it constitutes hostility toward Him and alienates us.

The way God reconciled us is through the human death of Christ. The physicalness of that is emphasized ("in his fleshly body through death" vs. 22), which speaks against the budding Gnostic thinking that physical matter is essentially evil. Spiritual enlightenment is not a matter of humans trying to shake off the physical nature in pursuit of absolute holiness and truth. God's reconciliation is perfect and restored us to "holy and blameless and beyond reproach" status with God.

This truth, this status, is contingent upon faith, a faith that endures and is rooted in the hope of the gospel. Now some people stumble on this verse, thinking that assurance of salvation is nearly impossible since we cannot know whether our faith is enduring until the end of our lives. However, "if" statements in the Bible can be understood in different ways. Paul is not questioning whether their faith endures. The translators insert the word "indeed" to reflect what might be called an "if" of certainty. In other words, if you continue in the faith—and for the sake of argument, we will assume that to be true—you will be presented before God. The Colossians had that kind of faith. It was not a dead faith (as James refers to in his letter), but an alive faith. Their being "firmly established and steadfast" comes from being made holy, blameless and beyond reproach. It is God's work. Ours is simply a response.

Lord, thank You for reconciling me from my rebellion against You. Rather than consigning me to an eternal hell, You rescued me through the Lord Jesus Christ.

Worth Suffering For

Colossians 1:24

²⁴ Now I rejoice in my sufferings for your sake, and in my flesh I do my share on behalf of His body, which is the church, in filling up what is lacking in Christ's afflictions.

T he Church occupies a high place in the affections of God and in the view of the apostle Paul. Put simply, it was worth suffering for. The psalmist reflects God's heart for His people, "As for the saints who are in the earth, they are the majestic ones in whom is all my delight" (Ps. 16:3). It was written of Jesus, ". . . who for the joy set before Him endured the cross" (Heb. 12:2). James encouraged the scattered believers to "Consider it all joy . . . when you encounter various trials" (James 1:1). The joy is not in suffering, as though there is efficacy in self-flagellation or any kind of masochism. Rather, joy has to do with knowing that some things are worth suffering for. God suffered to procure redemption and reconciliation. God's people suffer to remain faithful to God. Paul suffered as the Lord's messenger of reconciliation and hope.

This point to the Colossians is well orchestrated. We know from later history that Gnostics taught that the material world is unholy and sinful because it is distant from the absolute truth of the universe. Nothing good or holy could come from fleshly experiences; the object of spiritual devotion was to ascend above such base things. Yet here, the apostle extols the sufferings "in my flesh." This had value and was worth rejoicing over. His adamant assertion here indicates that such false thinking which was characteristic of later Gnosticism was also threatening the Christians at Paul's time.

In what sense does Paul's sufferings fill up "what is lacking in Christ's afflictions?" Clearly, it cannot refer to the atonement sufferings of Christ, for He died once for all. Nothing can be added to that! Paul acutely knew that any persecution against or suffering caused to Christians was effectively persecution against the Lord Jesus Christ. In his pre-conversion life when he was persecuting the Church, Jesus appeared in a vision asking, "Why are you persecuting me?" (Acts 9:4). The Lord identified the suffering of the Church with Himself. MacDonald puts it this way, "The Head in heaven feels the suffering of His body on earth." So, Christians who suffer in loyalty to Christ are very much, as His body, continuing in the suffering that Christ experienced.

One cannot help but remember the response of Peter and John to their suffering, ". . . they . . . rejoiced that they had been considered worthy to suffer shame for His name" (Acts 5:41).

Lord, help me take my place among those who consider it a great joy to suffer for You and Your people, whom You call "the majestic ones."

WEEKEND READING

Saturday – John 8:1-30
Sunday – John 8:31-59

_____
_____
_____
_____
_____
_____
_____
_____
_____
_____
_____
_____
_____
_____
_____
_____
_____
_____
_____
_____
_____
_____
_____
_____
_____
_____
_____

A Servant of the Truth—Part 1

Colossians 1:25-27

²⁵ Of this church I was made a minister according to the stewardship from God bestowed on me for your benefit, so that I might fully carry out the preaching of the word of God, ²⁶ that is, the mystery which has been hidden from the past ages and generations, but has now been manifested to His saints, ²⁷ to whom God willed to make known what is the riches of the glory of this mystery among the Gentiles, which is Christ in you, the hope of glory.

Paul's message was so revolutionary in its scope that nothing would stop him from spreading it. The message was new, unknown before then—he called it a mystery. Of course, now that he was spreading this truth, it was no longer a secret. Paul, however, did not figure it out, as though clever human intellect was capable of piecing together the plot line. As a mystery, it could only be known by God revealing it. The apostle was simply the steward of that truth.

Some words in this passage need clarification. Paul was a "minister." But, he does not use the word in the contemporary, non-biblical usage, that is, making a distinction between clergy and laity. He uses a simple word in the Greek, *diaconos*. In its original sense it had to do with waiting on tables, a server. To the Greek mind, "ruling not serving is proper to a man" (Plato). But to the Christian mind, being called a servant became a highly valued epithet. In time, the word came to describe the "deacons" who were recognized in the church for being helpers to the elders. Never was it used in New Testament times as a title for clerical privilege or authority, nor is there anywhere in the New Testament found any support for a separate ministerial class of Christians. All are simply brothers and sisters in Christ; in fact, all are "saints" (vs. 26). For Paul, his life was dedicated to serving the purpose of spreading the news of the now revealed mystery. It was a stewardship, not something he achieved.

What a marvelous truth this mystery turns out to be! Paul refers to it with terms like "the riches of the glory" and "the hope of glory." Why such illustrious descriptions? Because the mystery is this: Christ is in us (vs. 27). We have Him, in whom resides the fullness of Deity, living in our lives! How amazing is that? If that doesn't excite you, you must be completely devoid of emotion. The God of the universe does not just live among us; as believers, He lives in us. He is our "hope of glory." He brings to us the riches of His glory.

With this truth in mind, it now certainly makes sense why Paul would rejoice in his sufferings, because he knows how great the message of the mystery is. No amount of suffering would stop him from spreading the good news! Ever!

Lord, help me take my place among those who consider suffering for You and your people, whom you call "the majestic ones" a great joy.

A Servant of the Truth—Part 2

Colossians 1:25-27

[25] Of this church I was made a minister according to the stewardship from God bestowed on me for your benefit, so that I might fully carry out the preaching of the word of God, [26] that is, the mystery which has been hidden from the past ages and generations, but has now been manifested to His saints, [27] to whom God willed to make known what is the riches of the glory of this mystery among the Gentiles, which is Christ in you, the hope of glory.

Mystery, suspense—the makings of a great novel! I met a young man who set out on a spiritual journey, beginning with the reading of the Bible. He knew virtually nothing of the plot, but he was a literature major in college, so he read it like a piece of classical literature. As he indulged his literary and spiritual curiosity through the beginnings of God's working on the earth in the first five books of the Bible, he became enthralled. He couldn't put the book down.

As he moved from the foundations of the nation of Israel into the failures of God's people to keep their part of the agreement (or covenant) with God, the story captivated him. As he found himself working through poetic literature and into prophetic writings, his heart began searching for the solution to the divide between God and man. The sin problem was clearly laid out, the plot fully developed, but there was no resolution. Hints abounded but nothing concrete.

This young man struggled with a spiritual depression. Things seemed hopeless for humans. That is, until he turned to the New Testament! Light began to shine from the pages of Scripture. In Christ was the solution to mankind's dilemma. What was hidden in the first part of the story was revealed when the plot was fully worked out. Christ provided the sacrifice for the sin problem. And, not just for the Jews, the people through whom the message to the world came, but also to the rest of the world, the Gentiles!

That is the mystery of the church: hidden in the Old Testament, but now revealed to us in Christ, the grace of God fully explained in the writings of the apostle Paul. We have the privilege today of knowing what the people of God before Christ could not possibly have known. "As to this salvation, the prophets who prophesied of the grace that would come to you made careful searches and inquiries, seeking to know what person or time the Spirit of Christ within them was indicating as He predicted the sufferings of Christ and the glories to follow. It was revealed to them that they were not serving themselves, but you, in these things which now have been announced to you through those who preached the gospel to you by the Holy Spirit sent from heaven—things into which angels long to look" (1 Peter 1:10-12).

Lord, thank You for revealing to me Your grace, available to all who believe.

The Divine Commentary

Colossians 1:28

^{28} We proclaim Him, admonishing every man and teaching every man with all wisdom, so that we may present every man complete in Christ.

Jesus Christ is the prime focus of the Christian message. This would seem obvious today, but that is because we have had centuries of reading the letters of Paul. But, the first century church was just receiving this teaching for the first time. While the story of Jesus' life had circulated widely, Paul gave cogent commentary on what that life meant in the face of false teaching. (Often through church history, doctrine is extolled and refined in the confrontation of false teaching). It is not just a moral code or a religious system, or just a subject for theological debate. It is all about a Person and a relationship with Him, the One who is God in the flesh. Someone has said that, at the core of false teaching, there is a diminishing of the preeminence of Christ.

The proper response to false teaching is to exalt Christ, place Him at the center of all discussions, debates and refutations. Therefore, Paul never tired of proclaiming Christ. Further, he continually challenged people to consider the implications of Christ in their lives. Here, he "admonishes every man" using every ounce of wisdom God has given him. The goal is to "present every man complete in Christ." The Greek word here is *"teleios"* which can be translated "perfect, complete, mature." The Christian life is a progression toward that goal, and it cannot be done apart from Christ. No amount of tips or techniques, spiritual disciplines or rituals can move us toward spiritual maturity apart from being "in Christ." It is all about having Christ's presence actively and powerfully manifest in our lives.

That goal, namely "complete in Christ," is the desire of every Christian: to be completely unified with Him in every area of life; to be dead with Him, and to be alive with Him (as Paul writes later in this epistle). In one sense, we are already complete and have already identified with Christ in death and resurrection (see Romans 6). In that sense, we have nothing left to do in order to be accepted by God, forgiven and secure forever. However, as we progress through life, that knowledge of spiritual truth alters our daily lives.

Some religions are so other-worldly minded that they have no value for changing people's lives and souls. The message of Christ transforms, and life becomes a great unraveling of the mystery of Christ in us and us in Christ. So, this message of Christ is not just some cerebral or esoteric topic designed to make one feel "religious." The message is a Person, and He revolutionizes life!

Father, I exalt the Lord Jesus Christ in my life, and also I will exalt Him in my death. He is the anchor and the life line. His is life itself.

The Mighty Partnership

Colossians 1:29

29 For this purpose also I labor, striving according to His power, which mightily works within me.

Unabashed and confident was the apostle Paul in his purpose for living. His life was his ministry, and he had no other focus than Christ and proclaiming Him to everyone he met. Whether roaming the world freely or sitting in prison, every situation provided opportunity to make Christ known.

This otherwise innocuous verse contains tremendous insight into the apostle's psyche—what made him tick. First, his ministry was work—hard work. He said he labored. It wasn't a task for a lazy man. Serving the Lord is not just a career option for making money and enjoying life. The life Paul enjoyed was the life of Christ, but I am sure he didn't enjoy the painfulness of incarcerations and beatings. His life was not a journey of self-actualization or self-discovery. It was, rather, a life of laboring hard to discover more and more of Christ and His grace and to share that knowledge with others. He described this work as "striving." Not just putting in his hours or being committed only to the task at hand, he was striving for something far greater than just surviving the daily grind. He was on an eternal salary. In other words, the true benefits or rewards were future. He was motivated by an inward desire for "the goal of the prize of the upward call of God in Christ" (Phil. 3:14).

In all his striving and labor, he partnered with the far greater and more powerful "Partner" and served in the Partner's way. Yes, Paul discovered the balance, or should we say, the confluence of his own laboring and trusting in the power of God. Too many Christians whimsically say, "Let go, and let God." However, Paul would rather say, "I am going to hold on and move ahead, but I am going to do it in the power of God." That required resolve, sweat, pushing ahead—in short, it meant Paul needed to bring his natural initiative and industry to bear on the Lord's mission for him, and to align his efforts with the Lord, taking advantage of the superior strength of the Spirit. It is not a setting aside of his own work, but a superimposing of the strength and the will of God on it.

Christians err in one of two ways: 1) Serve the Lord in their own strength only, as though God weren't even there, or 2) Sit back passively waiting for God to imbue them with spiritual strength, as though sprinkling angel-dust and they will somehow become supernaturally motivated. We need to take our lesson from the one (Paul) who taught us about the strength of the Lord and commit to serving the Lord with all our strength and to do it in His strength.

Lord, thank You for giving me Your spiritual strength. I don't want to let that strength atrophy through my non-use of it. But, let it work mightily in me.

Sacrifice of Ministry

Colossians 2:1

¹ For I want you to know how great a struggle I have on your behalf and for those who are at Laodicea, and for all those who have not personally seen my face ...

S acrifice integrates seamlessly with serving the Lord. It is not just a by-product of the desire to aggressively share the faith. It is also a badge of honor conveying the depth of commitment to those receiving the message. Not that Paul was a spiritual masochist (that is, one who enjoys suffering in a weird sort of way), but hardships and trials were a means to an end. His life goal was not the elimination of difficulties but to get the message out even through the difficulties and persecutions.

The book of Acts records much of Paul's travels and hardship, punctuated by excerpts from his letters (e.g. 2 Cor. 1:8-10; 4:7-18; 11:23-33). Persecution began shortly after his conversion, when he began preaching fearlessly in the city of Damascus (Acts 9:23-25) and he needed to be let down from a window in the city wall in a basket for fear of the Jews. In 2 Corinthians 11:33, Paul concluded his litany of difficulties with that very first one, which may have left the most indelible and possibly embarrassing impression on him. At the least, it was a foretaste of greater persecution—and he was resolved to never be deterred by it.

During his first mission tour, when he circled through the area called Galatia minor on the northeastern coast of the Mediterranean Sea, he was confronted with physical persecution when he was dragged out of a city, pelted with rocks and left for dead (Acts 14:19-20). Then, in sight of the new believers, he got up and continued his mission in the nearby city of Derbe where he had just previously preached.

It was during his second mission tour, as he was revisiting the churches established on the first tour, that the Holy Spirit redirected him to Macedonia (in particular, Philippi). It was on his way from Galatia to his port of departure at Troas that he bypassed Colosse (he later visited the nearby city of Ephesus on his return trip). Laodicea was also in that area (known more for the letter written to it as recorded in Revelation 3:14). Interestingly, Paul's letter to the Colossians refers to Laodicea four times, indicating the close relationship of the believers in the two neighboring cities. None of the believers in these two cities had apparently ever met Paul in person, but they had most likely come to faith in Christ through those who had met Paul. Though they had not met, Paul still had a sacrificial affection for them, helping them grow through his writings.

Lord, thank You for all those godly individuals who have had an influence on my life, though having never met me in person: authors, speakers and leaders.

WEEKEND READING

Saturday – John 9
Sunday – John 10

PERSONAL
REFLECTIONS

_____
_____
_____
_____
_____
_____
_____
_____
_____
_____
_____
_____
_____
_____
_____
_____
_____
_____
_____
_____
_____
_____
_____
_____
_____
_____

Gaining Wealth

Colossians 2:2

... ² that their hearts may be encouraged, having been knit together in love, and attaining to all the wealth that comes from the full assurance of understanding, resulting in a true knowledge of God's mystery, that is, Christ Himself ...

Needed among Christians, at the top of the list, is encouragement. The English word, encourage, means "to inspire with courage, spirit or hope." Yet, with the plethora of Christian teaching, you would think there is enough spiritual encouragement. Teaching of the Word is prevalent over the radio, Internet and at churches every Sunday morning. Depending upon which polls or researchers you read, the average adult in North America is either well steeped or completely ignorant of basic biblical facts. But, Paul was writing to Christians who did know the basics. What they needed was the courage to live out their faith in the face of doctrinal aberrations. It is one thing to know the truth; it is entirely another to live the truth. The difference is one of courage.

The nearby city of Smyrna was faced with similar challenges, with the writer of Revelation even calling the opposition, "the synagogue of Satan." There, John writes to them, "Do not fear what you are about to suffer. Behold, the devil is about to cast some of you into prison, so that you will be tested . . ." (Rev. 2:10). The Colossians, like the Smyrnans, needed to be encouraged.

Is it not interesting that false teaching affects not just the mind but also the heart? It discourages people from walking in true faith. People are drawn away because there is an appeal to the flesh, the natural man in each of us. "It just seems so right, so good," a person might say. But, is it true to the Word of God? I fear many Christians decide on the church they attend, the speakers they listen to or the authors they read, based on how it makes them feel. When their hearts rule over their minds, they become prey to the false teacher who knows how to manipulate. Think about it, false teaching that is simply bland and has no appeal to the flesh will not go very far in attracting a following. But, a compelling communicator can skillfully adjust the facts to couch erroneous teaching in a way that sounds soothing and good, even wholesome—but completely wrong.

Christians must be encouraged, "having been knit together in love" (vs. 2), so that our attraction is to each other seeking the Lord together. The goal is the rich understanding that comes from a true knowledge of the Lord Jesus Christ. One of the signs of false teaching is that it denigrates the full uniqueness, supremacy and deity of the Lord Jesus Christ. If Jesus Christ is reduced to only a man, or just a prophet, or to just one of many gods (of which we all become), such teaching and those who propagate it are completely false.

Lord, I believe Your Son, the Lord Jesus Christ is God in the flesh. Amen.

Christian Enlightenment

Colossians 2:3

... ³ in whom are hidden all the treasures of wisdom and knowledge.

Jesus Christ is the "in whom." To initial onlookers, He appeared to be just a Jew, maybe ahead of His time in terms of moral teachings and peaceful, non-violent resistance in the face of class struggle. Possibly even a mystic or guru pointing people to a high consciousness. Certainly, those embracing the philosophy that came to be known in later years as Gnosticism found in Jesus a sort of spiritual being, that is, an enlightened individual, pointing toward truth. In its more developed form, Gnostic belief held that Christ was a created individual, in line with a succession of "emanations" radiating out from the Absolute Truth, the central Idea of the universe—that which is Holiness and Purity and Perfection in totality. The farther an emanation was from the Absolute, the less holy and, therefore, more material it was. The creator god of this earth, in Gnostic thinking, was a distant emanation, for Absolute Holiness could not have directly created that which is material, like the earth. In the same vein, Jesus could not have been deity, unless that deity was so distant from the Absolute Truth that it was sufficiently material to experience life as a man or even a savior of material man.

In the face of all this thinking that was forming in the surrounding culture and attempting to invade the church, Paul writes, "in whom are hidden all the treasures of wisdom and understanding." There is no wisdom or understanding outside of or beyond Christ. He is the central repository, the fountainhead. To use Gnostic terms, He is the Absolute Truth. He Himself said, "I am the way, the truth and the life . . ." (John14:6). John wrote of Him, "And the Word became flesh, and dwelt among us, and we saw His glory, glory as of the only begotten from the Father, full of grace and truth" (John 1:14). There is no truth or wisdom outside of Him. Knowing Christ is the object of every Christian's desire; it is the very goal of living. Paul expressed it this way, "That I may know Him . . ." (Phil. 3:10). He exclaimed, "Oh, the depth of the riches both of the wisdom and knowledge of God! How unsearchable are His judgments and unfathomable His ways!" (Rom. 11:33). This wisdom is found in Christ.

Enlightenment, therefore, occurs in knowing the Lord Jesus Christ. The Christian life is not primarily a self-help pattern of living. It is not essentially about how to do good and to avoid doing bad. It is not adapting a Christian worldview—all these things are good, but they are not the central thing. The central thing is knowing Christ "in whom is hidden all wisdom and understanding."

Lord Jesus, I seek You with all my being, for apart from You I can know nothing at all. I commit to knowing You more and more in all of my life.

Preventing Perverse Persuasion

Colossians 2:4

⁴ I say this so that no one will delude you with persuasive argument.

Persuasion takes a person where his will may initially be reluctant. It can be a force for good or for not-so-good. Jesus was a master persuader in that many people were compelled by His teaching and life to follow Him. As many as 5,000 followed Him at any given moment in His earthly ministry. He used healing, miraculous feedings, compelling stories and riveting teaching. His debates with the religious leaders were showcases for His superior reasoning abilities. Yes, Jesus was a very persuasive individual.

Carefully extending below the surface, though, His persuasion was found in the substance of doing the work the Father had given Him to do on the earth and the Holy Spirit's empowering His life and ministry, bringing conviction of sin to the people. The entire Trinity was at work—no wonder He was persuasive! And, it involved the work of God and the power of God and the love of God. Therefore, He used persuasion like a workman who uses everything in his power to accomplish his task.

Persuasion, however, can be used to influence people in a wrong direction. Paul wants us to be attuned when we are confronted with a persuasive teaching. Now, it is not always easy because by its very nature a person who is deceived does not know he is being deceived. So, we must on the first order admit to the very real possibility that we ourselves could be deceived, that is, deluded.

Proverbs counsels us, "Trust in the LORD with all your heart and do not lean on your own understanding. In all your ways acknowledge Him, And He will make your paths straight" (Prov. 3:5-6). We must admit that our own ability to understand can deceive us because of the deceptive nature of the sin problem in each of us. We must hold to an unreserved commitment to the revealed Word of God, the Scripture, which is our anchor in the face of deluding words.

For Christians, that means also an unreserved commitment to the Lord Jesus Christ, who, as Paul asserted in the previous verses, is the source of all treasures of wisdom and knowledge. Pre-Gnostic thinking sought after wisdom and knowledge as reserved for the spiritual elite, those with the secret mysterious knowledge of the Absolute Truth. But for the Christian, truth is found in Christ alone. He is the revelation of the mystery of God, not some esoteric religious experience. And, He is available to anyone who believes, not the religious elite. We need to avoid anyone who teaches or speaks persuasively if they in anyway denigrate the full revelation of the deity of Jesus Christ.

Father, thank You for inviting me to feast on the full knowledge
and revelation of the Lord Jesus Christ. I need nothing else.

Spiritual Presence

Colossians 2:5

⁵ For even though I am absent in body, nevertheless I am with you in spirit, rejoicing to see your good discipline and the stability of your faith in Christ.

"I am with you" is a common phrase in many cultures. Most notably in the ancient Hebrew context, during the time of Moses, the phrase spoken by God took on enormous significance. When Moses was commissioned by God to lead the people of Israel out of bondage in Egypt, he obsessed about his own inadequacy. "But Moses said to God, 'Who am I, that I should go to Pharaoh, and that I should bring the sons of Israel out of Egypt?' And He said, 'Certainly I will be with you, and this shall be the sign to you that it is I who have sent you: when you have brought the people out of Egypt, you shall worship God at this mountain'" (Ex. 3:11-12). God's presence was a promise. A few verses later, God said to Moses, "'I AM WHO I AM'; and He said, 'Thus you shall say to the sons of Israel, "I AM has sent me to you."'"

Repeatedly, God reminded them of that promise. And in fact, when Christ was born, He was called by God "Emmanuel" which means "God with us." And at the end, when He instructed His disciples with the great commission, Jesus said, ". . . lo, I am with you always, even to the end of the age" (Matt. 28:20b). We are reminded by the writer of Hebrews, "I will never desert you, nor will I ever forsake you . . ." (Heb. 13:5b).

With the presence of God, what else do we need? Why would we need the presence of anyone else? Why does Paul tell the Colossians, "I am with you in spirit"? First off, he is not evoking some kind of mystical presence in replacement of Christ's presence. Nor is he assuming a high-church "saintly" role. Paul knew very well his place in the grand scheme of things—he was a sinner saved by grace and a servant of Christ. His point is that although he was not physically present, he was still spiritually involved in their lives. We humans are so attached to the physical world that we tend to obscure spiritual realities. Our bodies are the medium through which we interact with the physical world around us. And, when someone is physically far away, the relationship suffers. But, not so with Paul. He was very much before the Lord on their behalf, through prayer and rejoicing. He was truly with them spiritually.

Jesus said that where two or more are gathered in His name, He is there in their presence. It seems to me that when we are gathered "spiritually" together, even when not physically present, we can know that the Lord is also in our presence spiritually. Oh, that we would open our eyes to this reality!

Lord, help me build up my brothers whom I have never met, but who are laboring under persecution. They are my kin, we are part of the same family.

The New Walk Again

⁶ Therefore as you have received Christ Jesus the Lord, so walk in Him ...

First instructions often set the tone for what follows. After Paul's introduction and lengthy prayer which turns into a rejoicing and a rehearsing of the great truths of God, all in chapter one, and telling the Colossians of his efforts on their behalf in the initial verses of chapter two, he turns to his first instruction to them. Teaching with the goal of change in their lives was at the heart of Paul's ministry. His doctrine, though, never changed. It was the lives of believers that needed to change.

The Colossians needed affirmation to continue living in the same way that they had received Christ. There was nothing new to add to the basic teaching of Christian living. He is about to remind them about who Christ is, but suffice it to say at this juncture, living the Christian life is the same as receiving Christ in the first place. "As you received Christ Jesus, so walk in Him." Very simple and very succinct. Yet, profound in the face of the false teaching confronting the Colossians!

There were many who were suggesting that belief in Christ was good, but there was so much more that they needed to know to arrive at the ultimate destination, that is, unity with the Absolute Truth, where there is pure knowledge. This pre-Gnostic thinking was a sort of mystery religion, that only the select few were initiated into the higher level of spiritual understanding. It was tempting to believers, that they could somehow gain more than what they already had, in terms of understanding knowledge and mysteries.

But, Paul has already made it clear that the mystery of God had previously been made known to believers (Col. 1:26) and that the mystery is made known in Christ (Col. 1:27). There is no other mystery, no greater knowledge than knowing Christ. Living the Christian life, then, is living in constant discovery of Christ, whom we already know. In the next verse, Paul further explains this, but let us stop for a moment to consider our present temptations.

There are many religions today that purport to contain the "true" knowledge of absolute truth. Some claim to build upon Christianity, asserting that Jesus was a great prophet and teacher, but more is needed. However, biblical Christianity teaches that Jesus is enough. In Him, God is fully revealed. Any religion or spiritual teaching that involves "truth beyond" Christ or implies that Christ is not God's complete statement to us is simply false.

Lord, help me to see Christ so completely, that all false teaching absolutely loses its appeal. I want to walk in Christ in the same way I received Him.

WEEKEND READING

Saturday – John 11:1-27
Sunday – John 11:18-57

PERSONAL REFLECTIONS

_____
_____
_____
_____
_____
_____
_____
_____
_____
_____
_____
_____
_____
_____
_____
_____
_____
_____
_____
_____
_____
_____
_____
_____
_____
_____
_____
_____
_____

Rooting For the Foundation

Colossians 2:7

... ⁷ having been firmly rooted and now being built up in Him and established in your faith, just as you were instructed, and overflowing with gratitude.

Paul had just exhorted the Colossian Christians to continue walking in Christ in the same way they received Him. Sanctification (the process of becoming more like Christ) is rooted in justification (the act of being made right before God). Both are the working of grace in our lives and take place "in Christ." Both are appropriated through faith.

"To be rooted" captures the image of a tree with a strong root system. Psalm 1 pictures a rooted man as one who builds his life on the Word of God. "His delight is in the law of the LORD, and in His law he meditates day and night. He will be like a tree firmly planted by streams of water, which yields its fruit in its season and its leaf does not wither; and in whatever he does, he prospers" (Ps. 1:2-3). Now "in Christ" our rootedness is not based on what we do (e.g. meditating on God's word), but on what God has done for us in Christ. We have already been made righteous and are now rooted "in Him."

Therefore, we are now being built up "in Him", and our faith is being established. What a strong combination. We are secured in Him, and we are assured in our faith! As believers in Christ, we are safe for all eternity. "He rescued us from the domain of darkness, and transferred us to the kingdom of His beloved Son, in whom we have redemption, the forgiveness of sins" (Col. 1:13-14, see Romans 8:28-39).

Unfortunately, not all Christians are assured, because either they lack knowledge or they lack mature faith. Paul just finished saying that our walk must be like our birth—in faith. Our faith was used by God to save us, and our faith is used for assuring us that we are secure. By faith we were saved, by faith we live the Christian life. This was engendered from Paul's earlier instruction and had already resulted in overwhelming gratitude on the Colossians' part.

So, how do we walk by faith? By believing God's Word! We believed the message of salvation through Christ, by His grace through our faith. This is the first and the greatest promise of God to us. Walking the Christian walk is simply a matter of continuing to believe the promises of God, believing in Him when He instructs us how to live. How much of our difficulties come from neglecting God's Word to us and living by our own fleshly sight, "thinking ourselves to be wise," without God's help? He knows best how we ought to live our lives, so we need to believe that when we follow His commands, we are living as He wants us to—and in the end, that kind of life brings Him the greatest glory!

Lord, help me live my Christian life the way I began it—by faith in You.

Beware the Deceivers

Colossians 2:8

⁸ See to it that no one takes you captive through philosophy and empty deception, according to the tradition of men, according to the elementary principles of the world, rather than according to Christ.

Where there are truth tellers, there are the truth perverters. In Paul's time, the Judaizers tried to infuse the Law into the message of Christ and grace, and the pre-Gnostics tried to mystify spirituality with their fanciful imagination. Paul warns repeatedly throughout his writings against anything that changes the gospel message or threatens it in any way.

Remember in Galatians he wrote rather acerbically, "But even if we, or an angel from heaven, should preach to you a gospel contrary to what we have preached to you, he is to be accursed! As we have said before, so I say again now, if any man is preaching to you a gospel contrary to what you received, he is to be accursed!" (Gal. 1:8-9). To the Corinthians, he wrote, "For though we walk in the flesh, we do not war according to the flesh, for the weapons of our warfare are not of the flesh, but divinely powerful for the destruction of fortresses. We are destroying speculations and every lofty thing raised up against the knowledge of God, and we are taking every thought captive to the obedience of Christ, and we are ready to punish all disobedience, whenever your obedience is complete" (2 Cor. 10:3-6).

So. here also, with the Colossians, he warns not to fall captive to religio-philosophical lies invented by humans. This is particularly concerning in our present day where we are witnessing a proliferation of religious philosophies competing for the minds of people. More and more, these worldviews are commonplace in academia and in popular culture, whether rooted in eastern religious thought or simply in the rehash of older philosophies disguised as new or post-modern thinking. They all have one thing in common: they originate in the imaginations of humans. Paul calls this "the tradition of men," and they are rooted in what he describes as "the elementary principles of the world." All false teaching originates on earth, rather than in heaven in Christ.

This warning of Paul's speaks to the very real possibility for genuine Christians to be deceived and led astray from truth, from right doctrine. False teachers can be skilled in manipulation and in framing their teachings in attractive, somewhat convincing ways—but their teachings are none-the-less false. Christians need to be on guard, examining every teaching, to determine whether it is biblical, that is, whether it comes from God or not.

Lord, help me to be discerning so that I and my fellow brothers and sisters in Christ would not be deceived but be able to actively confront false teaching.

The Ultimate Integration

⁹ For in Him all the fullness of Deity dwells in bodily form ...

Big things come in small packages. This short verse conveys a huge truth. God became a man! Fully God, fully man. The Nicene Creed captured this well when it referred to Jesus Christ as "true God from true God . . . he became truly human." Notice from our verse for today two very important observations. First, this truth involved the fullness of deity. There was nothing about God that did not inhabit the person of Jesus Christ. He was nothing short of God, not inferior to God in essence. Though the distinction between the Father and the Son is maintained, both the Father and the Son are fully and equally God.

The second observation is that God dwelt in Christ in *bodily* form. This was physical; He became part of His own creation. There was nothing un-bodily about Jesus Christ. He was not a phantom that just appeared to be human. He was physically born, grew bodily; he ate, drank, got tired, felt pain—he fully experienced life as a physical being. So, Jesus Christ was fully human. And, since He rose from the dead in bodily form, He continues to be fully human.

Some charge that it is impossible for a man to become God. We agree, actually. But, that is not what this passage is saying. Consider one simple clarification: a man did not become God, but God became a man! The concept that Deity dwelt in bodily form asserts that God became a man. The Scripture does not say that man dwelt in deity form. This changes the whole discussion. Whereas, we agree that it is impossible for a man to become a God, the reverse is not impossible, because God is God and He invaded His own creation.

Now, the idea that God could and did become a man is repulsive to some because they think that demeans the stature and holiness of God. God is too pure for that, they say. However, the incarnation of Christ (that is, God taking on human form) is precisely what is so amazing about God. He is able to relate to His creation, in what can be said to be the ultimate integration of God with His creation.

To be sure, now, we should not be surprised that the incarnation would tax our reasoning abilities. At the point of incarnation, eternity and time intersect. Who can fully comprehend the Infinite occupying space in the finite? How can we imagine the omni-present One, localizing Himself and, for example, walking along the road. It makes sense that in Christ, fully God and fully man, we would see an anomaly that boggles our normal conceptions of reality. God entering His own creation strains the fabric of creation itself. Not only does creation reflect His glory, but now in Christ, creation has become the home for His glory.

Lord, it is a good and pleasant thing for You to share reality with us, with me.

"In Him"

Colossians 2:10-12

[10] and in Him you have been made complete, and He is the head over all rule and authority; [11] and in Him you were also circumcised with a circumcision made without hands, in the removal of the body of the flesh by the circumcision of Christ; [12] having been buried with Him in baptism, in which you were also raised up with Him through faith in the working of God, who raised Him from the dead.

"In Him" provides one of the most assuring promises the Christian has. Christ is the all-sufficient One; therefore, being "in Him" meets all of our needs. In both the letter to the Ephesians and now to the Colossians, we are constantly brought back to Christ and the fact that we are "in Christ" and, therefore, securely placed in the most advantageous situation possible.

In our passage today, we see that "in Him you have been made complete." This could also be translated, "made full." What a tremendous truth coming after verse 9, where Christ is indwelt with the fullness of Deity. We have been made full "In Christ." This does not mean that we are, therefore, deities ourselves. But the fullness of Christ is ours; we do not need ritual circumcision, philosophy, human inventions or any human merit. There is nothing we need besides Christ. Since He is the "head over all rule and authority," there is no need for any other rule or authority. No religious system beyond faith in Christ is needed. Religions that teach there is more knowledge and insight than what God has revealed in Christ are, therefore, false. He is the be all and end all. And we are complete and full in Christ.

In fact, all that we had before Christ, that we hung our hopes upon, has been buried, put in the past as being useless and dead. That is what our baptism signified. But, now we have been raised with Christ, who Himself was raised from the dead by God. Paul weaves the complete package deal here.

Through the centuries, religions have risen that claim to possess a new or greater insight into spiritual things, but this implies that Christ is not enough. False religions in some way diminish the exalted nature of Christ as being fully God and fully man, who came to dwell among humans. But He is not just a prophet, a great moral teacher, a pointer of the way to God. Jesus Christ is God in the flesh, manhood and Deity in perfect harmony. And we who believe need nothing else. For in Him, we are complete, and we have been raised up with Him, as though being alive from the dead. What more could any religion offer us, now that we have Christ, and in Him, we have everything we need for life and godliness (see 2 Peter 1:3).

Lord Jesus, help me to know the depths of wisdom and insight found in You.
I want to know You better and all the glories of being raised with You.

Made Alive

Colossians 2:13-15

13 When you were dead in your transgressions and the uncircumcision of your flesh, He made you alive together with Him, having forgiven us all our transgressions, 14 having canceled out the certificate of debt consisting of decrees against us, which was hostile to us; and He has taken it out of the way, having nailed it to the cross. 15 When He had disarmed the rulers and authorities, He made a public display of them, having triumphed over them through Him.

I am alive, and so are you as a believer in Christ. Really alive! Verse 12 told us that we were buried and raised up with Him through faith. Paul now points out the true condition that required our "burial"—we were dead! Our "transgressions" (breeches of Law) rendered us the same as "uncircumcised" Gentiles. For Jews, this would have been shocking to hear. All the externals of their religion meant nothing to God, now that Jesus has risen from the dead. Our aliveness has nothing to do with religious behavior or rituals or disciplines.

Notice the descriptions of our pre-faith condition: we were dead (vs. 13), debtors (vs. 14a) and objects of hostility (vs. 14b). God has now taken care of these things completely. We are alive; our debt has been canceled, and the hostility has been taken away!

How did this happen? It was all nailed to the cross, as it were. The imagery is that of a written decree listing out our sins being taken and nailed to the cross on which Christ died. This was once vividly illustrated at a Christian summer camp where the campers were encouraged to write on a small piece of paper the sins with which they were currently struggling. Then, one by one, they walked up to a makeshift wooden cross and taking a hammer and nail, they fastened the "decree" to the cross. As each camper stood there watching, the cross was towed away on a trailer, symbolizing that the "debt consisting of decrees against us . . . He has taken it out of the way" (vs. 14). What a powerful picture of the illustration God has given to us of what took place on the cross.

Christ's death was not just an example of suffering for wrong done. Nor was it meant to be a sentimental act of love, showing Christ's commitment to the truth, or to be a catalyst of non-aggressive resistance to worldly religious authority imitated by the likes of Mahatma Ghandi or Martin Luther King, Jr. It was far more than that. Our Lord's death provided death and resurrection for all who would believe on Him. That was not just symbolism, but reality. We are now alive, no longer spiritually in debt, our enemy the devil has been disarmed in his accusations against us—all because of what Jesus has done!

Lord, I am overwhelmed when I think of what You have accomplished for me. Eternity will not be long enough for praising You.

WEEKEND READING

Saturday – John 12
Sunday – John 13

PERSONAL
REFLECTIONS

_____

_____

_____

_____

_____

_____

_____

_____

_____

_____

_____

_____

_____

_____

_____

_____

_____

_____

_____

_____

_____

_____

_____

_____

_____

_____

_____

Praise God, Free At Last

Colossians 2:16

[16] Therefore no one is to act as your judge in regard to food or drink or in respect to a festival or a new moon or a Sabbath day ...

The term "judging" is the Christian boogeyman, and rightly so. Jesus said, "Do not judge so that you will not be judged. For in the way you judge, you will be judged; and by your standard of measure, it will be measured to you" (Matt. 7:1-2). There is much of that going around today. But at other times, we are instructed to make judgments. For indeed, Jesus also said, "Do not judge according to appearance, but judge with righteous judgment" (John 7:24).

For example, I might observe a friend beginning to drink alcohol every night of the week and come to the judgment that he is descending into alcoholism with all its destructive behavior. Out of love, I confront the person to help stem the behavior. I am judging his behavior as counter-spiritual. However, if I approach him with the idea of calling his salvation into question, I begin wandering into Colossians 2:16-17 territory. I have made alcoholism into an additional sin that somehow needs to be paid for beyond the cross.

However, Paul just finished saying God has "canceled out the certificate of debt consisting of decrees against us, which was hostile to us; and He has taken it out of the way, having nailed it to the cross" (Col. 2:14). No law can stand up to that, even the man-made "Christian" law, "Thou shall not drink alcohol." Yet, so many churches require such total abstinence for membership, effectively making it a legalistic requirement. That's like saying no fat person can be a member of the church because gluttony is a sin.

True, excess and ceding control of our bodies to food or drink is not good. Paul says in another place, "All things are lawful, but not all things are profitable. All things are lawful, but not all things edify" (1 Cor. 10:23; see also 1 Corinthians 6:12). Alcoholism is a terrible waste of a human life, but for the Christian, it is nailed to the cross. The debt of that sin, along with all other sins, has been done away with. Jesus paid it all. Our standing with God is not in question.

So, therefore, Christians need to act in freedom, making our daily choices not on the basis of guilt or fear of how others might judge us or even the fear of losing our salvation. We should, rather, act in the freedom of those whose debt has been forgiven. That includes the freedom to walk in good conscience, even when others might criticize how we worship (observing or not observing special religious days, including Sundays). Our salvation is secure! We are free!

Lord, thank You for freeing me from the legalistic requirements of men. My debt has been paid and, praise to You, I am no longer judged by the Law.

Giving Way to Substance

Colossians 2:17

... ¹⁷ things which are a mere shadow of what is to come; but the substance belongs to Christ.

Shadow, that is how Paul describes the Law of the Old Testament. And, a shadow begs the question, "What casts the shadow?" The answer is very simply, "Christ!" The image is a surprising one, for one usually sees the thing first, then the shadow. But in this case, the shadow of Christ is found in the Law, which came first in time. The implications of this are huge!

First, the thing casting the shadow, in this case, Christ, is absolutely more significant than the shadow, in this case the Law. Therefore, if one has Christ, it is supremely inferior, then. to focus on the Law as a means for regulating life. The Law was a shadow of Deity, but in Christ, Deity resides (Col. 1:19; 2:9). In Christ, we are "complete" (Col. 2:10), fully accepted by God—so, we no longer need to keep the Law in order to find complete acceptance with God. We are now to "walk in Him" (Col. 2:6), not walk in the Law. Why, then, would any of us spend time focusing on the shadow when we can focus on Christ?

But, there is another implication—the Law cast a long shadow. Human nature, fallen as it is, always gyrates toward law. There is significant odor of self-promotion in trying to live by a set of rules. It goes something like this: "It is possible for me to become a good person by my own efforts. I just need to keep the rules in order to make it happen." The fallacy with such thinking is that the focus is in the wrong place, on the shadow, that is, the rules. Our focus should rather be on Christ, the thing casting the shadow. That takes our eyes off ourselves and puts the attention on Christ.

The book of Hebrews expands on the superiority of Christ over the Law. "[The priests] serve a copy and shadow of the heavenly things, just as Moses was warned by God when he was about to erect the tabernacle; for, 'See,' He says, 'that you make all things according to the pattern which was shown you on the mountain.' But now He [Christ] has obtained a more excellent ministry, by as much as He is also the mediator of a better covenant, which has been enacted on better promises" (Heb. 8:5-6). "For the Law, since it has only a shadow of the good things to come and not the very form of things, can never, by the same sacrifices which they offer continually year by year, make perfect those who draw near" (Heb. 10:1). "For by one offering He has perfected for all time those who are sanctified" (Heb. 10:14). So, in Christ, and not in the Law, we find perfect, complete acceptance with God.

Father, I am so thankful that Your Son is far superior to the Law. In Him, I am complete, and I choose to walk in Him and not by the regulations of the Law.

Prize Fighting

Colossians 2:18-19

[18] Let no one keep defrauding you of your prize by delighting in self-abasement and the worship of the angels, taking his stand on visions he has seen, inflated without cause by his fleshly mind, [19] and not holding fast to the head, from whom the entire body, being supplied and held together by the joints and ligaments, grows with a growth which is from God.

Prize fighting is what the apostle Paul was all about. Not the crude form of bare-knuckle boxing, but the struggle of which he spoke in another letter: "I press on toward the goal for the prize of the upward call of God in Christ Jesus" (Phil. 3:14). Literally, the word means "prize of conflict," and there is certainly a conflict in the Christian life in terms of how to live our lives. We either "walk in Him" (2:6) striving for the true goal of Christ, or we follow after a religious system of various sorts. The implications of what Paul has been saying thus far is that, since we are "complete" in Christ, all other religious systems, which are all based on some form of human achievement, are fallacious and counter-productive to genuine spiritual growth.

Now, he turns his application eye to specific teachings confronting the Colossians; many of which are universal "religious" things. The first is "self-abasement." Sanctification, or true spiritual growth, is not found in setting our goal to physically deny ourselves. Some religions promote self-flagellation, inflicting physical harm on one's body as a means of suppressing "the fleshly desires." Some obsess with angelic manifestations. Still others emphasize the experience of supernatural visions. All these have the ultimate effect of stroking a person's ego. And, the aforementioned things get bigger and better with the telling, i.e. exaggeration. It is entirely possible that such testimonies begin with some small impression or experience that is interpreted in a spiritual way, then "inflated" through the retelling, like an urban myth, or a Christian-myth. The tendency is for people to hold on to these kinds of experiences, to bolster their lagging faith. This describes Gnosticism, a system built on esoteric experiences, visions and insider knowledge.

However, all such ways of pursuing spiritual experiences, though appealing to the "fleshly mind," have this one big problem—they all gain acceptance only when a person lets go of "holding fast" to Christ. It is in Christ, and Him alone, that the church finds nourishment for faith and growth. There is no substitute, no supplement for truth. He is the Truth, the whole Truth, and spiritual growth comes through our "walking in Him."

Lord, help me to see when false thinking draws me away from Christ. I want to continue seeking for the prize of the upward call of God in Christ Jesus.

Fruitless Legalism

Colossians 2:20-23

20 If you have died with Christ to the elementary principles of the world, why, as if you were living in the world, do you submit yourself to decrees, such as, 21 "Do not handle, do not taste, do not touch!" 22 (which all refer to things destined to perish with use)—in accordance with the commandments and teachings of men? 23 These are matters which have, to be sure, the appearance of wisdom in self-made religion and self-abasement and severe treatment of the body, but are of no value against fleshly indulgence.

Cutting across the "religiousism" that pervades many people's church experience, Paul takes direct aim at living life legalistically. Why settle for a cheap substitute for walking "in Him" that does not satisfy? There is something strangely addicting to running life by a set of rules. It is so universal, so pervasive, that people assume it to be an elementary principle for life, a basic truism. Of course religion should define what a person can't do—everyone knows that, right? Paul disagrees! First of all, Christians have "died with Christ." Those are not just words, but it is true and has significant implications. Among other things, having died with Christ means we are dead to this world. Truly, we are "dead men walking," not in a ghoulish sort of way but in a spiritual way. The rules change now, in that we are no longer subject to the "elementary principles." Things which others take for granted no longer apply to us.

Paul, in a memorable way, sums up those principles as, "Do not handle, do not taste, do not touch." True, there were Old Testament laws given by God that ordered similar practices. But, religionists replace them with man-made versions that are not a means of understanding the holiness of God (as were the Old Testament laws), but which have become a means of attempting to attain righteousness. Therefore, these misapplications of the Law became man's efforts to turn the Law into achievements, failing to understand that they "are of no value against fleshly indulgence" (vs. 23).

The goal is not to keep a set of rules, but to live Christ-like lives. That kind of living begins with, and cannot be sustained apart from, the knowledge that as believers in Christ we are dead with Him. Without that, our efforts are reduced to "self-made religion and self-abasement." Even the most rigorous self-denials and self-imposed sacrifices don't suppress the desires of the flesh in reality, but only drive them underground. They may give the impression of godliness and wisdom, but in the end, they bring us no closer to being like Him.

Lord, I confess that sometimes I fall into living according to religious notions of self-sacrifice that are really efforts to appease my flesh rather than defeat it. Please give me the strength to embrace the death of Christ for daily living.

View From the Top

Colossians 3:1-2

¹ Therefore if you have been raised up with Christ, keep seeking the things above, where Christ is, seated at the right hand of God. ² Set your mind on the things above, not on the things that are on earth.

S anctification grows out of the constant pursuit of Christ. There are two great truths that form the bulwark of growing in Christlikeness, both found in our identification with the Son of God: "If you have died with Christ . . ." (Col. 2:20) and "If you have been raised up with Christ . . ." (Col. 3:1). The first frees us from the useless way, and the second directs us to the profitable pursuit. There is a choice to be made, focusing on our own efforts or focusing on Christ. This is not some "head-in-the-sky" mysticism reserved for the spiritual ascetics. As believers, we have been raised with Christ (see Romans 6:1-14). This is hugely significant and absolutely central to all of the Christian life!

Now, based on this truth, we are directed toward two imperatives. First, keep seeking the things above. Life is made up of pursuits of various sorts. People run after money, jobs, power or fame. Some have lives centered on gaining acceptance or protecting themselves from others. But, the only way to live the Christian life that has any traction for holiness is to seek the things of Christ. Paul calls these, "the things above, where Christ is." And, that place is at the right hand of God, the position of authority and preeminence.

All the things we seek here on earth are eclipsed in the pursuit of Christ, because He is far superior to them all. In Him, we find the power of God for salvation (Rom. 1:16) and for victory over sin (1 Cor. 15:56-57). He is the owner of everything—earthly possessions and money are trivial compared to being His heirs. We have the attention and love of the greatest Person in existence, and we have already been received as His children—therefore, we have far more security than any earthly person, thing or experience can provide.

The second imperative is to set your mind on things above, similar to the first, but emphasizing the use of the mind. The world would seek to capture the Christian mind back into its futile way of thinking, but we need to focus on that which is central to our lives—Jesus Christ. This is not self-effort in the sense of accomplishing a standing with God. Rather, it is strategic, for what we set our minds upon is what we pursue, what we give our time to. There are many self-help books, even those with a Christian flavor, complete with Scripture references. But, setting our minds on the Lord Jesus Christ is central to all Christian living and growth, and the only real way to true spiritual growth.

Lord, thank You for giving us the focus that will anchor our lives in a distracting world. I want to grow in my knowledge and understanding of Christ.

WEEKEND READING

Saturday – John 14
Sunday – John 15

PERSONAL
REFLECTIONS

The Hidden Reveal

Colossians 3:3-4

³ For you have died and your life is hidden with Christ in God. ⁴ When Christ, who is our life, is revealed, then you also will be revealed with Him in glory.

Three truths are found in our passage for today. We have died with Christ; our life is hidden with Christ, and we will be revealed with Him. Like three prongs on an anchor, they secure us to the Rock. Let's look at each of these.

We have died with Christ. This is a recurring theme with the apostle Paul. Not only is he building on the truth of Colossians 2:20-23 and our freedom from man-made rituals, but this truth forms the critical link in his teaching on sanctification in Romans. "Our old self was crucified with Him, in order that our body of sin might be done away with, so that we would no longer be slaves to sin . . . if we have died with Christ, we believe that we shall also live with Him, . . . consider yourselves to be dead to sin, but alive to God in Christ Jesus" (Rom. 6:6, 8, 11). Sanctification begins with our spiritual death. Obviously, Paul is speaking figuratively and spiritually here, but the imagery is powerful and conveys an enormous truth. We have spiritually died with Christ, when He died physically on the cross. God wants us to "set your minds on things above . . ." (Col. 3:2), namely, that from the spiritual perspective ("above") we are dead.

The second truth, our life is hidden with Christ in God, is equally important. Remember, the Colossians were being tempted toward the Gnostic way of thinking, that certain mysteries lay hidden to all but the elite, the spiritually initiated. However, as believers in Christ, we ourselves are hidden with Christ. We have already been initiated, through His death, into the mysteries of God, namely, that He has reconciled the church to Himself, regardless of whether Jew or Gentile. We are in Him, a new person, a collective whole, and not just certain "enlightened" ones. Since Christ is raised from the dead, we are not just spiritually dead to the world and sin, but we are alive in Him. Paul intoned this when he wrote, "Christ, who is our life" (vs. 4a). This new life will never end, since it is a raised life.

Finally, Paul explains that while our life in Christ may not be fully recognized here on earth, there is coming a time when Christ Himself will be revealed to all the world. It will be seen at that time that we believers have the "inside" relationship with Him, that we are part of the inner circle of fellowship, that we are in fact the true initiates. We take a backseat to no one in terms of knowing God. What a privilege we have in being hidden in Him with a glory that is to be revealed when He returns.

Lord, help me to live as a dead man who has been raised to life in Christ. I want to live in such a way that Christ is glorified.

Dead Members

Colossians 3:5

⁵ Therefore consider the members of your earthly body as dead to immorality, impurity, passion, evil desire, and greed, which amounts to idolatry.

"Consider"—that's the core activity of the Christian mind. We need to consider, to think, to interpret, to change our field of reference. As those with new lives hidden in Christ (vs. 3), we have been enlightened and no longer see the world the way we used to see it. Though we'd like to see this all happen automatically, it is rather a matter of putting us in a position to live differently. At the heart of it is the capacity to see things differently because we have been redeemed, because we have been raised up with Christ. So, the choice is ours in how we interpret life experiences. And, that choice is one of faith.

For example, when an enticing temptation confronts me, I can choose to interpret it as being more powerful than I am and, since I have fallen to that temptation before, what's the use, I can't resist. Or, I can choose to consider, as our passage for today teaches us, that my body is dead to temptation, that God is living out His holiness in me and, therefore, I don't have to give in to that temptation. Satan may intend it as a temptation for evil, but God intends it for my faith-building. The choice is one of interpretation based on faith.

This applies to whatever temptation or situation confronts me. The apostle Paul lists six vices, powerful ones at that. The draw of immorality is huge, especially in our time with the prevalence of the internet and media in our homes, and the loosening of traditional morals at an accelerating pace. Passion, by its very nature, is all consuming and difficult to resist. It covers a broad spectrum of behavior and thought. But, some things can only be described as "evil desires." Greed, disguised as rampant consumerism, has left many Christians in debt and enslaved by their desires for more and more.

All those things, Paul says, amount to idolatry, for they carry for us a god-like quality—we think that we can't live our lives without them. When a person holds on to greed, they are setting up an idol that their life depends upon—they can't live without that for which they lust. All else in their life bows in worship and subservience to that evil desire, passion, impurity or immorality.

Against all this, the Holy Spirit instructs us to "consider the members of your earthly body as dead." We need to picture in our mind and in our spirit that we are indeed dead to those influences, that they have no control over us. We are free, therefore, to walk in freedom as those alive from the dead.

Lord, thank You for giving me new spiritual eye-sight. Help me to see temptations as opportunities to work my spiritual-mind muscles.

Somber Warning

Colossians 3:6-9a

⁶ For it is because of these things that the wrath of God will come upon the sons of disobedience, ⁷ and in them you also once walked, when you were living in them. ⁸ But now you also, put them all aside: anger, wrath, malice, slander, and abusive speech from your mouth. Do not lie to one another ...

Warnings in Scripture come in different forms. Here the apostle Paul had just instructed the Colossians to avoid various kinds of immorality. Now, he gives the reason. Very clearly he does not hold over them the threat of judgment in hell. He is not teaching, as so many in Christendom do today, that believers can lose their salvation by falling under the wrath of God. We must parse this very carefully. The wrath that is spoken of here is that fierce anger of God directed to the "sons of disobedience." Is it possible for Christians to be disobedient? Absolutely! But, is Paul saying that when believers like the Colossians disobey, they are included then in the description "sons of disobedience?" I think not. He says that they are now characterized as those who had at one time "walked" in that way. A clear distinction is being made between believers and unbelievers.

So, what is the point that Paul is making then? Why warn them about something they would never experience? The answer is simple. Christians should not engage in behavior for which God brings eternal judgment on unbelievers! Why act in ways that God punishes unbelievers for? We know from many other Scriptures that believers are secure (see, for example, Romans 8:28-39, 1 Corinthians 3:10-15). The principle is still true, though: God is not mocked, what we reap we will sow (Gal. 6:7). For the unbeliever, it is grounds for eternal punishment. But, for believers, who are secure because of God's promises, there can still be a certain fear of reprisal and a loss of joy. The hymn writer points out the joy of obeying the Lord: "Yes, I to the end shall endure, As sure as the earnest is given. More happy, but not more secure, The glorified spirits in heaven." When a Christian gives in to temporal, fleshly "enjoyment," his security is not affected, but his joy here on earth certainly is diminished. So, we are left with the implication of Paul's admonition: Why would a Christian even want to engage in activities for which the unsaved are eternally condemned?

Now, the list of fleshly activities continues with anger, wrath, malice, slander, abusive speech, and lying. All of these things are enumerated in other places, but now they are put on the same level as the previous list of immoralities (Col. 3:5), in one respect. There is no distinguishing between "little" or venial sins and "big" or mortal sins. All incur God's displeasure.

Lord, help me to never take any sin lightly, for each one goes flatly against Your holiness and is a violation of Your righteous standards.

Living the Life

Colossians 3:9b-10

⁹ ... since you laid aside the old self with its evil practices, ¹⁰ and have put on the new self who is being renewed to a true knowledge according to the image of the One who created him ...

Warning gives way to rationale. Christians should avoid immoral behaviors not only because it displeases God, but also because that kind of living goes against the truth of the new life in Christ. In coming to faith, repentance means that we have "laid aside the old self with its evil practices." This is a reprise of Paul's earlier question, "If you have died with Christ to the elementary principles of the world, why, as if you were living in the world, do you submit yourself to decrees, such as 'Do not handle, do not taste, do not touch . . .'" (Col. 2:20-21). Fundamental to the Christian life is the death of self. There is the spiritual reality of it, and there is also the ongoing embracing of it. In dying to self, we lay aside the old behaviors and practices.

Unfortunately, at conversion we don't instantly change everything in our outward lives. Like a child that is born into a new life outside of the womb, there is still a lot of growing to do. We need to build on the new life, or in the words of verse 9, we need to build on the laying aside of the old self and not continue to live like that anymore. The positive side of this is putting on "the new self." The imagery is that of putting off a set of old clothes and putting on a new set. We Christians need to daily adorn ourselves with the new life and not go back to the old (which, if you remember, is the immoral behaviors and ways of relating to people discussed in the previous verses).

But how does this kind of effort differ from the usual religious or moral effort found in all religions and ethical sensibilities? What keeps this from being simply the virtue of self-control that all civilized, educated people pursue? Well, Paul is saying that, left to our selves, the "old self" will continually dominate and result in moral misbehavior, regardless of self-effort. But as believers in Jesus Christ, we are dealing with a different foundation. We operate from a different reality, a different perspective: "Therefore if anyone is in Christ, he is a new creature; the old things passed away; behold, new things have come" (2 Cor. 5:17). And further, God is at work renewing us continually as we grow in our knowledge of Christ. The more we know Him, the more we become like Him. How wonderful it is, then, to know that we have the mystery revealed to us that Christ is fully God (Col. 1:19; 2:9), and we are complete in Him (Col. 2:10). Let us, therefore, grow in our knowledge of Him.

Father, thank You for revealing Christ to me. I want to know Him so that I can grow in Him and become like Him.

Constant Upgrading

Colossians 3:10-12a

... ¹⁰ and have put on the new self who is being renewed to a true knowledge according to the image of the One who created him— ¹¹ a renewal in which there is no distinction between Greek and Jew, circumcised and uncircumcised, barbarian, Scythian, slave and freeman, but Christ is all, and in all. ¹² So, as those who have been chosen of God, holy and beloved, put on ...

The new self is what Christians have "put on," like a set of new clothes. The purveyors of false teaching at Colossae probably taught that Paul's teachings about Christ, though once new, were now getting old, and therefore, needed to be renewed with their new, mysterious (pre-Gnostic) teachings. But, the truth doesn't change. Christ is enough. And our "new self" in Christ is not static, but dynamic, being constantly renewed like a continuous upgrading, to being more and more like Christ. The more we know of Christ, the more we become like Him. Exposure leads to evolution into God-image likeness.

Now this "renewal" is blind to human distinctions. Prejudice dissolves before God's redemption; the world is no longer divided into Jew and non-Jew. The term Greek is virtually synonymous with Gentile in Paul's writings, for the Jews were a minority in predominantly Greek culture, even during Roman political ascendency. Further distinctions of cultural/political groupings mattered nothing to the spiritual renewal of believers. It does not matter to the spiritual point Paul is making whether a person is a barbarian (uncultured and considered savages), Scythian (the worst of the barbarians), slaves or non-slaves. The deepest human distinctions are obliterated in Christ. It is not that Christians have come to recognize through human wisdom the uncivilizedness of such animosities based on social status. Rather, the knowledge of Christ overwhelms and obliterates all such distinctions—like a high intensity floodlight extinguishes all shadows.

In God's eyes, there is no difference, but the new self in us is being renewed to increasing awareness and embracing of that truth. Christ is all and in all. Today, there is one church—there are not black Christians and white Christians, as though the defining attribute of a person is the color of his skin, and his beliefs are secondary. We are above all Christians—that is our central and most important identification. The point, then, is that Paul's instructions are based on that new life. Our moral behaviors, therefore, are not conditioned by those surface differences, but by our new life as "those who have been chosen by God, who are holy and beloved" (vs. 12a).

Lord, thank You that grace extends to even me. Help me to extend that grace of acceptance to all other Christians regardless of their ethnicity or background.

WEEKEND READING

Saturday – John 16
Sunday – John 17

PERSONAL
REFLECTIONS

_____
_____
_____
_____
_____
_____
_____
_____
_____
_____
_____
_____
_____
_____
_____
_____
_____
_____
_____
_____
_____
_____
_____
_____
_____
_____
_____

Spiffing Up the New Look

Colossians 3:12b-13

... ¹² put on a heart of compassion, kindness, humility, gentleness and patience; ¹³ bearing with one another, and forgiving each other, whoever has a complaint against anyone; just as the Lord forgave you, so also should you.

What does putting on the new self actually look like? Paul puts flesh to this lofty spiritual concept with seven specific applications to human relationships. So-called spiritual truth without changed behavior is nothing more than mystical meditation. The gospel that Paul taught was life changing. True, this message is epic in scope, eternal in duration and profound in spiritual insight. But, without practical outcomes in day-to-day living, putting on of the "new self" looks more like donning a monk robe. Hardly what God had in mind! The author James would add his Amen! (see James 1:27; 1:14-17).

So, in the putting on of the new self, we are to first of all put on a "heart of compassion." Is not this the heart of Christ when the multitudes came to Him for healing: "Seeing the people, He felt compassion for them, because they were distressed and dispirited like sheep without a shepherd" (Matt. 9:36)? In New Testament times, the word translated here in the English as compassion, referred to the center or seat of human emotions. According to one lexicographer, compassion "concerns and expresses the total personality at the deepest level." In Philippians 2:1, Paul treats compassion as fundamental to the foundation of Christian humility. So, at the heart of our new life in Christ, the new self ought to express itself first and foremost in compassionate actions toward others.

Kindness comes next, and this moves compassion from an inward feeling into action (see Romans 2:4 where "the kindness of God leads you to repentance"). Kindness is how we treat people. Humility is how we present ourselves in social contexts, not as those who crave attention but as those who treat others better than ourselves (Phil. 2:3). Again, do we not see this in our Lord? (see Philippians 2:5-11). Next comes gentleness, which was also characteristic of our Lord: "Take My yoke upon you and learn from Me, for I am gentle and humble in heart . . ." (Matt. 11:29). Patience is one of the seven virtues of the new self. This, too, is modeled in our God Himself: "The Lord is not slow about His promise, as some count slowness, but is patient toward you, not wishing for any to perish but for all to come to repentance" (2 Peter 3:9). The new self, sixthly, is characterized by forbearance (which trait the Lord showed toward us, Romans 3:25). This is the gracious, loving act of putting up with others' faults and sins. Finally, we are to forgive one another, just as the Lord forgave us.

Lord, help me be like You, putting on the new self in real practical ways in my relationship with others.

What Are You Wearing?

Colossians 3:14-15

¹⁴ Beyond all these things put on love, which is the perfect bond of unity. ¹⁵ Let the peace of Christ rule in your hearts, to which indeed you were called in one body; and be thankful.

The new Christian apparel takes on many hues. Romans 13:14 tells us to put on Christ. In Colossians 3:10, we are taught to put on the new self. Then, in yesterday's verse, 3:12, we are instructed to put on the seven Christian virtues. Now, we are exhorted to put on love, like a cloak that covers over all else. Being properly attired does matter for the Christian!

Keeping in mind that "God is love," as the apostle John asserts (1 John 4:8), Paul places love at the pinnacle of Christian virtues. This is agape love (sacrificial action) as opposed to philos love (brotherly affection). Putting on Christ is putting into action Christlikeness. And in Christ, God so loved the world that He gave—that's an action; His only Son—that's a sacrifice (John 3:16). Love is the Christlike trait that binds Christians together, so that our fellowship is more than just being members of the same organization. We are a family defined by love for one another. This is the "perfect bond of unity."

Paul's follow up about peace is intricately intertwined with love. For only where there is genuine Christlike love will there be peace in our relationships. Christians are not called to just tolerate one another. True, we are to be patient and forbearing (Col. 3:12-13), but God hasn't called us to do these things passively. We are to actively love by being patient and forbearing. We cannot just do our part, as though we love 50/50 with other people, meeting them halfway. No! Such a notion will result in a virtual traffic jam, where love gets queued up and the least negligence backs it all up—into open conflict. But, unconditional love more than compensates for each other's failings.

All these are needed in the body of Christ, the church. Indeed, as Paul has reiterated both in the book of Colossians as well as Ephesians, we as Christians are called to be the body of Christ, one body and thankful. Yet, so often we fight and bicker with each other, even while doing the Lord's work and worshipping the same God who is over all, our Master as well as our Savior. Each morning, we need to "put on Christ" and, throughout the day, to be constantly reminding ourselves of how Christ should look on us when we go through the struggles of relationships. When people observe our behavior and life style, they should see an uncanny resemblance to Christ. As for ourselves, we see how far short we fall. But, in hope, we know that He is at work conforming us to His image.

Lord, I don't want to wear the ragged, dirty clothes of my former life. But when I put on Christ, I walk in a new image. Thank You for Your grace.

Strategic Domicile

Colossians 3:16-17

---

[16] Let the word of Christ richly dwell within you, with all wisdom teaching and admonishing one another with psalms and hymns and spiritual songs, singing with thankfulness in your hearts to God. [17] Whatever you do in word or deed, do all in the name of the Lord Jesus, giving thanks through Him to God the Father.

Dress for the spiritual life—this is how Paul sums up his final general instructions before moving to specific applications for everyday relationships. Two summary mandates are laid out: allow God's Word to be central in your life, and do everything in Jesus' name. The first reflects what Peter had said years earlier, "Lord, to whom shall we go? You have words of eternal life" (John 6:68). His words are life; they are our daily sustenance. In the upper room, the Lord Jesus prayed, "The words which You gave Me I have given to them; and they received them and truly understood that I came forth from You, and they believed that You sent Me" (John 17:8). That Word has been received by us, and we need to continue receiving it so that it permeates every portion of our body, so that He actually dwells in us, like one would comfortably dwell in one's own home, with no hidden closets, no restrained resources, no out-of-bounds areas.

This dwelling of the Word of Christ can't help but find its outward expression in permeating our relationships with others—not so much an attitude of lecturing people with the Word, but teaching them through the melody of our lives. Certainly, Paul was using both the imagery as well as the actuality of singing in his instruction here. The melodious Christian is a singing Christian. And, that is why when Christians gather they sing songs.

The second summary statement is that all should be done "in the name of the Lord Jesus." This means we are conscious of our relationship as His ambassadors. "Therefore, we are ambassadors for Christ, as though God were making an appeal through us . . ." (2 Cor. 5:20). We represent Him; we act on His behalf, not our own. Everything, not just on Sunday mornings or at our daily devotional times. We represent Christ on our business trips, in the theater, when exercising, in the privacy of our home and bedrooms, everywhere, all the time. We represent Him when no one but the unseen angelic world is watching. Therefore, we ought to do everything with the view of how it honors the Lord.

Finally, did you notice the repetition of giving thanks to God in these two verses? A Christian in whom the Word of God dwells richly and who honors the Lord Jesus Christ is a thankful Christian, and has much to sing about.

Lord, thank You so much for Your Word. It gives me focus and motivation, and it helps me to know what honors Your Son, the Lord Jesus Christ.

All In The Family

Colossians 3:18-21

[18] Wives, be subject to your husbands, as is fitting in the Lord. [19] Husbands, love your wives and do not be embittered against them. [20] Children, be obedient to your parents in all things, for this is well-pleasing to the Lord. [21] Fathers, do not exasperate your children, so that they will not lose heart.

Dwelling in our hearts, the Word of God should also affect the relationships with those who dwell in our homes. Wives should continually place themselves under the husband's leadership. Unpopular as this teaching may be today, it is God's formula for a marriage in which the Word of Christ dwells richly (vs. 16) and Christ is honored (vs. 17). "For as the heavens are higher than the earth, so are My ways higher than your ways and My thoughts than your thoughts" (Isaiah 55:9, see also Ephesians 5:22-24).

This does not mean the husband is the master and the wife is the slave. The husband is to love his wife with an agape or self-sacrificing kind of love, as Ephesians 5:25-33 spells out in detail. Husbands, on their side, must resist the temptation to bitterness—which seems an odd thing to say at this juncture. Why would a man become that way with his wife? The word translated bitter is used in James, "Does a fountain send out from the same opening both fresh and bitter water?" (James 3:11). Some have suggested the concept of becoming irritable, incensed or provoked. The husband's leadership, rather, should be like a fountain of fresh water, to which the wife would run for refreshing love, in contrast to a world that would treat her as little more than an object, one who can never measure up to its superficial expectations.

Children are to obey parents in all things. Whereas the women's role is "fitting in the Lord," the children's role is "well-pleasing" to the Lord. Is that not the goal, to do everything in the name of Christ? And when men love their wives the way Christ loves the church, this honors the Lord.

Fathers also reflect the Word of God dwelling in their lives in the way they treat their children. Of all the things, Paul zeroes in on one aspect, exasperating their children. Fathers can exasperate their children in many different ways: setting expectations too high, having uncontrolled anger, being absent too much, being over bearing, being controlling, teasing excessively, being physically, emotionally or sexually abusive—all things that warp a child's view of themselves and life. The word exasperate can be translated to provoke, make resentful, irritate. Paul explains it as causing them to "lose heart" or become discouraged with life. The blame for this is laid at the feet of the father, not the children.

Lord, help me live out the new life in Christ in the midst of all my family relationships, for Your pattern is far superior to the world's ideas.

Condoning Slavery?—part 1

Colossians 3:22

22 Slaves, in all things obey those who are your masters on earth, not with external service, as those who merely please men, but with sincerity of heart, fearing the Lord.

Hot topic this is, for those of us in the western world, with our history of brutal slavery. Human depravity rarely sinks deeper than to subjugate another person to the humiliation of having his freedoms stripped and to be enslaved to the will of those more powerful. No darker blight rests on the history of mankind because of those who have not only propagated slavery, but who have also justified it from the Holy Bible or some other religious writing.

Historically, slavery was not always a matter of racism, as it is thought of today. It had more to do with power and economics. When one nation or tribe has the power to control another, this foments an environment that easily leads to slavery. In war, for example, one group exerts its superiority over another through military might, then imposes death, humiliation and/or economic reparations. Death represents elimination of the opponent. Humiliation takes many forms historically, from torture and mutilation to public exposure, which often ended in death. Kings and despots would use these means to celebrate and also to deter others from resistance.

Slavery represented the ultimate gloating ascension of one people over another. A lifetime of servility brought both enduring humiliation and deterrence, but it also brought economic benefit to the victors in the form of "free" labor. The weaker became servants of the stronger, according to the will of the strong, with no freedoms to speak of.

This, of course, is an overly simplistic analysis of slavery. Many shades of the practice can be found, from extreme forms to that which seems more like an employer/employee relationship with slaves experiencing considerable freedom. Even today, slavery exists in many forms, from Sudan to the sex-slave trade industry that spans the globe, to sweat house factories and indentured slaves who can never work off their "debt." So it is very difficult to speak of slavery in the context of Bible study, particularly with verses like Colossians 4:22.

Does the Bible condone slavery? Does the Scripture assume the legitimacy of slavery? Does the Bible contain any clear-cut denunciation of slavery? All valid questions. Suffice it to say that in our passage today, the apostle addresses those who are slaves and apparently have no ability to change their status. Can faith and grace operate in such conditions? And if so, how?

Lord, help me walk in faith and grace in those situations which I cannot change. I need Your power to live a Christlike response to those over me.

Weekend Reading

Saturday – John 18
Sunday – John 19

Personal Reflections

_____
_____
_____
_____
_____
_____
_____
_____
_____
_____
_____
_____
_____
_____
_____
_____
_____
_____
_____
_____
_____
_____
_____
_____
_____
_____
_____
_____
_____
_____
_____
_____
_____
_____

Condoning Slavery?—part 2

Colossians 3:22

[22] Slaves, in all things obey those who are your masters on earth, not with external service, as those who merely please men, but with sincerity of heart, fearing the Lord.

No, Scripture does not condone slavery. Period! But, living the Christ-like life is possible even within the context of slavery. This is God's fallback plan: don't sin, but if you do, here is what you should do next. By analogy, the Bible tells us not to offend others, and if we do offend, we are to confess to one another. But, God knows that people often fail at both those things, so He instructs, "Love covers a multitude of sins" (1 Peter 4:8). This kind of dichotomy is repeated throughout Scripture. For example, each of us should "bear his own load" (Gal. 6:5), but when someone does not, we should "bear one another's burdens" (Gal. 6:2). God hates divorce (Mal. 2:6), but He allows for it (Deut. 24:1-4) as a concession to hardened hearts (Matt. 19:8). To put it simply, God expects obedience to His authority, but He knows that humans will in fact rebel against that authority. He recognizes that we live in a fallen world and must live among fallen sinful people and, by extension, sinful institutions.

Slavery is a symptom of our fallen world. God certainly did not design it, nor does He condone it. But, living in slavery is no excuse for not living the Christ-like life, any more than other sinful situations in which we find ourselves. And, it is that to which the apostle speaks. And, if Christlike living is possible within something as extreme as slavery, Christlike living is possible within every other situation where our freedoms or rights are limited. In other words, living for Christ trumps anything this world can throw at us!

Christians today tend to apply this teaching about slaves to any hierarchy of human relationships where one person has authority over another (for example, employment). When Paul says, "Slaves, in all things obey those who are your masters on earth," that means employees should submit to their bosses who are their "masters" on earth, even when they are compelled by virtue of their employment to do tasks that they don't like to do, or when they disagree with their supervisors, or are tempted to criticize, resist or undermine their direct authority. They should genuinely do what is expected of them, for the Lord judges the heart, not just the outward behavior.

Is there a limit to this command? Yes, for we see in Peter and John an exception, when they chose to follow a higher, more direct command to obey the Lord in sharing the good news rather than earthly leaders (Acts 5:29).

Lord, help me learn to have an obedient attitude toward those in authority over me and to discern carefully when Your authority supersedes.

Transformative Service

Colossians 3:23-25

23 Whatever you do, do your work heartily, as for the Lord rather than for men, 24 knowing that from the Lord you will receive the reward of the inheritance. It is the Lord Christ whom you serve. 25 For he who does wrong will receive the consequences of the wrong which he has done, and that without partiality.

Scripture is clear, repetitive, consistent and adamant on this point: we are put on earth for one purpose, and one purpose only. That purpose can be stated in different ways, and theologians have written volumes on this subject. In one form or another, it all comes back to this: We exist to glorify God—that is ultimately why He created everything, including us humans. The first and foremost question in the Westminster Catechism states it well, "The chief purpose of man is to glorify God and enjoy Him forever." That captures the teaching of Scripture quite well.

What God gets out of the deal is that by creating mankind He gets to reveal Himself to something outside of Himself. He wants to be known—just like we all want to be known (which makes sense in light of the fact that we were created in His image). He wants us to enjoy Him. What an amazing thing!

But, how best can we enjoy the Creator God of the universe, who reveals Himself to us? The answer is by learning about Him and living our lives in accordance with that knowledge. This is why Paul says, "Whatever you do, do your work heartily, as for the Lord." He is the "Master," not our earthly masters or authority figures. Everything else is relative, limited. We live for Him. "It is the Lord Christ whom you serve."

Now, our existence in God's creation has consequences. We are not completely free to order our own universe. We were created to fit in with His plan—it's all about God! Therefore, it makes sense that when we live our lives within His purposes, we will experience His joy in the plan. Or, to use the words of the apostle Paul, we "will receive the reward of the inheritance." When we live under the direction of our own plan, we "will receive the consequences of the wrong which he has done." There will be the lack of joy, which God has created us to experience. What He designed us for is the pleasure of an intimate relationship with Him.

Therefore, the Spirit admonishes us to treat our work, whether it be the labor of a slave or our employment or cleaning the house or helping a neighbor or teaching Sunday school—to do it all with an active awareness of God as our ultimate Master. And, to do it with gusto as one who loves and pleases Him.

Lord, help me keep constantly in mind that I was created for You and that I can only find my real joy in serving and pleasing You.

Pointed Prayer

¹ Masters, grant to your slaves justice and fairness, knowing that you too have a Master in heaven. ² Devote yourselves to prayer, keeping alert in it with an attitude of thanksgiving; ³ praying at the same time for us as well, that God will open up to us a door for the word, so that we may speak forth the mystery of Christ, for which I have also been imprisoned; ⁴ that I may make it clear in the way I ought to speak.

One would think Paul should tell slave masters to set their slaves free and speak out against slavery. However, Paul's teaching, taken seriously, would radically transform the master/slave relationship—from within! The one in authority should treat those under him with "justice and fairness," in the same way he wants God to treat him. This is a sort of super golden rule for masters, "Treat others the way you would want God to treat you."

Interestingly, Paul goes on to talk about prayer, about being in communication with God. Consider three observations of the kind of prayer he speaks of: 1) devoted prayer, tenaciously seeking communication with the Lord, 2) alert prayer, being acutely aware of the needs of others and the mind of God, and 3) thankful prayer, being fully cognizant of the undeserved, but inestimable privilege of having an audience with and blessing from God.

Paul slips in a personal request at this juncture, speaking to his readers as mature Christians and, as it were, team members in the service of our Lord. He asks that they pray for God to "open up to us a door for the word." What an amazing attitude Paul had: "Lord, You open the door, and I will walk through!"

Consider the implication of his request: 1) doors open and close only at God's command, 2) Paul valued the teamwork of prayer 3) when a servant of God is committed to sharing the gospel, he need only ask for opportunities, 4) sharing the gospel may at times result in confinement, loss of our "freedoms" (Paul was imprisoned as he was writing, which fact gives us insight into his instructions to slaves, who had no freedoms), 5) when Paul asked for an open door, he may have meant the door of the physical imprisonment, but he surely meant also the figurative door into having a hearing for the gospel in many places. 6) besides an open door, Paul recognized the need for divine help "that I may make it clear in the way I ought to speak" (vs. 4). Open doors and clear communications—that is what we need and that should be the focus of our lives, no matter where God has called us to serve, whether as a husband or wife, parent or child—or even as a master or slave!

Lord, open a door today for me to speak clearly the gospel of the Lord Jesus Christ. I ask also for those who You have sent to the mission field that they too would have an open door for sharing the message of Christ.

Wisdom and Grace

Colossians 4:5-6

⁵ Conduct yourselves with wisdom toward outsiders, making the most of the opportunity. ⁶ Let your speech always be with grace, as though seasoned with salt, so that you will know how you should respond to each person.

Finally, before turning to his personal greetings and instructions, the apostle Paul gives one last burst of directions for the Christian life. He has covered much ground in this short letter, but he finishes with two parting admonitions.

First, their general manner of behavior among non-Christians, those outside of the community of faith, should be characterized by wisdom. There are only so many specifics Paul or any of the New Testament writers can lay down in writing. In some regards, the Scripture provides a framework, a skeleton for Christian maturity. To be sure, there are specifics that need to be obeyed, for all Scripture is inspired and is to be taken as our instruction manual for life (2 Tim. 3:16). However, the mandates of Scripture, which are given within certain contexts of the life and times of the 1ˢᵗ century church, don't always line up perfectly with the life situations we face today. Wisdom is the key for both interpreting Scripture as well as applying it to the specifics of our life situations. Paul prayed for this when he wrote earlier, ". . . we have not ceased to pray . . . that you may be filled with the knowledge of His will in all spiritual wisdom and understanding, so that you will walk in a manner worthy of the Lord . . ." (Col. 1:9b-10a).

Second, there are only so many things that can be taught about how we should communicate with others. The teaching has to be assimilated, internalized and applied in the individual episodes of life. For this, grace carries one beyond line-by-line speech principles. This comes with setting maturity as our goal. Grace is exhibited when we resist one-up-manship, when we resist stealing the attention away from another person's story; when we forbear another's humorless tedium, when we allow slights to slide off us like the proverbial water off a duck's back, when we turn our other cheek to insults and offenses, when we are quick to speak of another's good fortune and successes.

Wisdom and Grace—is that not the desire of every Christian? Jesus came into this world "full of grace and truth" (John 1:14). If we understand wisdom to be defined as truth applied, Christlikeness is tantamount to grace and truth in action. When we Christians behave with these characteristics, truly we then become like the salt of the earth (Matt. 5:13), salt that has not lost its flavor.

Lord, I want to live with wisdom and grace, the salted kind of life that makes others thirsty for knowing God.

Faithful Servant

⁷ As to all my affairs, Tychicus, our beloved brother and faithful servant and fellow bond-servant in the Lord, will bring you information. ⁸ For I have sent him to you for this very purpose, that you may know about our circumstances and that he may encourage your hearts ...

Paul often traveled with an entourage of young men he mentored along the way. He embodied what he conveyed to others, "The things which you have heard from me in the presence of many witnesses, entrust these to faithful men who will be able to teach others also" (2 Tim. 2:2). Tychicus was one of those young men. He was first mentioned on Paul's third missionary journey (Acts 20:4) as one of the band of seven who accompanied Paul from Greece up into Macedonia. From there, they went ahead to Troas while Paul took a side trip to visit the believers in Philippi. It was at Troas where Acts records that they held the Lord's Supper, followed by a lengthy sermon by Paul. Then, they travelled to Miletus where they met with the Ephesian elders and Paul gave his farewell speech and final instructions to those shepherds of the local church in Ephesus.

So, Tychicus was one of Paul's young charges with a ringside seat to fairly significant happenings. The apostle had high confidence in him, calling him a "beloved brother and faithful servant and fellow bond-servant in the Lord." Certainly, he fulfilled the qualifications of 2 Timothy 2:2 above. And, his faithfulness was demonstrated by being a fellow-prisoner of Paul in the faith (that is how we understand "fellow bond-servant"). It is an indication of the high respect that Paul had for the Colossians that he would send such a man to them. His task was simply to give them an update on the activities and circumstances of Paul.

However, Tychicus also was charged to "encourage your hearts." The Greek word employed here for "encourage" is related to the word used for the Holy Spirit, the paraclete, which can be variously translated as encourager, counselor, comforter or advocator (John 14:16). Tychicus would be the glove on the spiritual hand of the Holy Spirit in ministering to the Colossians. God uses His people to minister His grace, to be His hands, His feet, His encouraging arm around the shoulder. God's work in our lives is fleshed out by the members of His body serving one another according to their spiritual gifting. Oh, that more Christians would see this great truth, that we each have the opportunity to bring the Spirit of encouragement to one another, so that we all experience God's work in our lives and through us in others' lives.

Lord, I want to become worthy of the description: a "beloved brother and faithful servant and fellow bond-servant in the Lord."

WEEKEND READING

Saturday – John 20:1-18
Sunday – John 20:19-31

_____
_____
_____
_____
_____
_____
_____
_____
_____
_____
_____
_____
_____
_____
_____
_____
_____
_____
_____
_____
_____
_____
_____
_____
_____
_____
_____
_____
_____
_____

Faithful Companions

Colossians 4:9-10

... ⁹ and with him Onesimus, our faithful and beloved brother, who is one of your number. They will inform you about the whole situation here. ¹⁰ Aristarchus, my fellow prisoner, sends you his greetings; and also Barnabas's cousin Mark (about whom you received instructions; if he comes to you, welcome him) ...

Continuing on in his personal greetings, we discover some fascinating details about Paul's entourage, his traveling companions, the young brothers he was mentoring. At the time of writing, he had sent Onesimus along with Tychicus (vs. 7-8) to give a ministry update to the Christians at Colossae. There was an obvious emotional connection between Paul and the church there, even though Paul had never actually visited them before. It is highly probable that the relationship came through such young men as were native to Colossae, with whom he had spent time. The love and concern they shared with the Colossians may have given the apostle a sense of love for them as well.

Onesimus, of course, was a former slave of Philemon—in fact, the entire book of Philemon represents Paul's attempt at reconciling the slave and his earthly master, now that both were Christians. It is clear that Paul sees him as a free man and useful in the work of the gospel. He refers to him as "our faithful and beloved brother." This was not just Paul's feeling, but it was apparently shared with or at least would become obvious to the Colossians once he arrived. High commendation and affirmation of what Paul wrote elsewhere, "There is . . . neither slave nor free . . . for you are all one in Christ Jesus" (Gal. 3:28).

Aristarchus was a member of the group of seven who accompanied Paul on his third mission tour (Acts 19:29; 20:4) and even traveled with Paul as he went under arrest to Rome on his final recorded trip (Acts 27:2). At the time of writing this letter, he seems to have been a prisoner along with the apostle. One can sense that Aristarchus embraced a universal love for all believers, for although he was a Macedonian from Thessalonica, he joined with Paul in sending greetings to the Colossians who lived in Asia Minor (Acts 27:2). Ethnicity proved no barrier to the fellowship of God's people.

And then, there is Mark (also known as John Mark, Acts 12:25), noted here as a cousin to Barnabas, the same Mark who accompanied Paul and Barnabas on their first mission tour but bailed out part way through. Though Paul refused Mark as a team member on his second tour, now years later he has regained his stature in Paul's eyes, so the apostle commends him to the Colossians.

Lord, I simply want to be useful in service to You and Your people. Let it be said of me that I was faithful.

Servants of Excellence

Colossians 4:11-12

... ¹¹ and also Jesus who is called Justus; these are the only fellow workers for the kingdom of God who are from the circumcision, and they have proved to be an encouragement to me. ¹² Epaphras, who is one of your number, a bondslave of Jesus Christ, sends you his greetings, always laboring earnestly for you in his prayers, that you may stand perfect and fully assured in all the will of God.

The list goes on, as Paul mentions other traveling/ministry companions. He is quite fond of calling them "fellow workers" or "bondslaves" like himself (e.g. Rom. 1:1). The Greek word doulos is translated variously as servant, slave, bondslave or bondservant. At the heart of ministry is service to God and others.

The name Jesus, as can be seen here, was not isolated to our Lord Jesus Christ, but was common in that day (so also in some Latin cultures today). The name itself means "savior" (Matt. 1:21) and corresponds to the name "Joshua" in the Old Testament of the same meaning. However, the Jesus mentioned here also went by the name Justus, and he is one of the Jewish co-workers of Paul (he is probably not the same Justus also called Barsabbas in Acts 1:21). The noteworthy point here is that most of Paul's disciples were Gentiles. This makes sense in light of his mission being primarily to the Gentiles rather than the Jews. The few Jewish co-workers provided encouragement to Paul, probably because of their shared background and understanding of the Old Testament. It might also be inferred that the scant number of Jewish co-workers in Paul's ministry may indicate either the indifference of many Jewish believers toward reaching Gentiles, or possibly the difficulty in overcoming Jewish prejudice for many—at least, Paul found it important to point out there were only a few.

Epaphras was a fellow prisoner of Paul's, to whom he refers also in Philemon 23. Both letters (Colossians and Philemon) were probably written from prison and at the same time, so Epaphras was with Paul in both cases at the time of writing. He sends his greetings, being unable to go to them like some others that Paul sends. Epaphras was apparently a native Colossian and had a keen sense of serving on behalf of them. He may have been "commended" from them to missionary work as their representative. At any rate, Paul had a keen sense that Epaphras' work was credited to them as their ambassador to the ministry for which God had called him. And, he was a hard worker!

Paul's ministry was always personal. Ministry was about people. It was not just a career path for him or his partners. And so, his letters reflect that heart for people, even in the concluding remarks.

Lord, help me to never forget that serving You is about serving people. It was for people that You died, people that You love, not a religious institution.

Demas and the Doctor

Colossians 4:13-14

For I testify for him that he has a deep concern for you and for those who are in Laodicea and Hierapolis. Luke, the beloved physician, sends you his greetings, and also Demas.

E paphras, unsung outside the area of Colossae, was well known there because he was the one who brought them the gospel of grace (Col. 1:6-7). As we mentioned earlier in this study, Paul had not been there personally, but the ministry was the result of others who had heard the message from Paul.

For Epaphras, though, his relationship with them was not just a duty, but one of deep love. This is the true mark of a minister of the gospel—he does not serve in ministry simply as a career choice, or as a way to make money, nor to "make a name for himself." As someone has said, "There is no limit to what can be accomplished for God, if you don't care who receives the glory." In Epaphras' case, what mattered was the people, not himself.

His concern extended to the nearby cities of Laodicea and Hierapolis. Paul, likewise, shared that same concern, most likely due to the influence of Epaphras (Col. 2:1). Is it not true that passion is contagious? The city of Hierapolis, while only mentioned here in the New Testament, became significant in church history and in the formation of the canon of the New Testament. The writer Papias, reported to have been a disciple of the apostle John, wrote from Hierapolis around AD 130 what amounts to be the earliest information we have concerning the origin of the Gospel according to Mark. He recorded that Mark had compiled into a book the sayings of Jesus as he heard them from the apostle Peter.

The Laodiceans, on the other hand, became famous for their slide into luke-warmness, as documented in the book of Revelation (3:14-22). Though they began well, they drifted into a life that was neither hot nor cold. The Lord indicated He would "vomit" them out of His mouth (though most translations render the word in less unpleasant ways, the word has a sense of repulsion).

Dr. Luke, as he is often called today, was in fact a physician and a frequent companion of Paul's. He was the writer of the gospel according to Luke and also the book of Acts. Apparently, he was one of those kinds of Christians that had a reputation for exuding Christ-like love. Demas, at this time a faithful co-worker of Paul's, later separated and went back into a worldly life (2 Tim. 4:10)—no specific accolades are mentioned concerning him. Demas' mention here speaks to the grace of God, even in light of His foreknowledge.

Lord, I want to be Your faithful servant, one who has a deep love for all the Christians. Help me keep to Your way and not stray into the way of the world.

Final Greetings

Colossians 4:15

¹⁵ Greet the brethren who are in Laodicea and also Nympha and the church that is in her house. ¹⁶ When this letter is read among you, have it also read in the church of the Laodiceans; and you, for your part read my letter that is coming from Laodicea. ¹⁷ Say to Archippus, "Take heed to the ministry which you have received in the Lord, that you may fulfill it." ¹⁸ I, Paul, write this greeting with my own hand. Remember my imprisonment. Grace be with you.

Evidence of good church relations comes to light in Paul's closing comments, reflecting good fellowship between the area churches surrounding Colossae. The idea of a super-church that stood alone, completely independent from others, was not the norm during apostolic times. In particular, Paul's communication to them was to be shared.

His closing infers that Paul wrote other letters (e.g. to the Laodiceans), which have been lost to antiquity, and that did not find their way into the New Testament canon. In fact, we can piece together from the historical evidence found in his extant letters that he wrote at least two additional letters to the Corinthians, which also have not been preserved. Armchair theologians like to theorize what would happen if one of these were found, but such is only speculative at best. There is no way of validating any such find if it were to occur anyway. Suffice it to say, the Lord has preserved that which He desires for the church through the ages.

Archippus receives the final admonition to fulfill the ministry given to him— mentioned last but certainly not least.

Finally, as he did in some of his other letters (see 1 Corinthians 16:21 and 2 Thessalonians 3:17), Paul adds his own handwriting to the conclusion, as his personal mark of authenticity. Most likely, this implies that he had working for him what is called an amanuensis, that is, a personal secretary, to actually write down his communication. Why Paul didn't pen the whole letter is a matter of speculation, not the least possibility being limitations due to his imprisonment or maybe his eyesight. Regardless of whose physical hand was put to parchment, the letter was none-the-less his authorship. Despite the penchant of 18th and 19th century liberal theologians, no serious scholar today doubts the authenticity of Paul's letter to the Colossians as being his actual writing.

Finally, the apostle asks the Colossians to remember him in his imprisonment and closes with his signature saying, "Grace be with you." Paul, amidst all that he taught and did, in the final analysis was all about grace.

Lord, grant us the grace to share our Christian lives with others beyond the local church in which we are involved. We all together are the body of Christ.

Wrap-up

The apostle Paul was a prolific writer, having penned thirteen letters (or fourteen, depending on whether he was the author of Hebrews). The four we have studied in this devotional series, the letters to the Galatians, Ephesians, Philippians and Colossians, are shorter than his epic volumes to the Romans and the Corinthians, but their truth is no less significant for the church today.

Galatians was probably his first letter, written about the time of the Jerusalem council (Acts 15), at the end of his first mission tour. It has been called the "Magna Carta" of Christianity, in that it laid down a clear statement of the freedom we have in Christ, through justification by grace through faith, in contrast to justification by works of the law. Paul made it absolutely clear that any other "gospel," even a modification of His message of grace, was completely anathema (Gal. 1:8-9).

The other three of these letters (Ephesians, Philippians, Colossians) were written much later and from prison. They spoke to maturing Christians about growing in their faith, learning to apply grace in all of life. To the Ephesians, Paul wrote of the great truth, the unity of the church, that is neither Jewish nor Gentile—the mystery now revealed. The church at Ephesus had a storied history of being under Paul's teaching for over two years and also that of Apollos.

The letter to the Philippians challenged Christians who were living well, to grow in their knowledge of Christ, not just in breadth only, but also in depth. It was a joyful correspondence for Paul, as evidenced by his frequent references to joy and rejoicing. Indeed, the growing Christian has a great deal to be joyful about, and increasingly so as we grow in our knowledge of Christ.

Colossians is a letter dealing with the superiority of Christ over the prevailing drift toward a Gnostic perversion of the gospel message of grace. In Him, we are complete and don't need to pursue any other worldview or religious mysteries or insights. We have everything we need in Him, for the fullness of Deity dwells perfectly in Him in bodily form.

Finally, we close with pointing out that Paul's letters are authoritative for the Christian life, as the apostle Peter recognized when he wrote of the message of salvation about which, ". . . Paul, according to the wisdom given him, wrote to you, as also in all his letters, speaking in them of these things, in which are some things hard to understand, which the untaught and unstable distort, as they do also the rest of the Scriptures, to their own destruction" (2 Peter 3:15-16).

Lord, I praise You for using the faithfulness of the apostle Paul, whose ministry continues to this very day through his writings, which were inspired by Your Spirit. I commit to living according to the teachings of Your Word.

WEEKEND READING

Saturday – John 21:1-14
Sunday – 21:15-25

PERSONAL REFLECTIONS

Day by Day in the Gospel of Matthew
by Chuck Gianotti

When Matthew was called to discipleship by Jesus with the simple command, "Follow Me!" he was a Rome appointed tax collector and despised by his fellow Jewish countrymen. Now he holds a place of honor as one of the four authorized biographers of the life and ministry of Jesus Christ.

Matthew's gospel account portrays Jesus of Nazareth as the fulfillment of the Old Testament prophecies, giving ample proof that He was, indeed, the Messiah King whom God had promised to send to reign over His people, Israel.

These daily devotionals (spanning one whole year) follow the gospel of Matthew verse by verse. Each reading is accompanied by a brief commentary and a succinct, devotional prayer to ground your heart and will in an increasing desire to love, honor, and serve the Lord Jesus as one of His disciples today.

Call or go online for more information:
563-585-2070 or www.ecsministries.org

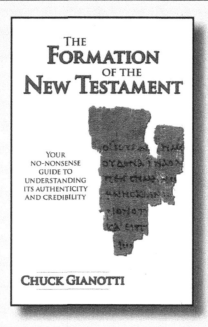

The Formation of the New Testament
by Chuck Gianotti

The Christian faith rises or falls on the historical credibility of the Bible, particularly the New Testament documents. In today's post-modern culture, Christians and those searching for answers face numerous questions including:

- ➤ Are the New Testament writings historically reliable?

- ➤ How do we know those books are authoritative?

- ➤ Who decided which documents to include?

- ➤ What about the apocryphal or deutero-canonical writings?

- ➤ Can we know for certain that the Bible is accurate and complete?

This book reduces the large volume of available (yet very technical) information on the subject by providing a concise analysis of the facts to help you gain confidence in the credibility of the New Testament canon.